Journey into the Heart of God

Credit: Portable icon depicting the Transfiguration, 11th-12th century (Mosaic), Byzantine/Louvre, Paris, France/ Giraudon

The Transfiguration recurs several times in this book and underlies the whole study. The traditional Byzantine representation of the event is basically unchanged since the sixth century.

Christ on the mountain emerges as "Light from Light, true God from true God." To our left Elijah points to Christ as the fulfillment of ancient prophecy. To our right Moses holds in his arm the Torah, the Law that leads us to Christ.

Below them are the three apostles who were "with him on the holy mountain." Peter is to our right, his left hand braced on the ground, his right hand reaching out to protect himself from the dazzling light. James is on our left, pointing in awe-struck wonder to Christ and thrown off balance by the force of the divine light. Between them is John, shrinking from the pure light of God.

The harmonious agreement of the two testaments promises the unity of the whole body of believers. Embracing all is the Holy Trinity: the Father represented by the blue from which the Son emerges and the Holy Spirit portrayed as rays proceeding from the Father and enlightening the whole world and all within it.

Journey Into The Heart Of God

Living the Liturgical Year

PHILIP H. PFATTEICHER

OXFORD
UNIVERSITY PRESS

OXFORD
UNIVERSITY PRESS

Oxford University Press is a department of the University of Oxford.
It furthers the University's objective of excellence in research, scholarship,
and education by publishing worldwide.

Oxford   New York
Auckland   Cape Town   Dar es Salaam   Hong Kong   Karachi
Kuala Lumpur   Madrid   Melbourne   Mexico City   Nairobi
New Delhi   Shanghai   Taipei   Toronto

With offices in
Argentina   Austria   Brazil   Chile   Czech Republic   France   Greece
Guatemala   Hungary   Italy   Japan   Poland   Portugal   Singapore
South Korea   Switzerland   Thailand   Turkey   Ukraine   Vietnam

Oxford is a registered trademark of Oxford University Press
in the UK and certain other countries.

Published in the United States of America by
Oxford University Press
198 Madison Avenue, New York, NY 10016

Library of Congress Cataloging-in-Publication Data
Pfatteicher, Philip H.
Journey into the heart of God : living the liturgical year /
Philip H. Pfatteicher. pages cm
ISBN 978-0-19-999712-1 (cloth : alk. paper)   1. Spiritual life—Catholic Church.
2. Church year meditations.   3. Church year—Prayers and devotions.   I. Title.
BX2178.P43 2013 263'.9—dc23
2012050011

1 3 5 7 9 8 6 4 2
Printed in the United States of America
on acid-free paper

To Lois
as always
and
to David Paul Gleason

Contents

Preface

RUDYARD KIPLING IN his poem "The English Flag" asked the incisive question, "What should they know of England who only England know?" A similar question might appropriately be put to those who know only one liturgical tradition. No matter how committed one may be to a particular denomination, it is essential for those who speak to and for the Church to know something of the breadth and richness of the whole Christian tradition. This study, therefore, while giving attention primarily to the Western Church, attempts to keep in view the Latin rite of the Roman Catholic Church, and the Anglican, primarily Episcopal, tradition, and the Lutheran movement, especially in North America. Some attention will be given also to the Byzantine churches. The liturgical texts and customs found in these places will be supplemented by the rich body of hymns that have developed in many denominations of Christianity and that may be said to express, even more than does the liturgy, the people's theology. (One of the purposes of this book is to encourage those individuals and denominations that historically have paid little attention to the liturgical calendar, except in its broad outline, to explore the richness and depth of the Church's year as it has developed across denominational lines.)

Old handbooks in the Roman Catholic tradition give the esoteric name Heortology (from the Greek "festival") to the study of the origins, development, and meaning of the feasts and seasons of the Church's distinctive year. Early medieval books used the term *ordo anni circuli*, the order of the annual cycle (of feasts, days, and seasons). The Lutheran pastor Johannes Pomarius introduced the term "Church Year" (*Kirchenjahr*) in 1589 (some trace his use of the term to 1585). Abbot Prosper Guéranger popularized the name "liturgical year" (*année liturgique*) in 1841. This book will use "Church Year" and "Liturgical Year" interchangeably.

This study, while respecting and building on historical inquiry, is an examination of the liturgical year as it has developed in the Church and is now received and lived. It progresses through the year, season by season, making use of insightful liturgical texts, many of which may not be familiar to many worshippers, especially the texts found in Daily Prayer, the Liturgy of the Hours. (One of the purposes of such references is to encourage the wider use of ordered Daily Prayer by more Christian people.) This study will also draw on the treasury of classic hymns as expressions of the themes of the Church year. Hymns provide the laity, who may not have the time or the inclination to study in a formal way the various branches of theology (systematic, historical, moral), with a course in theology that, while requiring attention and reflection, is accessible and, because of the poetic character of hymns combined with their tunes, memorable. Rich and profound poetic texts have nourished Christian people throughout the lifetime of the Church. (One of the purposes of the inclusion of classic hymns in this study is to draw people away from thin and repetitious songs toward more nourishing fare.)

In the Roman rite there are three presidential prayers that are part of the Proper of each Sunday or festival: the Collect, the Prayer over the Offerings, and the Prayer after Communion. Only the first of these is common to the three liturgical rites that are primary to this study. The other two will be referred to only occasionally in the following pages. The attentive reader will note that there is little attention given in these pages to the prayers in recent Lutheran books. The 1978 *Lutheran Book of Worship* revised many of the traditional Collects, not always to their improvement. *Evangelical Lutheran Worship* (2006) has introduced three prayers of the day for each Sunday and for some festivals corresponding to the three years of the lectionary cycle. That is simply too many to consider carefully in this study. Many of them are variations on the prayers in the *Lutheran Book of Worship*. The idea of a collect for each Sunday and feast of each year in the three-year lectionary cycle was attempted by the Roman Catholic Church and ultimately rejected. It is too early to tell how this abundance of prayers will shape the life of the Church, except to remark that the traditional purpose of the Collect was more than to reflect the teaching of the appointed lessons. The *Lutheran Service Book* (2006) unfortunately does not include the texts of the Collects, reserving them for the Altar Book.

This book has its immediate origin in an invitation extended to me by Nashotah House Theological Seminary to teach a course in the History and Function of the Liturgical Year during Petertide 2011. The roots of the study, however, go back behind that for half a century, to the first years of my parish ministry as I sought ways to make the Church Year touch and shape the lives of my people. I am grateful to Arnold W. Klukas, Professor of Liturgics and Ascetical Theology at Nashotah House, for the invitation, to the faculty and staff of the House for their gracious welcome, and to my students in that class (who represented five nations and some six denominations) for their work, insight, questions, and contributions. I must also record my gratitude to Philip S. Ramstad, then pastor of St. John of the Cross Lutheran Church in Dravosburg, Pennsylvania, who a dozen years ago encouraged me to write a liturgical commentary for the assistance of those who preach. This book is perhaps not unlike the volume that he had in mind.

The Very Revd. Dirk van Dissel, whose name appears from time to time in these pages, deserves identification. An Anglican priest, he is Dean of the Diocese of the Murray in Australia. His knowledge of the Church's treasury of collects is unsurpassed; his concern for accuracy and intelligibility in his translations and his sensitivity to the rhythms of English prose are exemplary.

My preparation of this study has increased my respect for the work, devotion, and insight of those predecessors, especially in the Lutheran tradition, who through their writings have been my teachers and have shaped my understanding of the Church and its central and eternal activity, the worship of the Triune God. If what I say now has any value, it rests solidly on their foundation. For them, my thanks. May they rest in peace and rise in glory.

The book is dedicated to my wife in thanksgiving for now more than fifty years of marriage and also to our pastor in celebration of his forty years of faithful and effective ministry that has enriched the whole Church.

Journey into the Heart of God

Introduction

WE ARE, ALL OF US, A FORGETFUL PEOPLE IN
CONSTANT NEED OF BEING REMINDED WHO WE ARE

Who We Are

WE ARE, FIRST of all, children of earth. In an increasingly urban world, the ecological dimension of our life is easy to forget. Most now live at a remove from nature and are able to ignore our connection with the natural world even as we are woven into the web of life and the cosmos. The idea that we human beings are independent is, in a word, a lie. We come from nature; we exist by the processes of nature; we live every moment of our lives in absolute dependence upon nature. We cannot live apart from nature, nor can we live against nature. We can only live with nature. If in our ignorance or aggressiveness or apathy we tear the fabric of which our own life is a part, we destroy ourselves as well as the mighty structure from whose womb we were born, in whose web we have had our unfolding history, and whose support and companionship is the primal place and ground of our existence.[1]

Biblical religion, especially Christianity, has not infrequently been blamed as the chief culprit in the exploitation of the natural world because in the very first chapter of the Bible humankind is given "dominion over the fish of the sea, and over the birds of the air, and over the cattle, and over all the wild animals of the earth, and over every creeping thing that creeps on the earth" (Gen. 1:26). Human beings have extended that dominion to include not just animals, birds, fish, and reptiles but the whole created order, and some have taken that passage as a divine authorization to exploit the entire planet and its solar system for the exclusive benefit of human beings. "Dominion," however, is not to be understood as "domination," as if humanity had been given authority to exercise absolute control over creation. "Dominion" does not mean the depredations of an unjust and irresponsible tyrant, but the careful stewardship of a good king. The natural world is to be governed by humanity as a nation is governed by a good monarch, that is, with justice, care, and concern.[2] The Bible "presents humanity not as the owner of nature but as its steward, strictly accountable to its true Owner (see Lev. 25:23–24).³

At the conclusion of the Book of Job (chapters 38–41), when God at last responds to his long-suffering servant, he reminds Job that a human being cannot control nature but rather is part of it. It is the view of the account of creation given in the second chapter of Genesis in which human beings, male and female together, are created out of the earth and remain part of it. Psalms such as Psalm 104 assert a common dependency of creation on its Creator. The awe-inspiring vision of Isaiah (Isaiah 6) allows the prophet not simply to look into heaven to see God on the throne surrounded by a glorious retinue of angels and swirling incense but also to hear the song of the angels, "Holy, holy, holy Lord God of Sabaoth; heaven and earth are full of your glory." Creation thus filled with the divine presence becomes a great sanctuary, and human beings may be regarded as priests serving that sanctuary.⁴ Such a powerful understanding ought to be especially vivid to Christians who at every celebration of the Eucharist join the angels' song and in the Sanctus sing, "Holy, holy, holy Lord, God of power and might. Heaven and earth are full of your glory." And at the end of the New Testament, St. John the Divine has a grand vision of the "new heaven and a new earth" in which the consummation of the kingdom of God is portrayed not as human beings taken out of this world for heaven, but rather as the renewal of all creation.

In several hymns Christians have sung of their utter dependence and consequent responsibility but have not always paid careful attention to what their words were saying. A widely used hymn by William Walsham How has the people sing,

> We give thee but thine own,
> Whate'er the gift may be;
> All that we have is thine alone,
> A trust, O Lord, from thee.

Less widely used but even more pointed is Somerset Corry Lowry's "Son of God, eternal Savior":

> Thine the gold and thine the silver,
> Thine the wealth of land and sea,
> We but stewards of thy bounty,
> Held in solemn trust for thee.⁵

If Daily Prayer were more widely used as the prayer of Christian people, the traditional introductory psalm (Psalm 95) at Matins (Morning Prayer) would remind them daily of the ownership of creation.

> For the Lord is a great God,
>   and a great King above all gods.
> In his hand are the caverns of the earth,
>   and the heights of the hills are his also.
> The sea is his, for he made it,
>   and his hands have molded the dry land.
> Come, let us bow down, and bend the knee,
>   and kneel before the Lord our Maker.

We need to be reminded of our place in the natural world: stewards entrusted with the care of what belongs to God.

Christians, secondly, need to be reminded that they are baptized children of God and therefore inheritors of a long history of which they are a part. Those who have been baptized are related to one another and to all the generations that have gone before them "with the sign of faith." Thus, the baptized can say, "The history of the Church is *our* history, a grand story in which we have but a small part."

The liturgical year brings the two often forgotten facts together and, properly understood, preserves the connection between the baptized children of God and their situation as children of the earth. In remarkable and diverse ways the Church's Year of Grace teaches us again and again who we are. One of the purposes of this book is to call attention to some of these reminders of the community of creation.

Called to the Pilgrims' Way

We are in need of being reminded of who we are. We are also in need of being reminded of who we are called to be: people on the Way. The Second Vatican Council of the Roman Catholic Church (1962-1965) renewed attention to the image of the pilgrim Church. The Constitution on the Liturgy, the first document approved by the Council, says,

> In the earthly liturgy, by way of foretaste, we share in that heavenly liturgy which is celebrated in the holy city of Jerusalem toward which we journey as pilgrims....[6]

The Constitution on the Church declares,

> The Church on earth, while journeying in a foreign land away from her
> Lord (cf. 2 Cor. 5:6), regards herself as an exile. Hence she seeks and
> experiences those things which are above, where Christ is seated at the
> right hand of God, where the life of the Church is hidden with Christ in
> God until she appears in glory with her Spouse (cf. Col. 3:1-4).[7]

Christians are portrayed as a people on the move, and that understanding
implies progress, change, and development. We are reminded that we have
ancestors who have walked this way before us; we have companions who walk
now beside us; and there will be after us generations yet to be born who will in
their time travel where we now go.

Among the millions of Semitic nomads migrating across the Fertile
Crescent, Abraham is regarded as different from all the rest and his travel
becomes the prototype of other biblical journeys: the wilderness wanderings
that made a nation out of freed slaves; the "psalms of ascent" (Psalms 120-134)
of pilgrims going up to Jerusalem (every male Jew was required to visit the
temple three times each year according to Ex. 23:17 and Deut. 16:16); the eschatological vision of Isaiah (2:2-3) and Micah (4:1-2) of the exaltation of the house
of the Lord with all the nations streaming up to it; the elaboration of this vision
in the New Testament book of Hebrews; the peripatetic ministry of Jesus who
had no fixed abode but whose ministry took him to Jerusalem and culminated
there. Since the destruction of Jerusalem in A.D. 70, homelessness and eventual return has been a central theme of Judaism, evocatively expressed in the
hopeful Passover declaration, "Next year in Jerusalem." The pervasive biblical
metaphor of pilgrimage warns against an easy acceptance of the world and its
ways, undermines pride, and preserves a sense of what is passing and of what
abides, as Jews and Christians journey through the world with all of its allure-
ments and temptations, on to the goal of the ancient pilgrimage. It suggests to
the pilgrims ever-new possibilities as they journey through ever-new territory.

Christianity has its roots in the profound sense of exile. The Faith reminds
us that we while on earth are aliens in a foreign land whose true home is
elsewhere. It is an idea that is nearly universal in the world's religions, which
speak of a pilgrimage, whether literal or spiritual, to the center. Pilgrimage,
moreover, is an image that occurs often in world literature: from Homer and
Virgil in classical times, through Chaucer's *Canterbury Tales* in the fourteenth
century, to James Joyce in the twentieth century. Behind the religious and literary appropriations of the metaphor is the basic human awareness of being
essentially transients on the land and the sense that the larger forces of life go

on independent of, and sometimes in spite of, us. In the long history of the universe, the human race is a transient, momentary visitor to a scene that will endure without us long after we are gone.

The pilgrimage has its focus on the goal: the experience of arrival must be earned by planning, preparation, the actual journey, and the arrival at the destination. In the most profound pilgrimages, such as Abraham leaving Ur of the Chaldees and the Israelites leaving Egypt, it is a one-way journey in search of a homeland. There is no interest in a return; in fact, longing for what had been left behind is seen as an act of cowardice and rebellion. Sometimes, however, the journey is interrupted and radically changed from its original intention. The classic example is St. Paul on his way to Damascus to round up followers of the Way, as many as he could find, both men and women. As a memorable hymn, "We sing the glorious conquest before Damascus' gate,"[8] has it, as he was about to enter the city that was his destination, Paul was confronted by the living Lord Jesus, knocked to the ground, temporarily blinded, and given new orders. The encounter transformed him from the leading opponent into the foremost follower of the very Way that he sought to exterminate. What he had expected to be a round-trip journey from Jerusalem to Damascus and back again was suddenly changed into a pilgrimage with an as yet unrevealed destination. Paul was made to emulate his ancestor Abraham.

The pilgrim's journey is both outward and inward. It is outward to strange new places, out of self-centeredness, which is the prominent characteristic of sin, into the natural world, into the society of other people. The journey is also inward to spiritual fulfillment, satisfying a longing planted deep in the human heart. The classic exposition in English of this double journey is John Bunyan's *The Pilgrim's Progress from This World to That Which is To Come* (First Part 1678, Second Part 1684). The progress of Christian (for that is the name of Bunyan's pilgrim) is outward from a shocking and radical break with his wife and children, leaving home, since they would not come with him, and making his way through this world in a series of physical dangers and crises until at last the gates of heaven open to receive him. These adventures are, however, outward and visible signs of the inward and spiritual struggle required of all who would be faithful to the biblical summons to venture forth.

Occasionally the transformed condition of the pilgrim who has returned home is reported. Margery Kempe (ca. 1373-1438) describes the "cryings" arising from compassionate contemplation that began to visit her when she was in Jerusalem and that continued after she had returned home to England. Moreover, she reports that she found subsequent pilgrimages to lesser places to be anticlimactic. More powerfully, T. S. Eliot's *Journey of the Magi* has one of the Magi late in his life, describe what the journey to Bethlehem had done to him and his companions. They came, they saw the beginning of the story, they made their offerings, and they returned home to those they now viewed as an alien people "clutching their gods." The Magi had been changed by their journey but changed in a necessarily incomplete and unsatisfactory way because they did not and could not yet know the whole story of the Child whom they saw, to whose cradle they had been led, and whose life and work had just begun.

The image of the pilgrimage, therefore, serves as a controlling metaphor for the living of the liturgical year, which might well be called The Pilgrims' Way. Such was the name of the principal roads leading to the shrine of our Lady of Walsingham in England, to the shrine of St. Thomas Beckett at Canterbury, and to the hugely popular shrine of St. James in Compostela, Spain. The name sets forth the truth that the people of God are a people on the move, unable to settle in comfortably by accommodation with the world and its culture. The people of the Way are ever directed ahead, to the future fulfillment of the promises of God. The celebration of the past, in the biblical perspective, is ultimately an incentive to search for the way ahead. For the Hebrews, the past was the exodus from Egyptian slavery, and in that formative past event they found the impulse to journey toward the land of promise and the messianic kingdom to come. Such a perspective as the liturgical year affords, therefore, properly understood, far from being confining in predictable routine, encourages open-mindedness and a readiness to be surprised.

Pilgrimage is thus a basic pattern for interpreting the entire biblical record and thus the life and ministry of the Church. The metaphor of pilgrimage serves to open and unfold to us the nature of the Church as year by year the Christian wayfarers make their way through the cycles of the seasons, ever constant yet ever-new, retracing yet again the great circle. The emphasis on movement, journey, progress maintains the essential eschatological emphasis of Christianity. Luther opposed a static view of Christianity and insisted that the saving works of God

have all been begun in such a way that from day to day they are achieved more and more. For this reason it is...called the Passover of the Lord, that is a passing through (Ex. 12:11-12), and we are called Galileans, that is, wanderers, because we are continually going forth from Egypt through the desert, that is, through the way of the cross and suffering to the Land of Promise. We have been redeemed, and we are being redeemed continually. We have received adoption and are still receiving it. We have been made sons of God, and we are and shall be sons. The Spirit has been sent, is being sent, and will be sent. We learn, and we shall learn. And so you must not imagine that the Christian's life is a standing still and a state of rest. No, it is a passing over and a progress from vices to virtue, from clarity to clarity, from virtue to virtue. And those who have not been en route you should not consider Christians either. On the contrary, you must regard them as a people of inactivity and peace, upon whom the prophet calls down their enemies.[9]

The Church's Gospel is enlivening because it is a message not of present possession but of promise. There is more to come; indeed, as Robert Browning's "Rabbi Ben Ezra" declares, "The best is yet to be."

In the great Eucharistic prayers of the Church, as in the Gospels, the narrative of the institution of the Holy Supper is connected with a keen sense of what is to come: "until his coming again" is the phrase in the Book of Common Prayer. The remembrance is set within anticipation, the narrative of a past action within the present expectation of the future. So the pilgrimage motif urges us ever forward until at last we are home.

The Church Year as a Collaborative Achievement

The liturgical year finds its power not only in the strength of its doctrine but in its character as a work of art, a compelling creation of the imagination. It is a collective composition, shaped over many centuries, even millennia, by diverse hands and many cultures. The Church has used and promoted many aspects of art, music most of all in the Church's own plainsong and in the glories of Russian Church music, but the organ has become and remains the premier instrument, after the human voice, of music in the Western Church. (The Eastern churches employ only the human voice.) Architecture, the design and construction of the "house of the church," is of clear importance to the work of the Church and its worship of God. Sculpture adorns the buildings, inside and out; painting has created altarpieces and large illustrations of biblical scenes and aspects of the Church's teaching; stained glass paints the air as the light comes through it into the church; dance has its own place in the carefully choreographed movements of the sacred ministers at a solemn high mass, ensuring that the necessary movement is graceful, harmonious, and unobtrusive. In addition to all these, the Church has its own distinctive creation: the liturgy, which incorporates the other arts and advances them in a coherent whole. Liturgical action in its largest sense is the most generally accessible statement of the experience of Christianity. The liturgy is the Church's peculiar literature, its imaginative appropriation of its own past, its present life, and its expectation of the future, which draws upon the whole experience of humankind of the divine and what the race has found of ultimate significance. This artistic creation is not merely the words and actions of the central rites, but the whole body of supporting material, which includes the conception of time enshrined in the liturgical year.

It is representative action. One sees it happening before one's eyes, one participates in the action, yet it stands for more than one sees and does. It points beyond itself to larger vision. The frequent recourse in these pages to some of the great hymns of the Church is a reminder that in hymns the essential music of poetry becomes more explicit. We are carried by melody and by words before we attend to their meaning.[10] So it is with the music that pervades and penetrates and gives life to the language and the doing of the liturgy of the Church. The intricate satisfactions of the liturgy are so complex that we require outside help to appreciate and embrace them. It was because our ancestors in the faith understood this necessity that the *Common Service Book* suggested, "A Hymn of Invocation of the Holy Ghost may be sung at the beginning of all Services."[11]

The liturgy, like drama and music, is preeminently a collaborative art. The words and music and actions enlist the cooperation of the participant in creating a living expression of the Gospel of Christianity. The aspect of the Church's liturgy, which is the subject of this study, the liturgical year, is of particular interest in the way it makes use of the diversity, complexity, and strangeness of human experience. It dramatizes a way of living with honesty, insight, even vulnerability that, when one looks carefully and receptively at it, is remarkably compelling.

The creation of the Church Year has been a collective achievement, for which no one person, no one group, no one age has been responsible. Robert Payne describes the creation of the Nicene Creed: "So there came about, by the slow processes of trial and error, as a poet will substitute a new word to a line or resurrect a word used formerly, continually revising his rhythms, an astonishingly beautiful summary of the Christian faith, such a summary as might have come full-grown from the mind of one of the apostles. But in fact this statement of faith came about arduously and slowly, after many bitter contests, and many subtle dialectical quarrels...."[12] It is not at all unusual for literary compositions to arise in this way. This is exactly how the English-Scottish border ballads were composed: by a process of telling and retelling, the ballads took on an increasingly effective and concise shape until they arrived at a more or less permanently satisfying expression that told all that needed to be told and omitted all but the absolutely essential elements of the story. "Sir Patrick Spens," perhaps the best-known of the ballads collected in the eighteenth century from the Scottish border, gives the outline of its tragic tale, suggests but does not pursue the motivation of Sir Patrick for the dangerous winter voyage, does not describe the shipwreck (for no observer was present), but is emotionally more effective by describing only the flotsam and the increasing anxiety of the women who waited the return of the ship's men. However such ballads first began, whether an individual or a communal composition, they have for the most part been subjected to a continued process of revision, both conscious and unconscious, by those through whose lips and memories they passed and are generally the better for it.

In many of the ballads, refrains provide for the listener as well as the singer a pause in the story while the repeated lines are sung, and thus a simple but powerful sense of suspense is built up. The narrative tension is regularly relaxed, and the progress to the usually tragic conclusion is made the more inevitable. In a similar way, the Sundays and great feasts of the liturgical year can be seen as the narration of the events of salvation, and the intervening weekdays as the refrain, the pause that heightens the power of the unfolding story. The great events are seen over against the ordinary events of everyday, and this counterpoint of the real and the routine enhances the power of those selected events that make and give sense, just as the narrative in a ballad gives sense even to the nonsense of ordinary trivial, uncontrolled speech (the nonsense of such refrains as "Hey, nonny, nonny...") So the movement of a ballad is from sense through pause to further sense. The movement of the liturgical year turns the usual view of the week upside down. To the secular world, Sunday and the occasional holy day are seen as pauses in the routine of daily life. In the Church's Year, however, it is the daily business that is the enforced pause in the recital of the formative happenings that enlighten the ordinary days. In his poem "Sunday," George Herbert praises the Lord's Day, "The week were dark, but for thy light."

There must be rhythm to life. One cannot feast continually; "Alleluia cannot always be our song while here below."[13] The necessary business of everyday has meaning only in the context of the archetypal events, and the routine gives space for meditation upon "those mighty acts" whereby God has "given us life and immortality."[14] As with the ballads, so with the rhythm of the week and the year. Apart from the events that reveal the Gospel, daily life cannot disclose] its full meaning. The ballad does not pause occasionally to ask the meaning of the nonsense words of the refrain, for of themselves they convey nothing. Instead, the nonsense words—the refrain that gathers meaning from its repetition in several contexts, now of this stanza, now of that—are themselves a pause that gives time and occasion to let the power of the words of the narrative do their work.

The unity of conception revealed in the liturgical year is, as Northrup Frye says of the Book of the Prophet Isaiah, "a unity not of authorship but of theme"[15] and consequently one does not go astray in examining the work, whether the Bible or the Church Year, as a whole artistic product, even if it was not originally conceived that way. The study that is presented in this book takes into account the present state of the understanding of the history and development of the Church's year, but the primary focus is not on origins but on the interpretation of the liturgical year as it currently exists and is lived by the liturgical churches primarily of the West. In this way it is similar to canonical criticism or to theological criticism of the Bible. One begins literary criticism not with historical questions of sources and the development of a text but with an effort to perceive the unique quality inherent in a work that attracts and moves the reader. Much of the power of a work resides in what the work suggests, in how it expands by unfolding new vistas, uncovering new insights, revealing new associations one had not been aware of before.

To enter into and benefit from such a demanding achievement, humility is required and an open and receptive spirit is essential. The reader familiar with the by-ways of Victorian literature may recall John Ruskin's plea to read humbly and attentively as through their books we enter into "the great concourse of the Dead." We must begin, he insists, with "a true desire to be taught by them, and to enter into their thoughts. To enter into theirs, observe; not to find your own expressed by them. If the person who wrote the book is not wiser than you, you need not read it; if he be, he will think differently from you in many respects. Very ready are we to say of a book, 'How good this is—that's exactly what I think!' but the right feeling is, 'How strange that is! I never thought of that before, and yet I see that it is true; or if I do not now, I hope I shall, someday.' But whether thus submissively or not, at least be sure that you go to the author to get at *his* meaning, not to find yours. ... And be sure also, if the author is worth anything, that you will not get at his meaning all at once;—nay, that at his whole meaning you will not for a long time arrive in any wise."[16] What Ruskin says of worthy books is also true of the work of art called the liturgy. (The demands that great art makes will return more explicitly in the concluding chapter of this book.)

In the liturgical year, as in every artistic masterpiece, everything holds together, every image reinforces the close-packed work so that several levels are experienced simultaneously. The fullness of the symbolism of the year may not always be readily apparent, but upon continued examination and reflection the symbols yield riches of suggestion. Some of the meaning may in fact lie hidden perhaps for generations until it rises again to conscious perception. Such is the wonderful treasury of the Church. The following pages seek to explicate some of that richness.

Anno Domini

TIME AND HISTORY

WHEN HE INSTITUTED the Feast of Christ the King in 1925, Pius XI made the wise observation, "[P]eople are instructed in the truths of faith, and brought to appreciate the inner joys of religion far more effectively by the annual celebration of sacred mysteries than by any official pronouncement of the teaching of the Church."[1] The pope understood the power of the liturgy as the school of the Church. The yearly celebration of the mysteries of the faith involves those who celebrate it mentally and physically and spiritually. By participation in the sacred year of the Lord we become part of what we celebrate, and it becomes part of us.

The Experience of Time

The liturgical year rests upon the most basic of all the universal experiences, an experience not only of humanity but of the whole cosmos: time. We experience time in at least three distinctive ways.

The first understanding that comes to mind is historical time, time in which recorded events take place. The image is linear, the familiar time line: out of the past through the present, into what lies ahead. Such linear, historical time is unrepeatable. A wise young man in the South Bronx said to me many decades ago in the middle of the week, "Not Saturday comin'; Saturday goin.'" His was a most vivid understanding of the passage of time. The Saturday that was a few days ahead of us was on its way toward us, but the previous Saturday was past and moving away from us as we stood in the present. Novelty also is associated with this unrepeatable passage of time. The remark attributed to Heraclitus (ca. 544-484 B.C.) to illustrate his basic assertion that "everything moves" is justly famous: "One can never step twice into the same river."[2] That image of time as a flowing river has been incorporated in the fifth stanza of Isaac Watts's paraphrase of Psalm 90, "O God, our help in ages past" [originally "Our God, our help in ages past"]:

> Time, like an ever-rolling stream,
> Bears all its sons away....

In such a linear view of history, the fullness of time is located either at the beginning, as for the ancient Greeks and the Golden Age, or at the end, as for Christianity and the expectation of the consummation. It is the conception of time that is traced in the Apostles' Creed (born of the Virgin Mary, suffered under Pontius Pilate, was crucified, died, buried, descended to the dead, rose again, ascended into heaven, will come again to judge) and is relived in the Church Year, following St. Luke's chronology in what has been called "the half-year of Christ" from preparation to birth, to the wondrous life, to suffering, death, resurrection, and forty days later, ascension and ten days after that the sending of the Holy Spirit; and then in "the half-year of the Church," the consequent spread of the Faith, by the work of the Spirit, from Jerusalem throughout Judea and Samaria and to the ends of the earth (Acts 1:8).

This figure of historical time, however, is not as basic as it may at first appear. J. B. Priestly, the English novelist and critic, wrote,

[I]n the ancient Egyptian *Book of the Dead*...the deceased asks the god Thoth, "How long shall I have to live?" And Thoth replies: "It is decreed that thou shalt live for millions of millions of years, a life of millions of years." In one jump we seem to have arrived in one of the shabbier corners of our own age. No esoteric wisdom here. This is the so-called eternity of our Bible Fundamentalists, spiritualists, and the like—a false eternity that is simply our passing time running on and on. It is time as we think we know it without any qualitative change, only more and more of it. Though in this life beyond the grave we may be invisible to mortal eyes, existing somewhere behind a veil, we are still in Time and History; there has been no fundamental change. We are asked to live in a brutally simplified universe.

...[P]rimitive men...could do better than this. The idea of the Great Time, the eternal dream time, with its qualitative difference, its *all-at-once* instead of *one-thing-after-another*, is infinitely more profound. Some wisdom seems to have been lost when the hunters and cave-men settled down to till the soil and then became not only farmers but civil servants, generals, high priests, soothsayers, and pharaohs. And a bad idea was born—the idea that eternity is simply a vast helping of passing time—an idea that makes mischief to this day. How many sensitive minds must have been first bewildered and then repelled by this false eternity offered them...?[3]

The all-at-once of the Great Time underlies the theological understanding of St. John the Divine (that is, John the Theologian) in his Gospel in which the resurrection, ascension, and sending of the Spirit all occur on one day. It is a view that we will encounter again and again in the liturgical year and its exploration and exposition of the great "mystery of our religion" (1 Tim. 3:16), most clearly of all in the Holy Triduum, the unified celebration (Good Friday, Holy Saturday, Easter Day) of the death, the rest in the tomb, and resurrection of Christ as one event. It is also to be found in the ancient celebration of the Epiphany, which weaves together the visit of the Magi to the infant Jesus, his baptism in the Jordan, and his first miracle at Cana in Galilee.

In addition to historical and Great Time, a third conception of time is what has been called cosmic time, nature's time, and its figure is the circle, the cosmic cycles and seasons.

The Turning of the Day

We encounter circular time most intimately in the turning of the day, the regular cycle of waking and rest, the basic rhythm of the world. Daily prayer is built on this fundamental pattern. The Second Vatican Council renewed the ancient pattern of prayer as the sun sets and prayer as the sun rises: "Lauds as morning prayer and Vespers as evening prayer are the two hinges on which the daily Office turns; hence they are to be considered as the chief Hours and are to be celebrated as such."[4] These two hours are the two poles, the two hinges on which the day turns. The pattern of Judaism has been continued in the Church: sunset marks the end of the day and also the beginning of the next day so that the days roll on without interruption, flowing in a continuous cycle. The hours of darkness are experienced as a time of waiting and watching. Negative emotions abound: the unknown, dissolution of perception and even of consciousness, isolation, fear, descent into nonbeing, death and the cosmic night. But night is not all negative, for it is also a time of stillness, rest, peace, and promise. The premier liturgical experience of night is Holy Saturday, the Great Sabbath, in which Christ rests in the grave and the tomb is transformed into the womb of new and unending life.

Dawn comes and brings with it fulfillment of the night of waiting and preparation. The emotions associated with the dawn are almost entirely positive: sunrise, light, the awakening from a world of dreams into the world of reality, a new beginning, gratitude for surviving the dangers of the night, and gratitude for fresh opportunities for being of service in the fulfillment of one's duty. Eighteenth-century and nineteenth-century hymns were especially keen on this idea. Bishop Thomas Ken's beloved morning hymn begins,

> Awake, my soul, and with the sun
> Thy daily stage of duty run;
> Shake off dull sloth, and joyful rise
> To pay thy morning sacrifice.[5]

And John Keble's "New every morning is the love" reminds us

> If on our daily course our mind
> Be set to hallow all we find,
> New treasures still, of countless price,
> God will provide for sacrifice.
>
> ...
>
> The trivial round, the common task,
> Will furnish all we ought to ask,—
> Room to deny ourselves, a road
> To bring us daily nearer God.[6]

The opening of a new day is to be consecrated by the sacrifice of praise and service gladly offered in thanksgiving for resurrection from sleep. Such is the personal appropriation of the significance of resting and rising. Christ's rest in the tomb is the preparation for the resurrection, and the daily rising of the sun is a proclamation of the resurrection of Christ, the rising Sun/Son.

In such a way Christianity accomplishes the sanctification of time, and participates in the unceasing praise of God that is the purpose of the Church's existence, weaving a continuous song of praise on earth as it joins the perpetual praise of heaven. Such a view is splendidly described in John Ellerton's evening hymn.

> The day thou gavest, Lord, is ended,
>   The darkness falls at thy behest;
> To thee our morning hymns ascended,
>   Thy praise shall sanctify our rest.
>
> We thank thee that thy Church, unsleeping
>   While earth rolls onward into light,
> Through all the world her watch is keeping,
>   And rests not now by day or night.
>
> As o'er each continent and island
>   The dawn leads on another day,

The voice of prayer is never silent,
    Nor dies the strain of praise away.

The sun that bids us rest is waking
    Our brethren 'neath the western sky,
And hour by hour fresh lips are making
    Thy wondrous doings heard on high

So be it, Lord; thy throne shall never,
    Like earth's proud empires, pass away;
Thy kingdom stands, and grows for ever,
    Till all thy creatures own thy sway.

The daily round of evening and morning, darkness and light, is a basic rhythm in the world, established at the beginning of creation ("evening and morning, the first day").

The Turning of the Seasons

A second basic rhythm is a larger cycle, the yearly round, the turning of the seasons. It, too, is rooted in the foundational book of Genesis (8:22).

As long as the earth endures,
    seedtime and harvest, cold and heat,
summer and winter, day and night,
    shall not cease.

Like the daily cycle, the yearly round is experienced by the whole human race and indeed by the entire creation. For more than thirty-five years Hal Borland (1900-1978) wrote a carefully crafted nature editorial for the Sunday *New York Times* and a quarterly essay for *The Progressive* magazine. The editors of *The Progressive*, a journal in the tradition of Robert M. La Follette of Wisconsin, regularly received complaints from readers who objected to wasting space for reports of leaves and bugs when there were such important matters crying for attention. The editors would regularly and gladly take up the challenge and defend their policy of setting social and political and economic issues of the moment in the larger context of the natural world. Borland wrote one spring in Connecticut,

So many are the demands and so loud the threats and the contention that it is easy to forget that the most important things happening right now are out of man's reach. The year is at that seasonal point where all the forces of earth and sky are going to get on with vernal business, no matter what man does or says. If they didn't, if buds didn't open and grass grow and flowers bloom, there would soon be no talk at all, and no talkers.

...We once knew these things almost instinctively. We grew up on the land knowing them. But arrogance and a short memory alienated us from the beginnings that are fundamental to life, isolated us from the showery truth of April and the green truth of May....[T]he annual miracle of spring is beyond our command.[7]

Although as December draws to a close we may speak of the old year ending and a new year about to begin, the year is in fact a circle, and therefore one can begin anywhere in its course and by following along arrive again at the place where one began. St. Paulinus of Nola (353-431) understood that. In a hymn for a patronal feast day he wrote

> Another year completed,
> The day comes round once more
> Which with our patron's radiance
> Is bright as heretofore....[8]

Moreover, no year is complete in itself. Each year overlaps the one ahead as well as the one behind in unbreakable continuity. Individual lives begin and end, but the enduring rhythms of the great cycle are the pattern of the earth and of the stars.[9]

Traces of the cosmic time of the natural year are embedded in the liturgical year. There are feasts on the solstices, the Nativity of St. John the Baptist (June 24) at the summer solstice and Christmas at the winter solstice. The spring equinox is associated with Passover and Easter. There are also the quarterly ember days, of obscure origin but with pre-Christian antecedents, observed at the turning of the seasons: in the fall (following Holy Cross Day, September 14), in the winter (following St. Lucy's Day, December 13), in the spring (following the First Sunday in Lent), and in the summer (following the Day of Pentecost).

The day is sanctified by the Liturgy of the Hours, the Daily Office of prayer as the sun sets and prayer as the sun rises, supplemented by the "little hours" at mid-morning, noon, and mid-afternoon, and Compline, "the way the Church says good night."[10] The year is sanctified by connecting it to the life of Christ and his Church. That life is all of one piece, but we benefit from the contemplation of it by stages, one event after another. Such sanctification is

not transforming something profane into something holy but rather conse-
crating it to a larger and deeper purpose. Better still, it is uncovering a significance that eludes those who see only the surface of things and revealing how
time in its many manifestations participates in the praise of God.

The Week

The arrangement of groups of days to comprise a week is not inherent in
the turning of the days or seasons or years. The seven-day week is an artifi-
cial construct, but it has become foundational for Judaism and therefore for
Christianity as well. Anthropologically, there are no exact parallels with other
Near Eastern cultures; the seven-day week may be connected with the phases
of the moon, but there are no resemblances to the manner in which the day of
the full moon was observed in Mesopotamia.

The seventh day of the Jewish week, the Sabbath, is the only day of the
week with its own name. In the Bible, the origin of the Sabbath is explained
in two ways: a commemoration of God's rest after the completion of creation
(Ex. 20:11 and 31:17), and a remembrance of the deliverance from Egypt (Deut.
5:15. Slaves cannot take a day off; free people can.) In the Bible, the Sabbath
observance is embedded in the Decalogue and is marked by complete abstinence from work (Ex. 20:10), by doubling the daily sacrifices (Numb. 28:9f),
and by special gatherings for worship (Lev. 23:2-3). It thus has a twofold purpose: a day of rest for people (especially slaves) and for cattle, and secondly a
day set apart for the worship of God (Ex. 31:12-17). Rabbinic definitions of what
constitutes work may seem excessively refined, but a classic definition is that
work is whatever requires changing the natural world, any interference in the
completed work of God. *Shabbat* is therefore an acceptance and enjoyment of
the world as God made it, a day of peace and gratitude, a participation in the
divine rest and satisfaction with creation. The Sabbath is thus a weekly correction of human relationship to nature, to God, to work, and to other people. It
makes and preserves space for God.

The early Christians, being Jews, continued to keep the Sabbath as a
day of rest and prayer, an eschatological event awaiting fulfillment in the
coming age. Liturgical observance of Saturday among Christians continued
or was revived in various places into the fourth century.[11] There were some
efforts to establish a liturgical observance of the Sabbath as well as Sunday;
at least from the time of Alcuin (d. 804), Saturday Mass has been a votive
of our Lady, the Lord's Day being preceded by our Lady's Day. Generally,
however, within the first generation of Christians, Sunday superseded the
Sabbath.

"From evening to evening you shall keep your Sabbath" (Lev. 23:32). The pattern begun in Genesis 1:5, "There was evening and there was morning, the first day," continues through the week of creation, and yields a continuity in which every hour is part of the pattern and nothing is left out. The evening marks the end of one day even as it is also the beginning of the next. The biblical understanding that evening, sunset, is both the end and the beginning underlies the central stanza of the Ambrosian hymn for the Ninth Hour *Rerum Deus tenax vigor* ("O Strength and stay upholding all creation"):

> Grant to life's day a calm, unclouded ending,
> An eve untouched by shadows of decay,
> The brightness of a holy death-bed blending
> With dawning glories of the eternal day.[12]

As life here comes to a close, eternity dawns.

Sunday, called the first day of the week in Syriac-speaking communities, was in Greek-speaking communities called the Lord's Day, in Latin *Dominica*, the name used in the calendars of the Western Church.[13] *Dominica*, the Lord's Day, perhaps derives from *Dominicum*, the Lord's Supper, celebrated on the first day of the week.[14] St. Paul and the Christians of Troas assembled "on the first day of the week, when we met to break bread" (Acts 20:7). The *Didache*, from the closing years of the first century, directs, "On the Lord's own day gather together and break bread and give thanks, having first confessed your sins so that your sacrifice may be pure" (14.1). Sunday is "the Lord's own day" because it is the day of resurrection and the day of his post-resurrection appearances; as in the Acts of the Apostles, "break bread" is at least becoming a name for the Lord's Supper; "give thanks" provides the name Eucharist; and it is noteworthy how early the name "sacrifice" is applied to the Eucharistic supper of the Lord.

Ignatius of Antioch (ca. 35-ca. 107), directing that Sabbath observance was to be replaced by the celebration of the Lord's Day, describes the day of resurrection as a joyful occasion on which there must be no kneeling, no fasting, its celebrants "no longer keeping the Sabbath but living in accordance with the Lord's Day, on which our life also arose through him and his death."[15] Sunday is the Christian weekly holy day because it is the day of Christ's resurrection and thus of ours in him.

Sunday, therefore, as the weekly commemoration of the resurrection, is the principal and basic festival of the Christian calendar. From the fourth century, the day began to be regulated by both Church and civil legislation. The first day of the week as a day of rest consecrated to the service of God was enjoined by canon 21 of the Council of Elvira (ca. 306) and by the emperor Constantine in the Peace of Constantine, promulgated March 3, 321, which forbade work on Sunday by townspeople, although permitting farm labor. Canon 29 of the Council of Laodicea (ca. 380) enjoined abstention from work as far as possible. Church legislation became increasingly strict from the sixth to the thirteenth centuries.

Sunday was the Christian weekly holy day because it is the day of Christ's resurrection. The first day of the week was also connected with the first day of creation (Genesis 1:1-5). Justin Martyr (ca. 100-ca. 165) described the twofold custom: "We assemble on the day of the sun because it is the first day, that on which God transformed the darkness and matter to create the world, and also because Jesus Christ our Savior rose from the dead on the same day."[16] The two events of creation and resurrection are joined in the first stanza of a Latin hymn attributed to Gregory the Great (d. 604), *Primo dierum omnium,*

> This day the first of days was made,
> When God in light the world arrayed;
> Or, when his Word arose again,
> And, conquering death, gave life to men.[17]

Later, St. Isidore of Seville (d. 636) connects the first day of the week with the coming of the Holy Spirit. Thus all three persons of the Holy Trinity came to be associated with the observance of Sunday—the resurrection of the Son, creation by the Father, the descent of the Holy Spirit—and eventually the Preface of the Holy Trinity came to be used on all Sundays after Pentecost that did not have a proper Preface of their own. A late (perhaps eighteenth-century) Latin hymn, *Die parente temporum,* makes the threefold connection:

> On this day, the first of days,
> God the Father's Name we praise,
> Who, creation's Lord and spring,
> Did the world from darkness bring.

> On this day the eternal Son
> Over death his triumph won;
> On this day the Spirit came
> With his gifts of living flame.[18]

Bishop Christopher Wordsworth (1807-1885) in his hymn "O day of rest and gladness"[19] praised the same "triple light" of creation, resurrection, and giving of the Spirit, as did Bishop William Walsham How (1823-1897) in "This day at thy creating word,"[20] in which each of the three creative actions is made the basis of a prayer for a personal blessing. The first stanza sets the pattern:

> This day at thy creating word
> First o'er the earth the light was poured;
> O Lord, this day upon us shine
> And fill our souls with light divine.

The first day of the week, moreover, took on eschatological dimensions.[21] The writer to the Hebrews warned, "And let us consider how to provoke one another to love and good deeds, not neglecting to meet together, as is the habit of some, but encouraging one another, and all the more as you see the Day approaching." (Heb. 10:24-25). More explicitly, the *Epistle of Barnabas*, written sometime between 70 and 135, explains, " 'I cannot stand your new moons and Sabbaths.' You see what he means: it is not the present Sabbaths that are acceptable to me, but the one that I have made; on that Sabbath, after I have set everything at rest, I will create the beginning of an eighth day, which is the beginning of another world."[22] Basil the Great (d. 379) said that the first day of the week was "the image of the age to come."[23] Augustine (d. 430) says "It prefigures eternal rest." Thus, as the eighth day, Sunday marks not simply the beginning of a new week but the beginning of a new creation. In his resurrection Christ has broken through the dimensions that limit this world and opened the gates into another world and so has inaugurated the new creation characterized by the day that has no end. (Because the baptized, who by the "water of rebirth" (Titus 3:5) are risen with Christ who lives in the unending eighth day, baptismal fonts are frequently octagonal, showing resurrection into the new creation.)

Sunday may be regarded as "a post-resurrection appearance of the Risen Christ in which he breathes his Spirit upon his disciples for the forgiveness of sins and for the life of the world." It is "the point at which all the central images of the Christian life converge and...the Christian Sunday may properly be claimed as the heart, not only of the liturgical year, but of the Christian life itself."[24]

Building on devout Jewish practice, Christians soon added two more days for religious observance during the week, directed as early as the *Didache*.[25] The Jewish fast days, not prescribed for first-century Jews but practiced by certain pious individuals, were Monday and Thursday; "I fast twice in the week," boasted the Pharisee in Luke 18:12. Christians chose two different fast days, the fourth day, Wednesday, and the day of preparation, Friday. Wednesday recalled the betrayal of Christ by Judas and Friday the crucifixion.[26] The use of different days and the significance that became attached to them are perhaps not intended to be understood as condemning Jewish practice but rather as emphasizing to Jewish converts the complete change that embracing the new faith required.[27] As time went by in the West, the fast (omitting food altogether) came to be reduced to abstinence (avoiding certain foods such as meat), and then Wednesday was omitted altogether except during Lent.

In the Middle Ages Thursday was kept as a day of rejoicing because it was the weekly commemoration of the Ascension and the day of the institution of the Eucharist. "Thus the events of Holy Week played an important role in developing the liturgical character of the weekdays."[28]

Living the History of Salvation

In the incarnation, God broke into human life and into our time, taking it all into himself, all the varying experiences and figures of time—historical, cosmic, "dream time." Thus the blessing of the Paschal candle declares, "All time belongs to him." Every year since his coming into the world is *anno Domini*, in the year of the Lord,[29] from whose nativity we reckon the years and count the centuries.

Long before the incarnation, however, God was at work in human history. Biblical religion is grounded in history, sacred history. Historical events are the vehicle of revelation. They mediate God and disclose the truth about God and ourselves as history and eternity meet. Therefore, the liturgy of the Church seeks to relate all time to the redemptive purposes of God, giving it meaning in time and in eternity. So the Church's year is not a mere pious recollection of past events, turning the clock back, imagining that the Church is present at a long-past day when one of the mighty acts of God was accomplished. In its year the Church relives its sacred days and appropriates their graces, bringing the past into the present, making all contemporary. The liturgical year is not a mere commemoration of the events of the Gospel; it is in fact the actualization of these events, their renewal upon earth.[30] Thus the act of salvation—begun in Bethlehem, accomplished on Good Friday, vindicated on Easter Day, crowned on Ascension Day—is an ever-continuing process as its fruits are made real in the lives of those who accept this redemption. The Church's calendar, its day-by-day observance of the liturgical year, is not only a pious recollection of historic events and people. The liturgical year is not a lifeless representation of the events of the past or a bare record of a former age. It is rather Christ himself who is ever living in his Church. Out of the past and distant antiquity such days as Christmas, Good Friday, Easter, Ascension, and Pentecost come alive when one realizes them as acts taking place in the world today and continuing until the final end of all days. The whole cycle of the incarnate Lord's life, in addition to its historic form, is regularly being reproduced in the lives of his people. He is constantly being reborn in those who accept him and who can say with the holy Virgin, "Let it be with me according to your word" (Luke 1:38) and who in Phillips Brooks's carol "O little town of Bethlehem" sing to the holy Child of Bethlehem, "Be born in us today." The Lord Jesus is being crucified afresh in those who deny and forsake him. He is again being resurrected in those who earnestly seek him in their early morning darkness. The liturgical year, therefore, is not just a memorial of events of twenty centuries ago. It is nothing less than Christ himself, living in his Church and working through it until the end of time in order to put human beings in contact with his life-giving mysteries and to make those people live through him. The redemptive events are timeless, their meaning eternal.

The liturgical year is more than a series of commemorations of past events. The events are experienced as living realities. Easter is in fact the resurrection of Jesus Christ from the dead. It is a remembrance of that morning in the garden when Mary Magdalene was troubled by the empty tomb and encountered one she first thought was the gardener, and at the same time it is a foreshadowing of the final hope of the Church and of each member of the Christian community. Those who participate in the liturgical celebration are witnesses of the resurrection.[31]

In the liturgical year the Church "lives always conscious of her past; perpetuating the life of her Founder in all the actuality of the present; her history in witness-bearer and witnessing; re-living it all as though it were a wholly new experience, for the testimony this may bear to the world, and the inspiration it will be to her children. In this she witnesses and worships, because it fully, harmoniously, and eloquently expresses her life."[32]

The events commemorated in the liturgical year are "not isolated episodes in the life of Christ, but links in a chain that is the paschal mystery.... [I]n each of these liturgical celebrations the Church looks to the one center of the Christian year: the death and resurrection of Christ, with his return at the end of time."[33] Melito Bishop of Sardis (d. ca. 190), long before, preached "the Passover mystery which is Christ."[34] The events of the Gospel that are celebrated in the Church's year are stages in a journey into the paschal mystery from which they derive their authenticity and effectiveness. "At every moment, then, we are journeying toward the definitive reconstruction of the world in accordance with the eternal plan of God."[35] The liturgical year regards each event in the life of Christ as having sacred significance, as nothing less than a revelation of God, a Theophany, which leads each believer out through a succession of events to a contemplation of and indeed a participation in the eternal action of God.

We who celebrate the Church's year are not expected to forget what we know or put out of our minds the entire story with which we are familiar. And year by year the story is ever-new. Paul Zeller Strodach (1876-1947) wrote of the First Sunday in Advent:

> The beginning a new *Anno Domini* in the real sense of that term, the Church's New Year's Day....
>
> The Church Year is vastly different from the common or civil year, not only in its divisions and the Days and Facts therein commemorated, but in that it is distinctively the *Christian* Year, in the fullest sense the *Year of Grace*. To grasp this is to understand its structure and purpose. For while it is built through the conjoining of various *Seasons* and marks certain *Holy Days* for observance, this is done with no mechanical or sentimental object in view, but entirely for the *believer's* benefit. For no Feast or Fast Day or Season will have any point or good in its coming or going unless it stirs one to remembrance and causes one to pass through the commemoration in such a way that one will be benefited thereby. Thus the entire Year wherein the Church lives and divides her time is one of great spiritual opportunity; not merely to review and remember, but to *see* therein more and more "what God has done for my soul."
>
> The portals are thrown wide, a Year of Grace! Will it be a *year*? Who knows? But in God's goodness to us all there opens before us again the way to the Green Pastures and the Still Waters...perhaps, too, to the Valley of the Shadow....The historical point of departure is this: The Church Year begins, one can almost say, picturing the Drama of Redemption. It is to be worked out according to God's plan. This is to be vivified in the Life of Christ and in the Birth of the Church, Christianity. It is to be developed in an orderly manner, step by step, Lord's Day on Lord's Day; a constant calling to remembrance all that has been done and won. But the genius of the Year is in that it develops this in such a way as if *we* were experiencing this for the first time, as though it were all for *me*;—dramatic perhaps, but it makes the contact, the effect, vivid. Hence the constant play of Lections, Introits, Collects, and Graduals and other minor "variables": all contributing some part in developing real contact with a moment which is to be to us an intensely real, personal experience with the Events.

> [W]e cannot go to Christmas Day with a mere thought of a Babe in our minds, nor that of celebrating an event marking an Anniversary. We have to approach and take that Day as part of a *Completed* Plan; and permit it to contribute its peculiar part in influencing us to realize how we stand, how we feel, what we really are at the Manger Throne in the light of that Completed Plan.[36]

The liturgical year is a confrontation with the one who said, "I am the first and the last, and the living one. I was dead, and see, I am alive forever and ever." (Rev. 1:17-18) The deeds and mysteries of that Living One are not things that are past and finished; they are living and present, even eternal. In Christ, and therefore in all the states and actions of Christ, history and eternity meet. And here the picture becomes more complicated and therefore more interesting.

Originally feasts did not commemorate a single discrete event in salvation history but rather a cluster of distinct events all at once. The antiphon to the Magnificat on the Epiphany declares,

> Three mysteries mark this holy day:
> today the star leads the Magi to the infant Christ;
> today water is changed into wine for the wedding feast;
> today Christ wills to be baptized by John in the river Jordan
> to bring us salvation.

The same idea is expounded in the fifth century by Coelius Sedulius in the hymn "When Christ's appearing was made known."[37] Pascha originally celebrated not just Easter morning but the entire mystery of Christ: his passion and death and descent into hell and resurrection on the third day (and in St. John's Gospel also the ascension into heaven and the sending of the Spirit). What was being celebrated was not a past event but an eternally present saving mystery: our present life in our Lord. With that understanding of "God's mystery, that is, Christ himself" (Col.2:2) we begin with what has become the beginning of the liturgical year, the season of Advent.

2

Advent

THERE ARE MANY beginnings of the year. There is the secular New Year, January 1, but the Church has taken little notice of that occasion except to condemn the excesses of its celebration, and there is, after all, no reason why the Church should follow the world. There is the practical new year, the beginning of the parish activity year that (in the northern hemisphere) begins in early September as congregants return from summer vacation and schools resume. For the Jews, Rosh Hashanah in September-October marks the beginning of the new year. In Eastern Orthodox practice the year begins September 1, which was the beginning of the tax year in the Byzantine Empire, showing Orthodoxy's frequent affinity with Judaism, whose new year also begins in the autumn. By an old reckoning, Septuagesima, the third Sunday before Lent, was a beginning of the year, echoing Pascha as the beginning of the year for ancient Hebrews: "This month [Nisan] shall mark for you the beginning of months; it shall mark the first month of the year for you" (Ex. 12:2). Pseudo Chrysostom in an ancient Easter homily observed, "The time of Passover...is taken to be the beginning of the year," and in the Eastern Orthodox tradition still the Fourth Sunday before Lent marks a kind of beginning of the new year. Since about the beginning of the seventh century, however, liturgical books begin with Advent, the latest and entirely Western addition to the Church's calendar.

The Origins of the Season

There is an almost innate pattern in human behavior of fast before feast, preparation followed by celebration, anticipation and preparation leading to feasting, but otherwise the origins of the season of Advent are obscure. Liturgical historians have in recent decades become notably skeptical regarding our knowledge of the origins and development of the seasons of the liturgical year.

We possess little sure and certain knowledge, only fragmentary and isolated pieces of evidence. It is like having a dozen or so pieces of a jigsaw puzzle and that basis attempting to imagine what the whole puzzle looks like. We will see with regard not only to Advent but also to Christmas, Epiphany, and Lent competing hypotheses with little agreement. Each hypothesis concerning the origins of Advent is of continuing interest; none is entirely credible.[1]

Advent may have its origins outside of Rome in preparation for baptism at Epiphany. There was in Gaul, attested by Hilary who died in 367, a three-week preparation for Epiphany and its baptisms. The Council of Saragossa in Spain in the year 380 speaks of a three-week observance from December 17 to January 6.

Perpetuus, Bishop of Tours (d. 490), decreed a fast in preparation for Christmas beginning on St. Martin's Day (November 11) consisting of three days of fasting per week. Sixth-century synodical documents and episcopal decrees enjoin penitence from St. Martin's Day (November 11) to the Epiphany, "St. Martin's Lent," continuing for eight weeks (fifty-six days, but no fasting on Saturday or Sunday gives a fast of forty days). These fasts had a penitential emphasis, suggesting that they were at least primarily a preparation for baptism. The Mozarabic rite in Spain and the Ambrosian rite in Milan have a six-week preparation. In the present Ambrosian rite Advent begins the Sunday after November 11. Northern Italian sources suggest a focus on the Incarnation rather than the Epiphany. Filastrius, Bishop of Brescia (d. 391), says that the Church observes four fasts during the year: at Jesus's birth, Easter, Ascension, and Pentecost. The pre-Christmas fast may have been newly established or perhaps had been shifted from a preparation for Epiphany. Maximus of Turin suggests that there are two Sundays of preparation for Christmas; the practice in mid-fifth century Ravenna is similar.

In pagan Rome there was a fast of the tenth month (December), one of the four season fasts of the year. Advent may have been in part the Church's response to this pre-Christian winter fast. The evidence suggests that until Gregory I (590-604), a six-week Advent was observed in Rome. The Church in Spain and Gaul perhaps gave the emerging season its penitential character. Gaul emphasized the eschatological character of the preparation, Adolf Adam suggests, through the influence of Irish missionaries who emphasized the coming judgment and the need for repentance before the return of the Judge.[2] Advent became a penitential season like Lent with the use of violet vestments and the exclusion of the Gloria in excelsis and Alleluias from the Mass and the Te Deum from the Office. The penitential character was brought to Rome in the twelfth century, but there the joyous Alleluia was retained, showing a less than complete acceptance of the penitential spirit. The practice of fasting varied in local communities: three weeks in Gaul and Spain in the fourth century, four weeks in the Gregorian sacramentary, five or six weeks in older Roman practice, six weeks in the Mozarabic and Ambrosian rites, eight weeks in Gaul in the fifth century, and three months, from the conception of John the Baptist, September 24, which was once the beginning of the civil year in Constantinople and throughout Asia Minor. This wide variation suggests a complex development of what began as more than a simple preparatory period before Christmas.

The seventh-century *Comes* (lectionary) of Würtzburg begins with the Vigil of Christmas, where the story began, and therefore the lessons at the end of the year tell of the end of the story: the last judgment and the reign of Christ. The Gelasian sacramentary (the manuscript is mid-eighth century) is the oldest known sacramentary in which the feasts are arranged according to the Church year. That collection begins with Advent; collects Epistles, and Gospels are provided for five Sundays before Christmas and also for the corresponding Wednesdays and Fridays.

Gregory the Great fixed the length of the preparatory period at four weeks, usually explained as a reliving of the four thousand years of waiting for the coming of the Messiah, the birth of Christ being widely thought to have occurred some four thousand years after creation began.[3] A Middle English lyric sings,

> Adam lay ybounden,
> Bounden in a bond;
> Four thousand winter
> Thought he not too long....

Thus there were propers provided for masses for the four Sundays before Christmas and for three Ember Day masses (Wednesday, Friday, and Saturday after the Third Sunday in Advent) that make use of Advent themes. The season is oriented toward preparation for the celebration of the Nativity.

The Meanings of Advent

The eschatological orientation that is found in some of these early sources continues to be a significant element in the proclamation of the season of Advent. Indeed the very name *Adventus*, "coming," "approach," suggests not only the coming of God into the world in Jesus but the approaching return of the risen Lord in all his heavenly splendor. Indeed, the Advent season and its hope should not be regarded purely or even primarily in terms of Christmas. It should not be seen as an introduction to the Incarnation but rather as the completion of the work of redemption. The spirit of the season is expressed in the impatient cry of a sometimes desperate people, "O that you would tear open the heavens and come down" (Isa. 64:1), echoed in the seventeenth-century German hymn *O Heiland reiss die Himmel auf*:

> O Savior rend the heavens wide;
> Come down, come down with mighty stride;
> Unlock the gates, the doors break down;
> Unbar the way to heaven's crown.[4]

The season gives voice to the impatience God's people feel at least from time to time but which they may be hesitant to express to God. The purpose of Advent is to rouse once again in the people of the Church the anticipation of the End and of the great Day of the Lord, and to bid them be prepared for it. In the Gospels, teaching about this approaching Day is always followed by a clear warning, "Keep awake therefore, for you do not know on what day your Lord is coming.... Therefore you also must be ready, for the Son of Man is coming at an unexpected hour" (Matt. 24:42, 44).

Since at least the time of Bernard of Clairvaux (d. 1153), Christians have spoken of the three comings of Christ: in the flesh in Bethlehem, in our hearts daily, and in glory at the end of time. The first of these comings was visible in the weakness of a human infant; the second is invisible but in spirit and power; the third in glory and majesty will be visible to everyone. Behind this threefold coming is a fourfold pattern expounded by Cyril of Jerusalem (315-386) in his justly famous catechetical lectures:

> There is a birth from God before the ages,
> and a birth from a virgin at the fullness of time.
> There is a hidden coming, like that of rain on fleece,
> and a coming before all eyes, still in the future.[5]

The manifold coming suggests an attractive complexity about the season. It is not just climbing back into the Old Testament and attempting a make-believe waiting, pretending that the Christ has not yet come. The waiting of Advent is a real waiting, an authentic expectancy of an event that has not yet taken place, an event that still lies out there ahead of us. Already, as the liturgical year begins, we are being introduced to a strange and profound idea that is inherent in ritual, not only among Christians. Our common distinctions are collapsed, past-present-future are made one and experienced as a single whole. It is what J. B. Priestly called "the all-at-once of the Great

Time, the eternal Dream time" as opposed to the more prosaic "one-thing-after-another." Mircea Eliade, the influential historian of religion, makes use of the traditional formula that introduced the reading of the Gospel in the old Latin Mass, *in illo tempore,* "at that time."[6] "That time" is the sacred time, a time essentially different from the profane succession of moments, a mythical time that is reattained by means of ritual or by the repetition of some action. Sacred time is a primordial mythical time made present. By participating in a ritual, one becomes contemporary with "that time," the *illud tempus,* the time of origins. So at the reading of the Gospel, the people stand as Christ speaks directly to them; they see the miracles happening before their very eyes; they are present with Christ and he is present with them. The people today stand in the crowd who stood around him then, "at that time," watching, listening.

"Stand up and raise your heads, because your redemption is drawing near." (Luke 21:28). The Church begins the year by looking forward to the birth of her Beloved, the Word made flesh. As an anxious bride, she counts the days, preparing, longing, constantly anticipating the joy that will be hers when the time will be fulfilled and Emmanuel will indeed be God-with-us. But the Church gives voice not only to the expectant joy of a bride or of a mother at the impending birth of her child. Mother Church expresses her deep longing for the coming of Christ in glory at the end of the ages. It is not a fearful dread that the Church wishes to instill in her members when through the psalms and hymns and readings and prayers she calls on us to think about the Parousia, the final coming, but rather she points us to the goal of our efforts to keep awake and to watch: unending union with Jesus Christ. All our work and study and prayer and living has one purpose and meaning: to bring us and all humanity into the kingdom of the Father and of the Son and of the Holy Spirit. So the central prayer of Advent is the one word, the concluding prayer of the Bible, *Maranatha,* Come, Lord Jesus.

The theme of Advent is waiting, waiting for God, waiting with sometimes rising impatience, deepening frustration, and frequent disappointment. We wait, we hope, we look. And in that attitude and perspective one finds the whole liturgical year's forward drive and direction. "Small wonder then that at this time, the beginning of the Preparation, the Message of Announcement is so completely illuminating and wide-reaching. It signalizes no individual event; it marks no one day or hour; it describes no single trait or act; but centralizes in its words the Whole Story and carries it home to the waiting heart."[7]

Advent begins (in the older rubric common to Roman Catholics, Anglicans, and Lutherans) "the nearest Sunday to the Feast of St. Andrew, whether before or after,"[8] or, now more straightforwardly, "The Sundays of Advent are always the four Sundays before Christmas Day, whether it occurs on Sunday or a weekday."[9] The Sundays during Advent were described in previous Anglican and Lutheran books as "in Advent" but now, following Roman Catholic use, are accounted "of Advent."[10] The four Sundays have clear themes. The First Sunday, sometimes called particularly among Anglicans "Advent Sunday," focuses on eschatology and the consummation, looking, as the season begins, to the end of all things. The lectionary previously in use in the early (seventh-century) Roman lectionaries, the Sarum Rite, and among Anglicans and Lutherans had as the Gospel for the First Sunday in Advent Matthew 21, the triumphal entry of Jesus into Jerusalem. It was an intriguing choice showing how the Church deals with history and the Bible. It took some time to explain that the "Palm Sunday story" was chosen not out of ignorance or disregard of chronology but symbolically as a vivid dramatization of the entrance of Jesus into his city and among his people amid the acclamation, "Your king comes to you."[11] And that cry was an anticipatory notice of his impending return in glory. This Gospel made a deep impression on European Lutherans and is the inspiration for many of the great Advent hymns of that tradition. One of the finest is by Paul Gerhardt (1607–1676).

> O how shall I receive thee,
>   How greet thee, Lord, aright?
> All nations long to see thee,
>   My Hope, my heart's delight!
> O kindle, Lord most holy,
>   Thy lamp within my breast,
> To do in spirit lowly
>   All that may please thee best.
>
> Thy Zion palms is strewing,
>   And branches fresh and fair;
> My heart, its powers renewing,
>   An anthem shall prepare.
> My soul puts off her sadness
>   Thy glories to proclaim;
> With all her strength and gladness
>   She fain would serve thy name.[12]

Another is by the Swedish bishop Frans Mikael Franzén (1772–1847),

Prepare the way, O Zion!
    Ye awful deeps, rise high;
Sink low, ye lofty mountains,
    The Lord is drawing nigh;
The righteous King of glory,
Foretold in sacred story.
        O blest is he that came
        In God the Father's Name!

O Zion, he approaches,
    Your Lord and King for aye;
Strew palms where he advances,
    Spread garments in his way;
God's promise faileth never,
Hosanna sound forever.
        O blest is he that came
        In God the Father's Name!

Fling wide your portals, Zion,
    And hail your glorious King;
His tidings of salvation
    To every people bring,
Who, waiting still in sadness,
Would sing his praise with gladness.
        O blest is he that came
        In God the Father's Name![13]

Komm, du wertes Lösegeld ("Come, O precious Ransom, come") by Johann Gottfried Olearius (1635-1711) in its third stanza welcomes the Savior,

My hosannas and my palms
Graciously receive, I pray you;
Evermore, as best I can,
Homage I will gladly pay you,
And in faith I will embrace
Life eternal by your grace.[14]

The picture also appears in the third stanza of Charles Coffin's hymn for the Paris Breviary (1736), *Instantis adventum Dei*. The Church is the new Israel going out to meet Christ as he comes toward his city:

> The Advent of our God
> Our prayers must now employ,
> And we must meet him on his road
> With hymns of holy joy.

The amazing condescension is described simply as the eternal God chooses to be incarnate in mortality and the Son becomes a slave in order to set free his sin-enslaved people.

> The everlasting Son
> Incarnate deigns to be;
> Himself a servant's form puts on
> To set his people free.

The invitation to rise and meet the King is renewed, for this is not a repetition of the entrance of the Lord on a lowly beast of burden twenty centuries ago but an event for which we still wait.

> Daughter of Zion, rise
> To meet thy lowly King,
> Nor let thy faithless heart despise
> The peace he comes to bring.
>
> As Judge, on clouds of light,
> He soon will come again,
> And all his scattered saints unite
> With him in heaven to reign.

There is still time, how much no one knows, to change one's life in preparation for meeting the King.

> Before the dawning day,
> Let sin's dark deeds be gone;
> The old life all be put away,
> The new life all put on.
>
> All glory to the Son,
> Who comes to set us free,
> With Father, Spirit, ever one,
> Through all eternity.[15]

The recognition of this hymnic tradition as well as the symbolic power of the Gospel of the triumphal entry led the drafters of the *Lutheran Book of Worship* (1978) to allow for the substitution of this story (from the corresponding synoptic gospel) for the gospel appointed in the three-year Common Lectionary. It was, however, a suggestion of which hardly any parish availed itself and it has now disappeared from the Sunday lectionary, although traces remain in the daily office.

The Second and the Third Sunday of Advent both focus on the ministry of the forerunner, John the Baptist. The Fourth Sunday takes as its theme the events that prepared immediately for Jesus's birth, sometimes summarized as the expectation of the Virgin Mary.

Advent as it is now observed is divided into two parts. Advent Sunday through December 16 has an eschatological thrust. The final week, December 17 through the 24th, looks toward the approaching birth, but it does so as a guarantee of the Second Advent; the eschatological orientation is not compromised or forgotten. The most notable liturgical feature of the final week is the use of the great "O" Antiphons to the Magnificat at vespers. In ancient Rome December 17 began the seven-day revels in honor of the god Saturnus. For Christians December 17 began a time of renewed and intensified devotion, each day having its proper Mass.

The liturgical color throughout Advent is violet, sometimes explained as symbolizing not penitence as it does in Lent but rather the royalty of the approaching King. Percy Dearmer observed, "The 'violet' for Advent does not of course mean the unpleasant colour (so remote from the violet flower) at present provided by the shops. There is no such restriction as to tints, and a rather dark blue, or purple is equally suitable for Advent."[16] In the Sarum use of Salisbury Cathedral the color was blue as also in Spain and in parts of Scandinavia and now revived especially among Lutherans. Blue is said to suggest hope as well as being the color associated with the Mother of Jesus. In the first recorded use of a sequence of liturgical colors, that of the Augustinian Canons of the Holy Sepulcher in Jerusalem in the early twelfth century, black was the color used in Advent. There has seldom in the Church been much attention given to uniformity in color use or to "correct" shades: violet, blue, and black seem interchangeable. In the Eastern Orthodox churches a wide variety may be seen, the general rule being only that brighter colors (or the best vestments) be used on great festivals. On "special occasions" the present Roman Catholic Church also permits the use of "more noble vestments," even if not the color of the day.[17]

Because Advent is a comparatively recent innovation in the liturgical year, there had not been a proper Preface appointed for the season until the middle of the twentieth century. The editors of *The Lutheran Hymnal* of the Lutheran Church— Missouri Synod (1941) drafted a preface for Advent in gloomy medieval style:

Through Jesus Christ, our Lord, whose way John the Baptist prepared, proclaiming Him the Messiah, the very Lamb of God, and calling sinners to repentance, that they might escape from the wrath to be revealed when He cometh again in glory.

A committee consisting of Paul Zeller Strodach, Edward Traill Horn III, and George Rise Seltzer prepared what is an excellent example of liturgical composition for the Lutheran *Service Book and Hymnal* (1958), drawing on Isa. 40:1, 43:1-21; Rev. 21:5 and the preface for Advent in the 1929 Scottish Book of Common Prayer and the 1940 *Book of Common Order* of the Church of Scotland:

You comforted your people with the promise of the Redeemer, through whom you will also make all things new in the day when he shall come again to judge the world in righteousness.

The 1979 Book of Common Prayer appoints the preface drafted for the Trial Liturgy of 1967:

Because you sent your beloved Son to redeem us from sin and death, and to make us heirs in him of everlasting life; that when he shall come again in power and great triumph to judge the world, we may without shame or fear rejoice to behold his appearing.

The Missal of Paul VI of the Roman Catholic Church appoints two prefaces corresponding to the two parts of the season. The first concentrates on The Two Comings of Christ:

Through Christ our Lord.
For he assumed at his first coming the lowliness of human flesh,
and so fulfilled the design you formed long ago,
and opened for us the way to eternal salvation,
that, when he comes again in glory and majesty
and all is at last made manifest, we who watch for that day
may inherit the great promise in which we now dare to hope.

The second preface, for December 17-23, is The Two-fold Expectation of Christ:

Through Christ our Lord.
For all the oracles of the prophets foretold him,
the virgin mother longed for him with love beyond all telling,
John the Baptist sang of his coming and proclaimed his presence
    when he came.
It is by his gift that already we rejoice at the mystery of his Nativity,
so that he may find us watchful in prayer and exultant in his praise.

Neither preface, being heavily didactic, is particularly impressive.

The First Sunday in Advent

The theme of the First Sunday in Advent is the return of the Lord in glory. In Matins (now called the Office of Readings in the Roman Catholic *Liturgy of the Hours*), for the First Sunday in Advent there is a magnificent responsory, a series of versicles and responses sung in answer to the reading of a Lesson, known by its Latin opening, *Aspiciens a longe*. It is an extraordinary text, familiar to many from the King's College Chapel service of Lessons and Carols for Advent Sunday, sung to music adapted from a Magnificat by Palestrina. This responsory is an imaginative combination and expansion of many biblical texts and allusions woven together in a remarkable composition that expresses the spirit of Advent. Its basic vision derives from such passages as Isaiah 52:8-10,

> Listen! Your sentinels lift up their voices,
>   together they sing for joy;
> for in plain sight they see
>   the return of the Lord to Zion....

The *Jewish Study Bible* comments, "[T]he prophet imagines that the lookouts on Jerusalem's higher buildings or fortifications will see God's Presence as it comes toward the city." The prophet Ezekiel reports, "Then he brought me to the gate, the gate facing east. And there, the glory of the God of Israel was coming from the east; the sound was like the sound of mighty waters; and the earth shone with his glory." (Ezek. 43:1-2) Those unknown liturgists who composed this text were so immersed in the language of the Bible that it was their own native tongue, and they could sometimes quote exactly certain passages and more often use texts that came to mind as the inspiration for a new but still faithful expression.

Responsory Aspiciens a longe	*sources*
Watching from afar,	*All people have looked on it [God's work]; everyone watches it from far away. Job 36:25 I am going to save you from far away Jer. 30:10*
I see the power of God coming	*The glory of the God of Israel was coming from the east…the earth shone with his glory Ezek. 43:2*
and a cloud covering the whole earth.	*You shall be like a cloud covering the land …like a cloud covering the earth. Ezek. 38:9, 16*
Go out to meet him and say,	*Come out to meet him Matt. 25:6*
Tell us are you the one who is to come	*Are you the one who is to come Matt.11:3*
To reign over your people Israel?	*He it is who shall rule over my people 1 Sam. 9:17 The Lord will reign over them in Mount Zion Micah 4:7*
High and low, rich and poor, one with another,	*High and low, rich and poor, one with another. Ps. 49:2 BCP pre-1979*
Go out to meet him and say,	*Matt. 25:6*
Hear, O Shepherd of Israel, leading Joseph like a flock,	*Hear, O Shepherd of Israel, leading Joseph like a flock Ps. 80:1*
Tell us are you the one who is to come	*Matt 11:3*
Open wide the gates, you princes,	*Open the gates Isa. 26:2*
That the King of glory may come in	*that the King of glory may come in. Ps. 24:7*
who is to reign over your people Israel.	
Stir up your strength, O Lord, and come	*Stir up your might, and come.… Ps. 80:2*
to reign over your people Israel. Glory to the Father, and to the Son, and to the Holy Spirit. Watching from afar, I see the power of God coming,	

and a cloud covering the whole earth.
Go out to meet him and say,
Tell us are you the one who is to come
to reign over your people Israel?

Although the theme of the First Sunday of Advent is vigilant waiting for the coming Lord,[18] here in this responsory the human element complicates the earnest expectation. John the Baptist, the prophet of the Advent who will be the focus on the next two Sundays, already speaks his hesitancy to acknowledge Jesus as the coming Lord because he does not fulfill what John expected. John's doubtful question is put in the mouth of the Church: "Are you the one who is to come, or are we to wait for another?" (Matt. 11:3) In these powerful verses we learn of the difference between the unconvincing certainty that leaves no room for mistaken human vision and the far more honest and realistic confidence that is born of a daring faith. Throughout Advent, and indeed throughout the authentic life of the Church, two points of view are held in tension. There is the prophetic view that preserves and relies on the promises of God, and there is what might be called the situational view reflecting the actual everyday experience of humanity.

Such honesty before God is profoundly rooted in the Tanakh, the Hebrew Bible, and John shows himself to stand in a noble line, indeed the last of the prophets. When God promised to Abraham a vast posterity, the patriarch boldly objects that he, a very old man, has no children and therefore the promise is surely impossible of fulfillment. Sarah joins in his skepticism and both laugh at the promise. (Genesis 15:1-18:15.) Realistic doubt challenges God's declaration. Christians look back over a long history and, when honesty prevails, can say that the world has not changed in any obvious way since the appearance of Christ. Thomas Hardy, who wanted to believe, put his doubtful hesitation in a little poem "Christmas 1924."

> "Peace upon earth!" was said. We sing it,
> And pay a million priests to bring it.
> After two thousand years of mass
> We've got as far as poison-gas.

It is a devastating observation as what at least appears to be reality intrudes upon vision. Advent and the liturgical year as a whole, while proclaiming the promise, make allowance for such honest doubt.

The texts for the First Sunday reflect an unusual unity and coherence.[19] The antiphons to the psalms in first vespers in the Roman Liturgy of the Hours announce the truth that although the arrival of the coming Lord may still be distant, it is certain:

> Proclaim the good news among the nations,
> our God will come to save us.   [see Isa. 35:4][20]

> Know that the Lord is coming and with him all his saints;
> that day will dawn with a wonderful light, alleluia.   [see Zech. 14:5-7][21]

> The Lord will come with mighty power;
> all mortal eyes will see him.   [see Rev. 1:7][22]

The antiphon on the Magnificat anticipates the opening of the great responsory at Matins:

> See the Lord is coming from afar,   [see Jer. 30:10]
> His splendor fills the earth.   [Isa. 6:3][23]

God's power is still far away, and yet the second line declares that that power and glory are here already, even now filling the earth as the Church sings in the Sanctus.

The psalm antiphons in Morning Prayer focus on the renewal of creation: the whole world participates in the change that God is bringing about:[24]

> On that day sweet wine will flow from the mountains,
> milk and honey from the hills, alleluia.   [Joel 3:18]

> The mountains and hills will sing praise to God;
> all the trees of the forest will clap their hands,
> for he is coming, the Lord of a kingdom that lasts for ever, alleluia.
>   [see Ps. 96:12]

A hymn that Charles Coffin composed for the Paris Breviary (1736), *Jordanis oras praevia* ("On Jordan's bank the Baptist's cry"), declares in its original second stanza,

> E'en now the air, the sea, the land
> Feel that their Maker is at hand;
> The very elements rejoice,
> And welcome him with cheerful voice.[25]

It is not only humanity that waits for the completion of the revelation of God; the whole natural world, as St. Paul knew, shares the expectation. "For the creation waits with eager longing for the revealing of the children of God;...the creation itself will be set free from bondage to decay and will obtain the freedom of the glory of the children of God." (Rom. 8:19, 21).

A third psalm antiphon at Morning Prayer recalls Moses's declaration that God would "raise up for you a prophet like me from among your own people" (Deut. 18:15, 18).

> A great prophet will come to Jerusalem;
> of that people he will make a new nation.   [see Deut. 18:15, 18][26]

The Gospels indicate that the expectation of the fulfillment of this promise was very much alive at the beginning of Jesus's ministry. When asked about his identity, John the Baptist denied that he was "the prophet" (John 1:21); the crowds experiencing the sign of the feeding of the five thousand, "began to say of Jesus, 'This is indeed the prophet who is to come into the world'" (John 6:14); later some said, "This is really the prophet" (John 7:40). Moses spoke of the need to listen to the coming prophet. The "new nation" of the antiphon is the Christian community, those who hear and obey the teaching of Jesus (Luke 8:21; 11:28).

Although there may be preliminary or preparatory actions, the Eucharist proper begins with the entrance of the ministers of the service and their taking their places near the altar. The action was once accompanied by the singing of an antiphon and psalm, the Introit. While often ignored in modern use (they never were included in the Book of Common Prayer), the classic Introits are still permitted in the Roman sacramentary and in Lutheran use.[27] Their function is not only to accompany the action of entrance of ministers and servers but also to sound a keynote for the day or feast. Many in this historic series are still strikingly apt.

The Introit[28] for the First Sunday of Advent (*Ad te levavi*) is drawn from Psalm 25, which with Psalms 80 and 85 is one of the three preferred Advent Psalms.

> *Antiphon [Ps. 25:1-3a].* To you, O Lord, I lift up my soul.
>   O my God, in you I trust;
>   do not let me be put to shame;
>   do not let my enemies exult over me.
>   Do not let those who wait for you be put to shame.

Psalm [25:4]. Make me to know your ways, O Lord;
teach me your paths. *Gloria Patri.*
The antiphon is repeated:
To you, O Lord...Do not let those who wait for you be put to shame.

This Introit is an excellent example of the way of the liturgy, taking an apparently bland biblical passage and giving it life by putting it into the context of the liturgical year. "Those who wait for you" are ourselves, the Church, waiting with sometimes impatient longing for God to do something. Here at the outset of the journey that is the Church year we are to learn a secret that is increasingly alien to current thought and practice. In the liturgy, carefully crafted over many centuries, in its best expression, every word counts, each word has a rich meaning to which worshippers should be attentive. Such a situation presents a dilemma. What Abraham Joshua Heschel said about Jewish liturgy is no less true of Christian liturgy. "A pilgrimage through the entire order of the daily morning prayer in its present form is like a journey through a vast collection of precious works of art. To absorb all their beauty, even to a small degree, would take many hours of concentration as well as the ability to experience an immense variety of insights, one after the other. But the time allotted to daily prayer is too brief, and all we are able to accomplish is a hasty glance."[29] No participant can take it all in at once; our hasty glance can sometimes linger on a particularly striking word or expression before our attention is required to move on. At another time we may be struck by some other word or expression. And not all participants will be impressed by the same words. No one can take in and absorb all that the liturgical year has to say and teach as we make its pilgrimage, but the consolation is that most of us will have many years to do it again and again and make more and deeper discoveries. Thus the Introit for the First Sunday teaches that Advent is a time of expectation, hope, and waiting, joined with a confidence of not being disappointed by God, who is attentive to his people's needs.

The Collect is a term once common to the three Western liturgical churches. Anglican use has always retained the word. In the English translation of the Roman sacramentary from 1970 until the revised translation introduced in 2011 the collect was called the "opening prayer"; now the traditional name Collect has been restored. The 1978 *Lutheran Book of Worship*, influenced in part by the Roman Catholic usage, introduced the term "prayer of the day," and the term continues in *Evangelical Lutheran Worship* (2006). The *Lutheran Service Book* (2006) retains the traditional word, Collect. The function and purpose of the Collect is to gather the thought and emphases of the day and express them in a concise and pointed way. The style is drawn from classical rhetoric and demands careful attention, especially by modern-day hearers. The structure is definite and exact, consisting of one sentence, usually short. The Collect offers one petition, always pleads the mediation of our Lord, and concludes with an ascription of praise to the blessed Trinity. It always begins with an address to God, sometimes, especially in the Latin original, just "God" [*Deus*], more usually with a brief descriptive phrase such as "Most merciful God"; secondly the collect may include, but need not always include, a statement of an antecedent reason, the ground on which the petition is to be offered ("you have given your eternal Word to be made incarnate of the pure virgin"); the actual petition, the heart of the prayer, follows ("grant to your people grace to put away the desires of the flesh"); the collect may include a statement of the desired result of the petition, the benefit that is hoped for ("so that they may be ready for your visitation") but this is not required in every collect; and the mediation ("through your Son, Jesus Christ our Lord") and doxology ("who lives and reigns with you and the Holy Spirit, one God now and for ever.")[30] This style of prayer differs markedly from the expansive style of the Eastern Orthodox liturgies. William Bright in wonderfully Victorian language extols the brevity and directness of the classic collect: "And doubtless the Collect-form as we have it, is Western in every feature; in that 'unity of sentiment and severity of style' which Lord Macaulay has admired; in its Roman brevity, and majestic conciseness; its freedom from all luxuriant ornament and all inflation of phraseology."[31]

It is to be noted that the use that one encounters frequently in modern compositions, "may we..." as a substitute for the petition of the Collect, is thus a departure from the classic form. It is not only an especially weak expression; it is merely a wish, not a petition. It does not ask anything.

The collect for the First Sunday in Advent that Thomas Cranmer composed for the first Book of Common Prayer (1549) and retained in every succeeding Prayer Book is a masterpiece of liturgical art. In its "contemporary" form in the present (1979) American Prayer Book, it reads:

> Almighty God, give us grace to cast away the works of darkness, and put on the armor of light, now in the time of this mortal life in which your Son Jesus Christ came to visit us in great humility; that in the last day, when he shall come again in his glorious majesty to judge both the living and the dead, we may rise to the life immortal; through him who lives and reigns with you and the Holy Spirit, one God, now and for ever.

The inspiration was the Epistle appointed in the previous lectionary, Romans 13:8-14, retained in the present three-year lectionary in Year A. The antitheses in the prayer are striking: cast away darkness, put on light; this mortal life, the life immortal; great humility, glorious majesty. The word "now" is crucial: remembering the first Advent and anticipating the second, we are now in this time, as St. Paul commands, to cast off the works of darkness and put on the armor of light.[32] The collect in this form consists of an address, a petition, the desired result, the mediation, and the doxology; there is in this collect no antecedent reason.

Archbishop Cranmer's collect replaced the one then in use in the Roman rite and still used by the Lutherans that came from the Gregorian and Sarum sacramentaries. In the English translation prepared for the (Lutheran) *Church Book* of 1868, it is:

> Stir up, we beseech thee, thy power, O Lord, and come; that by thy protection we may be rescued from the threatening perils of our sins and saved by thy mighty deliverance; who livest and reignest with the Father and the Holy Ghost, ever one God, world without end.

The prayer is addressed directly to the Son, who is implored to "come." The ancient rule was that prayer was to be offered to the Father, through the Son, in the Holy Spirit. This deviation from that rule marks this collect as a later composition. (Collects addressed to the Holy Spirit are extremely rare.) This is the first of three Advent collects beginning "Stir up," in Latin, *Excita*, "rouse," "excite." The urgent plea is for God to rouse himself and come to his people. The Collect voices the longing appeal of the Church in the single word "Come," addressed directly to Christ, which is particularly appropriate to this Sunday and this season.[33]

The Missal of Paul VI (1970) has moved the "Stir up" collect of the previous book to Friday in the first week of Advent and appointed in its place what was a post-Communion prayer in the Gelasian sacramentary:

> Almighty God, strengthen the resolve of your faithful people to go forth to meet your Christ with righteous deeds at his coming, so that, gathered at his right hand, they may be worthy to possess the heavenly kingdom; through Jesus Christ our Lord....

"Go forth to meet your Christ" is an allusion to cry of the bridesmaids in Matt. 25:6, a picture associated with Advent in the great chorale by Philipp Nicolai (1556-1608), "Wake, awake, for night is flying"[34] and the hymn by Laurentius

Laurenti (1660-1722), "Rejoice, all ye believers, and let your lights appear."[35] The "righteous deeds" of which the prayer speaks allude to Matthew 25:34-36, the blessing of the righteous at the Last Judgment. Other less direct allusions are to Titus 2:11-14 and 3:4-7.

The readings appointed in the Revised Common Lectionary for the First Sunday in Advent are these.

Year A

Isaiah 2:1-5. The exaltation of the house of God.

Psalm 122. Let us go to the house of the Lord.

Romans 13:11-14. Lay aside the works of darkness.

Matthew 24:36-44. The Son of Man is coming at an unexpected hour.

Year B

Isaiah 64:1-9. O that you would tear open the heavens and come down.

Psalm 80:1-7, 17-19. Restore us, O God of hosts.

1 Corinthians 1:3-9. Waiting for the revealing of our Lord Jesus Christ.

Mark 13:24-37. Keep alert; you do not know when the time will come.

Year C

Jeremiah 33:14-16. The fulfillment of the promise is surely coming.

Psalm 25:1-10. Prayer for guidance and protection.

1 Thessalonians 3:9-13. Blameless at the coming of our Lord Jesus with all his saints.

Luke 21:25-36. Cosmic signs at the coming of the Son of Man.

The central theme of each Sunday is found in the appointed Gospel: the return of the Lord in power and great glory attended by unmistakable terrifying signs.

The doctrine of Advent is brought home by some of the greatest hymns in the treasury of the Church. Perhaps the most thrilling of them all is Charles Wesley's powerful rewriting of a hymn by John Cennick on the second coming. Close behind the hymn lies the terrifying passage from Revelation 1:7,

Look! He is coming with clouds;
    every eye will see him,
even those who pierced him;
    and on his account all the tribes of the earth will wail,

as well as other New Testament texts on the glorious return of the Son of Man.

Lo! He comes with clouds descending
   Once for favored sinners slain;
Thousand, thousand Saints attending
   Swell the triumph of his train:
      Alleluia!
God appears, on earth to reign.

Every eye shall now behold him
   Robed in dreadful majesty;
Those who set at nought and sold him,
   Pierced and nailed him to the tree,
     Deeply wailing,
Shall the true Messiah see.

Those dear tokens of his passion
   Still his dazzling body bears,
Cause of endless exultation
   To his ransomed worshippers:
     With what rapture
Gaze we on those glorious scars.

Yea, amen! Let all adore thee,
   High on thine eternal throne;
Saviour, take the power and glory,
   Claim the kingdom for thine own:
     JAH, Jehovah! [Ps. 68:4 AV]
Everlasting God, come down!

The hymn is most often sung to the powerful tune *Helmsley,* which is said to have been adapted by Thomas Olivers, one of John Wesley's preachers, from a melody he heard whistled on the street; the *Hymnal 1982* ascribes the melody to Augustine Arne (1710-1778). The hymn presents an absolutely terrifying picture of the second coming but is expressed with masterful control by Wesley, so that it never descends into wild emotionalism. The vigor of the original form of Wesley's hymn has been too much for many modern editors, who in taming the vigor have drained the power from Wesley's words and thus from the biblical pictures as well. In the worst cases, all the terror has been removed and replaced with bland cheer.[36]

The language of the hymn is immersed in biblical quotation and allusion. When Christ the Lord returns he will not arrive alone but attended by "ten

thousands of his holy ones, to execute judgment on all, and to convict everyone of all the deeds of ungodliness that they have committed" (Jude 14-15).
When he returns it will be no longer hidden in humility but for "every eye"
to see in a majesty that instills fear and trembling. His now resplendent body
still bears the emblems of his passion, the wounds in his hands and feet and
side, wounds that are now to those who understand what he has accomplished
"dear" (both precious and also expensive) and the "cause of endless exultation"; the wounds have been transformed into precious ornaments on which
his people whom the wounds ransomed gaze with rapture. Therefore, Christ,
the everlasting God, is implored to come to claim his kingdom. The saints
of the old covenant and those of the new are in a similar position: looking to
God enthroned high in heaven, they plead with him to fulfill his promise and
come down.

A blessing of the people at the end of Mass was not common until the
later Middle Ages. Bishops, especially in Spain, France, and England, would
bestow a blessing after the Our Father and before the *Pax Domini*, "The
peace of the Lord be with you always." The blessings were collected in a book
called a Benedictional, the oldest extant copy of which appears to date from
the seventh century. The practice of such blessings was prevalent in Gallican
churches, and also in Ambrosian, Mozarabic, and Celtic liturgies, and was
extensively observed in the Anglo-Saxon church in England. The text of the
blessing varied according to the season or occasion; the termination was
invariable. The tripartite form of the blessing was doubtless inspired by the
form of the Aaronic benediction (Numb. 6:22-27).[37] Such solemn blessings
have been revived in recent Roman Catholic and Anglican books as a fitting
way of bringing the liturgies of the seasons of the Church Year to an appropriate close. The Episcopal Church has provided a series of such seasonal blessings in two forms, one the threefold pattern and the second a simple form.
The threefold blessing in the *Book of Occasional Services* is a free version of the
solemn blessing in the Roman sacramentary.

May Almighty God, by whose providence our Savior Christ came
among us in great humility, sanctify you with the light of his blessing
and set you free from all sin. *Amen.*

May he whose second Coming in power and great glory we await, make
you steadfast in faith, joyful in hope, and constant in love. *Amen.*

May you, who rejoice in the first Advent of our Redeemer, at his second
Advent be rewarded with unending life. *Amen.*
    or this

> May the Sun of righteousness shine upon you and scatter the darkness
> from before your path; and the blessing of God Almighty, the Father,
> the Son, and the Holy Spirit, be among you, and remain with you
> always. *Amen.*

The threefold blessing is carefully constructed. The first section looks to the
past coming in Bethlehem; the second to the return in glory; and the third
brings together the first and the future Advent. The briefer form is appropriate for the lessening of light (in the northern hemisphere) as winter comes
on, involving the natural world in the proclamation of the rising of the Sun of
Justice (Mal. 4:2).

In second vespers a psalm antiphon echoes the Gospel appointed for this
First Sunday in earlier lectionaries,

> Rejoice greatly, O daughter of Zion!
> Shout aloud, O daughter Jerusalem.[38]

A second antiphon gives John's testimony:

> Christ our King will come to us:
> the Lamb of God foretold by John.

It is followed by a third in which we hear the voice of Jesus:

> I am coming soon, says the Lord;
> I will give to everyone the reward his deeds deserve.

And then the daughter of Zion, the Blessed Virgin Mary, who is, one may imagine,
too afraid and bewildered to speak for herself, is addressed by the angel Gabriel:

> Do not be afraid, Mary, you have found favor with God;
> You will conceive and bear a Son.[39]

For the weekdays of Advent the Roman sacramentary has drawn principally
upon the riches of the Church's oldest sacramentary, called the Leonine (from
its attribution to Leo the Great who died in 461) or the Verona (where the manuscript was discovered). Notable prayers for the first week of Advent, however,
include two from the Gelasian sacramentary. The prayer appointed for Monday
is "Make us, we pray you, O Lord our God, watchful and heedful in awaiting the
Coming of your Son Christ our Lord; that when he shall come and knock, he

may find us not sleeping in sins, but awake and rejoicing in his praises; through the same Jesus Christ our Lord."[40] The biblical allusion is Rev. 3:20. The prayer appointed for Wednesday is "We entreat you, O Lord our God, to gird up the loins of our mind by your divine power; that at the Coming of our Lord Jesus Christ your Son, we may be found worthy of the banquet of eternal life and to receive from his hands the bread of heaven; through the same Jesus Christ our Lord."[41] The expectation of the season looks not in fear to the day of judgment but to the consummation and the messianic banquet. As here we receive the bread of heaven from the hands of a mortal minister of Communion, so we await the reception of the fullness of the presence of our Lord from himself.

The Second Sunday in Advent

The Second Sunday in Advent presents the preparatory work of John the Forerunner. The theme is the voice in the wilderness: Prepare the way of the Lord. The antiphon to the Magnificat at first vespers sets the tone of hopeful, even joyful expectation: "Come, Lord, visit us in peace, that we may rejoice before you with a perfect heart" (derived from Isaiah 38:3; 2 Kings 20:3).

The antiphons to the psalms in Morning Prayer express the tension between the now and the not yet, the presence,

> Zion is our mighty citadel,
> our saving Lord its wall and its defense;
> throw open the gates,
> for our God is here among us, alleluia   [see Isa. 26:1-2][42]

and the promise of a future return,

> Our God will come with great power
> to enlighten the eyes of his servants, alleluia.   [see Isa. 35:2-5]

A psalm antiphon at second vespers seeks to alleviate doubt about the Lord's coming, declaring confidently:

> The Lord will come; he is true to his word.
> If he seems to delay, keep watch for him,
> for he will surely come, alleluia.   [Hab. 2:3][43]

The Introit of the Mass (*Populus Sion*) is another example of the Church using its native tongue, the language of the Bible, to say something new and powerfully appropriate, leaving the original context and meaning behind and creating a new configuration. The resulting text does not contradict the original idea and is still faithful to the original intent; it simply imports it to a new situation.

> *Antiphon.* People of Sion, behold the Lord shall come to save the nations, and the Lord shall make the glory of his voice to be heard in the joy of your heart.
>   *Psalm* [80:1]. Give ear, O Shepherd of Israel, you who lead Joseph like a flock. *Gloria Patri.*
> *The antiphon is repeated:* People of Sion...joy of your heart.

The antiphon is a liturgical adaptation drawn from Isaiah 62:11, and 30:30, 29 where the address is to the daughter of Zion, now made collective and directed to the people of Jerusalem and in the present time to the people of the Church. The Lutheran liturgies are closer to the biblical text: "Daughter of Zion, See your salvation comes. The Lord will cause his majestic voice to be heard, and you shall have gladness of heart." The address can be understood to refer not only to Jerusalem but to the Virgin Mary, who sometimes bears the title "daughter of Zion."

The Lutheran and pre-Vatican 2 Roman liturgies use a Gelasian collect on the pattern of the collect of the First Sunday, but this time addressed to the Father:

> Stir up our hearts, O Lord, to make ready the way of thine only begotten Son, so that by his coming we may be enabled to serve thee with pure minds; through the same thy Son Jesus Christ our Lord, who lives and reigns with you and the Holy Spirit, one God, world without end.

The present Roman rite has moved the collect to Thursday in the second week of Advent and on the Second Sunday appoints a Gelasian collect that again makes use of the parable of the ten bridesmaids from Matthew 25.

> Almighty and merciful God, may no earthly undertaking hinder those who set out in haste to meet your Son, but may our learning of heavenly wisdom gain us admittance to his company, who lives and reigns....

Note the weakness of the repeated expression of a wish, "may...may...." The proposed translation by the International Commission on English in the Liturgy (ultimately rejected by the Vatican) is stronger and forthright:

> Almighty and merciful God, do not let our earthly concerns keep us from hastening to meet your Son, but teach us that heavenly wisdom which makes us his true companions; who lives and reigns with you and the Holy Spirit....[44]

The Book of Common Prayer introduces a new collect based on the collect assigned by the Church of South India to the Third Sunday in Advent on the theme "the Fore-Runner":

> Merciful God, who sent your messengers the prophets to preach repentance and prepare the way for our salvation: Give us grace to heed their warnings and forsake our sins, that we may greet with joy the coming of Jesus Christ our Redeemer; who lives and reigns with you and the Holy Spirit, one God, now and for ever.

The collects for this Sunday in the Roman, Episcopal, and Lutheran liturgies all place the responsibility not only on the ministers of God's message but on all the people to be prepared for Christ's return.

The readings appointed by the Revised Common Lectionary for the Second Sunday in Advent are these:

Year A
> Isa. 11:1-10. The peaceful kingdom.
> Psalm 72:1-7, 18-19. The kingdom of peace.
> Rom. 15:4-13. Hope, joy, and peace.
>> [This was the Epistle for this Sunday in the previous lectionary]
> Matt. 3:1-12. Repent, for the kingdom of heaven has come near.

Year B
> Isa. 40:1-11. Comfort my people, says your God.
> Psalm 85:1-2, 8-13. The age of justice and peace.
> 2 Peter 3:8-15a. The Lord is not slow to fulfill his promise.
> Mark 1:1-8. John's work in the wilderness.

Year C

Baruch 5:1-9. The restoration of Jerusalem.
  or Mal. 3:1-4. The Lord will suddenly come to his temple.
Psalm. Luke 1:68-79. The song of Zechariah.
Phil. 1:3-11. In the day of Christ may you be pure and blameless.
Luke 3:1-6. Prepare the way of the Lord.

A fifth-century Latin hymn by a follower of St. Ambrose, *Vox clara ecce intonat*, inspired by the Epistle for Advent 1 (Rom. 13:11-12), was rewritten for the 1632 Roman Breviary as *En clara vox redarguit* and made the office hymn for Sunday Lauds (Morning Praise) during Advent. It was translated by Edward Caswall (1814-1878), recasting the Prayer Book collect for the First Sunday in Advent (see p. 41). In its English dress it is a powerful expression of the essence of the preaching of John the Baptist.

> Hark! A thrilling voice is sounding;
>   "Christ is nigh," it seems to say,
> "Cast away the dreams of darkness,
>   O ye children of the day."
>
> Startled at the solemn warning,
>   Let the earth-bound soul arise;
> Christ, her Sun, all sloth dispelling,
>   Shines upon the morning skies.
>
> Lo, the Lamb, so long expected,
>   Comes with pardon down from heaven;
> Let us haste, with tears of sorrow,
>   One and all to be forgiven.
>
> So when next he comes in glory,
>   Wrapping all the earth in fear,
> May he then as our defender,
>   On the clouds of heaven appear.
>
> Honor, glory, virtue, merit,
>   To the Father and the Son,
> With the co-eternal Spirit,
>   While unending ages run.

A voice like a trumpet blast wakens a sleeping race with its thrilling sound. It is the voice of the bridesmaids announcing the approach of the Bridegroom. The slumbering soul is to wake from the world of dreams and enter the world of light and truth. The interpretation of what the voice says is, however, most careful. The speaker allows that the interpretation may be mistaken, but nonetheless embraces what the voice "seems to say." The circumspection reminds one of the conclusion of George Herbert's Poem "The Collar" in which the rebellious speaker's ranting is broken off abruptly:

> Methought I heard one calling, "Child!"
> And I replied, "My Lord."

The voice that breaks in may be only in the speaker's imagination, but it is received as the voice of God. The speaker's rebellion is broken, he is suddenly again in his right mind, and he submits not to the Father as a child but to the Lord as a servant. Behind both these poems is St. Augustine's account of his conversion. In his tormented spiritual struggle he hears what seems to be a child's voice calling at play, "Take up and read." Receiving the voice as a divine command, he takes up the New Testament and reads what his eye first falls upon, Romans 13:13-14 ("live honorably as in the day, not in reveling and drunkenness, not in debauchery and licentiousness, not in quarrelling and jealousy. Instead put on the Lord Jesus Christ, and make no provision for the flesh, to gratify its desires"), and in an instant "the light of confidence" flooded into his heart "and all the darkness of doubt was dispelled." He would become a Catholic Christian. Modern editors seem unable to tolerate such ambiguity in the identification of the divine voice,[45] but the uncertainty is true to authentic human experience, and Caswall's hymn is the more believable because of it.

Stanza two in the manner of an *Aubade*, rouses the soul from slumber and urges her (in traditional devotion the soul is always female) to get out of bed and greet the Sun/Son. Thomas Ken's "Awake, my soul, and with the sun/Thy daily stage of duty run" is a well-known example of such a morning song.[46]

The third stanza introduces a new image that explains the significance of the cry, "Christ is nigh." The long-expected Lamb comes down with pardon for those who seek forgiveness. This is now in our own time. The fourth stanza looks to the second coming in glory and the world is "wrapped" in fear, with the double meaning of both "bound up" and "rapt." Caswall's original first line had "Hark! An awful voice is sounding": the voice that startles and wakes is awe-inspiring as well as thrilling. He who comes as Judge is implored to come as Defender of his people. The plea is for terror to be replaced with love. The hymn is an impressive exposition of the immeasurable tension implicit in the expectation of the second Advent: the contrast between the things we experience, including the long delay, and the hope we nonetheless maintain.[47]

The antiphon on the Magnificat on Thursday in the second week of Advent comes from the testimony of John the Baptist (John 1:15, 27, 30).

> The one who is coming after me existed before me;
> I am not worthy to untie his sandals.[48]

The antiphon ponders the mystery of the One who is coming. John prepares the way for one who in fact precedes him: John, born into the world six months before Jesus's birth (June 24 is the feast of his Nativity), actually comes after the one who is coming, because the Son of God, begotten of the Father before all ages, existed from all eternity and thus precedes all creation. His birth as a human child marks not his beginning but his coming into the world. Thus the liturgy and its year disregard exact chronology. It is the theology that is paramount, theology expressed not in dogmatic definitions and treatises but in the suggestion of poetry and contemplation based on Scripture.

On Friday in the second week of Advent the Roman sacramentary appoints a Gelasian collect. "Grant, we pray, Almighty God, this grace to your people, to wait with all vigilance for the Coming of your only-begotten Son; that as he, the Author of our salvation, taught us, we may prepare our souls like blazing lamps to meet him, the same Jesus Christ our Lord."[49] The prayer derives from Jesus's parable of the wise maidens who were prepared for the approach of the bridegroom (Matt. 25:1-13). The bridegroom who comes at midnight is a clear figure of Jesus's birth, traditionally celebrated in the middle of the night, as well as his return at an unexpected hour. The blazing lamps anticipate the candlelight that fills Christian churches at the midnight Mass.

The Third Sunday in Advent

The Third Sunday in Advent sounds a note of anticipatory joy: rejoice, for the messianic age is here. The psalm antiphons at first vespers[50] voice an increasing certainty and reassurance, suffused with the joy that characterizes this Sunday.

Rejoice, Jerusalem, let your joy overflow;
your Savior will come to you, alleluia.   [see Isa. 52:9-10]

> I, the Lord, am coming to save you;
> already I am near;
> soon I will free you from your sins.

The antiphon to the Magnificat at first vespers has God declare, "There was no god before me, and after me there will be none; every knee shall bend in worship, and every tongue shall praise me." In this antiphon the voice of Christ is heard speaking, rather than the voice of the Father. (See Isaiah 43:10 and Phil. 2:10-11.) One remembers the celebration of Christ the King three weeks earlier and also the visit of the Magi some three weeks hence.

The Introit of the Mass gives its name to the third Sunday, *Gaudete*, rejoice. As the season developed as a winter Lent, the third Sunday was seen as comparable to the mid-Lent Sunday called *Laetare*, "Be glad," with its lessening of the somberness and discipline of the season, anticipating the approaching joy of the coming feast to encourage participants to continue in their discipline. Rose, brighter than the sober violet, became the liturgical color for Advent 3 as well as Lent 4. (When blue is used as the liturgical color for Advent it is not displaced by rose.) The antiphon of the Introit for Gaudete is taken from what was then the Epistle for the day, Philippians 4:4-6.

Antiphon [Phil. 4:4-6]. Rejoice in the Lord always; again I will say, Rejoice. [Let your gentleness be known to everyone.] The Lord is near. [Do not worry about anything, but in everything by prayer and supplication with thanksgiving let your requests be made known to God.]

Psalm [85:1]. Lord, you were favorable to your land; you restored the fortunes of Jacob. *Gloria Patri.*

The Antiphon is repeated: Rejoice in the Lord...made known to God.

The bracketed words in the antiphon are omitted when it is used as an Entrance Antiphon. In the Psalm past favors of God are taken to be a guarantee of future favor.

In the previous Roman missal and Lutheran books, the Collect was from the Gelasian sacramentary and was addressed to God the Son:

Lord, we beseech thee, give ear to our prayers and lighten the darkness of our hearts by thy gracious visitation; who livest and reignest with the Father and the Holy Ghost, one God, world without end.

The translation "lighten" is most felicitous. It means of course "enlighten," or "give light to/in," but the word can also suggest lifting the weight of sin from us, lightening the burden. This collect is "a typical example of the ancient Latin prayers which compressed spiritual thought of large significance in clear and terse phrase."[51] The 1549 Prayer Book retained the collect, but Bishop John Cosin in the 1662 book introduced a new collect based on the Epistle (1 Cor. 4:1-5), which focused on the holy ministry, looking forward to the Advent Ember Days that fell toward the end of this week, and likening the Christian ministry to that of John the Baptist.

O Lord Jesus Christ, who at thy first coming didst send thy messenger to prepare the way before thee; Grant that the ministers and stewards of thy mysteries may likewise so prepare and make ready thy way, by turning the hearts of the disobedient to the wisdom of the just, that at thy second coming to judge the world we may be found an acceptable people in thy sight, who livest and reignest with the Father and the Holy Spirit ever, one God, world without end.

The 1978 *Lutheran Book of Worship*, with its fondness for the 1928 Prayer Book, provides as an alternative prayer on this Sunday an adaptation of that prayer by Bishop Cosin. The 1979 American Prayer Book appoints instead the Gelasian collect assigned in previous Roman and Lutheran rites for the Fourth Sunday in Advent.

Stir up your power, O Lord, and with great might come among us; and, because we are sorely hindered by our sins, let your bountiful grace and mercy speedily help and deliver us; through Jesus Christ our Lord, to whom, with you and the Holy Spirit, be honor and glory, now and for ever.

The present Roman sacramentary appoints a Leonine collect.

O God, who see how your people faithfully await the feast of the Lord's Nativity, enable us, we pray, to attain the joys of so great a salvation and to celebrate them always with solemn worship and glad rejoicing, through our Lord Jesus Christ, your Son....

The focus on the joy of salvation is appropriate to the Gaudete theme.

The Revised Common Lectionary appoints these readings for the Third Sunday in Advent:

Year A

Isa. 35:1-10. The return of the redeemed to Zion.

Psalm 146:5-10. Praise of God's faithfulness

or Luke 1:46b-55. The Song of Mary.

Jas. 5:7-10. Be patient until the coming of the Lord.

Matt. 11:2-11. Jesus confirms John's work.

Year B

Isa. 61:1-4, 8-11. The good news of deliverance.

Psalm 126. Song of the returning exiles

or Luke 1:46b-55. The Song of Mary.

1 Thess. 5:16-24. The one who calls you is faithful.

John 1:6-8, 19-28. The testimony of John to the priests.

Year C

Zeph. 3:14-20. Sing aloud, daughter of Zion.

Psalm: Isa. 12:2-6. A song of Isaiah.

Phil. 4:4-7. The Lord is near.

Luke 3:7-18. One more powerful than John is coming.

The Final Week of Advent, December 17–23

The second part of Advent, its final seven days, begins on December 17. For over a thousand years this climactic week has been enriched and given its special character by the chanting of the "O" Antiphons with the Magnificat at vespers. These glorious antiphons are seven apostrophes to the promised Savior derived from Old Testament titles and figures. Their authorship is unknown; they seem to have originated in Rome[52] and are another example of the Church's way of weaving together phrases and images from many parts of the scriptures to create a new and yet faithful expression of the Word of God.[53] Their structure is similar to that of the classic collect: the invocation of the Messiah under an Old Testament title; the amplification giving an attribute of the Messiah and developing the invocation; an appeal beginning with "Come" and making reference to the invocation.

> December 17. *O Sapientia.*
>> O Wisdom, proceeding from the mouth of the Most High,
>>> [Sirach 24:3]
>>> pervading and permeating all creation,
>>> mightily ordering all things: [Wisdom 8:1]
>> Come and teach us the way of understanding.   [Isa. 40:14]
>>> [that is to say, the way of prudence, of
>>>> common sense]

1 Cor. 1:24 calls Christ "the wisdom of God," and the great church in Istanbul, dedicated to him, bears his title *Hagia Sophia,* Holy Wisdom.

> December 18. *O Adonai.*
>> O Adonai and ruler of the house of Israel,
>>> who appeared to Moses in the burning bush   [Exod. 3:1-6]
>>> and gave him the law on Sinai: [Exod. 20:1ff]
>> Come with an outstretched arm and redeem us.   [Exod. 6:6]

The antiphon carefully avoids the use of the sacred Name of God, the tetragrammaton YHWH, and, in accordance with Jewish custom, employs the substitute name, Adonai, preserving the mystery of the divine being and also, for now, of the identity of the One who is coming.

> December 19. *O Radix Jesse.*
>> O Root of Jesse, standing as a signal to the peoples,   [Isa. 11:10]
>>> before whom all kings are mute,   [Isa. 52:15]
>>> to whom the nations will do homage: [Ps. 22:27]
>> Come quickly to deliver us.   [Heb. 10:37]

The root of Jesse, the father of David, points to Jesus, born of David's line, who will rise as a standard or banner before the peoples of the earth. The "signal" or "standard" or "ensign" will be understood to point to the holy cross as the Passiontide hymn, "The royal banners forward go, the Cross shines forth with mystic glow" declares.

> December 20. *O Clavis David.*
>> O Key of David, and scepter of the house of Israel,
>>> [Num. 24:17; Heb.1:8]

you open and no one can close,
    you close and no one can open: [Isa. 22:22; Rev. 3:7]
Come and rescue the prisoners
who dwell in darkness and the shadow of death.

                                            [Isa. 42:7; Luke 1:79]

Key and scepter are symbols of messianic authority and power and anticipate the opening of the gate of heaven at the resurrection.

December 21. *O Oriens.*
        O Dayspring, splendor of light everlasting
            and sun of righteousness: [Mal. 4:2]
        Come and give light to those who sit in darkness
            and in the shadow of death. [Luke 1:79]

It is noteworthy that this antiphon addressed to Christ as the radiant dawn from on high is sung on December 21, the winter solstice and shortest day of the year.

December 22. *O Rex Gentium.*
        O King of the nations,   [Jer. 10:7]
            the ruler they long for,   [Hag. 2:7 (AV)]
            the cornerstone uniting all people:
                                    [Isa. 28:16; Ephes. 2:14, 20-21]
        Come and save us all,
            whom you formed out of clay. [Gen. 2:7]

Christ the ruler is described as the monarch the nations desire, fair and just, "the desire of all nations."

December 23. *O Emmanuel.*
        O Emmanuel, our king and lawgiver, [Isa, 7:14; 33:22]
            the desire of the nations and their savior: [Hag. 2:7 (AV)]
        Come and save us, O Lord our God.

The final antiphon in the series addresses Christ as "God with us." His approach is as good as complete, and moreover we recognize that he is already among us, as John the Baptist declared, "Among you stands one whom you do not know, the one who is coming after me" (John 1:26-27). This final antiphon gathers into a concluding prayer ideas and images from all the preceding antiphons. The Advent longing and promise, about to be fulfilled in the arrival of the one whom we await, is gathered into one evocative name and title: Emmanuel, God-with-us.

In the English use of Sarum (Salisbury cathedral), the O Antiphons began on December 16 and a final one on December 23 was addressed to the mother of the Savior, *O Virgo virginum:*

> O Virgin of virgins, how shall this be?
>> For neither before thee was any seen like thee,
>> nor shall there be after.
> Daughters of Jerusalem, why marvel at me?
>> The thing which you behold is a divine mystery.[54]

In Germany and Liège and Paris two other antiphons were added. The O Antiphons were not included in the 1549 Prayer Book due to the discontinuance of antiphons; they were restored in 1662. In the Missal of Paul VI, the O Antiphons, to give them more prominence in addition to their use at vespers, are used as the Alleluia verses of the daily masses December 17-23. Medieval devotion, which delighted in such things, was pleased to discover that the initial letters of the seven titles when read backward spelled ERO CRAS, "I will be there tomorrow."

The invitatory that opens each day's prayer changes on December 17th to signal the intensification of the preparation and the heightened expectation. From the First Sunday in Advent through December 16th, it is

> Come, let us worship the Lord,
> The King who is to come.[55]

From December 17th through the 23rd the invitatory is

> The Lord is close at hand;
> Come, let us worship him.

On December 24th it becomes still more assured and urgent:

> Today you will know the Lord is coming,
> And in the morning you will see his glory.

On each of the days of this final week of Advent, the propers are carefully woven together. The antiphon on the Benedictus, the Gospel Canticle at Lauds or Morning Prayer, is taken from the Gospel that will be read at the Eucharist later in the day, and the collect reflects those themes.

On December 17 the Gospel is Matt. 1:1-17, the genealogy of Jesus, telling the generations one by one, each name one step closer to the fulfillment of God's purpose determined from the foundation of the world. The antiphon on the Benedictus builds on that confidence, as if spoken by John the Forerunner (see Matt. 4:17).

> Believe me, the kingdom of God is at hand;
> I tell you solemnly, your Savior will not delay his coming.[56]

The collect for the day, from the Leonine sacramentary, identifies the purpose of this great work that God has begun: the "wonderful exchange."

> O God, creator and redeemer of the human race, it was your will that in the womb of the ever-virgin Mary your Word should take flesh: Mercifully hear our prayers, and grant that your only-begotten Son, who came to share our human nature, may lead us to share in his divine life; through the same Jesus Christ....[57]

On December 18 the Gospel is Matt. 1:18-24, the birth of Jesus, Son of David, born of Mary. The antiphon on the Benedictus is

> Let everything within you watch and wait,
> for the Lord our God draws near.

The completeness of the preparation through all the ages demands of us a complete expectation. All of our attention is to be directed to the approaching Lord, who "has come to his people and set them free." Slavery to foreign nations, slavery to sin is ended by his coming. Thus the appointed collect, new in the Missal of Paul VI, prays,

> Almighty God, grant that we who are oppressed and weighed down by the chains of our ancient slavery to sin may be set free by the long-awaited yet ever-new birth of your Son, Jesus Christ our Lord....[58]

The familiar story never ceases to teach and delight with new insights and applications. Jesus, whose name means Savior, has saved his people in the past and will continue to work liberation in wonderful ways. The old story is still fresh and able to surprise with its gift of freedom.

On December 19 the Gospel is Luke 1:5-25, the birth of John the Baptist foretold by an angel. The antiphon to the Benedictus derives from the gentle vision of Sirach 24:30-32,

> Like the sun in the morning sky, the Savior of the world will dawn;
> like rain on the meadows,
> he will descend to rest in the womb of the virgin.[59]

The gentleness of the descent is a frequent theme of the Advent season. Antiphons and hymns have been shaped by Isa. 45:8.

> Shower, O heavens, from above and let the skies rain down righteousness.
> Let the earth open, that salvation my spring up.[60]

The collect, from the Leonine sacramentary, reflects this gentle view, suggesting the perpetual virginity of the Blessed Virgin Mary, a virgin during the conception of Jesus and also during the act of childbirth.

> O God, in the child-bearing of the holy virgin you revealed to the world the radiance of your glory: Grant that we may celebrate with full and reverent faith this great mystery of the Word made flesh, your Son, Jesus Christ our Lord....[61]

As Luther explains in the Small Catechism Jesus is true God, "begotten of the Father in all eternity, and also a true human being, born of the Virgin Mary."[62] The "virgin birth" is the source of his humanity. In the collect we ask to join the praise of heaven and earth in proclaiming this wondrous birth.

On December 20 the Gospel is Luke 1:26-38, the angel Gabriel's annunciation to the Virgin Mary. The antiphon on the Benedictus is a straightforward quotation from that reading.

> The angel Gabriel was sent by God to the virgin Mary,
> who was engaged to a man whose name was Joseph.[63]

The collect, from the Leonine sacramentary, takes up the theme of Mary's acceptance of the will of God.

> O God, by accepting the message of the angel the pure virgin became the temple of your ineffable Word and was filled with the light of the

Holy Spirit: Give us grace to follow her example and be always ready to do your will; through your Son Jesus Christ our Lord....[64]

The salvation of the world hung on the word of acceptance from a perplexed young woman. The second lesson in the Office of Readings in the *Liturgy of the Hours* is from a justly famous homily in Praise of the Virgin Mother by St. Bernard of Clairvaux. As Advent reaches its climax, so the whole world, all history, awaits the Virgin Mary's acceptance of the angel's word. Bernard says, "The angel awaits an answer; it is time for him to return to God who sent him. We too are waiting.... Tearful Adam with his sorrowing family begs this of you.... Abraham begs it, David begs it. All the other holy patriarchs, your ancestors, ask it of you, as they dwell in the land of the shadow of death. This is what the whole earth waits for... for on your word depends comfort for the wretched, ransom for the captive, freedom for the condemned, indeed, salvation for all the children of Adam, the whole of your race."[65] The responsory that follows gives voice to our encouragement of the holy virgin to say *yes* to what God offers. "Receive, O Virgin Mary, the word which the Lord has made known to you...."[66]

On December 21 the Gospel is Luke 1:39-45, Mary's visit to her cousin Elizabeth. As we may imagine the two pregnant women supporting each other and counting the days until giving birth, so the Church counts the days to Christmas. The antiphon on the Benedictus is

> There is no need to be afraid;
> in five days our Lord will come to us.[67]

We are subtly reminded that not only Christmas but also the Second Advent may be that close. The collect, from the Gelasian sacramentary and also included in the *Common Service Book* and the *Service Book and Hymnal,* combines the first and the second comings.

> Lord, mercifully receive the prayers of your people, that as they rejoice in the advent of your only-begotten Son in human flesh, so when he comes a second time in his majesty they may receive the gift of eternal life; through the same Jesus Christ our Lord....[68]

In the midst of the joy of Christmas we await the second advent, made sure by the first advent.

On December 22, the Gospel is Luke 1:46-56, the song of the expectant mother Mary, the Magnificat. The antiphon on the Benedictus is Elizabeth's report of the work of her son, John, still in the womb, leaping for joy that the long-awaited time has come; already he points to the yet unborn Jesus.

> As soon as I heard the sound of your greeting,
> the child in my womb leapt for joy.[69]

The collect, from the Bergamo sacramentary, recognizing that the coming of God into the world was not a lonely event but was attended by Elizabeth and John, asks that we too may be counted as his companions.

> O God, when we had fallen into sin and death you turned toward us and rescued us by the advent of your only-begotten Son: Grant that we, who with reverent love acknowledge his incarnation, may also be found worthy to be counted as companions of him who is our Redeemer, Jesus Christ our Lord....[70]

John the Baptist is our example: he acknowledged the Incarnation, even while he was yet in Elizabeth's womb, and became therefore a companion of Jesus, not as one who walked with him but one who shared uniquely in the work of God. (It is worth remembering that "companion" comes from the Latin "to eat bread with.")

On December 23 the Gospel read at Mass is Luke 1:57-66, the birth of John the Baptist. The antiphon on the Benedictus, the song sung by his father at the birth of his son, recalls that Gabriel had told Mary that her aged and infertile cousin Elizabeth was six months pregnant and therefore nothing was impossible for God, not even the pregnancy of a virgin.

> All that God promised to the virgin through the message of the angel has been accomplished.[71]

Therefore the Leonine collect prays,

> Almighty and everlasting God, as the feast of the nativity of your Son draws near, grant that we may know the mercy of the eternal Word who took flesh of the Virgin Mary and came to dwell among us, Jesus Christ our Lord....[72]

We ask that we may know the meaning of the Incarnation: mercy.

Many texts in the Church's Daily Prayer during this final week of Advent reflect the immanent approach of the long-awaited and sometimes seemingly long-delayed Coming and are often stirring in their excitement. A psalm antiphon at Lauds (Morning Prayer) on December 17 pierces the air with a thrilling sound.

> Blow the trumpet in Zion, for the day of the Lord is near.
> Behold, he comes to save us.[73]

A responsory for December 19, echoing Jer. 31:10 and 4:5, extends the good news into the distant corners of the world:

> Hear the word of the Lord, O nations;
> and declare it to the ends of the earth.
>   Say to the far-off islands: our Savior is coming.
> Proclaim the good news, let it be heard;
> tell everyone, shout it aloud;
>   say to the far-off islands: our Savior is coming.[74]

Another responsory for the same date, drawing on Isa. 49:13 and 47:4, urges all creation, heaven and earth, to join in the celebration of the glad news.

> Sing for joy, O heavens, and exult, O earth;
> break forth, O mountains into singing!
>   The Lord has comforted his people,
>   and will have compassion on his suffering ones.
> Our Redeemer—the Lord of Hosts is his name—
> is the Holy One of Israel.
>   The Lord has comforted his people,
>   and will have compassion on his suffering ones.[75]

Not just all people, but all elements of creation, all created things, are to be joyful. The natural world has its part to play in the praise of God's saving work. That broadly inclusive view of the unity of creation will continue through Christmas and Epiphany.

The Fourth Sunday in Advent

The final seven days of Advent, each of which has its own Mass propers in the Roman sacramentary, are interrupted by the celebration of the Fourth

Sunday in Advent. The theme of the final Sunday before Christmas is the incarnation of the Word of God, the expectation of Israel, Mary, and the Church. A psalm antiphon at first vespers declares the fulfillment of the Advent waiting:

> The fullness of time has come upon us at last;
> God sends his Son into the world.[76]

Finally, at long last, the time has come. The idea comes from St. Paul in Gal. 4:4. A psalm antiphon at Morning Praise (Lauds) similarly announces the end of the waiting drawing upon the imagery of Isa. 9:6:

> The Lord is here; go out to meet him, saying:
> Great is his birth, eternal his kingdom,
> strong God, Ruler of all, Prince of peace, alleluia.[77]

The announcement "The Lord is here; go out to meet him" recalls the responsory with which the season of Advent began, *Aspiciens a longe*. Another psalm antiphon at second vespers derives from Isa. 9:7,

> Ever wider will his kingdom spread,
> eternally at peace, alleluia.[78]

The idea will be echoed in the Christmas Proclamation, which declares that when Christ was born the whole world was at peace. It derives from the vision of Zechariah 1:11, the report of the horses sent out from the heavenly court on a reconnaissance mission, "We have patrolled the earth, and lo, the whole earth remains at peace."

The Introit of the Mass *Rorate* focuses on the cosmic participation in the Incarnation.

> *Antiphon* [Isa. 45:8]. Shower [Drop down], O heaven from above, and let the skies rain down righteousness;
>> let the earth open, that salvation [a Savior] may spring up.
>> *Psalm* [19:1]. The heavens are telling the glory of God;
>> and the firmament proclaims his handiwork. *Gloria Patri*.
> *The antiphon is repeated:* Shower ... spring up.

It is foreshadowing of the work of the Savior who will unite heaven and earth as the Exsultet at Easter will proclaim. The Introit reaches far beyond the immediate occasion making final preparation for the celebration of the birth and carries us far ahead to the tree that will be set in the earth as a sign for all to see. God showers his love upon the world, and out of it grows the tree of life, which may be said to be planted at Christmas.

The Collect in previous Lutheran and Roman Catholic books was a Gelasian collect addressed to God the Son. (In the Gregorian sacramentary the collect is addressed to the Father.) In the translation prepared for the 1868 Lutheran book, it is:

> Stir up, we beseech thee, thy power, O Lord, and come, and with great might succor us, that by the help of thy grace whatsoever is hindered by our sins may be speedily accomplished through thy mercy and satisfaction; who livest and reignest with the Father and the Holy Ghost, ever one God, world without end.

The collect is similar in thought to the collect for the First Sunday in Advent. It is appointed, in a different translation, in the American Prayer Book for the Third Sunday.

The 1979 Book of Common Prayer provides on the Fourth Sunday of Advent this prayer from the Gelasian sacramentary in the translation from William Bright's *Ancient Collects*:

> Purify our conscience, Almighty God, by your daily visitation, that your Son Jesus Christ, at his coming, may find in us a mansion prepared for himself; who lives and reigns with you in the unity of the Holy Spirit, one God, now and for ever.

"Mansion" comes from the Authorized Version of John 14:2, "in my Father's house are many mansions." The word was introduced by William Tyndale in his translation and in Old English meant a "dwelling place," not necessarily palatial. The prayer joins the daily coming of God and the coming at the end of time and puts the believer in the situation of the Virgin Mary as a mansion prepared for the dwelling of the Son of God.

The Roman sacramentary appoints the collect used in Lutheran and Anglican books on the Feast of the Annunciation. In the Prayer Book translation, it is:

> Pour your grace into our hearts, O Lord, that we who have known the incarnation of your Son Jesus Christ, announced by an angel to the Virgin Mary, may by his cross and passion be brought to the glory of

his resurrection; who lives and reigns with you, in the unity of the Holy Spirit, one God, now and for ever.

The splendid collect, from the Gregorian sacramentary, joins the first Advent in Bethlehem to the culmination of the work of Christ in the Paschal events and drives into the eschatological future with the petition that at the second and glorious Advent we be granted a share in the resurrection.

The Revised Common Lectionary appoints these readings for the Fourth Sunday in Advent.

Year A
Isa. 7:10-16. The sign of Immanuel.
Psalm 80:1-7, 17-19. Plea for the return of God's favor.
Rom. 1:1-7. Called to belong to Jesus Christ.
Matt. 1:18-25. The conception of Jesus, the Messiah

Year B
2 Sam. 7:1-11, 16. God promises David a throne for ever.
Psalm: Luke 1:46b-55. The Song of Mary
    or Ps. 89:1-4, 19-26. God's faithfulness.
Rom. 16:25-27. The mystery, secret for ages, is made known to the
                  Gentiles.
Luke 1:26-38. The annunciation to the Blessed Virgin Mary.

Year C
Micah 5:2-5a. The Ruler from Bethlehem.
Psalm: Luke 1:46b-55. The Song of Mary
    or Ps. 80:1-7. Plea for the return of God's favor.
Heb. 10:5-10. Jesus the high priest.
Luke 1:39-45 (46-55). Mary visits Elizabeth.

A psalm antiphon for the final week of Advent from Sirach 36:21 summarizes the theme and the spirit of the season.

> Reward those who wait for you,
>   and let your prophets be found trustworthy.[79]

The theme of Advent is the answer that will be given at last to the people's continued prayers, and the fulfillment of the visions of the prophets, which will prove that they have been faithful declarers of the Word of God. The spirit of the season is confidence brimming with expectation and hope, underneath which runs a current of uncertainty. It is the acknowledgment that all this may be a delusion. The absolutely convincing proof is yet to come, when the hopes and dreams and prayers of the ages are fulfilled and the prophets are shown to have spoken the very truth of God. Only then can the confidence of Advent be replaced with absolute and undeniable certainty.

Ember Days

The turning of the four seasons of the natural world has been incorporated into the Church's calendar. These are the Ember Days, the name derived from the German *Quatember*, a corruption of *quattuor tempore*, "the four times," four groups of three days (Wednesday, Friday, and Saturday), marking the seasons by fasting and abstinence. Their origin is obscure. Originally there were just three groups (summer, autumn, winter), perhaps connected with pre-Christian celebrations of harvest (Summer), vintage (September), and sowing or seed-time (December), dating to the time of Pope Callistus I (ca. 220). The days were well established in Rome by the time of Leo the Great (440-461). From the fifth century the ember days were recognized as especially appropriate times for ordinations. They were the Wednesday, Friday, and Saturday following St. Lucy's Day (December 13), the winter ember days; the Leonine sacramentary included a prayer among its ember week masses marking sowing or seed-time, "that we may not only enjoy the fruitfulness of the earth but may also receive with purified hearts, the birth of the eternal bread." The summer ember days were the Wednesday, Friday, and Saturday following Pentecost. The autumnal days followed Holy Cross Day (September 14). The spring Ember Days were added later, following the First Sunday in Lent. In 1969 the Roman sacramentary, recognizing an increasing estrangement from the agricultural setting of the Church's calendar, replaced the Ember Days with days of prayer for various needs set by regional conferences of bishops. The 1979 Prayer Book notes when the Ember Days are "traditionally observed"[80] and provides collects and lessons under "Various Occasions. For the Ministry" "For use on the traditional days or at other times."[81] The Ember Days were retained on sixteenth-century Lutheran calendars, but eventually were replaced by quarterly lectures and examinations in the catechism.

The present Roman sacramentary preserves in the opening prayer on December 24, before the time of the vigil Mass, a collect from Ember Wednesday in the previous missal. With rising impatience, the day before Christmas, the Church cries out, "Come quickly, Lord Jesus, do not delay, that those who put their trust in your goodness may receive the consolation of your coming." The long wait for the Lord's Advent has reached its climax.

Advent Customs in the Home and Church

The appeal of the Church's Advent season encouraged the development of several customs in the home as well as in the church. The most common is the Advent wreath in which the approach of Christ is made visible. It employs pre-Christian symbols of enduring life: fire and evergreens. The modern use is attributed to Johann Hinrich Wichern (1808-1881), who in 1833 founded a settlement house in Hamburg (*Das Rauhe Haus*, the rough house) where he invented the Advent wreath to make the Christmas preparation and expectation real to the boys of the house. It first took the form of a tree with graduated rings fastened to it on which the lights were placed. Because of the danger of fire or perhaps to distinguish it from the Christmas tree, this arrangement was later replaced by a wooden ring suspended by chains, with room for twenty-eight candles. On the first Sunday in Advent a candle was lit, and the children recited the promise of the Seed of woman that would bruise the serpent's head (Gen 3:15). Each night another candle was lighted, and another messianic prophecy was read.[82] There is occasionally seen a variation in the form of an Advent log, four candles in a row giving a linear view of the approach of Christmas. The brightness afforded by electric lights lessens the effectiveness of the increasing candlelight, but the living flame still proclaims the reality of the One who is returning. The small seeds of light, planted as we may imagine in darkness, are an anticipation of the wonder that the Church will celebrate some months from now as life emerges from the darkness of the tomb. Each of the great days and seasons of the liturgical year is never celebrated in isolation from all the rest. We are to learn that in the final analysis darkness and light are not opposites arising from different sources. Psalm 18:9-11 says of the coming of God to the earth,

> He bowed the heavens, and came down;
>   thick darkness was under his feet.
> He rode on a cherub, and flew;
>   he came swiftly upon the wings of the wind.
> He made darkness his covering around him,
>   his canopy thick clouds dark with water.

Darkness is part of the wardrobe of God. Advent teaches us that God is present in darkness as well as in the light, and in this season the Church is like Moses who "drew near to the thick darkness where God was" (Exod. 20:21). Here again we confront the continuing complexity of the liturgical year. The darkness of night may seem threatening as it often is portrayed in daily prayer, and the decreasing daylight of the days of Advent (in the northern hemisphere) a reminder of the eventual end of the world, but in and through all the changes, God is present as Emmanuel.

The Advent calendar, a German custom now taken over by the secular world, helps children count the days until Christmas as each day a new window is opened revealing a mystery of faith, a religious symbol, or on December 6, St. Nicholas.

In the Moravian tradition, from the First Sunday in Advent until Epiphany, a three-dimensional paper star illuminated from within adorns homes and churches. The custom originated at Nietsky, Germany, during the fiftieth-anniversary celebrations of the Moravian movement, January 4th through the 6th, 1821, when an illuminated star with 110 points hung in the courtyard of the school. The Moravian star is a festive decoration, for Advent is observed not as a penitential time but a season of joyful anticipation.

The Jesse tree, a tree decorated with symbols of Old Testament figures, is found as early as the twelfth century. It is a portrayal of the root of Jesse (Isa. 11:1-2), "my servant the Branch" (Zech. 3:8), and God's promise to "raise up a righteous Branch" (Jer. 23:5).

The Tau cross (in the shape of a capital T) is sometimes called the cross of prophecy and associated with Advent because it is said by some to be the form raised by Moses in the wilderness (Num. 21:4-9), anticipating the cross of Christ.

The rose became a popular symbol in the thirteenth century based on Isa. 35:1-2. The rose came to be identified with the Virgin Mary as in the rose windows of Gothic churches and in the early fifteenth-century carol "There is rose of swych vertu/As is the rose that bare Jesu," familiar from Benjamin Britten's "Ceremony of Carols." But in other cases (such as the fifteenth-century hymn *Es ist ein Ros entsprungen,* "Lo, how a rose e'er blooming") the rose is Christ, sprung from the tender stem of his mother. Matthew Bridges (1800-1894) brought the two together in the second stanza of his hymn "Crown him with many crowns."

> Crown him the Virgin's Son,
>   The God incarnate born,
> Whose arm those crimson trophies won
>   Which now his brow adorn:
>   Fruit of the mystic Rose,
>   As of that Rose the stem,
> The root whence mercy ever flows,
>   The babe of Bethlehem.[83]

The Virgin Mary is the "mystic Rose," but Jesus Christ is the root and stem from which that rose springs.

Advent in the Modern World

A continuing problem for the Church is maintaining the expectant theme of Advent in a secularized world that has transformed some of the Church's symbols into merchandising encouragements. Perhaps the best response of committed Christians is to remember that they live *in* the world but yet are not part *of* it. Some may choose to make their testimony and deliberately turn their back on the frenzy of consumption and refuse to participate. Others may consciously allow the decorations and sometimes manufactured cheer to serve their part in the building expectancy and explore ever more deeply the meaning of the season of Advent and its promise of Jesus's return to judge the living and the dead. They will move in a quite different path from the secular society, knowing that the liturgical season is more satisfying than what the world in its blatant greed and shallow partying and hollow cheer can ever be. The Church will do its part by proclaiming with all the power and energy it can muster the thrilling mystery of this most profound season.

3

Christmas

THE ORIENTATION OF Advent toward the end of all things and the consummation of the work of God is not over when the season ends. The eschatological focus continues in the liturgical celebration of Christmas as the observance of the feast developed.

Development and Spread of the Feast

For the first three centuries of its life the Church observed a simple calendar. There was the weekly celebration of the resurrection, the Lord's Day, and there was the yearly celebration of Pascha (Easter). The situation changed at the beginning of the fourth century, as the legalization of Christianity brought enormous changes. Among those changes was an increasing interest in historical commemoration, following the Christian story step by step. Harald Buchinger puts it simply, "Except for the Christian Paschal celebration and its Pentecost, it is known that there is no sure evidence for a single Christian feast before the fourth century, while towards the end of the same century, a fully unfolded liturgical year with several circles of feasts seems to have spread across the entire Christian world." [1]

In the fourth century, December 25 was an observance in the churches of Rome of the birth of Jesus. In the earliest evidence from that city, the date of Jesus's birth begins the dates of the feasts of the martyrs given in the Philocalian calendar (so called because part of the document was illustrated by the artist Furius Dionysus Philocalus), an almanac compiled in 354, sometimes known as the Roman Chronograph. Internal dating indicates that the list was put together in 336; the observance of December 25 may be still older. The Feast of December 25 was taken up by many outside Rome and North Africa which zealously followed Roman liturgical custom. At this point in the fourth century it may be said that the liturgical year begins with Christmas.[2]

One may say simply, "Rome was the place where this feast was created."[3]
Roman lectionaries from the seventh century (after Advent had been created)
continue to give Christmas as the beginning of the liturgical year. Advent is
found at the end of the lists. This may reflect a certain resistance in Rome to
the introduction of the new season of Advent.

December 25 as the birthday of Jesus is not given in the Bible and the date
is, some suggest, not in accord with the "shepherds living in the fields, keeping watch over their flock by night" because that watch would be kept in the
spring when there were newborn lambs to protect. Two hypotheses regarding the origin and selection of December 25 compete. The first is what has
been called the "history of religions school," suggested by Hermann Usener
in 1889. According to this suggestion, December 25 was chosen to replace a
pagan festival, *Natale solis invicti*, the birth(day) of the unconquered sun. The
Roman emperor Aurelian, to unite and strengthen his vast empire, had established the festival in 274 in honor of the Syrian sun god on December 25, a
celebration of the winter solstice on the Julian calendar. The pagan festival was
noted on December 25 by the Roman chronographer on his civil (Philocalian)
calendar of A.D. 354. The popularity of the cult raised concerns in Leo the Great
and St. Augustine. The new Christian feast, it is argued, celebrated Christ as
the Sun of Righteousness (Mal. 4:2) and the light of the world (John 8:12), the
true Sun that knows no setting. "Thou its Sun which goes not down," William
Chatterton Dix (1837-1898) wrote in his hymn "As with gladness men of old."
This hypothesis was widely accepted and is found in the studies of the liturgical year by Adolf Adam, Adrian Nocent, and Edward Traill Horn III. The
hypothesis, it may be noted, was perhaps anticipated by Charles Wesley in the
third stanza of his familiar hymn "Hark! The herald angels sing," deriving
from the prophecy of Malachi:

> Risen with healing in his wings,
> Light and life to all he brings,
> Hail, the Sun of Righteousness!
> Hail, the heaven-born Prince of Peace.[4]

There is truth in the assertion that the rites of the Incarnation are influenced
if not actually governed by the solar year, as the rites of redemption, Pascha,
are governed by the lunar year.

Louis Duchesne, also in 1889, proposed an alternative origin, called the
"calculation" or the "computation" school, accepted by Paul Zeller Strodach[5]
and given new life in the latter twentieth century by Thomas Talley. From the
third century Christians had attempted to calculate the date of Jesus's birth.

There was a common belief that a perfect human life ought to begin and end on the same day to form a complete and perfect circle, the life thus yielding a whole number of years. Because Jesus lived a perfect life, the day of his death, it was thought, must also be the date of his conception, the beginning of his coming into the world. March 25 was widely held to be the date of the crucifixion, and therefore to fulfill the expectation of perfection, March 25 ought also to be the date of the Annunciation and his conception. Thus his birth would occur exactly nine months later, December 25.

Acceptance of the two hypotheses, it has been noted, divides largely on linguistic lines: the history of religions hypothesis appeals to continental Europeans, while the computation hypothesis appeals to English speakers. Both proposals have weaknesses. "On the historical level, it has become, on the one hand, unlikely that the origin of Christmas is to be explained as a Christian reaction to the birth feast of the unconquered sun, and on the other hand, the early calculations of the birth date of Christ are contradictory and can really no longer be offered as the basis for the introduction of the feast of Christmas."[6]

In any case, whatever its origin, the observance of Christmas spread throughout the Church. John Chrysostom, preaching in 386 in promotion of the new feast, notes that the date of Christ's birth had been known for less than ten years.[7] The earliest name of the feast seems to have been *Natalis* or *Nativitas Domini;* the French and the early English *Noel* derive from this Latin title. In German it is *Weinacht,* Holy Night, from Christmas Eve. In Scandinavia it is *Yule,* a feast of obscure Teutonic origin that also found its way into Old English use. *Christmas,* a name traceable to the twelfth century, is from Christ-Mass, the Mass of Christ's Day, analogous to Candlemas and Michaelmas.

The Meaning of Christmas

Christmas was created in Rome and there the fullness of its celebration developed. In the fourth century there was one Mass celebrated by the bishop of Rome on Christmas Day at 9 in the morning (long the preferred time in both East and West for morning liturgies). In the fifth century, a midnight Mass was added in the basilica of Santa Maria Maggiore (St. Mary Major), the principal church in Rome dedicated to the mother of Jesus. In the sixth century, a third Mass was introduced at St. Anastasia, December 25 being her feast day. Since then the Roman tradition has celebrated three Christmas Masses: (1) the midnight Mass of the angels' announcement of Jesus's birth; (2) the dawn Mass of the shepherds' visit to the Child in the manger; and (3) the daytime

Mass of the faithful, proclaiming the theological meaning of the Incarnation set out in the great prologue to St. John's Gospel. Thus, there is the declaration of the birth, the response to the announcement, and the interpretation of the event. Medieval mystics saw this three-fold celebration as an allusion to the "three-fold birth." John Tauler (d. 1361) wrote:

> The first and supreme birth takes place when the heavenly Father bears his only-begotten Son as one with himself in essence yet as also a distinct person. The second birth, which we commemorate today, results from the maternal fruitfulness which the chaste Virgin exercised in perfect purity. The third birth is this: that God is truly but spiritually born every day and at every hour in a good soul, as a result of grace and love. We celebrate these three births by means of the three holy Masses.[8]

Note the three-fold and four-fold Advent pattern given in the previous chapter. What is noteworthy here in the fourteenth century is the loss of the eschatological expectation. A more suggestive interpretation is that the three Christmas masses reflect the rising dawn: midnight, dawn, full daylight. The Sun of Righteousness is always rising, ever increasing, the "sun which goes not down."[9]

Pope Leo the Great (400-461) explained how the celebration of Christmas was to be understood. We are, he said, "to think of the Lord's birth, wherein the Word became flesh, not as a past event which we recall, but as a present reality upon which we gaze."[10] Christmas is "the day chosen for the sacrament of humanity's restoration," and as such it is not a duplicate of Easter but rather the starting point of our salvation. It is oriented toward our redemption, which it already contains.[11] The feast of the nativity renders present the beginning of salvation, the beginning in time of God's great act of redemption. With Christmas, therefore, the new creation has begun, our liberation is under way, so it is altogether correct to say that salvation has already been effected in the birth of Christ. If we object that the Incarnation itself was not redemptive, as some assert, we are captive to that compartmentalized thinking that undermines a proper understanding of the liturgical year, as if in its observance we move step by separate step through discrete events that led ultimately to salvation. Rather, salvation is all of one piece: without the birth, there could be no death; without the death, there could be no resurrection, without the resurrection, there could be no redemption. Leo preached,

> Today's festival renews for us the holy childhood of Jesus born of the Virgin Mary; and in adoring the birth of our Savior we are celebrating

the commencement of our own life. For the birth of Christ is the source of life for Christian folk, and the birthday of the Head is the birthday of the body. Although every individual that is elect has his own order, and all the offspring are separated from one another by intervals of time, yet as the entire body of the faithful being born in the font of baptism is crucified with Christ in his passion, raised again in his resurrection, and placed at the Father's right hand in his ascension, so with him they are born in this nativity. For any believer in whatever part of the world that is reborn in Christ, quits the old paths of his original nature and passes into a new being by being reborn; and no longer is he reckoned of his earthly family's stock but among the seed of the Savior....As the end of the ages is fulfilled that which was ordained from all eternity: and in the presence of realities, when signs and types have ceased, the Law and prophecy have become Truth. Abraham is found the father of all nations, and the promised blessing is given to the world in his seed: nor are they only Israelites whom blood and flesh begot, but the whole body of the adopted enter into possession of the heritage prepared for the heirs of faith.[12]

The whole of salvation history is already present in its beginning. Here is the great mystery of the Incarnation: Christ has come, and still we wait; God who revealed himself in Christ remains hidden. Christmas in its fullness, therefore, is nothing less than a proclamation of the Parousia. It is a confident declaration that he who came once to his waiting people will, with equal certainty, come again in glory.

The Proclamation of Christmas

The church historian Caesar Baronius (1538-1607), in the course of revising the Roman Martyrology, a portion of which was read in chapters and monasteries every day at Prime, prepared for the Vigil of Christmas the text of a proclamation of Christmas that made it clear that the Nativity was an historical event for which all history, both sacred and secular, had prepared. Its impressive text (1586) announces,

In the 5199th year of the creation of the world, from the time when God in the beginning created the heaven and the earth; the 2957th year after the Flood; the 2015th year from the birth of Abraham; the 1510th year from Moses, and the going forth of the people of Israel from Egypt; the 1032nd year from the anointing of David the King; in the 65th week according to the prophecy of Daniel; in the 194th Olympiad; the 752nd year from the foundation of the city of Rome; the 42nd year of the rule of Octavianus Augustus, all the earth being at peace, Jesus Christ, the Eternal God, and the Son of the Eternal Father, wishing to consecrate the world by his most merciful coming, being conceived by the Holy Ghost, and nine months having passed since his conception *[here the voice is raised and all kneel]* was born in Bethlehem of Judea of the Virgin Mary, made man. The Nativity of our Lord Jesus Christ according to the flesh.

Fernand Cabrol in his book *The Year's Liturgy* (1938) provided the text as "well worth printing here, for it is not given in Missals or prayer books and yet, in our judgment, it is the most eloquent introduction to the feast of Christmas, as it treats the Nativity of Our Lord as the greatest event in the history of the world since the creation."[13] The Roman Catholic Church has adapted the text, making it less precise in its dating of biblical events and including the names of Sarah and Ruth.

Today, the twenty-fifth day of December, unknown ages from the time when God created the heavens and the earth...several thousand years after the flood... twenty-one centuries from the time of Abraham and Sarah; thirteen centuries after Moses led the people of Israel out of Egypt; eleven hundred years from the time of Ruth and the Judges; one thousand years from the anointing of David as king....

An evocative detail toward the conclusion of the proclamation is the note "all the earth being at peace" in preparation for the entrance of God into the world. It is a reference to more than the Pax Romana, although that was understood as part of the great preparation. It derives from the vision of Zechariah (1:11), the angel's report of the reconnoitering of the world, "we have patrolled the earth, and lo, the whole earth remains at peace." The restoration of Judah and Jerusalem is at hand.

In a more popular description, Christ came in the middle of the centuries, at the depth of the year, in the middle of the night, in the depth of the earth (a cave).

The Vigil of Christmas

The liturgical celebration of the Nativity of the Lord begins on December 24 with the Vigil. The anticipation that has been building through Advent now reaches its climax. In the Roman Liturgy of the Hours, the invitatory in the Office of Readings announces the immanent appearing in a phrase derived from Exod. 16:7:

> Today you will know that the Lord is coming,
>   and in the morning you will see his glory.

This night you will know, and when morning comes with the full light of the sun you will *see*. Notice should be taken of the promise of the eschatological return inherent in the verse. On Christmas morning you will know not as Isaac Watts's great hymn "Joy to the World" has it that "the Lord is come," but "you will know that the Lord is coming." Christmas looks not backward to the past but ahead to a future event.

In a sermon for the Vigil of Christmas, St. Bernard explains the Church's creative yet faithful use of scripture.

> These words belong to a specific place and time in Scripture, but Mother Church has not unfittingly applied them to the Vigil of the Lord's Nativity.... When she modifies or applies a text taken from the divine Scriptures, her accommodation is weightier with meaning than the text was in its original context, as the truth is weightier with meaning than the prefiguration of it, the light than the shadow....[14]

Bernard explains the text as speaking of two days, the first from the fall of humanity to the end of the world; "The second will be the day that lasts for ever." This second day is the focus of Christmas, Bernard says clearly. "Today, the coming of the only-begotten Son lights in us the lamp of true knowledge, that is, the knowledge that the Lord will come again." There, one may see the fully developed intent of the celebration of the birth of Christ: Christmas is a proclamation of the Parousia. Christmas declares that Christ will come again in power and glory. This forward-looking character of Christmas is evident in a vigorous antiphon from Ps. 19:5, appointed for Christmas Eve,

> The Lord comes forth like a bridegroom out of his chamber;
>   he rejoices like a champion to run his course.[15]

And again,

> He comes in splendor, the King who is our peace;
> the whole world longs to see him.[16]

The first coming was hidden in humility; it is the second coming that will be splendor.

The entrance antiphon is from the Introit for the Vigil of Christmas (*Hodie scietis*) Exod. 16:6-7 and echoes the confidence of the invitatory in the Office of Readings.

> Today you will know that the Lord will come, and he will save us,
> and in the morning you will see his glory.
>   *Psalm 24:1*. The earth is the Lord's and all that is in it,
>   the world, and those who live in it. *Gloria Patri*.
> Today...his glory.

The king is about to enter his realm.

The Collect for the Vigil of Christmas gathers in its wide view the three-fold mystery of Christmas: Christ's coming to earth, the mystery of his death and resurrection for which he comes, and his return as judge.[17] The prayer is from the Advent masses in the Gelasian sacramentary, appointed in the Gregorian and Sarum and northern European sacramentaries for the Vigil. It was translated into English for the 1868 (Lutheran) *Church Book*:

> O God, who dost gladden us with the yearly anticipation of our Redemption: Grant that we who now joyfully receive thine Only-begotten Son as our Redeemer, may also behold him without fear when he cometh as our Judge; who liveth and reigneth with thee and the Holy Ghost, ever one God, world without end.[18]

The same collect, with a revised preamble[19], has appeared in the American Prayer Book since 1892, appointed for Christmas Day.

The richness of the Christmas celebration has been understood through the centuries by those with insight and imagination. Christina Rossetti (1830-1894) set out those ideas in a remarkable hymn. It begins in northern European cold, a reflection of the condition of humanity.

> In the bleak mid-winter
>   Frosty wind made moan,
> Earth stood hard as iron,
>   Water like a stone;

> Snow had fallen, snow on snow,
>> Snow on snow,
> In the bleak midwinter,
>> Long ago.

Already in the second stanza the poem looks to the second coming. The mighty God whom heaven cannot contain and whom earth cannot support will return as ruler, and heaven and earth will flee before his presence. But at his first entrance into the world in the winter a stable was sufficient for the Lord God Almighty.

> Our God, heaven cannot hold him,
>> Nor earth sustain;
> Heaven and earth shall flee away
>> When he comes to reign;
> In the bleak midwinter
>> A stable place sufficed
> The Lord God Almighty,
>> Jesus Christ.

A note of realistic modern doubt creeps in to the traditional picture of the ranks of angels thronging above the earthly scene, in which only the virgin mother dared to kiss the Holy Child.

> Angels and archangels
>> May have gathered there,
> Cherubim and seraphim
>> Throngèd the air;
> But his mother only,
>> In her maiden bliss,
> Worshipped the Belovèd
>> With a kiss.

The angels may have done their part, the mother surely expressed her affection for her Child, shepherds and Magi gave gifts. We too have a gift that we must give.

> What can I give him,
>> Poor as I am?

> If I were a shepherd
>   I would bring a lamb;
> If I were a wise man
>   I would do my part;
> Yet what can I give him—
>   Give my heart.

Throughout the poem, the carefully controlled irregularities of rhythm are resolved in the three-syllable final line of each stanza. In the last stanza the pause at the end of the next-to-last line is extended, giving time for consideration of an appropriate gift for the Beloved. The conclusion is to give him the best gift of all.

The Roman Catholic Lectionary appoints one set of readings for the Vigil of Christmas for all three years of the lectionary cycle.

> Isa. 62:1-5. The vindication and salvation of Zion.
> Psalm 89:4-5, 16-17, 27, 29. The goodness of the Lord.
> Acts 13:16-17, 22-25. Jesus, descendent of King David.
> Matt. 1:1-25. The genealogy of Jesus the Messiah.

The essential point, especially in the long list of, to us, mostly obscure names that is the appointed Gospel, is that God had been steadily preparing through the ages for the dawn of this new day.

The rising expectation and excited anticipation is clear in the antiphons in the daily office. A psalm antiphon from first vespers declares, "He comes in splendor, the King who is our peace; the whole world longs to see him."[20] An antiphon to the canticle (Phil. 2:6-11) in first vespers anticipates the proclamation of the day that is beginning, "The eternal Word, born of the Father before time began, today emptied himself for our sake and became man."[21] The process of salvation is underway. The Son of God has put off his heavenly glory and privilege and has been born a mortal like us. The antiphon to the Magnificat says, "When the sun rises in the morning sky, you will see the King of kings coming forth from the Father like a radiant bridegroom from the bridal chamber."[22]

Again the emphasis is not on the sight of the newborn Holy Child but the return of the Lord in glory to claim his bride, the Church.

The progressive unfolding of the Christmas mystery is evident in the color use employed in twelfth-century Jerusalem and elsewhere during the Middle Ages and continuing even in nineteenth-century France. Black was used for the first Mass, red for the second, and white for the third.

The Christmas Midnight Mass

The first Eucharist of Christmas is the popular midnight Mass that announces the holy birth. The Roman sacramentary appoints as the entrance antiphon a liturgical composition.

> Let us all rejoice in the Lord, for our Savior has been born in the world.
> Today true peace has come down to us from heaven.

The alternative is the antiphon from the traditional Introit (*Dominus dixit*) from Psalm 2:7, 1-2, 8.

> The Lord said to me, "You are my Son;
> today I have begotten you."
>> *Psalm.* Why do the nations conspire, and the peoples plot in vain? [The kings of the earth set themselves, and the rulers take counsel together, against the Lord and his anointed. Ask of me and I will make the nations your heritage, and the ends of the earth your possession.] *Gloria Patri.*
> The Lord said...begotten you.

Lutheran books until 1978 replaced the Psalm verse with the Psalm from the Mass at dawn, Psalm 93:1 in the King James Version: "The Lord reigneth, He is clothed with majesty: the Lord is clothed with strength, wherewith he hath girded himself." The Psalm verse "Why do the nations conspire, and the peoples plot in vain?" is given by itself in the Gregorian sacramentary; the bracketed verses are added in the Graduale Romanum. The verses from Psalm 2 are a solemn reminder, even at the magical midnight Mass, of the hostility that the coming of Christ into the world generated. Herod was not the only ruler to feel threatened. The liturgical year and its appointments always reflect a realistic view of the way of the world and will not let us escape the truth.

The Collect dates from the Gelasian sacramentary in which it was appointed for the midnight Mass and continues in use in the Roman, Anglican, and Lutheran rites. In the Prayer Book translation it is

> O God, you have caused this holy night to shine with the brightness of the true Light: Grant that we, who have known the mystery of that Light on earth, may also enjoy him perfectly in heaven; where with you and the Holy Spirit he lives and reigns, one God, in glory everlasting.

The light of God has come into the darkness of our world, and it is paradoxically at night that Jesus Christ, "Light from Light" the Nicene Creed calls him, is revealed. He has come to do battle with the forces of darkness, and that struggle begins even in his infancy. But already the outcome of that contest is sure. Here on earth we see the light of truth, the illumination of Holy Baptism, the dawning of the day that shall never end. "In your light we see light," says the psalmist (Ps. 36:9). In Christ the light of the world (John 8:12) we see the Father, the fountain from which water and life and light flow. (John 1:4).[23] As St. John says, "The darkness is passing away, and the true light is already shining" (1 John 2:8). Eternal life has even now already begun. To make vivid the entrance of light into the world, it was customary to illumine the churches with as many lights as possible. O. B. Hardison, Jr. in his study of the origins of the early drama *Quem quaeritis* notes a rubric from the Cathedral of Parma concerning the preparation of the building for the celebration of the Easter Vigil about 3 a.m., during which the brief drama would be enacted, "All the lamps of the church are illuminated as on the Nativity."[24] Those who accept the proposal that Christmas was instituted to be a rival festival to the pagan ceremonies of the birth of the unconquered Sun[25] may find support for the hypothesis in this collect.

> One set of lessons serves all three years of the lectionary cycle.
> Isa. 9:2-7. Light to a land and people in darkness.
> Psalm 96. The Lord, King, and Judge of the world
> Titus 2:11-14. The grace of God has appeared.
> Luke 2:1-14 (15-20). The birth of Jesus revealed to shepherds.

The wonderful account of the birth of the Savior has inspired a vast number of tender hymns[26] and paintings and sermons. One of the loveliest is Phillips Brooks's beloved carol written for the children of the Sunday school of the Church of the Holy Trinity on Rittenhouse Square in Philadelphia where he was rector. He had a few years earlier been to the Holy Land and had arranged his itinerary so that he could be in the little town of Bethlehem for Christmas. His hymn in a beautiful vision allows us to participate in the dark night in Bethlehem and the wondrous things that took place there.

> O little town of Bethlehem,
> How still we see thee lie!
> Above thy deep and dreamless sleep
> The silent stars go by;
> Yet in thy dark streets shineth

>   The everlasting light,
>   The hopes and fears of all the years
>   Are met in thee tonight.

J. R. Watson notes "the very attractive use of internal rhyme" in the third and seventh lines of each stanza (deep/sleep; fears/years) that "reminds us of the hymn's origins as a Sunday school carol, because those lines have a delightful charming quality (not unlike a nursery rhyme) which sweetens the seriousness."[27] This night, this very night, the first Christmas Eve, the hopes and fears of all the years of the whole world came to a unified focus in the little town. Old Testament and New are joined, the first creation and the new creation.

>   O morning stars, together   [Job 38:7]
>   Proclaim the holy birth,
>   And praises sing to God the King   [Luke 2:13-14]
>   And peace to men on earth;
>   For Christ is born of Mary;
>   And, gathered all above,
>   While mortals sleep, the angels keep
>   Their watch of wondering love.

Much of the wonder and beauty of this night is the silence in which the coming of the Savior takes place. There is none of the thunder and fire of Sinai, but the "sheer silence" of Elijah's encounter with God. (1 Kings 19:11-12).

>   How silently, how silently,
>   The wondrous gift is given!
>   So God imparts to human hearts
>   The blessings of his heaven.
>   No ear may hear his coming;
>   But in this world of sin,
>   Where meek souls will receive him, still
>   The dear Christ enters in.

The comma in the next-to-last line shows how the lines are to be read: "still" modifies not "receive him" but "enter in." The following stanza explains how he who that night in Bethlehem came into the world can still come to his people where there is prayer, grief, or acts of kindness. Any day can be Christmas.

(It is unfortunate that only the Episcopal *Hymnal 1982* includes this fourth stanza of the hymn.)

> Where children pure and happy
>   Pray to the blessed child,
> Where misery cries out to thee,
>   Son of the mother mild;
> Where charity stands watching
>   And faith holds wide the door,
> The dark night wakes, the glory breaks,
>   And Christmas comes once more.
>
> O holy child of Bethlehem,
>   Descend to us, we pray;
> Cast out our sin, and enter in,
>   Be born in us today.
> We hear the Christmas angels
>   The great glad tidings tell:
> O come to us, abide with us,
>   Our Lord Emmanuel.

The great nineteenth-century preacher has given a graceful and memorable description of the meaning of Christmas: Christ can be born in every heart.

The meaning of the Gospel in the context of the liturgy of the Church and the two lessons that accompany the Gospel is larger and more inclusive than an encouragement to welcome the holy child into the heart. The Gospel has a more expansive view that includes not only individuals but nations, ultimately all the nations of the earth, and that looks toward the return in glory of the King who at his first entrance into the world had a feeding trough for his cradle.

The Mass at Dawn

The Mass celebrated as Christmas Day dawns is an extension of the announcement of the birth to the shepherds. (Their response is included in the Revised Common Lectionary optional extension of the midnight Gospel to continue through Luke 2:20.) We see their response and are encouraged like them to come to the manger and see for ourselves the wonder of the person of this Child. Once again, as in the liturgy's sympathy in Advent with John the Baptist's question, "Are you the one who is to come or are we to look for another?" so here we find that same reluctance to leap into gullibility and quickly accept as fact what we would like to be true. The liturgy is deeply founded on honest experience and is hesitant to assume too much too quickly. A psalm antiphon at Lauds on Christmas morning, to encourage our own faith, asks for the testimony of the shepherds, and their reply is notably circumspect.

> Tell us, shepherds, what have you seen?
> Who has appeared on earth?
>> We have seen a newborn infant
>> and a choir of angels praising the Lord, alleluia.[28]

The bewildered shepherds are still trying to take it all in and make sense of what they have experienced. All they are sure of are two facts: they saw a newborn child and they heard a choir of angels. More than that, they are as yet unwilling to say. The meaning of this conjunction of the ordinary and the extraordinary will take time to become clear.

St. Jerome, after his visit to Palestine in 385, reported that some of the desert hermits venerated the manger in which Christ had lain and later laments that he did not himself see the Christmas crib. Nothing else is heard of the existence of the crib. The liturgical dramas of the twelfth and thirteenth centuries portrayed the crib, and St. Francis of Assisi made a replica of the manger to assist his followers in visualizing the beginning of salvation. Since then, especially in Italy and in Germany, such scenes have had a large part in popular devotion. The Episcopal *Book of Occasional Services* provides a form for a Station at a Christmas Crèche when the celebrant and other ministers, as they enter the church for the celebration of the Holy Eucharist, briefly stop the entrance procession at a representation of the manger-crib.

The Introit antiphon for the Mass at dawn (*Lux fulgebit hodie*) is drawn from Isaiah 9:2, 6 and Luke 1:33.

> Today a light will shine upon us;
> and he will be called wondrous God, Prince of Peace,
> Father of future ages,
> and his reign will be without end.
>> *Psalm 93:1.* The Lord is king, he is robed in majesty;
>> the Lord is robed, he is girded with strength.
> Today a light...without end.

At dawn the sun is just beginning to rise, and when the promise of full sunlight is fulfilled, the words of the ancient prophet will be seen to describe the newborn Child.

In the Roman sacramentary the Collect is Gregorian. In the translation in the Book of Common Prayer where it is appointed for the First Sunday after Christmas it is

> Almighty God, you have poured upon us the new light of your incarnate Word: Grant that this light, enkindled in our hearts, may shine forth in our lives; through Jesus Christ our Lord, who lives and reigns with you, in the unity of the Holy Spirit, one God, now and for ever.

As the day breaks and the sun rises in the sky, we ask that the Light of Christ shine forth increasingly in our lives.

> One set of lessons serves for each of the three years of the lectionary cycle.
> Isa. 62:6-12. See, your salvation comes.
> Psalm 97. Earth rejoices in its king.
> Titus 3:4-7. The water of rebirth and renewal.
> Luke 2:(1-7) 8-20. The praise of angels and shepherds.

The reading from Isaiah presents the double thrust of Christmas. God has remembered his people; "You shall be called, 'Sought out, A City Not Forsaken.'" And yet, the fulfillment is still in the future. The reading from Titus makes the connection with our baptism. The appearance of "the goodness and loving kindness of God our Savior" that led to our rebirth and renewal was the work of the Holy Trinity, Father, Son, and Holy Spirit, which made us "heirs according to the hope of eternal life." The Gospel in the Roman lectionary is limited to Luke 2:15-20, which is surely sufficient. It speaks to the ethical response to the announcement of the birth of the Messiah; the shepherds confirm by their own eyes what had been announced specifically to them, then told others what had been told them about the Child, and then went back to their sheep, to their regular responsibilities, "glorifying and praising God." The Invitatory in the Office of Readings in the *Liturgy of the Hours* is noteworthy. "Christ is born for us; come, let us adore him."[29] Christ's birth was for us; the angel told the shepherds, "To you is born this day a Savior." And the pleading of Advent, "Come," addressed to Christ, now becomes an invitation to one another, as we say with the shepherds, "Come, let us adore him." We are to join the shepherds in adoration and with them proclaim the wonders of what we see. "A little child is born for us today; little and yet called the mighty God, alleluia."[30]

In the fifth century, perhaps in Rome, Coelius (Caelius) Sedulius, of whom little is known, composed a twenty-three strophe abecedarian poem on the life of Christ. The opening stanzas of the poem, beginning *A solis ortus cardine,* ponder the paradoxes of the day that is dawning. The translation by John Ellerton (1826-1893) is given as a Christmas hymn in several hymnals.

> From east to west, from shore to shore,
>   Let every heart awake and sing
> The holy Child whom Mary bore,
>   The Christ, the everlasting King.
>
> Behold, the world's Creator wears
>   The form and fashion of a slave;
> Our very flesh our Maker shares,
>   His fallen creature, man, to save.
>
> For this how wondrously he wrought!
>   A maiden, in her lowly place,
> Became in ways beyond all thought,
>   The chosen vessel of his grace.
>
> She bowed her to the Angel's word
>   Declaring what the Father willed,
> And suddenly the promised Lord
>   That pure and hallowed temple filled. [Mal. 3:1]
>
> He shrank not from the oxen's stall,
>   He lay within the manger-bed,
> And he, whose bounty feedeth all,
>   At Mary's breast himself was fed.
>
> And while the angels in the sky
>   Sang praise above the silent field,
> To shepherds poor the Lord most high,
>   The one great Shepherd, was revealed.
>
> All glory for this blessed morn
>   To God the Father ever be;
> And praise to thee, O virgin-born,
>   All praise, O Holy Ghost, to thee.[31]

To save the fallen mortal race the Maker of the world in incomprehensible condescension came among us as a slave, born of a humble mother, with animals as his companions, and revealed his coming to those of the lowest occupation, taking their name as his own. It was from them, whom John Byrom (1692-1763) in his magnificent but demanding hymn for Christmas morning[32] called "the first apostles of his infant fame," that the good news spread eventually throughout the whole world.

The Mass of Christmas Day

The Mass of Christmas Day concentrates on the interpretation of the meaning of the birth and unfolds the great mystery of the Incarnation. The Introit antiphon (*Puer natus est*) is adapted from Isaiah 9:6,

> A child has been born for us, a son given to us;
> authority rests upon his shoulders;
> and his name shall be called Messenger [Angel] of great counsel.
> > *Psalm 98:1.* O sing to the Lord a new song,
> > for he has done marvelous things. *Gloria Patri.*
> A child...of great counsel.

The Lutheran liturgies gave the conclusion of the antiphon as it stands in Isaiah 9:6 "and he is named Wonderful Counselor, Mighty God, Everlasting Father, Prince of Peace."

The Roman sacramentary appoints a collect from the Leonine sacramentary, the oldest of the Roman books. The Book of Common Prayer appoints this collect for the Second Sunday after Christmas Day and translates it:

> O God, who wonderfully created, and yet more wonderfully restored,
> the dignity of human nature: Grant that we may share the divine life of
> him who came to share our humanity, your Son Jesus Christ; who lives
> and reigns with you and the Holy Spirit, one God, for ever and ever.

It is an impressive statement of the "wonderful exchange" described so memorably by Athanasius, "God became human so that humans might become God."[33]

The Collect that Thomas Cranmer composed for the 1549 Prayer Book and has been continued in every succeeding Prayer Book, is remarkably similar.

Almighty God, you have given your only-begotten Son to take our nature upon him, and to be born [this day] of a pure virgin: Grant that we, who have been born again and made your children by adoption and grace, may daily be renewed by your Holy Spirit; through our Lord Jesus Christ, to whom with you and the same Spirit be honor and glory, now and for ever.

Cranmer's Collect is similar to the proper Preface for Christmas Day, which he also composed for the 1549 book. That Preface, in the 1979 American Prayer Book, is "Because you gave Jesus Christ, your only Son, to be born for us; who, by the mighty power of the Holy Spirit, was made perfect Man of the flesh of the Virgin Mary his mother; so that we might be delivered from the bondage of sin, and receive power to become your children." Massey Hamilton Shepherd, Jr. says of Archbishop Cranmer's Christmas collect, "[I]t is of all the Prayer Book Collects the most notable for its theological content, for the whole of the doctrines of the Trinity and the Incarnation are encased in it. Specifically, the Collect is woven about three themes: (1) the birth of the Only-begotten Son of God in the substance of our human nature is linked with the idea of our rebirth in Baptism by 'pure' water and the Holy Spirit; (2) the eternal Sonship of Christ is contrasted with our adoption as sons by the free grace of God; and (3) the historic birth of our Lord at a specific time and place is spiritually renewed in the hearts of his followers daily. (Cf. 2 Cor. iv.16: 'Though our outward man perish, yet the inward man is renewed day by day'; note also Col. iii.10; Eph. iii.16.)"[34]

In the previous Roman Missal, in various northern European missals including Sarum, and in the Lutheran use, a Gelasian collect was appointed. The translation made for the (Lutheran) *Church Book* (1868) is

Grant, we beseech thee, Almighty God, that the new birth of thine only-begotten Son in the flesh may set us free who are held in the old bondage under the yoke of sin; through the same Jesus Christ, thy Son, our Lord, who liveth and reigneth with thee and the Holy Ghost, ever one God, world without end.

Paul Zeller Strodach comments,

In the midst of the great joy of this Holy Day comes the quietly sober note of the *Collect*.... The Church could pray for many things; no doubt her greatest desire would be to take up the Glory-song of the Angels and pour it forth in adoration and thanksgiving; but in deep quietness of heart she finds the very center of the Coming-into-the-world and carries that in her festal prayer to the Giver of the Gift Divine. As one prays, one thinks of "If the Son shall make you free, ye shall be free indeed" and the "God so loved the world." The play of the original language is not only extremely expressive but very beautiful, and very excellently rendered in the English translation. In addition to being our prayer, this *Collect* is a very concise and complete doctrinal statement of the Incarnation of the Son and the Goal set before him.[35]

The description in the collect of the Lord's birth as "new" may seem odd, but it is exactly right. The birth of the only-begotten Son of God in the flesh is active here and now, and is therefore ever new to us and for us. The Christmas mystery is not something old and getting older, receding further into the distant past with each passing year. It is a gift that is to be received as a new and fresh grace in our lives and in the world.

In the Revised Common Lectionary one set of readings is appointed for all three years of the lectionary cycle.

> Isa. 52:7-10. The Lord has comforted his people.
> Psalm 98. God, the ruler of the world.
> Heb. 1:1-4 (5-12). The Son: image of the Father, agent in creation, redeemer.
> John 1:1-14. The classic statement of the Incarnation.

The Epistle from Hebrews is a summary of the creed. The opening words of the Gospel, "In the beginning," is a reminder that Christmas was originally the beginning of the liturgical year.

The Anglican proper Preface of the Incarnation is provided above in connection with Cranmer's Collect. The Roman sacramentary provides three prefaces. The first, "Christ the Light," from the Gregorian sacramentary, is also used in the Lutheran rite where it is translated:

> In the wonder and mystery of the Word made flesh, you have opened the eyes of faith to a new and radiant vision of your glory; that, beholding the God made visible, we may be drawn to love the God whom we cannot see.

The second preface provided in the Roman rite, the restoration of all things in the Incarnation, derives from a sermon of Leo the Great.

> On the feast of this awe-filled mystery,
> though invisible in his own divine nature,
> he has appeared visibly in ours;
> and begotten before all ages, he has begun to exist in time;
> so that, raising up in himself all that was cast down,
> he might restore unity to all creation
> and call straying humanity back to the heavenly kingdom.

The third preface in the Roman sacramentary, divine and human exchange in the Incarnation of the Word, is from the Leonine sacramentary.

> Through him the holy exchange that restores our life
> has shone forth today in splendor:
> when our frailty is assumed by your Word
> not only does human mortality receive unending honor,
> but by this wondrous union we, too, are made eternal.

An early Latin hymn, *Corde natus ex parentis* (literally, "Of the Parent's heart begotten") by Aurelius Prudentius Clemens (348-ca. 413), a Spanish lawyer who in retirement wrote poetry for which he is still known, gathers the whole sweep of the Christmas proclamation in its impressive power. The Latin text, from the ninth section of his *Cathemerinon* on the Christian day, where its title says it is a hymn appropriate for every hour of the day, is found in various medieval rites and is described as "a hymn for all hours" [of the daily office]. The English translation is by John Mason Neale (1818-1866) and Henry Williams Baker (1821-1877).

> Of the Father's love begotten
>   Ere the world began to be,
> He is Alpha and Omega,
>   He the source, the ending he,
> Of the things that are, that have been,
>   And that future years shall see,
>   Evermore and evermore.

The Son of God was eternally begotten of the Father. "There was never a time when the Son did not exist," was the Orthodox response to the Arian heresy that denied the eternity of the Son. And his being exists throughout all eternity. He is not just eternal; he is the source of all that exists and of all that has existed in past ages and of all that will exist in the future. The birth from the virgin is praised and then declared to be the fulfillment of the vision of the psalmists and poets of the Bible and promised by the prophets. God's word is always sure.

O that birth forever blessèd,
    When the Virgin, full of grace,
By the Holy Ghost conceiving,
    Bore the Savior of our race;
And the Babe, the world's Redeemer,
    First revealed his sacred face,
    Evermore and evermore.

This is he whom seers in old time
    Chanted of with one accord;
Whom the voices of the prophets
    Promised in their faithful word;
Now he shines the long-expected;
    Let creation praise its Lord,
    Evermore and evermore.

The ranks of angels in heaven sing in praise of the wondrous birth, and everyone on earth is called upon to echo the angels' endless praise, their tongues expressing what is sung in their hearts.

Let the heights of heaven adore him,
    Angel hosts, his praises sing;
Powers, dominions, bow before him,
    And extol of our God and King;
Let no tongue on earth be silent,
    Every voice in concert ring,
    Evermore and evermore.

Thee let old men, thee let young men,
    Thee let boys in chorus sing;
Matrons, virgins, little maidens
    With glad voices answering:
Let their guileless songs re-echo
    And the heart its music bring
    Evermore and evermore.

> Christ, to thee with God the Father,
>   And, O Holy Ghost, to thee,
> Hymn and chant and high thanksgiving,
>   And unwearied praises be;
> Honor, glory, and dominion,
>   And eternal victory,
>   Evermore and evermore.

The concluding doxology is a reminder that the work that was begun in Bethlehem was completed on Calvary; the birth and the passion and the resurrection all part of one great work of redemption, and so its praise will never end.

The Christmas solemn season blessing, adapted from the Roman sacramentary by the Episcopal Church, in its threefold form gathers the principal ideas of the celebration of the holy birth (the first line echoing the beginning of Archbishop Cranmer's Collect for Christmas Day): The darkness flees at the coming of the Light (we are to be transformed); the work of the angel-heralds is to be our model as we are to be heralds of the Gospel (the glad festival brings not only joy and comfort but responsibility); and the mystery of Christmas joins heaven to earth and earth to heaven, making the two one.

> May Almighty God, who sent his Son to take our nature upon him, bless you in this holy season, scatter the darkness of sin, and brighten your heart with the light of his holiness. *Amen*
>
> May God, who sent his angels to proclaim the glad news of the Savior's birth, fill you with joy, and make you heralds of the Gospel. *Amen*
>
> May God, who in the Word made flesh joined heaven to earth and earth to heaven, give you his peace and favor. *Amen*

The outline of the blessing derives from the familiar Christmas story in Luke's Gospel: there is the heavenly light, the angel's announcement of the birth, and the angels' song of peace and favor.

The briefer form of the blessing makes use of the most striking insight of the feast:

> May Christ, who by his Incarnation gathered into one things earthly and heavenly, fill you with his joy and peace; and the blessing of God

Almighty, the Father, the Son, and the Holy Spirit, by among you and remain with you for ever. *Amen.*

The idea of joining heaven and earth is developed from Ephesians 2:13-14 (God making Jews and Gentiles one in Christ) and Colossians 1:20 (through Christ "God was pleased to reconcile to himself all things, whether on earth or in heaven"). Earlier verses of that hymn (vv. 15-17) form part of the foundation of Prudentius's great Christmas hymn.

The antiphons in the daily office proclaim again and again the preexistence of the Son, praising together the begetting and the birth as two aspects of one truth. The Son of God was begotten of the Father before time began and was born into time in Bethlehem. The birth or even the conception of this child was not his beginning.

You have been endowed from your birth with princely gifts;
in eternal splendor, before the dawn of light on earth, I have begotten you.[36]

In the beginning, before time began, the Word was God;
today he is born, the Savior of the world.[37]

This pledge of new redemption and promise of eternal joy,
prepared through ages past,
has dawned for us today.[38]

The wonderful story of God's work has its origin before time began, is prepared through many ages in many ways, is at last made known, and will continue through all ages of ages. The wonders of that fulfillment abound as the antiphons attempt to express in human speech mysteries beyond our comprehension. The birth brings the created world together in unity.

Christ the Lord is born today; today the Savior has appeared. Earth echoes songs of angel choirs, archangels' joyful praise. Today on earth his friends exult: Glory to God in the highest, alleluia.[39]

St. Ambrose said that the Church came into existence at the moment of Christ's birth. "Christ is born and the shepherds begin their watch, gathering into the Lord's house his flocks, that is, the nations that hitherto had been living like beasts."[40] The mystical words of the Book of Wisdom 18:14-15 (*Dum medium silentium*) are used to describe in hushed awe the wonders of the holy night:

> While gentle silence enveloped all things,
> and night in its swift course was now half gone,
> > your all-powerful Word leaped down from heaven,
> > from the royal throne.[41]

In the anticipatory quiet of the "silent night, holy night," without a sound the eternal Word and Son of God leaped from his heavenly throne and from the royal hall of his mother silently enters the world that he had made.

Central to the wonder of Christmas is the all-encompassing embrace of God who enfolds heaven and earth in a single peace. Contrasts become one:

> Helpless, he lay in a manger;
> glorious, he shines in the heavens.
> > Humbled, he lived among mortals,
> > eternal, he dwells with the Father.[42]

Apparent contradictions are overcome:

> Marvelous is the mystery proclaimed today:
> > Human nature is made new as God becomes flesh;
> He remains what he was
> and becomes what he was not;
> > yet each nature remains distinct
> > and for ever undivided.[43]

The wonder and mystery of the Incarnation lingers through the Second Sunday after Christmas Day,

> By the power of the Holy Spirit the Virgin Mary has conceived a child; she carries in her womb this mystery which she cannot comprehend.[44]

The vast mystery that her (or any human) mind cannot comprehend is contained within her womb. An early English carol (ca. 1420) sang of the "marvelous thing,"

> There is no rose of such virtue
> As is the rose that bare Jesu;
> > Alleluia.
> For in this rose contained was
> Heaven and earth in little space;
> > Res miranda.

Language struggles to express what the mind cannot comprehend in its fullness.

A responsory for Christmas Day gathers the wonders and suggests the scope of the work that has begun.

> Today true peace came down to us from heaven.
>> Today the whole earth was filled with heaven's sweetness.
> Today a new day dawns, the day of redemption,
>> prepared by God from ages past,
>> the beginning of our never-ending gladness.
>>> Today the whole earth was filled with heaven's sweetness.[45]

Another responsory suggests the scope of the praise for the great work.

> Today for our sake
> the King of heaven chose to be born of his virgin mother
> to reclaim the lost for his heavenly kingdom.
>> All the angels cry aloud with joy
>> for God has come himself to save humanity.
> Glory to God in the highest,
> and peace to his people on earth.
>> All the angels cry aloud with joy
>> for God has come himself to save humanity.[46]

Heaven and earth are made one in the new creation that is now dawning, prepared by the Creator when the first creation was corrupted by human defiance and rebellion and paradise was lost. The new creation is even more wonderful than the first.

In the garden of paradise until the fall the man and the woman lived in harmony with the rest of creation, vegetation and animals. In the new paradise, the harmony will be restored. A responsory at Matins on Christmas Day in the previous Breviary, *O magnum mysterium, et admirabile sacramentum*, included the animals in the mystical adoration.

> What a great mystery, what a wonderful sign,
>> that animals should see the Lord, new-born,
>> lying in a manger!
> Blessed is the Virgin whose womb was privileged to carry
>> Christ the Lord.[47]

What had been in the mind of God from before the foundation of the world was coming into being.

Companions of Christ

As the celebration of Christmas developed, the heavenly birthdays of three "companions of Christ" came to be associated with the feast.[48] In previous Roman, Lutheran, and Anglican books the Propers for St. Stephen, St. John, and the Holy Innocents immediately followed the Propers for Christmas Day.

December 26 is "the feast of Stephen," the "proto-martyr" celebrated since the fourth century. St. Augustine notes that many churches were named for Stephen,[49] indicating his great popularity during that time. The story of "The martyr first, whose eagle eye could pierce beyond the grave,/who saw his master in the sky and called on him to save"[50] joins Christmas, the Death and Resurrection, the Ascension, and martyrdom in one profound proclamation. Fulgentius of Ruspe (468-533) in a sermon for this day shows how the work of Christ the King and Stephen his soldier are intertwined. "Yesterday our King, clothed in his robe of flesh, left his place in the virgin's womb and graciously visited the world. Today his soldier leaves the tabernacle of his body and goes triumphantly to heaven."[51] A responsory for the feast presents the same thought.

> Yesterday the Lord was born on earth
> so that Stephen might be born in heaven.
> > The Lord entered into our world
> > so that Stephen might enter into heaven.
> Yesterday our King, clothed in our flesh,
> came forth from the virgin's womb to dwell among us.
> > The Lord entered into our world
> > so that Stephen might enter into heaven.[52]

Stephen's noble death, in which he emulated the death of his Lord, had its effect on Saul who presided over the execution and for whom Stephen prayed. "Strengthened by the power of his love, [Stephen] overcame the raging cruelty of Saul and won his persecutor on earth as his companion in heaven."[53]

The collect in the Roman, Anglican, and Lutheran rites is from the Gregorian sacramentary. It is freely translated in the 1979 Book of Common Prayer.

> We give you thanks, O Lord of glory, for the example of the first martyr Stephen, who looked up to heaven and prayed for his persecutors to your Son Jesus Christ, who stands at your right hand; where he lives and reigns with you and the Holy Spirit, one God, in glory everlasting.

The reference to Jesus's standing not only refers to what Stephen saw as he died (Acts 7:56) but also suggests that Jesus stood up from his throne to welcome his first martyr into the heavenly mansions. The antiphon on the Benedictus in Morning Prayer declares,

> The gates of heaven opened out to blessed Stephen,
> and he was crowned first of martyrs.[54]

St. Stephen, Protomartyr, is celebrated by the Church as a martyr both in will and in deed.

The next day, December 27, St. John is celebrated as a martyr in will although not in deed. Although he was willing to die for his Lord, he was, according to tradition, the only one of the Twelve Apostles not to die a martyr's death. John, who with his brother James bore the nickname "sons of thunder," (Mark 3:17) is also identified as the "beloved disciple," the disciple whom Jesus loved, and is honored on the second day after Christmas, indicating his special nearness to Jesus. The Collect, common to the Roman, Anglican, and Lutheran rites, is from the Leonine sacramentary, abbreviated in the Gregorian sacramentary. The Book of Common Prayer translates it:

> Shed upon your Church, O Lord, the brightness of your light, that we,
> being illumined by the teaching of your apostle and evangelist John,
> may so walk in the light of your truth, that at length we may attain to
> the fullness of eternal life; through Jesus Christ our Lord, who lives and
> reigns with you and the Holy Spirit, one God, for ever and ever.

The prayer reflects the image of light that is emphasized in the prologue to John's Gospel and in such sayings as "I am the light of the world." The phrase "attain to the fullness of eternal life" suggests the Johanine view that eternal life is not a distant reward off in the future but is a present possession of believers.

The antiphon to the Magnificat on December 27, addresses the mother, "Virgin Mary, all that the prophets foretold of Christ has been fulfilled through you: as a virgin you conceived, and after you gave birth, a virgin you remained."[55] (The tradition is that St. John also was a virgin.)

December 28 is the Feast of the Holy Innocents of Bethlehem, celebrated as martyrs in deed although, since they were all infants, not in will. They have been celebrated since the fourth century and on this date since the sixth century. The day is out of chronological sequence; on that basis it should be observed after the Epiphany visit of the Magi. But strict chronology has not been a determining factor in the liturgical year. (That attitude is another borrowing from Judaism. Talmudic sages, untroubled by chronological irregularities in the account of the Exodus, declared that "there is no earlier or later in the Torah."[56]) The remembrance of the Holy Innocents of Bethlehem on the third day after Christmas is explained by the understanding that they died for Christ, that is, in place of Christ, making possible the salvation of the world. The Invitatory for the feast in the Roman *Liturgy of the Hours* is "Come, let us worship the newborn Christ who crowns with joy these children who died for him."[57]

Precisely what to make of the death of the Innocents has been a continuing conundrum for the Church. The various collects that have been appointed by the several rites through the years and their revisions and evasions are evidence of that discomfort in making sense of the commemoration. The Gelasian and Gregorian Collect, still used in the Roman rite, was translated in the 1549 Prayer Book, "Almighty God, whose praise this day the young innocents thy witnesses hath confessed and showed forth, not in speaking but in dying: Mortify and kill all vices in us, that in our conversation [i.e., conduct], our life may express thy faith, which with our tongues we do confess...." Many wondered how infants can give praise by being killed. The 1662 Prayer Book had, "O Almighty God, who...madest infants to glorify thee by their deaths...." It was not an improvement. The 1958 Lutheran *Service Book and Hymnal* took the path of evasion, abandoning the traditional collect and replacing it with a prayer of unknown provenance:

> O God our Father, who by the birth and infancy of thy Son didst sanctify
> and bless childhood: We commend to thy love all children, and beseech
> thee to protect them from every hurt and harm, and to lead them in the
> knowledge of thyself and the obedience of thy will; through the same
> Jesus Christ our Lord, who....

The prayer, in the judgment of the eminent liturgical scholar Luther Reed, failed "to capture any of the tragedy of the Gospel or the glory of the Epistle."[58] (The appointed Epistle was Rev. 14:1-5, the 144,000 redeemed.) The bland collect had no evident connection with the event being commemorated.

The 1979 American Prayer Book tried another approach (borrowed by the *Lutheran Book of Worship* and *Evangelical Lutheran Worship*), making explicit reference to the deaths of the infants but expanding the commemoration to include "all innocent victims" and praying for the "rule of justice, love, and peace." *Lutheran Worship* (1981) replaced the BCP-LBW prayer with a notable revision of the traditional collect:

> Almighty God, whose praise was proclaimed on this day by the wicked death of innocent children, giving us thereby a picture of the death of your beloved Son, mortify and destroy in us all that is in conflict with you that we who have been called in faith to be your children may in life and death bear witness to your salvation; through our Lord Jesus Christ....[59]

Its predecessor, *The Lutheran Hymnal* (1941), gave two versions of the traditional collect.

A traditional antiphon provides a picture of playful children, "Lord, these little ones praise you and skip with joy like lambs, for you have set them free."[60] The idea derives from Prudentius's hymn *Salvete, flores martyrum*, translated by Henry Williams Baker, "Sweet flow'rets of the martyr band," which in the previous Roman breviary was the office hymn at Lauds on December 28.

> First victims for th' incarnate Lord,
> A tender flock to feel the sword;
> Beside the very altar, gay,
> With palm and crown ye seemed to play.[61]

The hymn introduces the pleasant conceit of children playing with their signs of victory, palms and crowns, as children do, under the very altar of God, their laughter transforming the grim picture provided in Revelation 6:9-11.

The Magnificat antiphon on Holy Innocents' Day joins those infants with the holy child: "The holy virgin gave birth to God who became for us the frail, tender baby she nursed at her breast. Let us worship the Lord who comes to save us."[62] A responsory for the feast offers consolation from Isa. 65:19 and Rev. 21:4,5.

> I will rejoice in Jerusalem and delight in my people.
> No more shall the sound of weeping be heard
> or the cry of distress.
> Death will be no more;
> mourning and crying and pain will be no more,
> for behold, I am making all things new.

No more shall the sound of weeping be heard
or the cry of distress.[63]

In medieval times when the Holy Innocents' Day fell during the week, it was treated like a weekday in the penitential season of Lent, with Alleluias and the Gloria in excelsis omitted. The color was violet; the color for Stephen was red for his martyrdom; for John it was white, because he died a natural death. Since in medieval times each day had an octave, there was a complex interweaving of the propers at vespers: on St. Stephen's Day the collects were said in the following order: St. Stephen's Day, St. John's Day (being the eve), Christmas Day (commemorating the season); on St. John's Day the sequence was St. John's Day, Holy Innocents' Day, Christmas Day, St. Stephen's Day.[64]

The Sunday within the Octave of Christmas

The Sunday within the Octave of the Nativity in current Roman Catholic use is celebrated as the Feast of the Holy Family. The feast was established in 1893, suppressed in 1911, reintroduced in 1920 (on the Sunday within the octave of the Epiphany), and linked to the Octave of Christmas in the Sacramentary of Paul VI in 1969. In Anglican and Lutheran use, the day is accounted the First Sunday after Christmas Day.[65]

The Roman sacramentary appoints a new collect for the Feast of the Holy Family of Jesus, Mary, and Joseph:

O God, who were pleased to give us the shining example of the Holy Family, graciously grant that we may imitate them in practicing the virtues of family life and in the bonds of charity, and so, in the joy of your house, delight one day in eternal rewards; through our Lord Jesus Christ....

These readings are appointed for the feast:

Year A(BC).
      Sirach 3:2-6, 12-14. Duties toward parents
      Col. 3:12--21. Instructions for the household
      Matt. 2:13-15, 19-23. The escape into Egypt
Year B optional
      Luke 2:22-40. The Presentation of Jesus in the Temple
Year C optional
      Luke 2:41-52. The boy Jesus in the Temple.

The collect for the First Sunday after Christmas Day in the Book of Common Prayer is the collect from the Gregorian sacramentary given above as the collect for the Mass at dawn on Christmas Day. In the previous Prayer Book it had been assigned to the Second Sunday after Christmas Day. The *Lutheran Book of Worship* follows the 1928 Prayer Book and keeps this prayer on the Second Sunday after Christmas.

In the Revised Common Lectionary, the appointed readings for the First Sunday after Christmas are

Year A
> Isa. 63:7-9. The mercy of God
> Psalm 148. Cosmic praise
> Heb. 2:10-18. Christ became like us
> Matt. 2:13-23. The escape to Egypt

Year B
> Isa. 61:10-62:3. Vindication and salvation
> Psalm 148. Cosmic praise
> Gal. 4:4-7. Adoption as God's children
> Luke 2:22-40. Jesus presented in the temple

Year C
> 1 Sam. 2:18-20, 26. Samuel's service as a child
> Psalm 148. Cosmic Praise
> Col. 3:12-17. Clothed in love, living in peace
> Luke 2:41-52. The boy Jesus in the temple.

The first reading in Year A was introduced as the (Old Testament) Lesson for the First Sunday after Christmas in the 1958 Lutheran *Service Book and Hymnal*; the second reading in Year B was appointed in that book, in the 1928 Prayer Book, and in the previous Roman lectionary; the Gospel in Year B was appointed in the *Service Book and Hymnal* following medieval and the Roman lectionary. The Gospel in Year A is an expansion of the Gospel for the Second Sunday after Christmas Day in the 1928 Prayer Book (Matt. 2:19-23).

The Octave of Christmas

In the liturgical calendar as revised in the twentieth century, only two feasts have octaves, Christmas and Easter. In the present Roman calendar, January 1, the Octave of Christmas, is the Solemnity of Mary, the Mother of God. It is the oldest celebration of the virgin in the Roman Church, dating from the seventh century. It was restored to the calendar in 1931 and to January 1 in the 1969 Missal. The Marian feast may be understood as the culmination of three responses by the Church to the secular New Year celebration. The first response was to ignore it; then, since that was difficult to do, to counter it with penitential liturgies; and then finally to convert it, making it a feast of the Mother of God. The collect, from the Roman Missal, is

> O God, who through the fruitful virginity of Blessed Mary bestowed on the human race the grace of eternal salvation, grant, we pray, that we may experience the intercession of her through whom we were found worthy to receive the author of life, our Lord Jesus Christ....

One set of readings serves for all three years.

> Num. 6:22-27. The Aaronic benediction
> Gal. 4:4-7. God's Son, born of a woman
> Luke 2:16-21. The circumcision and the Name of Jesus.

The Anglican and Lutheran churches retain the medieval association of the octave with the circumcision and the giving of the holy Name. The Circumcision of Christ, eight days after his birth in accordance with Jewish custom, was celebrated in Spain and Gaul during the sixth century. The feast was accepted in Rome at the end of the thirteenth century. It had the shortest Gospel of the entire year: one verse that told the story, Luke 2:21. The festival of the Holy Name of Jesus originated in the fifteenth century; the date of its observance fluctuated. The collect for the combined feast of the Circumcision and Name of Jesus was taken from a Gregorian episcopal blessing for the octave of Christmas and translated in the 1549 Book of Common Prayer:

> Almighty God, which madest thy blessed Son to be circumcised, and obedient to the law for man; Grant us the true circumcision of thy spirit; that our hearts, and all our members, being mortified from all worldly and carnal lusts, may in all things obey thy blessed will.

The collect was adapted by Lutheran rites (*Church Book, Common Service Book, Service Book and Hymnal*) making it not a commemoration of circumcision as such but a celebration of the Jewishness of Jesus, subject to the Law, and our spiritual share in that obedience.[66]

> O Lord God, who, for our sakes, hast made thy blessed Son subject to the Law, and caused him to endure the circumcision of the flesh: Grant us the true circumcision of the spirit, that our hearts may be pure from

all sinful desires and lusts; through the same thy Son, Jesus Christ our Lord....

The prayer recalls Rom. 2:29 ("real circumcision is a matter of the heart—it is spiritual and not literal") as well as Col. 3:5 and Titus 2:12.

The 1979 Prayer Book has dropped the circumcision from the title of the day and has made it the Holy Name of Jesus. A new collect, revised from the *Cambridge Bede Book* (1936), is appointed:

> Eternal Father, you gave to your incarnate Son the Holy Name of Jesus to be the sign of our salvation: Plant in every heart, we pray, the love of him who is the Savior of the world, our Lord Jesus Christ; who lives and reigns with you and the Holy Spirit, one God, in glory everlasting.

The prayer has been borrowed by the Lutheran rite.

The Revised Common Lectionary provides one set of readings for all three years.

> Num. 6:22-27. God's Name put on his people
> Psalm 8. The majesty of the Creator
> Gal. 4:4-7. Our adoption as God's children
> 　 or Phil. 2:5-11. The Name of Jesus
> Luke 2:15-21. The circumcision and the naming of Jesus.

The Gospel focuses on Mary but also includes Jesus's circumcision (the first shedding of his blood) and the bestowal of the Name Jesus, Savior.

A Latin hymn *Gloriosi salvatoris nominis praeconia*, from the fifteenth century when the celebration of the Holy Name was spreading across Europe, gives thanks for the gift of revelation.

> To the Name of our salvation
> Laud and honor let us pay,
> Which for many a generation
> Hid in God's foreknowledge lay;
> But with holy exultation
> We may sing aloud today.[67]

What was long hidden has now been made known (Rom. 16:25-26). What generations before us did not know or only dreamed of or longed for, we now call by his Name.

The Second Sunday after Christmas Day

The Second Sunday after Christmas Day is a reflection of the light of Christmas. The old Missals provided no propers for a Second Sunday after Christmas Day. (It occurs four years out of every seven.) The 1552 Prayer Book extended the use of the propers for the Circumcision until the Epiphany. The Roman Church observed this Sunday as the Feast of the Holy Name of Jesus. The Lutheran rite was the first to make provision for the observance of this Sunday. Early in the seventeenth century Lutheran Church Orders appointed the only Gospel of the infancy not otherwise appointed, Matt. 2:13-23, the flight into Egypt (the observance of Holy Innocents' Day having been dropped by many of the church orders despite Luther's insistence that the narrative "should not be permitted to disappear from the churches for any reason."[68]) For the Epistle, 1 Peter 4:12-19 was added as a companion to the Gospel. The Introit, Collect, and Gradual for the First Sunday after Christmas were repeated on the Second Sunday. In the Anglican tradition, only with Prayer Book revisions of the 1920s (1928 in the United States) were propers provided for this Sunday.

The present Roman sacramentary now provides propers for this Sunday. The Entrance Antiphon is the wonderfully evocative passage from Wisdom 18:14-15,

> While gentle silence enveloped all things,
> and night in its swift course was now half gone,
> your all-powerful word leaped from heaven, from the royal throne.

The Collect is from the Gregorian sacramentary.

> Almighty and everlasting God, the glory of those who believe in you: Fill the world with your splendor and show to every nation the radiance of your light.

The Incarnation is for the whole world. It is as if the light that dawned in the birth of Jesus continues to rise in an unfolding day that will have no end and will not reach its zenith until every nation is brought into the light of the kingdom of God. The Prayer Book uses the Leonine collect appointed in the Roman sacramentary for the Christmas Day Mass.

> O God, who wonderfully created, and yet more wondrously restored, the dignity of human nature: Grant that we may share the divine life of him who humbled himself to share our humanity, your Son Jesus Christ....

In part because of the excellence of the prayer, the *Lutheran Book of Worship* gave the prayer greater prominence by assigning it to the First Sunday after Christmas, reversing the order of the collects in the Prayer Book for the First and Second Sundays after Christmas Day.

In the Revised Common Lectionary one set of readings serves all three years.

> Jer. 31:7-14. The joyful return of the exiles
> *or* Sirach 24:1-12. In praise of Wisdom
> Psalm 147:12-20. God's personal care of Israel.
> *or* Wisdom 10:15-21. Wisdom's guidance
> Eph. 1:3-14. Spiritual blessings in Christ
> John 1:(1-9) 10-18. The Word became flesh.

The Gospel, like the collect, reflects the proclamation of Christmas Day.

A "spectacular hymn"[69] for Christmas by Charles Wesley (1744) not found in any American hymnal and not well-known outside of British Methodism, deserves to be better known. It begins with familiar language echoing, as might be expected, Luke 2:14.

> Glory be to God on high
> And peace to earth descend!

Charles Wesley at his best is deceptively ordinary, and already in the second line as the hymn describes the descent of peace, it becomes interesting. Wesley picks up on something often overlooked by commentators, the up and down movement of the angels' song, praise ascending and peace descending. Peace here is not the wan dream of peace on earth, but the entire focus is on the coming of the God of peace to earth. It is all God's doing. The stanza continues,

> God comes down, He bows the sky,
> And shows Himself our Friend.
> God the invisible appears!
> God, the blest, the great I AM,
> Sojourns in this vale of tears,
> And Jesus is his Name.

The paradoxes continue as we come to the remarkably powerful lines drawn from Philippians 2:

Emptied of his majesty,
Of His dazzling glories shorn,
Being's Source begins to be,
And God Himself is born!

In an act of almost imaginable humility, the God of dazzling majesty lays aside that glory; and the great and overwhelming wonder is that what has happened to each of us, being born, has now happened to God. Since Christmas night, all of us, including even God our maker, have been born. Eternity now has a beginning.

The Continuation of Christmas

There is no clear and specific conclusion to the celebration of Christmas, which is in fact "the beginning of our never-ending gladness."[70] It continues through the Octave, the eighth day. The practice of observing the eighth day of a feast began with Easter and Pentecost; in the East with the Epiphany. From the seventh century, saints' days were dignified with octaves. In the twelfth century the practice of observing all eight days of the octave was introduced. In England, by the decree of King Alfred the Great in the ninth century, Christmas continues for twelve days, Christmas Day through the eve of the Epiphany, called "Twelfth Night." The day following Christmas Day, December 26, is called "Boxing Day," that is, a day for giving Christmas boxes or presents. In Germany, reflecting ancient practice, Christmas Day is reserved for church, "second Christmas Day" (December 26) and sometimes "third Christmas Day" (December 27) for family. By other reckoning, as in the present Roman calendar, "The feast of the Lord's baptism brings the Christmas cycle to a close" and Ordinary Time begins the next day.[71] The longest extent of Christmas is forty days, continuing until Candlemas, February 2. (This feast will be treated in the next chapter in connection with the Epiphany.)

Popular Symbols and Customs

Christmas has been an inexhaustible source of folk traditions, many preserved from pre-Christian custom.[72] Most common are the Christmas greens. Hal Borland wrote,

We follow the Druids with their sacred mistletoe, the early Norse with their firs, the Saxons with their holly, even the Greeks with their laurel.

But there is one common denominator in all of them—the veneration for green life that outlives the winter. And at root this is and always was a veneration of life, a belief in life's persistence. The green itself is the recurring symbol of enduring life.

Even beyond the symbolism of the fir tree, the laurel branch, and the sprig of holly or mistletoe, at the dark crisis of the solstice are the enduring truths of those real ancients, the running pine and the ground cedar. They, remnants and reminders of a past the geologists measure in hundreds of millions of years, are green symbols of life that not only outlasts the winter but outlasts the eons.

So we gather the greens and we hang the wreath, festoon the mantel and deck the tree to bring green reassurance into our lives. We reach for the belief that is at the heart of every festival ever celebrated in the dark solstice days of the year. We look to the greens of this earth for proof that the continuity we see in the stars is no illusion.[73]

His words are most effective in the northern latitudes of the northern hemisphere.

In medieval mystery plays in England and on the continent a fir tree was hung with apples on the feast of Adam and Eve, December 24, to represent the garden of paradise; it was called the Paradise Tree. (The custom and the name *Paradeisbaum* persists to this day in Bavaria.) Thus the first parents were paired with the Second Adam and his lady.[74]

The beginnings of European drama are to be found in the church, as a simple dialogue growing out of the liturgies of the Easter Vigil or Easter Matins early in the tenth century. The famed Easter dialogue, *Quem quaeritis in sepulchro*, gave rise to similar dialogues for the Nativity and the Ascension. The Christmas dialogue *Quem quaeritis in praesepe* was connected to the Introit of the Mass. The shepherds are asked whom they seek, and they reply, giving testimony to what they have seen.

> Whom do you seek in the cradle, O shepherds, tell me?
> Christ the Lord and Savior,
> The infant in swaddling clothes, as the angel has said.
> The babe is here with Mary his mother....[75]

The *Second Shepherds' Play* of the Towneley cycle of plays from Wakefield, England, is a superb example of a fully formed drama representing the

Officium Pastorem,[76] the service of the shepherds, with its comic realism progressing from winter cold to the joyful birth, having left the church building and its liturgy and moved outside to entertain and instruct the people.

A study of the liturgical year inevitably leads to an examination of its interaction with popular culture and customs.[77] In England, for example, there were the revels of Twelve Days, when little work needed to be done and the long cold and dark invited a time of festive celebration. The "boy bishop" is a conspicuous example of such revels, involving "lords of misrule" who were chosen to preside over the mid-winter festivities that were a version of the Feast of Fools celebrated in many parts of Europe at the turn of the secular year. In England in the fourteenth century the *episcopus chorustarum* (chorister bishop) was chosen by his fellows on St. Nicholas' Day (December 6; Nicholas was the patron saint of children) and from then until Holy Innocents' Day bore the title and habit of a bishop with cope and miter, pectoral cross and crosier. The function of the Boy Bishop was to mock and humble and thereby instruct the authentic bishop. Despite the often exaggerated buffoonery and irreverence, even occasional blasphemy of these revels, behind them lies an awareness of the underlying solidarity of the community, revealed by the temporary relaxation of the inhibitions that usually confine such emotions. The misrule was only temporary and was tolerated only within strict limits, from December 5 through 28 at most, often just Holy Innocents' Day, December 28. Such strictly limited disorder can be culturally healthful for a community, for misrule implies rule; without order the disorder of carnival festivities makes no sense.[78] Nonetheless, in defense of the faith the practice was suppressed in England by Henry VIII, restored by Mary, and finally abolished by Elizabeth I.

Hope and Expectation

The sentimentality of the secular celebration of "the holidays" still retains something of a hope for peace, as vague and distant a dream as it may be for the world. Even that is worth preserving. The Church, however, proclaims a concrete experience, God with us in the person of Jesus, an infant and a king, human and divine, who reconciles the nations with each other and the world with God. We may well enjoy the sentimentality of Christmas, religious and secular, but it is the realism of the feast that gives lasting meaning. Indeed, it may well be that it is in the obligations and responsibilities, the disappointments and frustrations of "ordinary life" that we come to know the Holy Child best.

Thomas Hardy's poem "Yuletide in a Younger World" looks back on the "doings of delight" that once characterized the celebration Christmas, a time when phantoms could be seen and dreams read and "the still small voice" of far-off prophets could be heard. The poem asks with sad skepticism in the final line, "Can such ever have been?" Much of the sentimental associations of Christmas look backward to an imagined and idealized time and lament the inevitable decline and loss of simplicity and belief. The recurrent, indeed persistent, theme of the liturgical year, however, is the acknowledgment of a deep longing arising from a discontent with the world as it is and a conviction that there must be more. As the writer to the Hebrews put it, "Here we have no lasting city, but we are looking for the city that is to come" (Heb. 13:14), "the city that has foundations, whose architect and builder is God" (Heb. 11:10) in the heavenly country. Advent has set the tone and the theme of all that follows. We wait, wait for what is to come, not knowing exactly what it is for which we long, but nonetheless sure not only of its arrival but also of its surpassing satisfaction of our deepest needs.

4

The Epiphany

ONE RESPONSE OF liturgical Christians to the secular recapturing of Christmas is to emphasize the older and original celebration of the Epiphany. The increased attention to the feast can help bring the Eastern and Western churches closer together in one of the glories of the Eastern calendar.

The oldest and most specific name of this feast, still used in the Eastern Churches, is "Theophany," the incarnation as the manifestation, the revelation of God. In the West, another, more general Greek title is used, Epiphany, derived from the state visit of a king or emperor to a city of his realm in the Greco-Roman world, especially when he showed himself publicly to the people. The 1928 American Book of Common Prayer added a subtitle to the word, making the word "epiphany" specific, "the manifestation of Christ to the Gentiles."

Origins of the Feast

The feast originated in the East before Christmas developed in the West. The earliest evidence comes from ca. 215 in the writings of Clement of Alexandria in Egypt, who reports its observance among the Basilidians, a sect with Gnostic tendencies, who commemorated the baptism of Jesus on that day. By the fourth century the feast was being celebrated by orthodox Christians, its focus having been extended to include the nativity of Christ and also his manifestation to the Magi and at the wedding at Cana in Galilee, his "first sign" (John 2:11).

The reason for the choice of the date of January 6 continues, as in the Christmas controversy, to be debated. The older "history of religions hypothesis" proposes that the Epiphany was introduced to oppose a pagan feast. Epiphanius (ca. 315-403) notes that in Egypt there was a night festival on the 11th of Tybi (January 5-6) celebrating the birth of the god Aion from a virgin, Kore; the waters of the Nile were thought to acquire miraculous powers and turned to wine that night. Pliny the Younger mentions a festival in honor of Dionysus, the god of wine, on January 5, *Pater Liber*. Noting the obvious similarities, one might conclude that Epiphany was a reaction to such a celebration. Careful study of the sources, however, fails to establish a close relationship between these festivals and the Epiphany.

Thomas Talley in the twentieth century therefore revived interest in "the computation hypothesis."[1] Christians in Asia Minor celebrated their paschal festival at the same time as the Jewish Passover on the 14th day of Nisan, the first month of spring in the Jewish lunar calendar. The Christians followed a solar calendar and set their paschal feast on the 14th day of Artemesios, the first month of spring on the solar calendar. When the Asian date was replaced with the Roman version of the Julian calendar, the result was April 6 as the date of the paschal feast. Since it was widely believed that Jesus's perfect life should be perfect in every aspect and should not admit fractions, it therefore must have begun and ended on the same date. His conception was thus thought to have taken place on April 6, which was also the date of his crucifixion. His birth would have been exactly nine months earlier, January 6.

Neither hypothesis has entirely commended itself to the scholarly community. At the end of the twentieth century, Merja Merras made a third proposal suggesting that the Epiphany was a Christianization of the Jewish Feast of Tabernacles. What is known for sure is that already in the late second or early third century January 6 was associated in Egypt both with Christ's birth and his baptism.[2]

In the East, the Epiphany always had a more theological and less historical character than in the West, and so Jesus's baptism was emphasized as showing the manifestation of God to the world in his Son. In the waters of the Jordan the Spirit descends upon the Son, and the Father testifies to his identity. The event is the work of the Holy Trinity.

The absence in the East of an emphasis on the birth of Jesus and a focus instead on his baptism has been explained by the fact that St. Mark's Gospel is traditionally associated with Alexandria, he being regarded as the founder of the Church there. At the beginning of the year the Egyptian church began the in-course reading of the Gospel according to St. Mark, and this account makes no mention of the birth but begins directly with the baptism of Jesus by John. In this sense the liturgical year therefore may be said to begin with Epiphany, a feast of Jesus's beginnings at the opening of the (secular) year.

In the second half of the fourth century, a popular description has it, an "exchange of feasts" took place, the West adopting the Eastern celebration of the Epiphany, and the East adopting the Western celebration of Christmas. It was not a quick transaction but took place over many decades. In the West, in the earliest extant sermons for the feast of the Epiphany the manifestations encompass the nativity, the visit of the Magi, the baptism, and the first miracle at Cana. Rome and its close follower North Africa were an exception to the process and resisted the introduction of the new feast of the Epiphany, observing only December 25.

When the East adopted December 25, the themes of the nativity and the Magi were both assigned to that date; the focus of January 6 was the baptism and the miracle at Cana. When Rome eventually accepted the feast of January 6, the only narrative it associated with the day was the adoration of the Magi (the transfer of their relics from Constantinople to Milan took place in the fifth century), although the narratives of the baptism and the first miracle were assigned to nearby days, the baptism on the octave of the Epiphany (January 13) and the first miracle on the Second Sunday after the Epiphany.

The Themes

For the Western Church, the adoration of the Magi provides sufficient material for devotional attention on the Epiphany. Tertullian (ca. 160-ca. 225) called them *fere reges,* "almost kings," and from the sixth century referring to them as kings became general; they were seen as a fulfillment of Psalm 72:10-11,

> The kings of Tarsish and of the Isles shall pay tribute,
>   and the kings of Arabia and Saba offer gifts.
> All kings shall fall down before him,
>   all nations do him service.

Origin (ca. 185-ca. 254) was the first to speak of *three* Magi, probably from the three gifts they offered. Later the three came to represent the three races of humanity: Asian, African, and European.[3] By the late fourth century their gifts acquired symbolic meaning: gold for a king, incense for a God, myrrh for his burial, as is explained in the hymn *O sola magnarum urbium* by Prudentius (348-410). In an English translation, it is "Earth hath many a noble city."[4] The fourth stanza explains the three gifts.

> Sacred gifts of mystic meaning:
> Incense doth their God disclose,
> Gold the King of kings proclaimeth,
> Myrrh his sepulcher foreshows.

The same interpretation is given by each of the Magi explaining the significance of his gift in the carol by John Henry Hopkins, Jr. (1820-1891), "We three kings of orient are."[5]

> Born a king on Bethlehem's plain,
> Gold I bring to crown him again,
>   King for ever,
>   Ceasing never,
> Over us all to reign.
>
> Frankincense to offer have I:
> Incense owns a Deity nigh;
>   Prayer and praising,
>   Gladly raising,
> Worship him, God Most High.
>
> Myrrh is mine; its bitter perfume
> Breathes a life of gathering gloom;
>   Sorrowing, sighing,
>   Bleeding, dying,
> Sealed in the stone cold tomb.

The three voices then join in praise of the threefold office of the One they come to worship, looking ahead to the confirmatory culmination of his work, the resurrection.

> Glorious now behold him arise,
> King and God and Sacrifice;
> Heaven sings alleluia:
> Alleluia the earth replies.

Leo the Great (d. 461) noted of the Magi that "They are conscious of honoring the divine nature and the human nature as united in a single being. For what was proper to each nature was not divided in the exercise of power."[6] Modern reflection is less theological. These Gentiles, obedient to their profession as astrologers-astronomers, came and saw the beginning of a story they did not and indeed could not understand, and returned to their own country changed men, discontented, and even unhappy ever afterward. (See their portrayal in T. S. Eliot's poem "Journey of the Magi.")

The Epiphany is a manifestation of Christ the Lord to the world and the world's adoration of its infant King. The Magi represent the nations, and their adoration anticipates all the peoples of the world acknowledging the kingship of the Savior. The same promise will be made on the last Sunday of the liturgical year, Christ the King.

A second emphasis of the Epiphany is the interaction of the revelation of Christ and the natural world. Gregory the Great declared that the very elements of the world recognize him.

> All the elements bore witness that their Maker had come. In terms customary among mortals, we may say that the heavens acknowledged this man as God by sending the star; the sea acknowledged him by turning into solid support beneath his feet; the earth acknowledged him by quaking when he died; the sun acknowledged him by hiding its rays; the rocks and walls acknowledged him by splitting at the moment of his death; hell acknowledged him by surrendering the dead it held.[7]

Such a relationship is most clearly evident in the Eastern churches in which the emphasis on Jesus's baptism remains central. The Epiphany is the time for the blessing of the waters of the earth,[8] often accompanied by dramatic actions in the Greek tradition such as throwing a gold cross into the waters for divers in competition to recover. Traces of this ecological interest in the natural world remain in the West as well.

> Mighty seas and rivers, bless the Lord;
> springs of water, sing his praises, alleluia.[9]

In another translation,

> You wells and springs, bless the Lord,
> You rivers and seas, praise him for ever.[10]

Bishop Maximus of Turin preached on the Epiphany,

> Christ is baptized, not to be made holy by the water, but to make the water holy, and by his cleansing to purify the waters which he touched. For the consecration of Christ involves a more significant consecration of the water. For when the Savior is washed, all water for our baptism is made clean, purified at its source for the dispensing of baptismal grace to the people of future ages. Christ is the first to be baptized, then, so that Christians will follow after him with confidence.[11]

Again and again the liturgy of the Church enlarges our understanding of the scope of the great work of God that is celebrated in the liturgical year. All creation is to be redeemed, and all creation is to participate in the celebration of that redemption. A hymn by St. Germanus (ca. 634-734) offers the invitation concerning the newborn Savior and Lord,

> Since all he comes to ransom,
> By all be he adored.[12]

It is not only that every human being is to worship the Maker and Redeemer of all; every created thing in the world of nature is to add its voice to the chorus of the redeemed.

In the fifth century Coelius (or Caelius) Sedulius in *Hostis Herodes impie*, drawn from the same abecedarian poem (stanzas 8, 9, 11, and 13) that is the source of the Christmas hymn "From east to west, from shore to shore," prefaced the three Epiphany mysteries with Herod's fear of a competitor.

> When Christ's appearing was made known,
> King Herod trembled for his throne;
> But he who offers heavenly birth
> Sought not the kingdoms of this earth.

Then follow in order the adoration of the Magi, who presented gifts that showed more perhaps than the Magi could know.

> The eastern sages saw from far
> And followed on his guiding star;
> By light their way to Light they trod,
> And by their gifts confessed their God.

Then the baptism, the purpose of which was not Jesus's purification (since he was without sin) but rather the purification of his people.

> Within the Jordan's sacred flood
> The heavenly Lamb in meekness stood,
> That he, to whom no sin was known,
> Might cleanse his people from their own.

(An antiphon for the feast of the Baptism of Our Lord explains the baptism of Jesus as our baptism, washing away our sin.

> A wondrous mystery is declared for us today:
>> the Creator of the universe
>> has washed away our sins in the waters of the Jordan.[13])

John Mason Neale's translation of Sedulius's hymn, on which the above version is based, makes clearer the reason for Jesus's baptism as explained by Bishop Maximus.

> Within the Jordan's crystal flood
> In meekness stands the Lamb of God
> And, sinless, sanctifies the wave
> Mankind from sin to cleanse and save.[14]

The sinless one came to the Jordan[15] to make water the agent of new birth. Finally the first sign at Cana in Galilee is praised.

> Oh, what a miracle divine,
> When water reddened into wine!
> He spoke the word, and forth it flowed
> In streams that nature n'er bestowed.

John Mason Neale's translation "when water reddened into wine" is a suggestive description of the silent miraculous process.[16] As Jesus baptized the water in which he was baptized, so too he consecrated the water at the marriage feast. Its transformation showed the surpassing re-creation of nature that his passion was to effect. The hymn was the office hymn for the Epiphany in the Roman, Mozarabic, and Sarum breviaries. In Christopher Wordsworth's 1862 hymn "Songs of thankfulness and praise" the three mysteries are expanded to include all the epiphanies of the former lectionary for the Epiphany season: the birth in Bethlehem and the adoration by "the sages from afar"; the baptism showing him to be prophet, priest, and king; the wedding feast at Cana (Epiphany 3); the healing "palsied limb and fainting soul" (Epiphany 4); the "quelling all the devil's might" (Epiphany 5); and generally "ever bringing good from ill." The final stanza, echoing the Prayer Book lessons for Epiphany 6 (Epistle 1 John 3:1-9; Gospel Matt. 24:23-31), applies these manifestations to our life now as we hear and read the Bible, looking to Christ's final Epiphany.

> Grant us grace to see thee, Lord,
> Mirrored in thy holy Word;
> May we imitate thee now,

And be pure, as pure art thou;
That we like to thee may be
At thy great epiphany;
And may praise thee, ever blest,
God in man made manifest.

In the final line, which is the concluding line of each stanza, the repetition of "man" in "manifest" is to be noted.

The Daily Office for the Epiphany

Antiphons in the Daily Office retain the varied themes of the Epiphany as observed in the East, sometimes weaving together in wonderful ways the seemingly unrelated themes. The antiphon to the Benedictus at Lauds on the Epiphany is

Today the Bridegroom claims his bride, the Church,
   since Christ has washed away her sins in the waters of the Jordan;
the Magi hasten to the royal wedding;
and the wedding guests rejoice, for Christ has changed water into wine,
   alleluia.[17]

The antiphon to the Magnificat at second vespers is more straightforward.

Three mysteries mark this holy day:
   today the star leads the Magi to the infant Christ;
   today water is changed into wine for the wedding feast;
   today Christ wills to be baptized by John in the river Jordan
      to bring us salvation.[18]

A wonderfully vigorous antiphon sees in the baptism of Jesus the great struggle with Satan that will be seen more clearly in the next event in Jesus's life, the temptation in the wilderness, and most clearly of all in the passion. The battle begins here, and already the victory is sure.

In the Jordan river our Savior crushed the serpent's head
   And wrested us free from his grasp.[19]

Other antiphons focus on the revelation of the great mystery of the manifestation of Christ.

Begotten of the Father before the daystar shone or time began,
   the Lord our Savior appeared on earth today.[20]

The eternally existent Son of God, "eternally begotten of the Father" the Nicene Creed describes him[21], present with the Father before the sun shone, even before time was made, has now made himself known on earth.

> The star burned like a flame, pointing the way to God, the King of kings;
>> the Magi saw the sign
> and brought him their gifts in homage to their great King.[22]

The three kings from the east, compelled by the flame of the star offer their gifts to their King. The image appears again at Lauds the next morning, extended to include all rulers of this world.

> He comes in splendor, the King who is our peace;
>> he is supreme over all the kings of earth.[23]

At midmorning we are reminded of the gift of the revelation of what had been hidden in the heart of God through ages past.

> This mystery, which has been hidden through all ages
>> and from all generations,
> is revealed to us today.[24]

The various themes and emotions are gathered into a responsory in the office of Readings in the Roman *Liturgy of the Hours.*

> This is the glorious day on which Christ himself,
>> the Savior of the world, appeared;
> the prophets foretold him, the angels worshiped him.
>> The Magi saw his star
>> and rejoiced to lay their treasures at his feet.
> God's holy day has dawned for us at last;
> come, all you peoples, and adore the Lord.
>> The Magi saw his star
>> and rejoiced to lay their treasures at his feet.[25]

Advent ("the prophets foretold him") and Christmas ("the angels worshiped him") find their fulfillment in the Epiphany, which invites all the nations of the earth to come and worship the Savior of the world.

The coming of Christ into the world has turned the natural order upside down. An antiphon at Morning Prayer on the Baptism of our Lord declares:

The soldier baptizes his King,
the servant his Lord,
John his Savior;
    the waters of the Jordan tremble,
    a dove hovers as a sign of witness,
    and the voice of the Father is heard,
        This is my Son.[26]

Hierarchies are reversed, water trembles in awed excitement, a sign is visible and a voice is heard. Peter Chrysologus (ca. 400-450), Bishop of Ravenna, preached in similar wonderment: "So the Gentiles, who were the last, become the first: the faith of the Magi is the first fruits of the belief of the Gentiles. Today Christ enters the Jordan to wash away the sin of the world.... Today a servant lays his hand on the Lord, a man lays his hand on God, John lays his hand on Christ, not to forgive but to receive forgiveness. Today, as the psalmist prophesied: 'The voice of the Lord is heard above the waters.' What does the voice say? 'This is my beloved Son, in whom I am well pleased.'"[27]

The Epiphany Eucharist

The Eucharist for the Epiphany proclaims the glory of Christ. The Introit of the Mass *Ecce Advenit* employs a liturgical text as the antiphon, loosely based on Mal. 3:1; Micah 5:2; Sirach 10:4. The Psalm verse is 72:1 (the NRSV "a king's son" translated in the Book of Common Prayer as "the king's son").

Behold, the Lord, the Ruler, has come:
and the kingdom and the power and the glory are in his hand.
Psalm. Give the king your justice, O God,
    and your righteousness to the king's Son.

Already the infant King begins to draw the whole world to himself. An approaching caravan of Magi, vaguely "from the east," draws near, and they come to worship the King.

The Gregorian collect, used in all three rites (Roman, Lutheran, Anglican), translated in the Book of Common Prayer is simple and straightforward:

O God, by the leading of a star you manifested your only Son to the peoples of the earth: Lead us, who know you now by faith, to your presence, where we may see your glory face to face; through Jesus Christ our Lord, who lives and reigns with you and the Holy Spirit, one God, now and for ever.

Although now "we walk by faith, not by sight" (2 Cor. 5:7), we pray that we may imitate the experience of the Magi, and be led to look into the face of God. *Here* by faith we know; *there* we will see. Strodach notes that while the Magi were led by the star to see the Holy Child in his infancy, the prayer of the Church is that we be led to "the revelation of all-giving Love in the darkness of the Cross" and through that, the original final clause of the prayer reads, "be led on till we come to gaze upon the beauty of thy Majesty."[28] (The original Prayer Book translation had the sonorous but opaque "may after this life have the fruition of thy glorious godhead.")

In the Revised Common Lectionary one set of readings serves all three years of the lectionary cycle.

> Isa. 60:1-6. The nations will be drawn to the light of God
> Psalm 72:1-7, 10-14. The kingdom of peace
> Eph. 3:1-12. Paul's mission to the Gentiles
> Matt. 2:1-12. The nations come to worship their Lord

All are obvious and traditional selections.

The Proper Preface appointed in the 1979 Book of Common Prayer is drawn from the Gelasian sacramentary (no. 59).

> Because in the mystery of the Word made flesh, you have caused a new light to shine in our hearts, to give the knowledge of your glory in the face of your Son Jesus Christ our Lord.

The *Lutheran Book of Worship* has

> ...through Christ our Lord. Sharing our life he lived among us to reveal your glory and love, that our darkness should give way to his own brilliant light,

derived from the previous (1928) Prayer Book, "through Jesus Christ our Lord; who, in the substance of our mortal flesh, manifested forth his glory; that he might bring us out of darkness into his own glorious light." Behind that lies the *Common Service Book* (1917) translation of the same: "And now do we praise Thee, that Thou didst send unto us thine Only-begotten Son, and that in Him, being found in fashion as a man, Thou didst reveal the fullness of Thy glory." (Lutheran books before 1917 did not include a preface of the Epiphany.) The Anglican and Lutheran rites use the proper preface of the Epiphany through-out the season, showing their understanding of the time after the Epiphany as a distinctive season of the liturgical year.

The Roman sacramentary provides a proper preface for the Feast of the Epiphany (the Roman rite no longer recognizes an Epiphany season) that is a combination from the Gelasian and the Leonine sacramentaries, to which it gives the heading Christ the Light of the Nations.

> Today you have revealed the mystery of our salvation in Christ as a light for the nations, and when he appeared in our mortal nature, you made us new by the glory of his immortal nature.

The fundamental image of light runs through many of the Epiphany texts.

The prayer after Communion in the Roman sacramentary is dense but rewarding to those who pay close attention and who ponder what it asks.

> Guide us always and everywhere, O Lord, with heavenly light, that we may perceive with clear sight and treasure with deep affection the mystery in which you have willed us to participate; through Jesus Christ our Lord.

The prayer was the post-Communion for the Octave day of the Epiphany (January 13) in the 1570 Roman Missal.

The solemn blessing for the Epiphany in the Roman sacramentary keeps its focus on the star and the light of Christ and provides a separate blessing for the Baptism of Our Lord. The version provided in the *Book of Occasional Services* makes use of the three events anciently associated with the Epiphany: the Magi, Jesus's baptism, his first sign at Cana in Galilee:

> May Almighty God, who led the Wise Men by the shining of a star to find the Christ, the Light from Light, lead you also, in your pilgrimage, to find the Lord. *Amen.*
>
> May God, who sent the Holy Spirit to rest upon the Only-begotten at his baptism in the Jordan River, pour out that Spirit on you who have come to the waters of new birth. *Amen.*
>
> May God, by the power that turned water into wine at the wedding feast at Cana, transform your lives and make glad your hearts. *Amen.*
>
> And the blessing of God Almighty, the Father, the Son, and the Holy Spirit, be upon you and remain with you for ever. *Amen.*

The alternative simple form employs the image of light.

May Christ, the Son of God, be manifest in you, that your lives may be a
light to the world; and the blessing of God Almighty, the Father, the Son,
and the Holy Spirit, be among you, and remain with you always. *Amen.*

A rubric notes that the solemn blessing is for use on the feast of the Epiphany
through the following Sunday, and in Year C on the Second Sunday after the
Epiphany (when the Gospel is the miraculous change of water into wine at Cana.)

Associated Customs

In ancient times before calendars were not easily accessible it became the
practice of the Church on the Feast of the Epiphany to announce the dates
of the events that lay ahead in the liturgical year. Before the reforms of the
Second Vatican Council and still in certain Lutheran circles the announcement is made thus:

> Dear brothers and sisters, we have celebrated with great joy the birth of
> our Lord Jesus Christ. Now by the mercy of God I am able to announce
> to you the happiness which will come from the Resurrection of our
> Savior. February 22 will be Ash Wednesday, the beginning of the holy
> season of Lent. On April 8 we shall celebrate with great joy the holy
> festival of the Resurrection of our Lord Jesus Christ. May 17 is the
> Ascension of our Lord Jesus Christ. May 27 is the Day of Pentecost.
> December 2 will be the First Sunday of the Advent of Our Lord, to
> whom be honor and glory, now and for ever. Amen.[29]

In the present Roman sacramentary the announcement is

> Dear brothers and sisters, the glory of the Lord has shone upon us, and
> shall ever be manifest among us until the day of his return. Through
> the rhythms and times and seasons, let us celebrate the mystery of
> salvation. Let us recall the year's culmination, the Easter Triduum of the
> Lord: his Last Supper, his crucifixion, his burial, and his resurrection
> celebrated between the evening of the 5th of April and the evening
> of the 8th of April. Each Easter, as on each Sunday, the holy Church
> makes present the great and saving deed by which Christ has for ever
> conquered sin and death. From Easter are reckoned all the days we
> keep holy. Ash Wednesday, the beginning of Lent, will occur on the
> 22nd of February. The Ascension of our Lord will be commemorated

on the 17th of May, and the joyful conclusion of Easter, the Day of Pentecost, will be celebrated on the 27th of May. Likewise the pilgrim Church proclaims the Passover of Christ in the feasts of the holy mother of God, in the feasts of the apostles, martyrs, and saints, and in the commemoration of the faithful departed.

To Jesus Christ, who was, and who is, and who is to come, the Lord of time and history, be endless praise, for ever and ever. Amen.

The revised form is an attempt to take what may seem to be a pointless list of dates that anyone can check on a church calendar and transform it into a teaching device reflecting modern liturgical theology. The announcement of the year (it is traditionally read after the Gospel) is a wise and helpful addition to the liturgy. It reminds the congregation of the unity of redemption. The story is not yet finished with the completion of the Christmas cycle and the real point of it all lies still ahead in the year. But also in a real sense our redemption has already been effected in the birth of Christ.[30] The birth, death, resurrection, ascension, and return are all one whole story, not as successive stages in the progress of the narrative, but all the events containing in themselves the fullness of the story. And all of it is present now, in each believer.

The announcement of the year takes place in church during the liturgy. In the West there arose a popular custom that extended the Epiphany celebration into the homes of the people. Probably because of the detail in the day's Gospel, that the Magi entered "the house" where the Holy Family then resided, the practice arose of blessing chalk during or after Mass and either the clergy or the people themselves taking that chalk and blessing the houses in which the parishioners lived. The mark was placed over the entrance door in this form for the year 2012:

20+C+M+B 12,

the initials indicating the supposed names of the Magi (Caspar [sometimes Kaspar or Gasper], Melchior, Balthasar, preceded by a cross showing their sainthood). Another interpretation was that the initials stood for *Christus mansionem benedicat,* [May] Christ bless this house.

In the East, as was noted above, there is the custom of blessing the waters in celebration of the baptism of Jesus.

In England the Monday after the Epiphany was celebrated as "Plough Monday." Plowing the land began following the festive Twelve Days of

Christmas; in the thirteenth century the return to work often began with a plough race or, reminiscent of pre-Christian customs, drawing a plough around a fire. In the mid-fifteenth century the holiday time did not end until the Sunday after the Epiphany, and the following Monday became "Plough Monday." Ploughs were blessed, and the remainder of the day was spent in money-raising tomfoolery and mumming. The holiday was celebrated into the nineteenth century and was revived in some places in the twentieth century.[31]

Candlemas. The Fulfillment of Advent

The celebration of Christmas may be understood to extend at its fullest length until February 2, the Presentation of Our Lord in the Temple and the Purification of St. Mary the Virgin, often called Candlemas from the custom of blessing candles on that day, inspired by the Gospel, Luke 2:22-40, which includes the Song of Simeon that praises Christ as "a light to lighten the Gentiles and the glory of your people Israel."[32] The block of the liturgical year that began with the successive lighting of the candles of the Advent wreath finds its fulfillment in the blessing and procession with lighted candles in celebration of the arrival of the Lord in his temple. The antiphon of the Introit (Ps. 48:8-9 BCP psalter) identifies our experience of waiting in the house of God with the expectant waiting of the aged Anna and Simeon and the old man's vision of the enlightenment of the Gentiles:

> We have waited in silence on your loving-kindness, O God, in the midst of your temple. Your praise, like your Name, O God, reaches to the world's end; your right hand is full of justice.[33]

The responsory in the *Liturgy of the Hours*, derived from Ezekiel 43:5 and Luke 2:22, declares,

> The glory of the Lord entered the temple by the eastward gate,
>   and the house of God was filled with his splendor.
> His parents took the child Jesus into the temple,
>   and the house of God was filled with his splendor.[34]

Old texts take on new significance. "Arise and shine, Jerusalem, for your light has come," (Psalm antiphon in the Office of Readings.) Christ the light has come to his city.

Johann Franck (1618-1677), a lawyer and Burgomeister of Guben, translates the historical event of the Presentation into the situation of worshippers gathered in the church awaiting the revelation of their Lord.

> Light of the Gentile nations,
>   Thy people's Joy and Love!
> Drawn by thy Spirit hither,
>   We gladly come to prove
> Thy presence in thy temple,
>   And wait with earnest mind,
> As Simeon had awaited
>   His Savior God to find.
>
>   . . .
>
> Let us, O Lord, be faithful,
>   With Simeon to the end,
> That so his dying song may
>   From all our hearts ascend:
> "O Lord, let now thy servant
>   Depart in peace for aye,
> Since I have seen my Savior,
>   Have here beheld his day."[35]

The hymn is set to the tune *Wie soll ich dich empfangen*, echoing the tune of Paul Gerhardt's Advent hymn "O how shall I receive thee," thus bringing to a satisfying close the extended celebration of Christmas. Two mid-nineteenth-century hymns take their point from the Collect and ask that we be presented by Christ to the Father, celebrating in similar ways the Lord's coming to his temple. Henry John Pye (1825-1903) describes the scene and offers a prayer.

> In his temple now behold him,
>   See the long-expected Lord;
> Ancient prophets had foretold him,
>   God has now fulfilled his word.
> Now to praise him, his redeemèd
>   Shall break forth with one accord.
>
> In the arms of her who bore him,
>   Virgin pure, behold him lie,
> While his agèd saints adore him,
>   Ere in perfect faith they die.

Alleluia! Alleluia!
  Lo, the incarnate God Most High!

Jesus, by thy Presentation,
  Thou who didst for us endure,
Make us see thy great salvation,
  Seal us with thy promise sure;
And present us, in thy glory,
  To thy Father, cleansed and pure.[36]

John Ellerton's hymn retains lingering echoes of Christmas, with Joseph standing in silent adoration and the child called the Light of the world.

Hail to the Lord who comes, comes to his temple gate;
Not with his angel host, not in his kingly state;
No shouts proclaim him nigh, no crowds his coming wait;

But, borne upon the throne of Mary's gentle breast,
Watched by her duteous love, in her fond arms at rest,
Thus to his Father's house he comes, the heavenly guest.

There Joseph at her side in reverent wonder stands;
And, filled with holy joy, old Simeon in his hands
Takes up the promised child, the glory of all lands.

O Light of all the earth, thy children wait for thee!
Come to thy temples here, that we, from sin set free,
Before thy Father's face may all presented be![37]

The antiphon to the Magnificat at first vespers on Candlemas is strikingly evocative:

The old man carried the child,
  but the child guided [*regebat*] the old man.
The virgin gave birth to the child
  yet remained a virgin for ever.
She knelt in worship before her child.[38]

The first two lines of the antiphon, derived from St. Augustine, are repeated in the Alleluia of the Mass for the Presentation: "Alleluia, alleluia. The old man

carried the child, but the child guided (or governed) the old man. Alleluia."
(The biblical text does not say explicitly that Simeon was an old man, but his
association with the aged Anna, who was either eighty-four years of age or
lived as a widow for eighty-four years, suggests that they were similar in age.)
The Presentation of the Lord in the Temple may be seen as the fulfillment of
the Advent waiting. We are one with Anna the prophet and with Simeon who
held the promised Child in his arms, and Christmas is complete.

But yet there is more. Simeon told Mary that a sword would pierce her
soul; the feast day looks ahead to the crucifixion and functions as a bridge
between the Nativity and the Passion. James Montgomery (1771-1854) in his
hymn "Angels from the realms of glory" goes through the events of Christmas
and Epiphany one by one. First the angels "who sang creation's story" are
now praised for proclaiming the birth of the Messiah. Next, the "shepherds in
the field abiding" are invited to "come and worship"; then the Magi are called
upon to "seek the great Desire of nations" and worship the one whose natal
star they have seen. Finally, the prophecy of Mal 3:1 ("the Lord whom you seek
will suddenly come to his temple") is invoked in the Presentation of our Lord
in the Temple as Anna and Simeon at last see the long-awaited Savior of his
people.

> Saints before the altar bending,
>   Watching long in hope and fear,
> Suddenly the Lord, descending,
>   In his temple shall appear:
>   Come and worship,
> Worship Christ, the new-born King.[39]

The description of the Lord "descending" to appear in his temple suggests
that the appearance of the Lord in his temple is not only as an infant held by
St. Simeon but as the one who is yet to come as Lord of glory. The event is
understood as a declaration of the certainty of the second coming. Christmas
is a proclamation of the Parousia.

The blessing bestowed on this day is the blessing of all the candles to be
used in the church in the year ahead (like the blessing of oils on Maundy
Thursday), and so the custom extends the festival into the future in the ever-
forward-looking way of the liturgical year. The Roman Catholic prayer of
blessing the candles has a similar forward thrust, asking that we may advance
toward the light: "O God, true light and source of light eternal, pour into the
hearts of your faithful people the clarity of perpetual light that all those in this

your holy temple, enlightened by these candles may advance with joy toward the light of your glory." Christmas is complete, and yet there is more to come.

In the present calendar, the celebration of the Epiphany concludes with the Sunday of the Baptism of Jesus. On the following day what the Roman calendar calls "ordinary time" begins, and the white color of Christmas-Epiphany is replaced with green. Anglican and Lutheran use, however, continues in a muted way the former practice of an Epiphany season lasting through the Last Sunday after the Epiphany (the Sunday before Ash Wednesday). In the 1979 Prayer Book, "The Titles of the Seasons, Sundays, and Holy Days observed in this Church throughout the Year" (p. 31) explicitly identifies the "Epiphany Season"; the *Lutheran Book of Worship* (p. 9) and the *Lutheran Service Book* (p. x) do likewise. The Last Sunday after the Epiphany is called explicitly in Lutheran use the Transfiguration and in Anglican use has the Transfiguration theme in the appointed Propers, although not the title. That event is understood as a final epiphany of the nature of Christ before Lent begins three days later. These Sundays between the Baptism and the Transfiguration are numbered "after the Epiphany" but are clothed in the color green. For this section of Ordinary Time, see chapter 8.

5

Quadragesima. Lent

THE EXHORTATION APPOINTED in the 1979 Book of Common Prayer for Ash Wednesday to introduce the imposition of ashes provides a good summary of the history and purpose of Lent.

> Dear People of God: The first Christians observed with great devotion the days of our Lord's passion and resurrection, and it became the custom of the Church to prepare for them by a season of penitence and fasting. This season of Lent provided a time in which converts to the faith were prepared for Holy Baptism. It was also a time when those who, because of notorious sins, had been separated from the body of the faithful were reconciled by penitence and forgiveness, and restored to the fellowship of the Church. Thereby, the whole congregation was put in mind of the message of pardon and absolution set forth in the Gospel of our Savior, and of the need which all Christians continually have to renew their repentance and faith.
>
> I invite you, therefore, in the name of the Church, to the observance of a holy Lent, by self-examination and repentance; by prayer, fasting, and self-denial; and by reading and meditating on God's holy Word. And, to make a right beginning of repentance, and as a mark of our mortal nature, let us now kneel before the Lord, our maker and redeemer. [p. 265]

The address is a slight revision of the description prepared for the Canadian Prayer Book to replace the homily found in previous English and Canadian books.

The Purpose and Development of Lent

The Exhortation recognizes the primacy of the holy Triduum, the sacred three days of Good Friday, Holy Saturday, and Easter Day, celebrated as one extended observance: "the days of our Lord's passion and resurrection." The varied development of the preparatory period, gradually extended to forty days, is compressed to the phrase "it became the custom of the Church to prepare for them," and the dual purpose of the preparatory period is noted: converts were prepared for baptism and notorious sinners were returned to the fellowship. The whole body of the Church—new Christians, lapsed Christians, faithful Christians—is seen as one people to whom the Gospel of pardon and forgiveness is addressed.

The second paragraph describes the threefold practice of Lent: self-examination resulting in repentance; the personal discipline of prayer, fasting, and self-denial; reading and pondering the Bible.

The address prepared for the 1978 *Lutheran Book of Worship* is comparable. To counter a prevailing understanding that Lent was a season of gloom, the address opens with an allusion to the joyful paradise that was and remains God's intention for his creation and an understanding of how sin is destructive of that happiness.

> Brothers and sisters: God created us to experience joy in communion with him, to love all humanity, and to live in harmony with all of his creation. But sin separates us from God, our neighbors, and creation, and so we do not enjoy the life our creator intended for us. Also, by our sin we grieve our Father, who does not desire us to come under his judgment, but to turn to him and live.
>
> As disciples of the Lord Jesus we are called to struggle against everything that leads us away from love of God and neighbor. Repentance, fasting, prayer, and works of love—the discipline of Lent—help us to wage our spiritual warfare. I invite you, therefore, to commit yourselves to this struggle and confess your sins, asking our Father for strength to persevere in your Lenten discipline.[1]

The opening sentences derive from Genesis 1-3, God's good will for his creation and human corruption of that intention. By the rebellion described in Genesis 3, the man and the woman set themselves against God, against each other, and against the natural world. Driven from the garden of paradise, their original equality broken, the man ruling over the woman, the earth would yield its fruit to the man only after hard labor, childbearing would no longer be entirely pleasurable, hostility between the woman and the serpent emerged. None of this was in accordance with the will of God. With sin, however, came the knowledge of God not only as Creator and Master but as a loving parent, grieved by the children's destructive rebellion, whose good desires for the whole creation remain unchanged.

The second paragraph describes the Lenten discipline by the "evangelical counsels" identified in the medieval period—fasting, prayer, and good works—to which is prefixed "repentance," recalling Luther's recovery of the New Testament primacy of *metanoia*, turning around, changing the direction of one's life. "When our Lord and Master Jesus Christ said, 'Repent' [Matt. 4:17], he willed the entire life of believers to be one of repentance."[2] Prayer is the chief activity of Lent, the penitential season a time for renewal in the practice of prayer.[3] Fasting is employed to support the practice of prayer, and almsgiving is service directed outward toward others to prevent self-absorption and to express the heart of the Christian life, self-giving in the service of others.[4] In the Roman sacramentary the opening prayer for Friday after Ash Wednesday implores, "Support us, O Lord, with your gracious favor through the fast we have begun; that as we observe it by bodily self-denial, so we may fulfill it with inner sincerity of heart."[5] The Gospel-commanded actions are intended to change our life, to turn us outward toward God and then toward others. A responsory for Ash Wednesday sets forth the purpose of fasting and self-denial.

> The Lord says, This is the fast that I choose:
> To share your bread with the hungry.
>   Then you shall call, and the Lord will answer;
>   you shall cry for help, and he will say, Here I am.
> When the Son of Man comes in his glory,
> he will say to those at his right hand,
> Come, you that are blessed of my Father, inherit the kingdom,
> for I was hungry and you gave me food.
>   Then you shall call, and the Lord will answer,
>   you shall cry for help, and he will say, Here I am.[6]

One is to fast in order to have something to share with those in need. John Chrysostom preached,

> Fasting consists not merely in abstinence from food, but in withdrawing from sinful practices. Since he who limits his fasting only to an abstinence from meats is one who especially disparages it. Do you fast? Give me proof of it by your works. If you see a poor man, take pity on him. If you see an enemy, be reconciled to him. If you see a friend gaining honor, do not envy. Let not the mouth only fast but also the eye, the

ear, the feet, the hands.... Let the hands fast by being pure from rap-
ine and avarice. Let the feet fast by ceasing from running to forbidden
pleasures. Let the eyes fast by learning never to fix themselves rudely
on handsome faces or busy themselves with strange beauties.... Let the
ear fast also... [by] not listening to evil speaking and calumnies.... Let
the mouth fast from disgraceful speeches and railing.[7]

The liturgical expression of the fast of the eyes is the practice of veiling crosses,
statues, and paintings in the Church during part or all of Lent. The fast of the
ears is expressed by the suppression of the use of the organ during the final
days of the season.

The concept of spiritual warfare is rooted in St. Paul's description of the
armor that protects combatants in the battle against "principalities, powers,
and world rulers of this present darkness, and the spiritual hosts of wickedness in the heavenly places" (Eph. 6:10-17). Behind that lies the Hebrew picture of the Lord God of Sabaoth, the Lord of Hosts, the Leader of the angelic
armies and the God of battles. The idea of spiritual warfare was prominent
in the early Church and through the Middle Ages. It is honored in the
much-misunderstood Islamic idea of *jihad*, the struggle primarily within
the self, involving commitment, even to giving one's life. Lorenzo Scupoli's
Combattimento Spirituale (1589) is a classic spiritual writing of the Counter-
Reformation period and was received, adapted, and revised according to the
ancient traditions of the Eastern Church as well.[8] Spiritual warfare is therefore
a vigorous, active, and compelling metaphor for the work of Lent. That mortal
combat is dramatically portrayed on the first Lenten Sunday, which focuses
on Jesus's struggle with Satan in the desert, recapitulating his ancestors' forty
years in the wilderness and giving us his example and courage in our own
testing and struggle against temptation. "Like a roaring lion your adversary
the devil prowls around, looking for someone to devour," Peter warned (1 Peter
5:8). One is reminded of Samson and also David who both battled beasts (Jud.
14:5-6; 1 Sam. 17:34-36.) St. Mark in his brief report of Jesus's temptation gives
the detail that "he was with the wild beasts" (1:13). This may be intended to
emphasize the fearsomeness of the time of testing and struggle, or it may
suggest that in Jesus the messianic peaceable kingdom has arrived (Isa. 11:6-
9); animals will not prey on others nor threaten human beings; all will live in
perfect harmony as at the beginning of creation. It is in fact likely that Mark,
perhaps remembering the account of the safety of Daniel in the lions' den
(Dan. 6:16-24, "My God sent his angel and shut the lions' mouths so that they
would not hurt me, because I was found blameless before him"), has both
interpretations in mind.

The entire Church is involved in the struggle as it is in the support of candidates for baptism. Ultimately, the struggle is for the sake of the world. Penance is inward and individual but it is also outward and social, and so the season is suffused with optimism and confidence.[9] A responsory for the Third Sunday in Lent exhorts,

> Save the weak and the orphan,
> defend the humble and needy.
>   Rescue the weak and the poor;
>   deliver them from the power of the wicked. [Ps. 82:3-4]
> God chose the poor in the world to be rich in faith
> and to be heirs of the kingdom
> that he has promised to those who love him. [Jas. 2:5]
>   Rescue the weak and the poor;
>   deliver them from the power of the wicked.[10]

The responsibilities of Lent are not peculiar to the season. They are the duties of the Christian life, intensified during the Forty Days.

The season was first called, as it still is in Latin, *jejunium*, "the Fast." In German it is *die Fasten* ("the Fast") or *Fastenzeit* ("fasting time"). The English name "Lent" derives from the Old English *lencten*, "lengthen," that is, spring when the daylight begins to lengthen. (German *Lenz*, spring.) Lent is therefore to be understood as the Church's springtime of renewal. This renewal is not just of the people of God, Church, but the renewal of the whole world of which the human race is a part.

Sources of Lent

Explanations of the early history of Quadragesima, the Forty Days, divide along language lines, English *versus* European, even more sharply than on the question of the origins of Christmas. Two models stand directly opposed to each other. The traditional view has supposed a gradual growth of the time of preparation for Easter from one day to two days, then three days to the whole week before Easter, to a three-week intermediate stage, and then in the fourth century a general acceptance of a forty-day period, variously reckoned.

This growth model was opposed by Thomas Talley, whose research in Syriac and Arabic sources understood Quadragesima to be not the result of a gradual extension of the preparation for Easter, but a forty-day period originally independent of Easter that had arisen in Egypt in connection with the Epiphany as the feast of the baptism of Jesus. The model was Jesus's temptation in the wilderness, but the period was understood as a preparation for baptism celebrated afterward in the middle of February. The Council of Nicaea (325) moved the period to just before Pascha; at the same time Easter became fixed as the preferred time for the baptism of catechumens. This theory rests, critics say, on late and inconsistent sources and bears traces of anachronistic reconstruction.

Harald Buchinger has suggested that in view of the opposing theories, we are dealing apparently not with successive stages of the development of the preparatory period of Lent but with perhaps four separate phenomena: (1) the extension of Paschal fasting as an individual ascetic practice; (2) the carving out of Holy Week under the influence of pilgrims to Jerusalem in the second half of the fourth century; (3) a three-week time of intensive preparation for baptism in various Western liturgies; (4) Quadragesima as a biblically inspired period of preparation for Easter introduced in the thirties of the fourth century.[11]

Whatever is the precise historical development of the season,[12] one of the strands woven into Quadragesima is preparation for baptism. As adult baptism declined, the baptismal aspect of Lent became less prominent and eventually disappeared almost entirely until the twentieth century, when the Roman Catholic Church in the Rite for the Christian Initiation of Adults restored the catechumenate and recovered the baptismal character of Lent.

A second strand of what was to become the present Lent is a penitential fast before Pascha. Penance was originally for those under discipline in preparation for their reconciliation on Maundy Thursday. They were enrolled for their penance on the First Sunday in Lent, and when Lent was extended to Ash Wednesday, ashes were put on their heads as a sign of their mortality and repentance. The practice was later extended to all the faithful and became common by the tenth century. It was an impressive sign of community support of the penitents and of solidarity with them.[13] By the end of the eleventh century, Pope Urban II extended the practice to the whole Western Church, when the practice of public penance had disappeared. The Lenten fast was a single meal daily, usually in the evening; later it included abstinence from meat and wine, as well as dairy products. During the high Middle Ages the strictness was relaxed and the focus shifted to the Passion of Christ. The Lutheran Common Service (1888) inherited this tradition and appointed as the Proper Preface for the season of Lent the Preface of the Cross, then in use in the Roman rite for Passiontide (the last two weeks of Lent), and in the *Common Service Book* (1917) provided the History of the Passion, a harmony of the four Gospel accounts divided into seven sections to be read at vespers on the days of Holy Week or during Lent.[14] In both East and West, Lent was a "closed time" for marriages since the fourth century.[15] There is no restriction in the 1983 Roman code of canon law.

The one observation that may securely be made about the origins of Lent is that there were multiple sources.[16] One indication that Lent had multiple origins is the comparative lack of striking liturgical texts associated with the season. Antiphons are drawn largely from Scripture, taken straight, and not subject to poetic elaboration or creative combination as, for example, are many of the texts of Advent and of Christmas-Epiphany.

The development may perhaps have been something like this. There was the original observance of the Paschal Vigil in which Christ's death, burial, and resurrection were understood and experienced as one continuous celebration, preceded by a varying number of days of fasting. By the end of the second century the celebration of Easter was prolonged for fifty days, "the Pentecost." In the third century one finds a six-day pre-Paschal fast in Alexandria and Syria that may be the origin of Holy Week. In view of the fifty days of Easter, however, even a week may have seemed inadequate as preparation, and so in Jerusalem, Rome, and elsewhere, three weeks were set aside for fasting, a week for each of the three days of the Triduum. The first reference to a forty-day Lent is Canon 5 of the Council of Nicaea (325), where it is not seen an innovation. By the end of the fourth century, the forty days of pre-Paschal preparation for Easter and for baptism at Easter seem to have become nearly universal,[17] deriving perhaps, in part, from a forty-day post-Epiphany fast, in imitation of Jesus's forty days in the desert following his baptism. The days were variously counted. Sundays were always excluded (the Lord's Day of resurrection was never a fast); in Antioch and Cyprus and Jerusalem,[18] Saturdays were also excluded in addition to Sundays. Good Friday and Holy Saturday came to be also excluded from the forty days and then also all of Holy Week. By the time of Leo the Great (440-461), Lent was six weeks long; Good Friday and Holy Saturday had been separated from the Triduum and added to the preparatory fast, making six weeks of six days each, thirty-six days, a tithe of the 365 days of the year.

In the West, the penitential period came to consist of the pre-Lenten preparation, the penitential time of Lent (Ash Wednesday and the following four weeks), and then a two-week Passiontide beginning on the Fifth Sunday in Lent, comparable to the final week of Advent, from December 17 to the Vigil of Christmas.

The development of liturgies on the weekdays of Lent was gradual. Initially there was the Eucharist on Sundays and a service of the Word on the fast days of Wednesday and Friday. In the fifth century services on Monday, Tuesday, and Saturday were added. In the sixth century all these became Eucharists. At last in the eighth century Thursday was provided with formularies for Mass.

In the Eastern churches, the preparatory period is called Great Lent to distinguish it from the three lesser Lents, i.e., times of fasting: of the Apostles from All Saints Sunday (the Sunday following Pentecost) until the Feast of SS. Peter and Paul, June 29; the fast of the Theotokos, August 1-14; and Christmas Lent, November 15 until December 24. Great Lent begins on the Monday before the Western Ash Wednesday and concludes in the evening of the sixth Friday of Great Lent, the Vigil of Lazarus Saturday, the day before Holy Week begins. Although Saturday and Sunday (the Sabbath and the Lord's Day) are not fast days in the Eastern tradition, they are nonetheless included in counting the forty days.[19] The Great and Holy Week is considered in the Eastern churches as a separate unit of preparation.

Pre-Lent

The Gelasian sacramentary denotes Ash Wednesday as *caput jejunii*, the beginning (head) of Lent, adding the four weekdays preceding the First Sunday in Lent, making exactly forty days, excluding Sundays. At the beginning of the sixth century the fast was extended to seven weeks, adding Quinquagesima ("fifty"), the Sunday before the First Sunday in Lent, resulting in fifty days of preparation for the fifty days of Easter. By the end of the sixth century another Sunday was added to the preparatory period, called Sexagesima ("sixty"), and by the beginning of the seventh century yet another Sunday was added, Septuagesima ("seventy"). Thus, by the time of Gregory the Great (d. 604) a season of pre-Lent had been added to the beginning of Quadragesima, and the preliminary period was sometimes referred to as a narthex to the Quadragesima. The stational liturgies for those three preparatory Sundays were celebrated in the famous churches of Rome's patron saints: Lawrence (Septuagesima), Paul (Sexagesima), and Peter (Quinquagesima). Moreover, repeated attacks by Goths and Lombards encouraged extended periods of prayer and penitence. The perils of the times mark some of the prayers composed during the invasions and threats and which are still in use. An example is the collect from the Leonine sacramentary *Da nobis, quaesumus, Domine, ut et mundi cursus*, appointed in the previous lectionary for the Fourth Sunday after Pentecost in the Roman rite, the Fourth Sunday after Trinity in Lutheran use, and the fifth Sunday after Trinity in the Book of Common Prayer.

> Grant, O Lord, we beseech thee, that the course of this world may be
> so peaceably ordered by thy governance, that thy Church may joyfully

serve thee in all godly quietness; through thy Son Jesus Christ our Lord....

Canon William Bright said of the prayer, "It seems to have been suggested, like several others in the Leonine, by the disasters of the dying Western Empire."[20] What the Anglican and Lutheran rites call the Collect for Peace, which they both use at the conclusion of Evening Prayer, *Deus, a quo sancta desideria*, from the Gelasian sacramentary, has proved to be one of the most popular prayers in the Church's treasury, used in the pre-Reformation Latin rite votive Mass for Peace, Lauds, Vespers, and the Litany. In the Prayer Book translation, borrowed by the Lutherans, now differently revised in the current liturgies, it is:

> O God, from whom all holy desires, all good counsels, and all just works do proceed: Give unto thy servants that peace which the world cannot give, that our hearts may be set to obey thy commandments, and also that by thee, we, being defended from the fear of our enemies, may pass our time in rest and quietness; through the merits of Jesus Christ our Savior....[21]

"We cannot but think of the troublous times in the latter half of the fifth century when it was composed—'when sieges and barbaric invasions made men's hearts fail for fear, when Rome but narrowly escaped the Huns and did not escape the Vandals; when the Western Empire itself passed away before Odoacer, and Odoacer was overthrown by Theodoric.'"[22]

The Latin names of the three Sundays of pre-Lent were retained in Anglican and Lutheran use: Septuagesima ("seventy," more exactly the Sunday within seventy days of Easter, actually sixty-four days before Easter; *septuagesima quarta* to be precise); Sexagesima ("sixty," the Sunday within sixty days of Easter, actually fifty-seven days before Easter; *quinquagesima septimus* to be precise); and Quinquagesima ("fifty," which is exactly right, fifty days before Easter). "And so in her wisdom and in order to avoid long and cumbersome tags, the Church decided to number by tens rather than by sevens. Who cares if it's accurate? It is easier to say."[23]

The season functioned as a preparation for Lent, a preparation for a preparation, and so the current Roman, Anglican, and Lutheran calendars have eliminated pre-Lent as unnecessary. The logic is simple. Since Lent is itself a season of preparation, to observe an additional time of preparation before Lent seems redundant. Why prepare to prepare? The argument may seem persuasive, but it is not entirely true psychologically or spiritually, because, in fact, we often, in many areas of life, need to prepare to prepare. In the instance of Lent that is especially true. We need, before Lent actually begins, to begin thinking about how we will keep the season. How will we use the time to our spiritual benefit? How will we exercise ourselves so that we grow in grace during Lent? The three Sundays before Lent can serve as a warning that the holy season is near and that it is time to give it some thought.

In earlier times pre-Lent was understood as the fast of the clergy, the ministers of the Church leading the way; the people's fast began two-and-a-half weeks later on Ash Wednesday. Strodach, who recognizes that "There did not seem to be any universal rule in the early period of the Church either as to the length, or manner, of the Lenten Fast," quotes "one of the medieval writers" who declares that "the monastic orders began the fast with Septuagesima, the Greek Church with Sexagesima, and the secular clergy with Quinquagesima."[24] Strodach suggests that the varying length of the preparation may be attributed to differing ways of counting fast days, some omitting Sundays, Thursdays, and Saturdays from the fast, but all counting forty days of actual fasting.

Pre-Lent was observed as an extension of Lent: the liturgical color was violet (although in Lutheran use the color often was green to distinguish the season from Lent itself[25]); the *Gloria in excelsis* and alleluia were omitted from the Mass, the *Te Deum* omitted from the Office. This expansion of the penitential season of Lent, deemed already sufficiently long, is a further reason for the suppression of pre-Lent. Maxwell Johnson has suggested that in the Roman rite, the days from Ash Wednesday to the First Sunday in Lent may be understood as the remains of pre-Lent, Lent understood as extending from the First Sunday to the evening of Maundy Thursday and the beginning of the Triduum.[26]

In the East, there is a corresponding four-Sunday (three-week) preparation for Lent. The fourth Sunday before Lent, the Sunday of the Publican and the Pharisee, teaches humility; the third Sunday before Lent, the Sunday of the Prodigal Son, teaches repentance; the second Sunday before Lent, the Sunday of the Last Judgment (Meatfare Sunday), begins the abstinence from meat; and the Sunday before Lent, the Sunday of Forgiveness (Cheesefare Sunday), begins the abstinence from dairy products. The Great Fast begins on the following day, Clean Monday (the Monday before the Western Ash Wednesday when the Eastern and Western date of Easter coincides).

A related feature of the development of the season was the cultural celebration of Mardi Gras ("fat Tuesday") in Gallic lands, a time to use up any remaining fat in preparation for Lent, and Carnival (farewell to meat) in Southern Europe[27] and Germany (*Karneval; Fasching* in Bavaria and Austria, from *Fastschank,* pouring the fast-tide drink) extending for some days before Lent. In more sober England, the day before Ash Wednesday was Shrove Tuesday, a day for being shriven, absolved of sin, before the penitential time began.[28] A socially useful time of release before the onset of the Lenten discipline, Carnival may be understood as more than a period of feasting and revelry. It is also a celebration of the common fate of the members of the human race. Its laughter is an act of acceptance, protesting the fact of universal mortality and laughing in acceptance of the democracy of death.[29] Thus, Carnival may be understood as an appropriate transition to Ash Wednesday and Lent.[30]

Ash Wednesday

In the present form of the Church's calendar, without a pre-Lenten period, Ash Wednesday (and therefore Lent) may be seen as a beginning of the liturgical year. Without any preparation, Ash Wednesday always comes as an unexpected interruption. Into the richness and pleasure of living suddenly comes the grim reminder, "You are dust, and to dust you shall return." It was God's word to our first parents in the garden of paradise after their disobedience, and it is God's word still to us all. Abruptly cutting into life when we are enjoying it the most comes the warning, "You too must die." It is a fact of life that we would rather not face, so we turn aside and raise our voices and laugh a little louder and quicken the pace of our pleasure; but still the hollow voice insists, "You too shall die." The certainty that no life lasts forever is always there, jumping out from behind an automobile in a near-accident, waiting in the corner of a hospital room. There is an inevitability about this unwelcome fact that makes it upsetting, sometimes frightening. The truth that Ash Wednesday will not let us forget is that life—our life—will someday end.[31]

Ash Wednesday with its disruptive intrusion into our pleasure may well be considered the real beginning of the liturgical year. It marks the one abrupt change in the yearly cycle. Advent follows without a break from the final weeks after Pentecost and takes up the proclamation of Christ the King on the Sunday immediately following, which is the First Sunday in Advent, "Behold your King comes to you." The secular New Year's Day does not mark a new beginning in the Church's calendar; for the Church, January 1 is the eighth day of Christmas. But Ash Wednesday is not a continuation or extension of the themes of the time after the Epiphany or even a bridge between Epiphany and Easter. It is not related to the recalling of the stages in the life of Christ. It comes as an unexpected interruption, almost without warning. It always catches us up short with its unwelcome message of mortality. But it is with the reminder of this solemn day, "Remember that you are dust, and to dust you shall return," that Lent begins, and with it, in a sense, a new Church year. The Jews conclude the High Holy Days marking the beginning of their new year with the most solemn day of the year, Yom Kippur, the Day of Atonement. For Christians, the year may be understood to begin with what may be described as the Christian version of the Day of Atonement, Ash Wednesday.

It is in keeping with this understanding of the character of the day that the 1978 *Lutheran Book of Worship* introduced the use of black as the liturgical color for Ash Wednesday. In Roman and in general European use, the color of Lent beginning with Ash Wednesday is violet (purple), the color of penitence and mourning. In English practice, Lent was often marked by the use of the Lenten array, unbleached white linen vestments, paraments, and veils for statues, crosses, and paintings, sometimes embroidered with a simple red cross. The intent was to make the items so covered blend into the white walls of the interior of the church. The leaves of a triptych were often painted the same white on the outside so that, when closed throughout Lent, the altarpiece would, in effect, be blotted out. The intent was to encourage the interior life during the holy season.[32]

The Revised Common Lectionary and the Roman liturgy have restored the early baptismal emphasis of Lent. The First Sunday in Lent was the time for the enrollment of candidates for baptism at the Easter Vigil. The celebration six days later of Ember Saturday with six prophecies and Epistles and Gospels took place the night between Saturday and Sunday, making the Second Sunday in Lent a "vacant" Sunday, a day without its own appointed Propers.[33] The Third, Fourth, and Fifth Sundays in Lent were occasions for the scrutinies (exorcisms and instruction) as part of the final preparation of the "elect" (see Matt. 24:31) for baptism at the Vigil of Easter. Often accompanied by exorcism to expel the demons and insufflation to breathe in the Holy Spirit to replace the unholy spirits who had been driven out (see Matt. 12:43-45; Luke 11:24-26), the scrutinies were designed to scrutinize the candidates, examining them closely to determine whether any aspects of their lives still needed to be set free from the influence of sin and evil. Generally the scrutinies were public examinations of the progress made by the elect in their conversion to Christ and the Church. A descendant of the scrutinies lingered into modern times in the public examination of candidates for Confirmation in Lutheran churches.

The number of scrutinies varied. In Rome there were originally three, celebrated on the third, fourth, and fifth Sundays in Lent in close connection with the readings from John's Gospel appointed for those Sundays. By the Middle Ages the scrutinies had become seven and were shifted to the weekdays during the last three weeks of Lent. The adult catechumenate declined and eventually disappeared, and the scrutinies were compressed into the pre-baptismal rites at the church door at the beginning of the baptismal liturgy for infants.

During the twentieth century the baptism of infants could no longer be assumed, and unbaptized adults sought admission to the Church. This encouraged the restoration of the original baptismal pattern in the 1972 Roman Catholic *Rite of Christian Initiation of Adults*. As in early Roman practice, the scrutinies include intercessions, prayers of exorcism, and dismissal from the Eucharistic assembly. During the week the scrutinies are followed by the *traditio symboli,* the "handing over" of the [Apostles'] Creed, that is, teaching it to the candidates and having them "hand it back" (*redditio*) by repeating what they have memorized; the presentation of the Lord's Prayer (week five) in the same manner; (by the end of the sixth century in Rome the Gospels were also handed over, the deacon reading the beginning of each Gospel and giving a brief commentary); and the final rites of preparation on Holy Saturday morning.

The ashes that give Ash Wednesday, in Latin *dies cinerum* (day of ashes), its name are an extraordinarily rich symbol. They speak of judgment and God's condemnation of sin; of human frailty and our total dependence on God for life. They anticipate what will be said at the burial of every Christian, "earth to earth, ashes to ashes, dust to dust." Ashes remind us and all who see them of humiliation and of repentance. Moreover, ashes were an ancient material for cleansing in the absence of soap; therefore ashes show cleanness and purification. They may serve as a penitential substitute for water. Water is essential for existence and for the maintenance of life. Water both stifles and refreshes, drowns and makes alive; so ashes tell of both death and renewal. They have therefore a healthful, medicinal effect: ashes can heal. In the previous Roman Catholic form for the blessing of the ashes the first prayer asks,

> Almighty and everlasting God, we beseech thee to spare them that are penitent, and to be favorable to them that call upon thee. Vouchsafe, we pray thee, to send thy holy Angel from heaven to bless and sanctify these ashes, that they may be a wholesome medicine to all them that humbly call upon thy holy Name...."[34]

The sobering exhortation of Ash Wednesday actually conceals something hopeful and encouraging. The words associated with the imposition of ashes transport us back to the moment of the fundamental break in our relationship with our Creator and therefore to the possibility of a fundamental healing in that relationship. We are dust, but dust lovingly formed by God, dust into which he has breathed his Spirit. Receiving the ashes on our head is an act of humility, but it also at the same time lays claim to the life-giving love and grace that was bestowed on that dust. God's love for us does not end when we in death return to the dust. He who formed us once out of dust will do so again. Our life, now and in the resurrection, is the love of God that can make even dust live.[35] Thus the imposition of ashes cannot be fully understood unless it is seen in the light of Easter.

There is also an urgency about the call to repentance. It is not to be delayed or put off. The responsory sung at the blessing of ashes in the Roman Missal urges, "Let us change for the better those things wherein we have sinned in ignorance, lest suddenly, overtaken by the day of death, we seek a place of repentance, and cannot find any." A verse from Baruch 3:2 provides words to say: "Hear, Lord, and have mercy, for we have sinned against you," and Psalm 79:9, "Help us, O God of our salvation; and for the honor of your Name, O Lord, deliver us." Lutherans with long memories may remember the absolution in the Order for Public Confession in the *Common Service Book* (made optional in the 1958 *Service Book and Hymnal*), "I therefore declare unto you who do truly repent and believe in him the entire forgiveness of all your sins: in the Name of the Father, and of the Son, and of the Holy Ghost. On the other hand, by the same authority, I declare unto the impenitent and unbelieving, that so long as they continue in their impenitence, God hath not forgiven their sins, and will assuredly visit their iniquities upon them, if they turn not from their evil ways, and come to true repentance and faith in Christ, ere the day of grace be ended" (pp. 242-3). Others may remember Isaiah's warning, "Seek the Lord while he may be found, call upon him while he is near" (Isa. 55:6). We are to take up the work of Lent while we have opportunity, before it is too late.

At the time of the Reformation, both the Anglican and Lutheran reformers discontinued the imposition of ashes. It is often said that they did so because they disapproved of the blessing of *things* rather than people. More likely, since the very use of ashes was discontinued, not simply their blessing, it was because of the apparent contradiction of Jesus's injunction in the Gospel for the day [Matt. 6:16-21], "wash your face." In the 1549 Book of Common Prayer, what was called Commination against Sinners replaced the traditional medieval rites, drawn from the penitential portion of the medieval rites of ashes and intended for use "Divers [i.e., diverse] Times in the Year." The form began with an exhortation during which the curses were solemnly recited.

Brethren, in the primitive Church there was a godly discipline, that, at the beginning of Lent, such persons as were notorious sinners were put to open penance and punished in this world, that their souls might be saved in the day of the Lord; and that others admonished by their example might be more afraid to offend. In the stead whereof, until the said discipline be restored again (which thing is much to be wished) it is thought good, that at this time (in your presence) should be read the general sentences of God's cursing against impenitent sinners, gathered out of the twenty-seventh chapter of Deuteronomy, and other places of Scripture; and that ye should answer to every sentence, Amen....

Cursed is the man that maketh any carved or molten image, an abomination to the Lord, the work of the hands of the craftsman, and putteth it in a secret place to worship it. *Amen.*
Cursed is he that curseth his father and mother. *Amen.*
Cursed is he that removeth away the mark of his neighbor's land. *Amen.*
Cursed is he that maketh the blind to go out of his way. *Amen.*
Cursed is he that letteth [hinders] in judgment the right of the stranger, of them that be fatherless, and of widows. *Amen.*
Cursed is he that smiteth his neighbor secretly. *Amen.*
Cursed is he that lieth with his neighbor's wife. *Amen.*
Cursed is he that taketh reward to slay the soul of innocent blood. *Amen.*
Cursed is he that putteth his trust in man, and taketh man for his defense, and in his heart goeth forth from the Lord. *Amen.*
Cursed are the unmerciful, the fornicators, and adulterers, and the covetous persons, the worshipers of images, slanderers, drunkards, extortioners. *Amen.*

Psalm 51, suffrages, and prayers follow. The form was modified in the 1892 and 1928 American Prayer Books, omitting the curses, as "A Penitential Office for Ash Wednesday."[36]

The Ash Wednesday liturgy in the Roman sacramentary, the Book of Common Prayer, and *Evangelical Lutheran Worship* (2006) follows the sermon, giving the preacher an opportunity to explain and reflect on the meaning of the ashes. The 1978 *Lutheran Book of Worship*, following the 1570 Roman Missal, puts the imposition of ashes at the very beginning of the liturgy, making it the first act of Lent.

The Collect in the Prayer Book, also in English-speaking Lutheran use since 1888, is by Archbishop Cranmer and is "a prayer of rare beauty and balance...a prayer which is one of the gems of collect literature."[37]

Almighty and everlasting God, you hate nothing that you have made and forgive the sins of all who are penitent: Create and make in us new and contrite hearts, that we, worthily lamenting our sins and acknowledging our wretchedness, may obtain of you, the God of all mercy, perfect remission and forgiveness; through Jesus Christ our Lord, who lives and reigns with you and the Holy Spirit, one God, for ever and ever.

The prayer is drawn in part from the antiphon of the Introit of the Mass for Ash Wednesday (*Misereris omnium*), Wisdom 11:24, 23, 26, "You love all things that exist, and detest none of the things you have made. You overlook people's sins, so that they may repent, and spare all things, O Lord." The opening prayer in the Roman sacramentary, from the Leonine sacramentary, provides insight into the purpose of Lenten fasting.

Grant us, O Lord, to enter on the service of our Christian warfare with holy fasting; that, as we are to fight against spiritual powers of wickedness, we may be fortified by the aid of self-denial; through Jesus Christ our Lord....[38]

In the 1570 Roman Missal this collect concluded the imposition of ashes; the Mass then began with the Introit.

The Revised Common Lectionary provides one set of readings for all three years of the lectionary cycle.

Joel 2:1-2, 12-17. Return to the Lord your God
  or Isa. 58:1-12. Is such the fast that I choose?
Psalm 51:1-17. Prayer for cleansing and forgiveness
2 Cor. 5:20b-6:10. Now is the day of salvation
Matt. 6:1-6, 16-21. Beware of practicing your piety to be seen by others

The reading from the Hebrew Bible and the Gospel continue the appointments in the previous lectionaries of the Roman, Anglican, and Lutheran churches: Joel 2:12-19 (12-17 in the Prayer Book); Matt. 6:16-21. The alternative reading from Isaiah 58 is from the lectionary in the 1979 American Prayer Book.

The 1979 Book of Common Prayer was the first American Prayer Book to include proper prefaces for Lent. The first, especially appropriate for the First Sunday in Lent, is:

"through Jesus Christ our Lord; who was tempted in every way as we are, yet did not sin. By his grace we are able to triumph over every evil, and to live no longer for ourselves alone, but for him who died for us and rose again."

The sources are Heb. 4:15; 2 Cor. 5:15; the 1929 Scottish revision of the Prayer Book; the *Book of Common Worship* of the Church of South India (1963); and the 1967 Liturgy of the Lord's Supper. The second preface is, "You bid your faithful people cleanse their hearts, and prepare with joy for the Paschal feast; that, fervent in prayer and in works of mercy, and renewed by your Word and Sacraments, they may come to the fullness of grace which you have prepared for those who love you." It is a paraphrase by Howard Galley of the first preface for Lent in the Roman sacramentary and especially appropriate for Ash Wednesday and most Sundays in Lent, expressing "powerfully the meaning and purpose of the season and the disciplines which it entails."[39] The *Lutheran Book of Worship* borrowed this preface, altering it slightly; *Evangelical Lutheran Worship* made further alterations. Previous Lutheran books during Lent used the Preface of the Cross appointed in the Roman Missal for Passiontide and feasts of the Holy Cross. The Roman sacramentary now provides a proper preface for each of the five Sundays in Lent based on the traditional themes of those Sundays and four others for Lenten weekdays and Sundays in Years B and C.

In Lent, in place of a seasonal blessing, a solemn prayer over the people is used, the deacon, or in the absence of a deacon the celebrant first saying, "Bow down before the Lord." The people kneel, and, on Ash Wednesday, the celebrant says,

> Grant, most merciful Lord, to your faithful people pardon and peace, that they may be cleansed from all their sins, and serve you with a quiet mind; through Christ our Lord.

The prayer is from the Gelasian sacramentary and was appointed in previous Prayer Books for the twenty-first Sunday after Trinity (the twentieth Sunday after Pentecost in the Roman Missal and the twentieth Sunday after Trinity in Lutheran books.) "The mercy of God is two-fold: pardon, or the compassionate overlooking of our sins; and peace, or freedom from the torment of sin and from anxiety and worry."[40] This prayer is appointed in the Episcopal *Book of Occasional Services*.

Lent as Pilgrimage

A principal organizing image for Lent is the evocative picture of a pilgrimage. It is, of course, an important image for the Bible. Abraham is the archetypal pilgrim, directed by God to leave his home and relatives, all that was familiar and comfortable, and go on an epic journey in search of spiritual truth. Without hesitation he set out, not yet knowing the destination and not yet comprehending the purpose of the long and difficult journey. His condition became the condition of all his descendants, who are described by the writer to the Hebrews as "strangers and pilgrims" (Heb. 11:13 AV) on earth, "resident aliens" living on land owned by God (see Gen 23:4; Lev. 25:23; 1 Chron. 29:15). A ninth-century Latin hymn sings of the church building, "strangers and pilgrims, seeking homes eternal, pass through its portals."[41] This world is not our home; the promised land of heaven is "our true native land" (as the Eucharistic hymn "O saving Victim"[42] calls it). Our life here is a journey through this passing world to our heavenly home. The Prayer of the Day for the First Sunday in Lent in the *Lutheran Book of Worship* derives from this image. "O Lord God, you led your ancient people through the wilderness and brought them to the promised land. Guide now the people of your Church, that, following our Savior, we may walk through the wilderness of this world toward the glory of the world to come." (The prayer would be improved by a request not simply to walk toward but to arrive safely at the intended destination.)

The journey begins, as it did for Abraham and his family, with turning in a new direction, with what the Greek New Testament calls *metanoia*, turning around, conversion. It requires a separation from one place and set of conditions and putting in place of them a concentration on the goal of the journey. It requires not just looking around but looking ahead with focus and determination. The Lenten pilgrimage is a journey to a specific holy place, Jesus's cross and tomb and to the life that lies beyond.

We may make the trip without actually leaving our city or town and accomplish the journey as a spiritual pilgrimage made in heart and mind. We are called to leave those places in our lives where we are not truly at home or at peace. One of the great purposes of Lent is to bring us to ourselves, so that, like the prodigal son in Jesus's parable (Luke 15:11-32), we may recognize that the condition in which we find ourselves is not our true home and that as comfortable as we may usually feel, we are in fact aliens in a foreign land and need to come home. So the Lenten pilgrimage is made with a clear purpose in mind. It is a journey home, although, as it was for Abraham, the home to which we go is a place we have never yet been.

This Lenten pilgrimage is accomplished not merely within our mind without leaving our present location. It requires (if we are able to make it) a physical journey. We must decide to leave home and get to a specific holy place, our church. There ritually we are in Jerusalem, and at the cross and tomb of Jesus. The journey is repeated week after week, year after year, but, one hopes, it is an ever-new experience with still more discoveries to be made, still more insights to be gained, still greater depths to be explored each time we make the journey.

The pilgrimage, we learn as we walk along, becomes an all-embracing, all-consuming activity. When we are on a pilgrimage, everything can be understood to be part of the way. Every step is as important as the last. Everyone and everything we encounter along the way is part of the pilgrim experience. A good bit of the route may seem ordinary and prosaic, but that does not mean that it is insignificant.

When God renewed the covenant with Abraham, changing his name from "Abram" to "Abraham" (Gen. 17, the Revised Common Lectionary first reading for the Second Sunday in Lent), God said to Abraham, "Walk before me, and be blameless" (Gen. 17:1). The verb "to walk" is used in this way throughout the Bible, in both Testaments, and it is often translated or interpreted as "to live." Walking, however, is a more active and suggestive verb. It implies movement: living is not a static activity. Walking also implies having a clear direction. Walking is not a casual stroll or an aimless meandering; it is going to a specific place with a specific intention. Walking before God (Ps. 116:9) is walking in God's law, going in the way of God's commandments, walking carefully along a prescribed path. "And when you turn to the right, or when you turn to the left, your ears shall hear a word behind you saying, 'This is the way; walk in it' " (Isa. 30:21). It is walking with God as with a friend (Micah 6:8). Nearly always, it should be noted, such walking is a community activity. "It is you, my companion, my familiar friend, with whom I kept pleasant company; we walked in the house of God with the throng" (Ps. 55:13-14). Such companionship on the journey affects our behavior. "Whoever walks with the wise becomes wise, but the companion of fools suffers harm" (Prov. 13:20).

In the New Testament, the counterpart to Abraham is the Virgin Mary. She was, like Abraham, summoned by God to be the progenitor not just of a new family but of a new race, those who become part of her Son, the new Adam. Abraham was called to leave home and to travel to a distant and as yet unrevealed place. Mary, too, received a transforming visit from God, but it was not necessary for her to travel far geographically. Her vocation was to be carried out where she was. There was a visit to her cousin Elisabeth in the hill country and the flight into Egypt to escape Herod's murderous orders, but mostly she stayed home. Her spiritual journey, however, was no less revolutionary than that of her distant ancestor Abraham. The pilgrimage of Lent, therefore, need not be geographical, but that does not lessen its call to a radical redirection and transformation of our lives.

Worshippers across denominational lines are familiar with the stirring Welsh hymn "Guide me, O thou great Jehovah" ("Guide me, O thou great

Redeemer" in *Hymns Ancient and Modern* and *The English Hymnal*) with its imagery of the signs of God's care in the wilderness, bread from heaven (manna), water from the rock, the pillar of fire and cloud, the epithets of God as Strength (Ps. 46:1; 73:26; 1 Sam 15:29 in the AV; Ps. 140:7) and Shield (Gen 15:1; Ps. 33:20; 84:11; 115:9; Deut. 33:29). The English translation dates from 1771.

Less widely known is a hymn that Christian Gregor (1723-1801) recast from two one-stanza hymns by Nicolaus Ludwig, Count von Zinzendorf (1700-1760), creating a new hymn *Jesu, geh' vor an,* which took the biblical image of pilgrimage as the basis for an impressive portrayal of the Christian life. The hymn, which became a favorite of Moravians and Lutherans, was translated by Jane Laurie Borthwick in 1846.

> Jesus, still lead on,
> Till our rest be won;
> And, although the way be cheerless,
> We will follow, calm and fearless;
> Guide us by thy hand
> To our fatherland.

We go by often cheerless paths through fearsome places following our Leader, by whom we are urged forward despite our faltering steps and weary condition. The memory of Jesus in the wilderness tempted by Satan is close at hand.

> If the way be drear,
> If the foe be near,
> Let not faithless fears o'ertake us,
> Let not faith and hope forsake us;
> For through many a foe
> To our home we go.

What keeps us going on the long and difficult path are the two gifts of faith and hope, both centered on the goal of the journey, our home, described with the evocative German word, *Vaterland,* our fatherland.

> When we seek relief
> From a long-felt grief,
> When temptations come alluring
> Make us patient and enduring;
> Show us that bright shore
> Where we weep no more.

We need both patience and endurance on the long pilgrimage, repeatedly refreshed by the glimpse of the bright shore where all sorrow is forgotten and where unending joy abounds.

> Jesus, still lead on,
> Till our rest be won;
> Heavenly Leader, still direct us,
> Still support, console, protect us,
> Till we safely stand
> In our fatherland![43]

The direction, support, consolation, and protection of Christ, who in his human nature has gone this way before us and who now leads us home, is continually invoked until we stand safe in our home and native land.

The pilgrimage image and the praise of the natural world are joined in a striking hymn by Katherine K. Davis (1892-1980). We are put in the company not only of ancient Israel in their wilderness travel but also of everything in creation.

> Let all things now living
> A song of thanksgiving
> To God the creator triumphantly raise,
> Who fashioned and made us,
> Protected and stayed us,
> Who still guides us on to the end of our days.
> God's banners are o'er us,
> His light goes before us,
> A pillar of fire shining forth in the night,
> Till shadows have vanished
> And darkness is banished,
> As forward we travel from light into light.
>
> His law he enforces,
> The stars in their courses
> And sun its orbit obediently shine;
> The hills and the mountains,
> The rivers and fountains,
> The deeps of the ocean proclaim him divine.
> We too should be voicing
> Our love and rejoicing;

> With glad adoration a song let us raise
> Till all things now living
> Unite in thanksgiving:
> "To God in the highest, hosanna and praise!"[44]

We are reminded that as the sun and stars always obey the laws of God, so should we, and that as the mountains, rivers, and seas praise the divine majesty of their maker, so we must join their proclamation of God's praise until all created things, the natural world and we who are a part of it, unite in one grand hymn.

In a sense, Lent does not bring anything new, only an intensification of what are already the constant themes and elements of the Christian life. The solemn season begins with a call to conversion, a summons to travel a different road, the way that leads to God. It is a road that leads out of the confinement of our mundane existence and into the uplands where wide vistas open before those who travel this way. The difficult path expands the horizon that has been reduced and limited by sin, which warps sinners into themselves. Lent encourages us to stand spiritually upright (see Luke 13:11-13) and open our eyes to see others who travel with us, to perceive larger possibilities for our lives, to feel the exhilaration of making our way to our true home.

It is customary in many places to begin the liturgy on the First Sunday in Lent, and sometimes also on subsequent Lenten Sundays, with the Great Litany, sung in procession. Singing a litany in procession is an action as ancient as the litanaic form itself. Since litanies were often prayed for a specific purpose, the people would process from the church to the place where that purpose manifested itself. If, for example, the intention was to pray God's blessing on the harvest, the procession would move from the church out into the fields and back again. Thus, movement became associated with this form of prayer, and to this day when the Litany is prayed, it is usually accompanied by movement. Moreover, such a practice, walking while praying, is a vivid dramatization of the passage through this world toward the world to come. The eventual arrival of the procession at the altar where it concludes is a promise of our safe arrival in heaven if we walk in the appointed way of God.

A text that may well be set over the journey of Lent is Psalm 84:5, in the NRSV translation, "Happy are those whose strength is in you, in whose heart are the highways to Zion." In the Prayer Book Psalter, also included in the *Lutheran Book of Worship*, it is verse 4,

> Happy are the people whose strength is in you!
> whose hearts are set on the pilgrims' way.

It is a song of pilgrims longing for the courts of the Lord, making their annual pilgrimage to Jerusalem for Passover, literally going up to the temple set prominently on the temple mount. Their desire to be in the Lord's house is so strong that even in the demanding journey they can find refreshment: "Those who go through the desolate valley will find it a place of springs" (BCP Ps. 84:5). The yearly pilgrimage looks forward to a greater ascent to an exalted temple described in the similar visions of Isaiah (2:2-4) and Micah (4:1-4):

> In days to come
>> the mountain of the Lord's house
> shall be established as the highest of the mountains,
>> and shall be raised above the hills;
> all the nations shall stream to it.

It will be a time of obedience to the ways of God, a time of justice and peace in all the earth. Thus the yearly Lenten journey is part of the larger and more inclusive pilgrimage.

An extra-liturgical devotion, the Way of the Cross, developed during the later Middle Ages, arising from the custom of pilgrims in Jerusalem following the traditional route that Jesus took from Pilate's house to Golgotha, continues its popularity as another method of prayer while moving from station to station throughout the church, following in the steps of Jesus from his condemnation to his burial.[45] A vivid yet tender thirteenth-century hymn often accompanies the movement, *Stabat mater dolorosa*, "At the cross her station keeping." The hymn gains its power from its point of view, seeing the crucifixion through the eyes of the Victim's mother.[46] The noble hymn, originally intended for devotional use, was popular among the flagellants in the fourteenth century. In the fifteenth century it entered various missals as a sequence in preparation for the reading of the Gospel and from 1727 by decree of Benedict XIII was used on the Friday after Passion Sunday (the Fifth Sunday in Lent), the Seven Sorrows of the Blessed Virgin Mary. The biblical sources include John 19:25 (Mary "standing near the cross") and Luke 2:35 ("a sword will pierce your own soul").

The First Sunday in Lent

The First Sunday in Lent in all three years of the lectionary cycle focuses on Jesus's temptation in the wilderness. The Introit (*Invocabit*[47] *me*) is drawn from Psalm 91 in which may be heard the Father speaking to the Son his temptation. The New Revised Standard Version has made the pronouns plural to avoid the masculine form and has thus blocked the connection with the principal theme of this Sunday. The antiphon is Psalm 91:15, 16; in the Authorized Version it reads,

> *Antiphon.* He shall call upon me, and I will answer him: I will deliver him and honor him. With long life will I satisfy him: and show him my salvation.
>> *Psalm 91:1.* He that dwelleth in the secret place of the Most High: shall abide under the shadow of the Almighty. *Gloria Patri.*
> *The antiphon is repeated.* He shall call upon me...my salvation.

The words that strengthened Christ also give strength to his people. In this song of assurance and trust, earthly blessings mingle with the blessings of the life to come; temporality intersects with eternity. The secret of such confidence is abiding in the shelter that God has provided as sanctuary, the Church.

The Collect in the Gregorian, Sarum, and Roman missals was:

> God, you cleanse your Church by the annual observance of Lent: Grant to your family that what they strive to obtain from you by abstinence, they may secure by good works.

"Good works" suggested to the Reformers, Anglican as well as Lutheran, what they condemned as "works righteousness," "works" being the offensive word and idea. (Perhaps "good deeds" would have softened the offense.) Thomas Cranmer radically revised the ancient Collect "without the Pelagian overtones or the implication that we must strive to obtain the gifts which God is anxious to give to those who seek".[48] In its original (1549) form, the prayer was

> O Lord, which for our sake didst fast forty days and forty nights: Give us grace to use such abstinence, that, our flesh being subdued to the spirit, we may ever obey thy godly motions in righteousness, and true holiness, to thy honor and glory, which livest and reignest....

In the twentieth century, the dualism of body and spirit became suspect, being derived from Greek philosophy rather than from the Bible, and Cranmer's prayer was replaced in the 1979 American Prayer Book with a revision of an original collect from William Bright's *Ancient Collects* (pp. 237-8).

Almighty God, whose blessed Son was led by the Spirit to be tempted by Satan: Come quickly to help us who are assaulted by many temptations; and, as you know the weaknesses of each of us, let each one find you mighty to save; through Jesus Christ your Son our Lord, who lives and reigns with you and the Holy Spirit, one God, now and for ever.

The prayer reflects the Gospel for all three years "and is particularly fitting as we enter this season of penitence in preparation for baptism or for renewal of baptismal vows."[49]

Lutheran books replaced the offending medieval collect with another from the Gregorian sacramentary found in the Bamberg (1498), Constance (1505), and Nuremberg (1484) missals:

O Lord, mercifully hear our prayer, and stretch forth the right hand of thy Majesty to defend us from them that rise up against us; through Jesus Christ thy Son, our Lord, who liveth and reigneth with thee and the Holy Ghost, ever one God, world without end.

The translation was made for the 1868 *Church Book*. The collect was appropriate for the First Sunday in Lent; "Them that rise up against us" could in this context refer to Satan rising up and testing Jesus in the wilderness, and the right hand of God's majesty can suggest the angelic protection given to Jesus. The 1978 *Lutheran Book of Worship* introduced the prayer of the day cited above.

The present Roman sacramentary (1970) uses a collect from the Gelasian sacramentary, which is an invitation to the imitation of Christ:

Grant us, almighty God, that through the yearly observance of Lent we may enter more deeply into the mystery of Christ and follow his mind by conduct worthy of our calling; through the same Jesus Christ our Lord, who lives and reigns with you and the Holy Spirit, one God, now and for ever.

The translation used here is from William Bright's *Ancient Collects*.[50]

The Revised Common Lectionary appoints these readings for the First Sunday in Lent.

Year A

    Gen. 2:15-17; 3:1-7. The fall: sin enters the world

    Psalm 32. The joy of being forgiven

    Rom. 5:12-19. The old Adam and the new Adam

    Matt. 4:1-11. Jesus rejects Satan's temptation

Year B

Gen. 9:8-17. The covenant with Noah

Psalm 25:1-10. Prayer for guidance and protection

1 Peter 3:18-22. Victory for the baptized

Mark 1:12-15. Temptation and ministry

Year C

Deut. 26:1-11. The gift of the promised land

Psalm 91:1-2, 9-16. God's protection

Rom. 10:8b-13. Salvation for all

Luke 4:1-13. Jesus's initial rebuff of the devil

Joseph Sittler made the observation,

> It is an ancient requirement of the Church that we enter the forty days of Lent through the dark wilderness where Jesus confronted the devil. Here two absolute wills met. The will of Jesus was unity, obedience, the world as God meant it, sacrifice, and the service of God. The will of the devil was disunity, arrogance, the world as man would have it, accommodation, and the will of man. The Church knows exactly what it is doing when it takes us this way, into and through the wilderness.
>
> This wilderness-meeting...is both report and re-enactment. It is report: for this struggle of the Servant of God...actually took place. And it is re-enactment too. For that old...story from God is for my story. It is then—and it is now. And we preach it and hear it and ponder it to the end that we may re-enact it.[51]

In the Eastern Orthodox churches, at vespers on Cheesefare Sunday, the day before Great Lent begins, a hymn is sung in which the voice of Adam is heard speaking for the whole human race. First he praises the extraordinary and unmerited kindness of God.

> The Lord my creator took me as dust from the earth,
> and formed me into a living being,
> breathing into me the breath of life.
> He honored me,
> setting me as ruler upon earth over all things visible,
> and made me companion of the angels.

Then comes the fall.

But Satan the deceiver,
  using the serpent as instrument,
  enticed me by food,
  separated me from the glory of God,
  and gave me over to the earth,
  and to the lowest depths of the earth.
  But as Master and compassionate, call me back again.
  …bring me into Paradise again.

It was by food, the forbidden fruit, that Satan ruined us, and so during Lent we fast and abstain from various kinds of food, as Jesus, whom Satan attempted also to entice with food, suggesting that Jesus in his hunger turn stones into bread. By fasting we are one with Jesus in the desert, who is one with us in our desolation. Food separated us from our creator, but in the wonderful way of God food, abundant food, will be characteristic of the heavenly kingdom, the messianic banquet when all will be restored.

A sixth-century Latin hymn has not yet been infected with the gloom that later came to shadow the season of Lent and speaks of the celebration of the glory of these forty days.

The glory of these forty days
  We celebrate with songs of praise;
  For Christ, through whom all things were made,
  Himself has fasted and has prayed.

Christ gathered into himself the experience of his people through the ages, and the hymn continues, naming the exemplars of fasting and prayer.

Alone and fasting Moses saw
  The loving God who gave the Law;
  And to Elijah, fasting, came
  The steeds and chariots of flame.

The references are to Exod. 24:15-18 and 2 Kings 2:1-12 (The biblical account does not speak of Elijah fasting in preparation for his being taken up to heaven, but it does note his going without food for forty days in 1 Kings 19:8.) Further examples are provided, Daniel and John the Baptist (as "the friend of the bridegroom" see John 3:29).

So Daniel trained his mystic sight,
  Delivered from the lions' might;

And John, the Bridegroom's friend, became
The herald of Messiah's name.

Then grant us, Lord, like them to be
Full oft in fast and prayer with thee;
Our spirits strengthen with thy grace,
And give us joy to see thy face.[52]

We are not alone in our struggle against the forces of evil. Joshua in his fare-well address to the people of Israel encouraged them, "One of you puts to flight a thousand, since it is the Lord your God who fights for you, as he prom-ised you" (Joshua 23:10).[53]

A hymn attributed to Gregory the Great (540-604) encourages those who begin the observance of Lent by reminding them that they are not alone in their struggle,

Now let us all with one accord,
In company with ages past,
Keep vigil with our heavenly Lord
In his temptation and his fast.[54]

A further source of strength is keeping the goal of the season of penance always in view: Easter. Claudia Frances Hernaman's familiar Lenten hymn does that effectively.

Lord, who throughout these forty days
For us didst fast and pray,
Teach us with thee to mourn our sins
And close by thee to stay.

. . .

Abide with us, that so, this life
Of suffering overpast,
An Easter of unending joy
We may attain at last.[55]

The Responsory appointed for the Office of Readings on the Thursday after Ash Wednesday teaches

This time of fasting opens the gates of heaven to us.
Let us welcome it and pray
    that when Easter comes
    we may share the joy of the risen Lord.

In all we do let us show that we are the servants of God,
        that when Easter comes
        we may share the joy of the risen Lord.[56]

Throughout the time of penance the eyes of the faithful who attend to the voice of the Church are to be fixed on the goal of the journey.

The prayer over the people for the First Lenten Sunday given in the Episcopal *Book of Occasional Services* is: "Grant, almighty God, that your people may recognize their weakness and put their whole trust in your strength, so that they may rejoice for ever in the protection of your loving providence; through Christ our Lord." The antiphon to the Magnificat at vespers on the First Sunday in Lent, remembering the Gospel read at the Eucharist, asks, "Watch over us, eternal Savior; do not let the cunning tempter seize us. We place all our trust in your unfailing help."[57] In our struggle against sin and Satan, we are to imitate the trust in God's strength shown by Christ in his temptation.

The First Sunday in Lent serves as an overture to the Paschal mystery of Easter: Jesus's struggle in the wilderness (fasting, hunger, temptation) but also his victory over powers hostile to God, as well as an anticipation of his glorification ("angels came and ministered to him").[58]

The Second Sunday in Lent

The theme of Christ's hidden glory is presented in the varying liturgical traditions on this Sunday. The Second Sunday in Lent in the previous as well as the present Roman lectionary repeats the Gospel of Ember Saturday, the Transfiguration. The three figures, Jesus, Moses, and Elijah, are all models of fasting: Jesus alone in the desert for forty days, Moses alone on Mount Sinai for forty days (Exodus 24:18), Elijah alone encountering God at Mount Horeb (1 Kings 19:8-18) after a forty-day journey. The sight of Jesus transfigured is to strengthen his followers in their Lenten discipline by a proleptic vision of the Son of Man raised from the dead (Matt. 17:9).

The antiphon of the Introit in previous books, *Reminiscere*, comes from Psalm 25:6, 2b, 22 and calls upon God to remember the promises of protection heard the previous Sunday.

> *Antiphon.* Remember your mercy, O Lord, and your steadfast love,
> for they have been from of old. Do not let my enemies exult over me.
> God of Israel, deliver us out of all our troubles.
> *Psalm 25:1, 2a.* To you, O Lord, I lift up my soul. O my God, in you

I trust; do not let me be put to shame. *Gloria Patri.*
The antiphon is repeated. Remember your mercy...our troubles.

The Collect appointed in previous Roman, Anglican, and Lutheran books, reflecting its assignment to this Sunday in the Gregorian sacramentary, continued the plea of the Introit. Its Lutheran form is close to the Latin; the Prayer Book expanded several phrases (see below, where the Collect is appointed in the present American Prayer Book for the Third Sunday in Lent).

> O God, who seest that of ourselves we have no strength: Keep us both outwardly and inwardly; that we may be defended from all adversities which may happen to the body, and from all evil thoughts which may assault and hurt the soul; through thy Son, Jesus Christ our Lord....

It is another prayer in which the troublous times in Italy are reflected. The collect in the present Roman sacramentary is a very fine Mozarabic prayer that further explicates the selection of the Transfiguration theme for this Sunday.

> O God, you commanded us to listen to your beloved Son: Nourish us inwardly with your Word of life, and purify the eyes of our spirit, that we may rejoice in the sight of your glory; through your Son Jesus Christ our Lord....[59]

The Gospel for each of the three Sundays of the lectionary cycle reports the Transfiguration.

> Year A. Matt. 17:1-9. Transfiguration
> Year B. Mark 9:2-10. This is my beloved Son
> Year C. Luke 9:28-36. Transfiguration of Christ.

Moses and Elijah both fasted forty days, both ascended the holy mountain, both are appropriately here with Jesus in lofty conversation. And, at least in earlier times, those who are preparing to be baptized will wear the white robes of baptism at Easter.

The Anglican and Lutheran calendars have employed the Transfiguration theme on the Last Sunday after the Epiphany, two weeks prior to this Sunday. The 1979 American Prayer Book appoints a Collect from the Missale Gallicanum vetus, Gelasian, and the Gregorian sacramentaries in which it is used in the Good Friday Bidding Prayer for schismatics and heretics. Here "it refers to those who have abandoned the practice of the Christian faith."[60]

> O God, whose glory it is always to have mercy: Be gracious to all who have gone astray from your ways, and bring them again with penitent hearts and steadfast faith to embrace and hold fast the unchangeable truth of your Word, Jesus Christ your Son; who with you and the Holy Spirit lives and reigns, one God, for ever and ever.

The *Lutheran Book of Worship* adapted the prayer for its own use.

The Revised Common Lectionary appoints these readings.
    Year A
            Gen. 12:1-4. The call of Abraham
            Psalm 121. Assurance of God's protection
            Rom. 4:1-5, 13-17. The example of Abraham
            John 3:1-17. Nicodemus visits Jesus
                or Matt. 17:1-9. The transfiguration
    Year B
            Gen. 17:1-7, 15-16. God's covenant with Abraham
            Psalm 22:23-31. Dominion belongs to the Lord
            Rom. 4:13-25. God's promise realized through faith
            Mark 8:31-38. Jesus foretells his passion
                or Mark 9:2-9. The transfiguration
    Year C
            Gen. 15:1-12, 17-18. God's covenant with Abram
            Psalm 27. Song of confidence
            Phil. 3:17-4:1. Citizenship in heaven
            Luke 13:31-35. Jesus' lament over Jerusalem.
                or Luke 9:28-36 (37-43a). The transfiguration

The role of Father Abraham, ancestor of all the faithful, is prominent in these readings, but other themes are also introduced, notably the passion.

The prayer over the people for the Second Sunday in Lent in the Episcopal *Book of Occasional Services* is the prayer over the people appointed in the 1570 Roman Missal for Saturday of the second week in Lent. "Keep this your family, Lord, with your never-failing mercy, that relying solely on the help of your heavenly grace, they may be upheld by your divine protection; through Christ our Lord."

The Third Sunday in Lent

Having diverged for a Sunday the three rites come together with a common point of view on the Third Sunday in Lent. The antiphon of the Introit (*Oculi mei*), like the previous Introit, is from Psalm 25, this time verses 15 and 16.

> *Antiphon.* My eyes are ever toward the Lord, for he will pluck my feet out of the net. Turn to me and be gracious to me, for I am lonely and afflicted.
> *Psalm 25:1, 2.* To you, O Lord, I lift up my soul. O my God, in you I trust; do not let me be put to shame. *Gloria Patri.*
> *The antiphon is repeated:* My eyes... and afflicted.

The individual petitioner is a frail creature, a small bird caught in a net, helpless unless God intervenes.

The collect in the Roman sacramentary is from the Gelasian sacramentary.

> O God, source of all mercy and goodness, in almsgiving, fasting, and prayer you have shown us a remedy for sin: Mercifully hear us as we confess our weakness, and, when we are bowed down by the burden of our guilt, lift up our hearts with the assurance of your mercy; through our Lord Jesus Christ, your Son....

The Book of Common Prayer appoints a Collect from the Gregorian sacramentary where it was appointed for the Second Sunday in Lent as it was in previous Anglican and Lutheran books.

> Almighty God, you know that we have no power in ourselves to help ourselves: Keep us both outwardly in our bodies and inwardly in our souls, that we may be defended from all adversities which may happen to the body, and from all evil thoughts which may assault and hurt the soul; through Jesus Christ our Lord, who lives and reigns with you and the Holy Spirit, one God, for ever and ever.

In Lutheran use, the collect was strengthened by the deletion of redundancies: "O God, who seest that of ourselves we have no strength: Keep us both outwardly and inwardly; that we may be defended from all adversities which may happen to the body, and from all evil thoughts which may assault and hurt the soul." The Latin original has the strength of sharp antithesis tersely put in a verbal parallel: *Muniamur in corpore…mundemur in mente,* defended in body…cleansed in mind.[61]

The Revised Common Lectionary appoints these readings.
Year A
> Exod. 17:1-7. Water from the rock
> Psalm 95. A call to worship and obedience
> Rom. 5:1-11. The results of justification
> John 4:5-42. The woman of Samaria at the well

Year B
> Exod. 20:1-17. The Ten Commandments
> Psalm 19. God's glory in creation and the Law
> 1 Cor. 1:18-25. Christ the power and wisdom of God
> John 2:13-22. Jesus cleanses the temple

Year C
> Isa. 55:1-9. An invitation to abundant life
> Psalm 63:1-8. Comfort and assurance in God's presence
> 1 Cor. 10:1-13. Warning from Israel's history
> Luke 13:1-9. Repentance and the barren fig tree.

The Gospel in Year A is the traditional reading for this Sunday in ancient lectionaries preparing candidates for baptism. Jesus is the well of living water; the woman, an outsider and of sullied reputation, responds in faith to Jesus's reaching out to gather her as a promise of forgiveness and of the inclusion of the nations in the kingdom.

The prayer over the people is simplicity itself. "Look mercifully on this your family, Almighty God, that by your great goodness they may be governed and preserved evermore; through Christ our Lord." It is the Gregorian collect appointed in previous Anglican, Lutheran, and Roman books for Passion Sunday, the Fifth Sunday in Lent. The Roman sacramentary appoints a collect assigned in the 1570 Roman Missal to Thursday in the third week of Lent. "Direct the hearts of your faithful people, O Lord, and in your mercy grant that they, abiding in love of you and of their neighbors, may fulfill the whole of your commands; through Christ our Lord." The prayer reflects Rom. 13:10, "Love is the fulfilling of the law," and such love of God and neighbor is one of the principal works of Lent.

The Fourth Sunday in Lent

When Lent began on the Monday following the First Sunday in Lent, the Fourth Sunday marked the exact mid-point of the season: eighteen weekdays preceding (Monday through Saturday of weeks 1, 2, and 3) and eighteen weekdays to follow (Monday through Saturday of weeks 4, 5, and 6). When Lent was extended to make a full forty days, this Sunday continued to be observed as mid-Lent. The Mass and the Sunday bore the name *Laetare*, from the first word of the Introit, "Rejoice with Jerusalem and be glad with her, all you who love her" (Isa. 66:10). It was celebrated as Refreshment Sunday (the Gospel was John 6:1-15, the feeding of the multitude), a brief lessening of the intensity of the discipline of Lent as an encouragement to the faithful not to lose heart, to persevere, and to continue the arduous journey to its goal. In England this Sunday was Mothering Sunday, from the Epistle then appointed, Gal. 4:21-5:1a ("the Jerusalem above...is our mother"). The day was observed by visiting the cathedral, the mother church of the diocese, and also the church where one was baptized, and also one's own mother.

> The Antiphon of the Introit, *Laetare Jerusalem,* is from Isa. 66:10.
> *Antiphon.* Rejoice with Jerusalem, and be glad for her, all you who love her; rejoice with her in joy, all you who mourn over her—that you may nurse and be satisfied from her consoling breast.
> > *Psalm 122:1.* I was glad when they said to me, "Let us go to the house of the Lord." *Gloria Patri.*
> *The antiphon is repeated:* Rejoice with Jerusalem...her consoling breast.

The invitation to joy is not only an encouragement to those undergoing Lenten discipline and a correction to those who find it gloomy and depressing. In it may be heard the conversation of the Church and the catechumens who were being prepared during Lent for their baptism. Children were coming to their mother for necessary nourishment; catechumens were being invited into the embrace of the Church and the house of God. An insight attributed to Leon Bloy declares, "Joy is the surest sign of the presence of God."

The collect in the previous rites was drawn from the Gregorian sacramentary.

> Grant, we beseech thee, almighty God, that we, who for our evil deeds deserve to be punished, by the comfort of thy grace may mercifully be relieved; through thy Son Jesus Christ our Lord....

The prayer was thought too gloomily medieval and inappropriate for Refreshment Sunday and was therefore replaced in all three rites. The opening prayer in the Roman sacramentary combines a Gelasian collect with phrases from a sermon by Leo the Great.

> Lord God, in a wonderful manner you reconcile humankind to yourself through your only Son, the eternal Word: Grant that your Christian people may press on toward the Easter sacraments with lively faith and ready hearts; through our Lord Jesus Christ....[62]

The people are reminded of the goal of their Lenten pilgrimage and encouraged by the thought of the celebration of Easter and its sacraments of baptism and Eucharist. The American Prayer Book, which appointed John 6:4-15 as the Gospel in Year B (continued from the previous lectionary), Jesus's feeding of the great crowd, uses a revision of a prayer by Frederick Brodie Macnutt in *The Prayer Manual* (1952).

> Gracious Father, whose blessed Son Jesus Christ came down from heaven to be the true bread which gives life to the world: Evermore give us this bread, that he may live in us, and we in him; who lives and reigns with you and the Holy Spirit, one God, now and for ever.

The living bread from heaven sustains the people through their Lenten fast. The *Lutheran Book of Worship* radically revised the traditional collect.

> God of all mercy, by your power to heal and to forgive, graciously cleanse us from all sin and make us strong; through your Son Jesus Christ our Lord....

The result was a remarkably bland prayer.

The Revised Common Lectionary appoints these readings for the Fourth Sunday in Lent.

    Year A
        1 Sam. 16:1-13. David is anointed king
        Psalm 23. The Lord is my shepherd
        Eph. 5:8-14. Live as children of light
        John 9:1-41. The healing of the man born blind
    Year B
        Numb. 21:4-9. The bronze serpent lifted on a pole

Psalm 107:1-3, 17-22. Thanksgiving for deliverance

Eph. 2:1-10. From death to life

John 3:14-21. The Son of Man must be lifted up

Year C

Josh. 5:9-12. Passover in the promised land

Psalm 32. The joy of being forgiven

2 Cor. 5:16-21. Everything has become new

Luke 15:1-3, 11b-32. The prodigal son and his brother

RC John 8:1-11. The woman taken in adultery.

The Gospel appointed for Year A is the ancient reading for this Sunday addressed to the catechumens. The washing in the pool of Siloam is a type of baptism; the progress of the man born blind and of catechumens is from darkness to enlightenment; the theme is spiritual sight and faith. In the course of the long Gospel, conflict between Jesus and his opponents makes its appearance. The baptized are thus taught that they, too, can expect trouble in their new life as Christians. Their spiritual warfare will continue to be waged.

The Episcopal prayer over the people for this Sunday is, "Look down in mercy, Lord, on your people who kneel before you; and grant that those whom you have nourished by your Word and Sacraments may bring forth fruit worthy of repentance; through Christ our Lord."

The Fifth Sunday in Lent

With the Fifth Sunday in Lent the Church enters "deep Lent." In the previous calendar it was called Passion Sunday, the beginning of a two-week period called Passion Time (in Roman Catholic books) or Passiontide (in certain Anglican circles), which focused on the passion and death of Christ. It was marked often with a distinct liturgical color, usually red; crosses and statues were veiled (a "fast of the eyes").[63] In English use, the white veils of the Lenten array were replaced with Passiontide red.[64] The emphasis was on preparing to mourn the suffering and death of Christ. Entering a veiled church was like entering a house of mourning with the curtains drawn.[65] Traces of this distinctive character remain in the Propers of the Roman rite. The Proper Preface for the Fifth Sunday in Lent in Years B and C tells of the Power of the Cross. "The suffering and death of your Son brought life to the whole world, moving our hearts to praise your glory. The power of the cross reveals your judgment on this world and the kingship of Christ crucified." The present liturgy in these final two weeks of Lent still turns toward the cross, but it is not to mourn but to ponder more intensely the Paschal mystery, Jesus's passage through death to life beyond.

The antiphon of the Introit for what was previously called Passion Sunday, *Judica me,* is from Psalm 42:1, 2a.

> *Antiphon.* Vindicate me, O God, and defend my cause against an ungodly people; from those who are deceitful and unjust deliver me! For you are the God in whom I take refuge.
>
>   *Psalm 43:3.* O send out your light and your truth; let them lead me;
>
>   let them bring me to your holy hill and to your dwelling. *Gloria Patri.*
>
> *The antiphon is repeated:* Vindicate me ... I take refuge.

As Lent draws toward its close and Holy Week approaches, it is impossible not to hear in these psalm verses the voice of Christ. And we know how the anguished prayer will be answered. The Father will indeed bring him to the holy hill called Golgotha and then beyond that in the Ascension to his dwelling.

The collect in all three rites before the twentieth-century revisions was from the Gregorian sacramentary.

> We beseech thee, almighty God, mercifully to look upon thy people [literally "family"], that by thy great goodness they may be governed and preserved evermore, both in body and soul; through thy Son Jesus Christ our Lord....

Although it was reminiscent of the Collect then appointed for the Second Sunday in Lent and was anticipatory of the Collect for Good Friday, modern books have replaced it with a prayer thought more suitable to the season. The objections to the prayer were not new. Paul Strodach early in the twentieth century knew what they were and provides a response.

> When one comes to the Day's *Collect* perhaps one feels like saying it is inadequate; but one should hesitate, read it again very quietly and slowly, ponder it; and then that first opinion will not remain, but become the opposite. It *is* simple, yet transcendingly beautiful and so complete in its single little sentence crowded full of soul petition. Perhaps the fathers who prepared these Offices—and we owe these unknown lovers of God a debt which only our appreciation and worshipful use can repay—felt, as many unhappily do not, how empty mere words are to

express the truly deep things of the soul. It is not the quantity of words, or the length to which it may be drawn out, that makes a prayer. These men were pray-ers; they prove it when they leave such devotional treasures as these Collects. A Collect such as this Day's can be born only of the deepest contemplation; it was not "written"; it prayed itself into the very spirit of the Day with the soul as the goal of the great High Priest's Ministry and sacrificial Death.[66]

Modern worshippers are not so patient nor are they equipped with a facility in the Latin language, and so have difficulty appreciating such understated and compressed prayers. (This is not necessarily sufficient reason to abandon them. It is rather to be taken as encouragement to careful explanation and exploration of the unfamiliar.) The Roman sacramentary appoints a collect from the Mozarabic rite.

> Come to our aid, Lord God, that we may walk courageously in that love with which, out of love for the world, your Son handed himself over to death; who now lives and reigns with you and the Holy Spirit, one God, for ever and ever.

The 1979 American Prayer Book appoints the Collect previously used in the Roman Missal, the Book of Common Prayer, and the Lutheran rite on the Fourth Sunday after Easter. It comes from the Gelasian and Gregorian sacramentaries in which it was assigned to the third Sunday after the Octave of Easter.

> Almighty God, you alone can bring into order the unruly wills and affections of sinners: Grant your people grace to love what you command and desire what you promise; that, among the swift and varied changes of the world, our hearts may surely there be fixed where true joys are to be found; through Jesus Christ our Lord....

The prayer only subtly looks through the cross toward the joys of Easter.

The Revised Common Lectionary appoints these readings.
    Year A
        Ezek. 37:1-14. The valley of dry bones
        Psalm 130. Out of the depths
        Rom. 8:6-11. Life in the Spirit
        John 11:1-45. The raising of Lazarus from the dead

Year B
>
> Jer. 31:31-34. A new covenant
> Psalm 51:1-12. Prayer for cleansing and pardon
> or 119:9-16. Teach me your statutes
> Heb. 5:5-10. The Son made perfect through suffering
> John 12:20-33. The hour has come for the Son of Man to be
> glorified

Year C
>
> Isa. 43:16-21. I am about to do a new thing
> Psalm 126. A harvest of joy
> Phil. 3:4b-14. Breaking with the past
> John 12:1-8. Six days before the Passover Jesus is anointed.

The Gospel for Year A is the ancient reading for this Sunday directed to the catechumens. It teaches the power of prayer, new life through Christ, and a promise of resurrection in him. In the Eastern churches "Lazarus Saturday," the day before Holy Week begins, exactly one week before Holy Saturday, is kept as a foreshadowing of the resurrection.

The prayer over the people for the Fifth Lenten Sunday is "Look with compassion, O Lord, on this your people; that, rightly observing this holy season, they may learn to know you more fully, and to serve you with a more perfect will; through Christ our Lord." The prayer has similarities to the prayer over the people for Thursday in Passion Week in the 1570 Roman Missal. To distinguish it from Holy Week, the fifth week in Lent, before the calendar reforms of the later twentieth century, was called Passion Week (despite the assertion of W. K. Lowther Clarke that "Passion Week is an incorrect phrase"[67]).

Lenten Weekday Collects

The Roman sacramentary assigns a collect for each weekday of Lent. Finding or composing thirty-three collects inevitably means a certain repetitiveness and predictability, but it does provide a place for the inclusion of some classic prayers not otherwise contained in the revised missal. Thursday after Ash Wednesday has as the Collect the great all-purpose prayer, appropriate not only for Lent but for any number of occasions.

> Direct us, O Lord, in all our doings with your most gracious favor, and further us with your continual help; that in all our works, begun, continued, and ended in you, we may glorify your holy Name, and

finally, by your mercy, obtain everlasting life; through Jesus Christ our Lord.[68]

The prayer is Gregorian, and in that sacramentary it is appointed for the Saturday in the fourth week in Lent. In the setting of Lent, it places all our self-discipline under God's direction so that all we do will be for his glory, even the gift of everlasting life.

For Saturday after Ash Wednesday the Roman sacramentary appoints the Gregorian collect that in previous books of the Roman, Anglican, and Lutheran rites had been used on the Third Sunday after the Epiphany.

> Almighty and everlasting God, mercifully look upon our frailty, and in all our dangers and necessities, stretch forth the right hand of your majesty to help and defend us; through Jesus Christ your Son our Lord....

In the earlier context there was an obvious connection with the Gospel, Matt. 8:1-13, the account of Jesus stretching forth his hand to heal a leper. Now it may be understood to anticipate the Gospel for the next day (Lent 1) asking God's protection in our temptations.

A Gregorian collect that was used in the Roman Missal continues in use on the Monday after the First Sunday in Lent.

> Turn our hearts back to you, O God of our salvation; grant us the grace of true conversion, and, that we may fully benefit from the Lenten fast, shape our minds with your heavenly teaching; through Jesus Christ our Lord.

The biblical understanding of repentance, turning around from darkness to light, recognizes that conversion is ultimately God's work. As Luther teaches in the Small Catechism, explaining the Third Article of the Apostles' Creed, "I believe that by my own understanding or strength I cannot believe in Jesus Christ my Lord or come to him, but instead the Holy Spirit has called me through the gospel, enlightened me with his gifts, made me holy and kept me in the true faith...."[69]

For Thursday after the First Sunday in Lent the Roman rite assigns a Leonine collect previously used on the Eighth Sunday after Pentecost in the Roman Missal, the Ninth Sunday after Trinity in the Prayer Book, and the Eighth Sunday after Trinity in the Lutheran rite. The Book of Common Prayer now assigns this Collect to Proper 14.

> Grant to us, Lord, we pray, the spirit to think and do always such
> things that are right; that we, who cannot exist without you, may by
> you be enabled to live according to your will; through Jesus Christ our
> Lord....

Luther Reed observes that the collect "exhibits a fine balance of phraseology
which it is almost impossible to preserve in translation."[70] Strodach's comment reveals that good prayers take on new meaning in new contexts. "The
hindrances are many, great and constant; they also are attractive, seductive.
The false spirits would lead away; and, while seemingly attractive and harmless, will only prove themselves to be hard masters of a slavery that leads to
destruction! The believer dare not pause or look back, or permit himself to be
drawn away from that end for which he is striving, where such a wonderful
promise awaits...."[71] He is relating the collect to what was then the Epistle,
Romans 8:12-17, but the same remarks are also appropriate to those making
the Lenten journey and who have recently heard the account of Satan's temptation of Jesus in the wilderness.

For Tuesday of the second full week in Lent, the Roman sacramentary
assigns the Gelasian collect used previously in the Roman Missal on the fourteenth Sunday after Pentecost, in the Book of Common Prayer on the fifteenth
Sunday after Trinity, and in the Lutheran books on the fourteenth Sunday after
Trinity.

> Watch over your Church, O Lord, with your unfailing mercy, and,
> because human frailty without you will surely fall, protect us by your
> help from every harm, and lead us to all things that work for our good;
> through Jesus Christ our Lord....

The collect is unusual in that the very first word in Latin voices the petition,
before the usual invocation.[72] The Episcopal *Lesser Feasts and Fasts* (2003)
appoints this collect to the Thursday after the Third Sunday in Lent.

On the Monday following the Third Sunday in Lent the Roman sacramentary assigns the Gelasian collect used previously in the Roman Missal on the
fifteenth Sunday after Pentecost, in the Book of Common Prayer on the sixteenth Sunday after Trinity, and in Lutheran books on the fifteenth Sunday
after Trinity.

> Let your continual mercy, O Lord, cleanse and defend your Church;
> and, because it cannot continue in safety without your help, protect and
> govern it always by your goodness; through Jesus Christ our Lord....

The collect, notably similar to the one above, is in the 1979 Book of Common Prayer assigned to Proper 13. The English translation cannot preserve the triple play on the Latin words *mundet* (cleanse), *muniat* (defend), *munere* (goodness).[73]

On Friday of the fifth full week in Lent the Roman sacramentary appoints the Gregorian collect used formerly in the Roman Missal for the twenty-third Sunday after Pentecost, in the Book of Common Prayer on the twenty-fourth Sunday after Trinity, and in Lutheran books on the twenty-third Sunday after Trinity in which the Church pours out its ardent plea: loose us from the slavery of service to this world and the captivity of pleasing ourselves and set us free.[74]

> Absolve, we beseech thee, O Lord, your people from their offenses; that from the bonds of our sins, which by reason of our frailty we have brought upon ourselves, we may be delivered by your bountiful goodness; through Jesus Christ our Lord, who....

The same collect was also used in the Lutheran rite on the Last Sunday after Trinity of each year.

In addition to the reassignment of some of the classic collects, the Roman rite has introduced some notable newly appointed prayers. A Gelasian collect is used on the Saturday after the Second Sunday in Lent in the Roman sacramentary and on Monday following the Fourth Sunday in Lent in the Episcopal *Lesser Feasts and Fasts* (2003).

> O God, in your holy sacraments you have given us, while still on earth, a foretaste of the good things of heaven: Guide us, we beseech you, in this present life, and lead us to that everlasting light in which you yourself dwell; through Jesus Christ our Lord....

We pray that, encouraged by the sacraments, we may be led from the darkness of this world to the land of light and life. The biblical reference is 1 Tim. 6:16.

A collect from the ninth-century Bergamo sacramentary is appointed in the present Roman sacramentary for Thursday in the third full week in Lent.

> We humbly implore your majesty, O Lord, that as the Paschal festival draws nearer, we may prepare ourselves with ever greater devotion to celebrate the mystery of the death and resurrection of our Lord; who lives and reigns....

Near the middle of Lent we are reminded of the approach of the goal of our journey, Easter, and the necessity of increased attention to our preparation for its worthy celebration.

A prayer composed of a collect from the Ambrosian rite together with a passage from a sermon of Leo the Great is appointed in the Roman sacramentary for Monday in the fifth full week in Lent.

> O God, by whose amazing grace we are enriched with every blessing: Grant us so to pass from the old life of sin to the new life in Christ, that we may be made ready for the glory of your heavenly kingdom; through Jesus Christ our Lord....

The prayer reminds us of the purpose of Lenten discipline: the passage from the old life to the new.

The English translation of these three prayers is by Dean Dirk van Dissel.

Lazarus Saturday

The last Saturday before Holy Week in the calendar of the Eastern churches is observed as Lazarus Saturday. One week before the central liturgy of Christianity, the Great Vigil of the Resurrection, the calling back of Lazarus from the dead (John 11:1-45) is remembered in anticipation of the greater and more permanent victory of Christ over the forces of death. It is an ancient association. The pilgrim Egeria (ca. 381-384) describes a procession from Jerusalem to Bethany on the Saturday before Palm Sunday to the church erected over the tomb of Lazarus of Bethany. (In the current Western lectionary the story of Lazarus is heard on the Fifth Sunday in Lent in Year A.) Lazarus, recalled from the dead, resumed his life in this world, but he had to die again and return to the grave. Jesus, in a greater triumph, did not come back from the dead but rather, having entered the tomb, went through it and out the other side into new and unending life. He was raised never to die again (Rom. 6:9). Many Eastern Fathers see in the description of Lazarus emerging from the tomb still in his grave clothes an indication that he will need them again. Jesus, on the other hand, they note, left his grave clothes in the tomb. The raising of Lazarus, especially when proclaimed on this last Saturday before Holy Week and exactly one week before the Easter Vigil, prefigures not only the resurrection of Christ but also the new life of each of the baptized and the general resurrection of all the dead. With the assurance of the declaration that Jesus gives life to the dead we are prepared to enter the Great and Holy Week.

6

The Great and Holy Week

AS LENT HAD developed through the centuries, there had come to be an impressive progression as the season unfolded. There were three Sundays of preparation, Pre-Lent. Then Lent itself began with Ash Wednesday and continued for four Sundays, the fourth of which, called Laetare ("rejoice"), marked a lightening of the severity of the discipline before the final effort, the two weeks of Passiontide, itself intensified in the second week, Holy Week, and that week intensified in its final days, Maundy Thursday and Good Friday. There had been some criticism of such a prolonged period of Easter preparation as more and more difficult to observe in an increasingly secular and busy world. Some[1] suggested the compression of Lent into its final two weeks, Passiontide. In 1955 the Roman Catholic Church, motivated by pastoral as well as liturgical and historical principles, revised its rites for Holy Week.[2] The revised rites commended themselves to Anglicans and Lutherans, and many parishes beyond the Roman Catholic Communion adopted them in whole or in part. The drama of Palm Sunday was made more vivid; Good Friday more forceful; and most of all the Easter Vigil was restored to the evening of Holy Saturday and its rich meaning became powerfully clear.

Holy Week is called in the East "Great Week," the name explained by John Chrysostom as referring to "the great things wrought at this time by the Lord." This central week of the Christian year is the Church's way of proclaiming and reexperiencing the events that changed the world. The purpose of religion is to push back the boundaries of the world, to expand the horizon of reality, to enlarge our view. From a limited human perspective the world has not changed after the death and resurrection of Christ. But the Great and Holy Week enlarges our understanding of what went on then and what continues to go on in the present time. The combat between death and life occurs in places and ways one might not expect. It is, Bishop Melito of Sardis (d. ca. 190) said, "the Passover mystery which is Christ."[3]

This week above all other weeks of the year is celebrated with remarkably rich liturgical actions that enhance and reinforce the biblical texts. The preacher has abundant help in proclaiming the central message of Christianity: the liturgies and the readings mutually interpret each other.

The Sunday of the Passion

Holy Week begins with the Sunday of the Passion. *Now,* Passiontide begins, the intense and exclusive concentration on the suffering and death of our Lord Jesus Christ. In the former calendar Passiontide was a two-week period. The Roman Catholic revision of the calendar and lectionary following the Second Vatican Council reduced the medieval two-week Passiontide to one week, the Holy Week. In the present calendar, the focus of Lent is Holy Baptism and its implications for daily living, including almsgiving, fasting, and prayer, the disciplines of the Christian life. Holy Week is the appropriate time to concentrate attention on the cross. This attention is intense, limited to one week instead of two, and it is exclusive, for no other celebrations are appropriate during this time. No holy days that fall during this week are celebrated, no weddings. All that can be postponed is moved out of these seven days (and also the next seven, Easter Week) to make room for the concentrated meditation and reflection upon the suffering and death of the Son of God.

The liturgies of Holy Week have their inspiration in third- and fourth-century Jerusalem, where great effort was made to follow the last days of Jesus's earthly life by visiting the holy places connected with his final actions, following step by step, incident by incident through the Great Week.[4] Egeria, a woman thought to be a nun or an abbess, perhaps from Spain or Gaul, who traveled to the Holy Land ca. 381-384, has left a diary describing in significant detail the services in Jerusalem in which she participated daily and Sunday, during Epiphany, Holy Week, Easter, and Pentecost. Her description of Palm Sunday indicates that it was celebrated as just that: the entry of Jesus into Jerusalem, reenacted with a procession from the Mount of Olives. About five in the afternoon the Gospel passage is read "in which the children bearing palms and branches came forth to meet the Lord, saying, 'Blessed is he who comes in the Name of the Lord.'" The bishop, surrounded by children of all ages and accompanied by "distinguished ladies and men of consequence" on foot, all carrying psalms or branches of olive, at a leisurely pace rides down from the mount and into the city "as far as the Anastasis," the location of the resurrection. There vespers is sung, "a prayer is said at the Cross" (the site of the crucifixion), and the people are dismissed. The procession with palms was imitated in Spain in the fifth century, in Gaul by the seventh century, in England by the beginning of the eighth century.

The procession began at some place outside the main church and moved into the church building, which was symbolically Jerusalem. In the early Middle Ages the focus of the procession was the Book of the Gospels, representing the presence of Christ; it was later supplemented by carrying relics of holy people. In England and Normandy the focus was the Host itself, Christ present among his processing people. In Germany a *Palmesel* (palm donkey), a wooden donkey on wheels with the figure of Jesus on its back portrayed the Lord's presence. The people carried palm branches or branches of evergreen or catkin willows (pussy willows) or other spring shrubs, as signs of life, hope, and victory,[5] showing, among other things, the participation of the natural world in acclaiming its king. In Luke's account (19:39-40) Jesus responds to the Pharisees' insistence that he tell his disciples to cease their messianic acclamation, "I tell you, if these were silent, the stones would shout out." Richard Wilbur's hymn "A stable lamp is lighted" promises the participation of the cosmos, "The stars shall bend their voices,/And every stone shall cry."[6]

In Rome the observance of the final Sunday of Lent, called "the Sunday of the Lord's Passion" was marked by the reading of St. Matthew's passion account (Matt. 26-27). At the end of the seventh century and in the eighth the name "Palm Sunday" (*dies palmarum*,[7] the day of palms) is given to the day, although the procession was not introduced in Rome until the eleventh century. Throughout the Middle Ages, flowers were blessed along with palm and olive branches[8]; the custom suggested, among other things, that beauty, like the glad welcome by the people on that Sunday, is transient.

The anticipatory joy of the procession finds a place in the Daily Office as well as at the entrance of the Mass. At first vespers on the eve of the final Sunday in Lent, the antiphon on the Magnificat is

> Praise to our king, the Son of David,
>   the Redeemer of the world;
> praise to the Savior,
>   whose coming had been foretold by the prophets.[9]

At morning prayer the references to the procession are more explicit. A psalm antiphon asks,

God grant that with the angels and the children
  we may be faithful and sing with them to the conqueror of death:
Hosanna in the highest.[10]

The reference to the children, prominent in Egeria's description, is also found
in the refrain of the familiar ninth-century processional hymn:

All glory, laud, and honor to thee, Redeemer, King!
To whom the lips of children made sweet hosannas ring.

The children do not appear in the familiar accounts of the procession read
at the blessing of the palms, but they appear a few verses later in Matthew's
account, repeating joyfully, as children do, what they have just heard others saying, "Hosanna to the Son of David" (21:15-16). The antiphon on the
Benedictus in Morning Prayer extends the invitation to take up branches and
join the angels and children.

With palms let us welcome the Lord as he comes,
with songs and hymns let us run to meet him,
as we offer him our joyful worship and sing:
  Blessed be the Lord![11]

What for many centuries had been known and observed as Palm Sunday has
in the present calendar been transformed into the Sunday of the Passion. The
palm ceremonies, especially the procession with palms and other branches, a
popular and conspicuous feature of this Sunday, dramatizing the triumphal
entry of Jesus into Jerusalem for the culmination of his ministry, are now in
all the rites clearly a prelude to the Eucharist, an overture to the events of the
Great Week. The procession is an act of praise to Christ the King, a sovereign
who reigns and triumphs paradoxically on the tree of the cross. The procession is also an expression of willingness to take up the cross and to follow
the Lord of glory along the way of sorrows, through death to the life that lies
beyond. This dramatic introduction to the week is an announcement of the
theme of victory over the forces of sin and death, which is the grand and over-
arching theme of this Great Week.

This week is the culmination of God's coming to humanity in power and
might, concealed in humility and apparent weakness (2 Cor. 12:9). It is this
humility that paradoxically *reveals* the might of God. The triumphant and victorious King rides not on a horse, not in a chariot, but on a beast of burden, a
donkey. Such is God's way of working the transformation of the world.

If this story of Palm Sunday is all that we know, we cannot yet understand it. We need the events of the entire week, taken together, to be able to see the meaning of what Jesus was acting out in this entrance into the city. What was said of his first followers applies equally to us all: "His disciples did not understand these things at first; but when Jesus was glorified, then they remembered that these things had been written of him and had been done to him" (John 12:16).

The procession with palms, therefore, is but the introduction to the chief purpose of this Lord's Day: the proclamation of the passion of Christ read from one of the synoptic Gospels. On this day of resurrection we read about how Jesus died. The story of the death is not reserved until Good Friday. In the richness of the liturgical year we are not just walking in Jesus's steps from entrance (Sunday) to controversy (Monday and Tuesday) to betrayal (Wednesday) to the Holy Supper (Thursday) to death (Friday) to sleep in the tomb (Saturday) to resurrection (Sunday). We do that, but in a complex way, for today, the Sunday of the Passion, we ponder what it means that this lowly king came to die. The Advent hymn speaks with new and pointed relevance to us this day.

> Daughter of Zion, rise
> To meet thy lowly King.
> Nor let thy faithless heart despise
> The peace he comes to bring.[12]

The peace he brought was purchased at an immense price, as St. Paul reminded the Corinthians and us (1 Cor. 6:20, 7:23).

In the 1570 Roman Missal the blessing of palms, like the blessing of ashes on Ash Wednesday, was exceedingly elaborate and complex. There was an antiphon, a collect, a reading (Exod. 15:27; 16:1-7), a responsory, the Gospel (Matt. 21:1-9), a collect, the preface verses with the Sanctus, and six prayers of blessing. It was in fact a "dry Mass," a form imitating the order of the Mass but without the consecration of bread and wine, suggesting that the rite was once a separate liturgy at a separate location. In the present Roman sacramentary, the blessing is simple, clear, and straightforward, and it has commended itself to the Anglicans and Lutherans as well. The point of the blessing and procession is our going up with Jesus to the holy city. It is Christ's journey, together with his people, to Golgotha and the great central act of redemption there.[13]

An antiphon is sung or said at the beginning of the rite of blessing. The Book of Common Prayer (and the Lutheran rite) provides Luke 19:38, "Blessed is the King who comes in the name of the Lord. Peace in heaven and glory in the highest." It echoes the song of the angels at Christmas, tying together the birth and the death and resurrection. The Roman rite uses Matt. 21:9, "Hosanna to the Son of David! Blessed is he who comes in the name of the Lord! O King of Israel: Hosanna in the highest." The collect that follows marks the beginning of Holy Week. The Prayer Book (followed by the Lutheran books) uses the Collect, derived from the Gelasian sacramentary and the Sarum breviary, appointed in the 1928 American Prayer Book for Wednesday in Holy Week to begin the week of meditation on the passion. In the 1570 Roman Missal it was the prayer over the people on Monday in Holy Week.

> Assist us mercifully with your help, O Lord God of our salvation, that we may enter with joy upon the contemplation of those mighty acts, whereby you have given us life and immortality; through Jesus Christ our Lord.

Worthy of note is the joy that is to characterize the weeklong contemplation of the mighty acts of redemption, joy because the end is life. The Roman Missal provided this prayer at the beginning of the blessing:

> O God, whom to love with heart and mind is righteousness, multiply in us the gifts of thy transcendent grace; and since by thy Son's death thou hast given us hope of those things in which we believe, grant us by his resurrection to reach our journey's end.[14]

The prayer directs our attention to the goal of the Lenten pilgrimage and well as the end of the journey of our life.

The processional Gospel is read. There are slight variations in the verses selected, but the Revised Common Lectionary appoints these:

> Year A. Matt. 21:1-11
> Year B. Mark 11:1-11a
> Year C. Luke 19:28-40.
>   *or* John 12:12-16.

The detail given in Mark's and Luke's accounts, "a colt that has never been ridden," makes clear that the procession was to have a sacred character.[15]

Palms and other branches such as olive, pussy willow, and yew are then blessed so that they may be carried by the people in procession.[16] The procession, a demonstration of loyalty to Christ the King, is our entry with Jesus into Jerusalem. It also tells of resurrection and ascension, Jesus's entry into the heavenly Jerusalem, and so looks toward the final fulfillment of all that Jesus came to do.[17] This eschatological understanding explains why the "Palm Sunday Gospel" was appointed in the medieval lectionaries for the First Sunday in Advent. The hymn sung during the procession, which has become virtually one of the Propers for the day, is *Gloria, laus, et honor* "All glory, laud, and honor to thee Redeemer, King," composed by Bishop Theodulph of Orleans (ca. 750-821),[18] it is said, while he was imprisoned at Angers on a charge of conspiring against King Louis the Pious. The fine processional hymn describes the completeness and universality of the praise offered to the King of Israel, "David's royal Son."

> The company of angels is praising thee on high
> And mortal men and all things created make reply.

Angels and mortals, the Hebrews with their palms and we in our time, together with all created things, the paving stones and the carpeting branches, all join in impressive melody. The hymn recognizes that we know more of the story than did the people who then accompanied Jesus: we know that soon will come the crucifixion and after it the resurrection and glorification of Jesus.

> To thee before thy passion they sang their hymns of praise;
> To thee, now high exalted, our melody we raise.

Another hymn that enhances the procession is "Ride on, ride on in majesty" by Henry Hart Milman (1791-1868), a powerful hymn that captures the drama of the day.[19] The majesty of Christ's entrance into his city is contrasted with the manner of his entry.

> Ride on! Ride on in majesty!
> Hark! All the tribes hosanna cry;
> Thy humble beast pursues his road
> With palms and scattered garments strowed.

"The whole occasion is filled with dramatic irony, because as the hymn is sung, the conclusion of the story is clearly in the singer's mind."[20] We are allowed to forget neither the tragedy nor the victory. The hymn, although filled with foreboding, looks beyond the triumphal entry and "the approaching sacrifice" to the resurrection and ascension. The coming death will be in fact a triumph.

Ride on! Ride on in majesty!
In lowly pomp ride on to die;
O Christ, thy triumphs now begin
O'er captive death and conquered sin.

The angels knew then what we know now, but even they were unable to prevent what was beginning to take place.

Ride on! Ride on in majesty!
The wingèd squadrons of the sky
Look down with sad and wondering eyes
To see the approaching sacrifice.

The road leads to death, but beyond it the Father awaits the return of his Son to the place he left to engage in this combat.

Ride on! Ride on in majesty!
Thy last and fiercest strife is nigh;
The Father on his sapphire throne
Expects his own anointed Son.

The approaching death is the path to glory.

Ride on! Ride on in majesty!
In lowly pomp ride on to die;
Bow thy meek head to mortal pain,
Then take, O God, thy power, and reign.

When the procession enters the church, it is in Jerusalem.

The mood abruptly changes from a major to a minor key; the liturgical color changes from bright red to oxblood, showing the kingship of Christ, whose hour of glorification has come and who is soon to reign from the tree of the cross, and showing, too, the Church's joy in the Lord's great work for the life of the world. The Mass of the Passion begins directly with the Collect of the Day used in all three Western liturgical traditions (Roman, Anglican, Lutheran). It is translated in the Book of Common Prayer:

Almighty and everliving God, in your tender love for the human race
you sent your Son our Savior Jesus Christ to take upon him our nature,
and to suffer death upon the cross, giving us the example of his great

humility: Mercifully grant that we may walk in the way of his suffering, and also share in his resurrection; through Jesus Christ our Lord, who lives and reigns with you and the Holy Spirit, one God, for ever and ever.

The prayer is from the Gelasian and Gregorian sacramentaries, inspired by the traditional Epistle for this Sunday, Phil. 2:5-11, the hymn on the humility of Christ. Luther Reed calls this "a noble and beautiful prayer which perfectly summarizes the divine plan of redemption."[21] The words "in your tender love for the human race" were added by Archbishop Cranmer in his translation (1549); he also replaced "may deserve to have" with what is now rendered "walk" and "share" to avoid the suggestion of merit, which was a principal issue of the Reformation. Massey Shepherd comments that "This Collect is the nearest thing to a statement of the doctrine of the Atonement to be found in the Prayer Book, and it is significant that it associates it with Christ's Incarnation no less than his Passion."[22] The collect is closely kin to the appointed Epistle, Phil. 2:5-11, in which both the incarnation and the passion are aspects of the humiliation of Christ, "who, though he was in the form of God, did not regard equality with God something to be exploited, but emptied himself, taking the form of a slave, being born in human likeness. And being found in human form, he humbled himself and became obedient to the point of death—even death on a cross." This emptying himself of his divine glory and privilege is not just to be wondered at; it is to be imitated by those who call him Lord, for the way of the cross is the path to life.

The focus of the Mass is the reading of the long (two-chapter) Passion Gospel. The first and second lessons and the intervening Psalm are the same in each of the three years of the lectionary cycle; only the Gospel selection changes so that all three synoptic accounts are read in the three-year period. From medieval times until the revision of the lectionary in 1970, Matthew's Passion was read on Palm Sunday, Mark's on Tuesday in Holy Week, Luke's on Wednesday, and John's on Good Friday.

> Year A-B-C. Isa. 50:4-9a. Humiliation and vindication of the Servant
>   Psalm 31:9-16. Prayer for deliverance
>   Phil. 2:5-11. Christ's humiliation and exaltation
> Year A. Matthew 26:14-27:66. The Matthew Passion
> Year B. Mark 14:1-15:47. Mark's Passion account
> Year C. Luke 22:14-23:56. Luke's Passion account.

In many places, to bring the long reading to life, parts are assigned in a dramatic reading, the people taking their part in the story.

The Roman sacramentary provides a separate proper preface for each Sunday in Lent. For the Sunday of the Passion the preface is, in the English translation of the Roman sacrmentary introduced in 2011,

> ...though he was innocent, he suffered willingly for sinners,
> and accepted unjust condemnation to save the guilty.
> His Death has washed away our sins,
> and his Resurrection has purchased our justification.

Anglican and Lutheran liturgies provide a proper Preface for Holy Week. The Book of Common Prayer provides this:

> through Jesus Christ our Lord. For our sins he was lifted high upon the cross, that he might draw the whole world to himself; and, by his suffering and death, he became the source of eternal salvation for all who put their trust in him.

The biblical references are John 12:32 and Heb. 5:8-9. The preface, new to the 1979 Prayer Book, is based on the 1929 Scottish revision of the Prayer Book. The *Lutheran Book of Worship* appoints as the Preface of the Passion the Gregorian Preface of the Cross that had in previous Lutheran use been appointed for the entire season of Lent:

> through Christ our Lord, who on the tree of the cross gave salvation to all, that, where death began, there life might be restored, and that he, who by a tree once overcame, might by a tree be overcome.

The translation used in the Lutheran Common Service from 1888 until 1978, it may be noted, was addressed to the Father, who is credited with giving salvation on the cross, and making clear that the victory over death and Satan was won "through Christ our Lord."

> O Lord, holy Father, Almighty, Everlasting God: who on the Tree of the cross didst give salvation unto mankind; that whence death arose, thence life also might rise again; and that he who by a tree once overcame, might likewise by a tree be overcome, through Christ our Lord.

In the (Lutheran) *Church Book* of 1868, the translation was through Jesus Christ, Thy dear Son, our Lord and Saviour; who for the redemption of our sinful race was lifted up upon the Cross; to the end that where death began, there also life might be restored; that he who overcame at the tree of the garden should also be overcome on the tree of the Cross.

The ancient preface relates the tree of the cross (Acts 10:39) to the tree in the garden of paradise that Satan used to bring death into the world through the disobedience of the first human beings. "He who by a tree once overcame" is to be understood as the devil, whose name the Church does not deign to speak as the holiest part of the Eucharist begins, overcome by the death of Christ on the tree of life. Behind this remarkable Preface is a complex of medieval legends that traced the wood of the cross back through Jewish history to the Garden of Eden. The traditions vary greatly. In some, Adam brought wood from the tree of life or from the tree of the knowledge of good and evil when he was expelled from Eden and used it as his staff throughout his life. Others say that Adam, dying, had his son Seth return to the Garden to beg from the sentinel angel balsam to relieve the agony of death. Seth received three seeds of the tree of life, which he put in Adam's mouth at his burial. Three trees—cedar, cypress, and pine—grew and merged into a single trunk. The wood became Moses's rod; it became a beam in Solomon's temple; it made its way to Joseph's carpenter's shop where Judas acquired it and eventually turned it over to the Roman executioners. Other accounts have the wood discarded by Solomon's builders because they found it unworkable, and they buried it where the Pool of Bethesda was later dug, giving the pool its miraculous qualities. When Jesus was condemned to die, the wood rose to the surface of the pool and was taken by the Roman soldiers for Jesus's cross.[23] The core of the legends is that the very wood of the forbidden tree was used to fashion the cross of the Second Adam. The legends thus proclaimed in a memorable way the essential point of the death of Christ. According to another insightful legend, Adam's bones were buried under what was to become Golgotha, "the place of a skull," and at the death of Christ the Second Adam, the rock split open to expose the bones of the first Adam. Thus, Adam's skull is frequently found at the foot of medieval crucifixes and shown in Byzantine icons, "for as all die in Adam, so all will be made alive in Christ" (1 Cor. 15:22). What was lost through the disobedience of the first Adam was restored through the obedience, even to death, of the second Adam. The fall and the restoration, paradise lost and paradise regained, are to be understood together.

A powerful hymn that has passed from Latin through German to English ponders the meaning of the crucifixion. A long medieval poem, *Salve mundi salutare*, addresses the various parts of the body of Christ hanging on the cross from the point of view of a disciple kneeling before the cross or crucifix and slowly raising the eyes to the feet, then the knees, the hands, the side, the breast, the heart, and finally daring to look into the face of the dying man. The hymn has been attributed to St. Bernard of Clairvaux (1091-1153), although the earliest known appearance of the poem is in fourteenth- and fifteenth-century manuscripts.[24] Luther thought highly of Bernard, and in the mid-seventeenth century (1676) Paul Gerhardt (1607-1676), the greatest of Lutheran hymn writers, translated the final part of the poem, which addressed the sacred head of Christ, *Salve, caput crucentatum*, into German, *O Haupt voll Blut und Wunden*. In 1830 an American Presbyterian minister who held the chairs of Rhetoric and Church History at Princeton University, James Waddell Alexander (1804-1859), produced an English translation that, slightly altered, has appealed to English-speaking Lutherans.[25]

> O sacred Head, now wounded,
>   With grief and shame weighed down!
> Now scornfully surrounded,
>   With thorns thine only crown:
> O sacred Head, what glory,
>   What bliss till now was thine!
> Yet, though despised and gory,
>   I joy to call thee mine.

The contrasts continue in the second stanza, culminating in the concluding assertion of the singers' guilt.

> How art thou pale with anguish,
>   With sore abuse and scorn;
> How does that visage languish
>   Which once was bright as morn!
> Thy grief and bitter passion
>   Were all for sinners' gain;
> Mine, mine was the transgression,
>   But thine the deadly pain.

Language fails in the attempt to express proper gratitude for what Christ has done, and the only response is to ask for a still further gift: continued love for the "dearest friend" to correspond to his endless concern for us.

What language shall I borrow,
  To thank thee, dearest friend,
For this thy dying sorrow,
  Thy pity without end?
O make me thine for ever,
  And should I fainting be,
Lord, let me never, never
  Outlive my love to thee.

Christ's death leads inevitably to thoughts of our own last hour. It was an old custom in the Church, still in use among Lutherans in the seventeenth century, to put a crucifix in the hands of a dying person as a focus of devotional meditation and consolation.

Be near when I am dying,
  O show thy Cross to me!
And, for my succor flying,
  Come, Lord, to set me free.
These eyes, new faith receiving,
  From thee shall never move;
For he who dies believing
  Dies safely in thy love.[26]

The hymn is sung to the tune "Passion Chorale" (*Herzlich tut mich verlangen*), written about 1600 by Hans Leo Hassler (1564-1612) for a love song, "Mein Gmüt ist mir verwirret, das macht ein Jungfrau zart," and attached in 1613 to a funeral hymn by Christoph Knoll, "Herzlich thut mich verlangen,"[27] from which is derived the name of the tune. The tune was combined with Gerhardt's text in Johann Crüger's *Praxis Pietatis Melica*, 1656. The tune was a favorite of Johann Sebastian Bach and was used five times in his St. Matthew Passion.[28]

The Prayer over the People for the Sunday of the Passion (Roman sacramentary) and through Maundy Thursday (Episcopal *Book of Occasional Services*) is, "Almighty God, we pray you graciously to behold this your family, for whom our Lord Jesus Christ was willing to be betrayed, and given into the hands of sinners, and to suffer death upon the Cross; who lives and reigns for ever and ever." The prayer is from the Gregorian sacramentary and was the Collect appointed for Good Friday in the Lutheran liturgies.

The historical commemoration of Palm Sunday soon gives way to the larger and more comprehensive contemplation of the Passion of Christ as a whole. Throughout this week there is less emphasis on a day-to-day chronology than one might expect. This is partly because the chronology is uncertain, but most of all it is because the passage from death to life must be taken as a whole story and proclamation. In the Roman Catholic calendar, Monday, Tuesday, and Wednesday in Holy Week are treated simply as ferias (weekdays) in Lent; the liturgical color is violet. In the Eastern churches the Great and Holy Week is considered a separate unit and is not counted as part of the forty days, which conclude on the evening of the Sixth Friday in Great Lent. In Anglican and Lutheran use also, Holy Week is treated separately from the preceding weeks of Lent, having its own character;[29] the liturgical color is crimson.

For all the somberness of this Great Week, the names given the Book of Common Prayer (until 1979) to its various days, Sunday through Thursday, look beyond the passion to its victorious goal. "The Sunday next before Easter, commonly called Palm Sunday"; "Monday before Easter"; "Tuesday before Easter"; "Wednesday before Easter"; "Thursday before Easter, commonly called Maundy Thursday." Friday, as everywhere in the English-speaking Western tradition, is simply "Good Friday"; Saturday is "Easter Even."

Monday in Holy Week

On Monday in[30] Holy Week, the chronological commemoration observed liturgically, Mary anointing the feet of Jesus, is described in the appointed Gospel as taking place "six days before the Passover." Monday is not six days before the Passover that was celebrated by Jesus on Thursday of this week (or Friday in John's chronology). Monday is, however, six days before Easter Day, the Christian Passover, and this explains how the phrase and event are to be understood in its liturgical setting.

The traditional Introit (*Judica, Domine*) draws upon Psalm 35:1-3, a psalm for God's help by a person who is persecuted and falsely accused.

> *Antiphon.* Contend, O Lord, with those who contend with me;
> fight against those who fight against me!
> Take hold of shield and buckler, and rise up to help me!
> > *Psalm.* Draw the spear and javelin against my pursuers;
> > Say to my soul, "I am your salvation." *Gloria Patri.*
> *The Antiphon is repeated:* Contend, O Lord...help me!

The voice of Christ is heard imploring his Father to stand up for him metaphorically, pleading the case of his innocence, and literally, taking up the shield and standing between him and the enemy. The great battle is about to be joined.

The Collect in Roman Catholic and Lutheran use is from the Gregorian sacramentary. In the Lutheran translation, used from 1868 to 1978, it is:

> Grant, we beseech thee almighty God, that we, who amid so many adversities do fail through our own infirmities, may be restored through the Passion and Intercession of thine only-begotten Son, who liveth and reigneth....

Paul Strodach comments on the contrast between our adversities and His; "that we fail, and fail so terribly, through our reliance, so often misplaced on our own strength in our own will, is all the more sharply brought home to us as we pray and think of Him....[I]n these hours we can only think of ourselves as failures when we find ourselves in His Company; and only as strong to endure or able to overcome in and through Him Who has loved us and given Himself for us."[31] Canon Joseph W. Poole has unpacked the terse Latin in his translation of the Collect:

> Grant, we beseech thee, Almighty God, that we, who in our times of trial often grow weak and falter, may take heart again and find new strength, seeing that Christ is his Passion has offered for us the obedience we are too frail to offer thee; through the same Jesus Christ....[32]

The Book of Common Prayer uses a Collect written by William Reed Huntington in 1882 (the passage "went not up to joy...before he was crucified" was taken from the exhortation formerly contained in the Visitation of the Sick and is therefore probably by Cranmer) and which was introduced into the 1928 American Prayer Book.

> Almighty God, whose most dear Son went not up to joy but first he suffered pain, and entered not into glory before he was crucified,: Mercifully grant that we, walking in the way of the cross, may find it none other than the way of life and peace; through Jesus Christ, your Son our Lord....

It is an elegant statement of the necessity of cross before crown and the paradox of the way of the cross being the only way of life and peace. Massey Shepherd comments, "Notice the fine balance between 'joy' and 'glory' at the end of our Lord's *via dolorosa,* and 'life and peace' at the end of ours."[33]

A Responsory in the Office of Readings declares,

> We worship your cross, O Lord;
> we recall your glorious passion.
>> Have mercy on us for whose sake you endured so much.
> You have redeemed us with your precious blood;
> hear the prayer of your servants, and come to our help.
>> Have mercy on us for whose sake you endured so much.[34]

The focus is relentlessly on the crucifixion.

The Revised Common Lectionary appoints one set of readings for all three years of the lectionary cycle.

> Isa. 42:1-9. The gentle servant, a light to the nations
> Psalm 36:5-11. The priceless love of God
> Heb. 9:11-15. Christ the High Priest enters the Holy Place
> John 12:1-11. Mary anoints Jesus six days before the Passover.

The Gospels have little concern for exact historical chronology, and so, while there have been attempts to assign various activities of Jesus to particular days of Holy Week, the actual events of Monday, Tuesday, and Wednesday remain uncertain. But that is no defect in Scripture or in liturgy. This week, to say it once again, is not primarily a chronological walking with Jesus from triumphal entry to crucifixion to burial to resurrection. It is rather an intense meditation on the meaning and significance of Jesus's passion and death. That meditation, which began on Sunday, continues with varying emphases on the succeeding days of Holy Week.

Tuesday in Holy Week

The traditional Introit for Tuesday in Holy Week (*Nos autem*) is unusual in having a passage from the New Testament as its antiphon, Gal. 6:14. The Lutheran liturgy uses it straight (in the Authorized Version, "God forbid that I should glory: save in the Cross…"); the Roman rite, as it is wont to do, paraphrases slightly ("We should glory in the cross….") The second part of the antiphon is not from the Bible, although it is surely biblical, and is an example of "farsing," the medieval custom of taking a phrase and enlarging upon it, as was not uncommonly done with the Kyrie.

> *Antiphon.* We should glory in the cross of our Lord Jesus Christ. In him is salvation, life, and resurrection from the dead: by him we are redeemed and set at liberty.

Psalm 67:1. May God be gracious to us and bless us and make his face to shine upon us. *Gloria Patri.*
The antiphon is repeated: We should glory... set at liberty.

The focus is now on our response to the deeds of the Great and Holy Week; we should glory, boast, rejoice, for by this dread sacrifice we have life and salvation, redemption and freedom from slavery to sin. The other Propers continue the thought.

The Collect for Tuesday in Holy Week in the Roman and Lutheran rites is from the Gregorian sacramentary. In the English translation of the Lutheran *Common Service* of 1888 it is:

Almighty and everlasting God, grant us grace so to contemplate the Passion of our Lord, that we may find therein forgiveness for our sins; through the same Jesus Christ our Lord....

The *Church Book* (1868) had its own translation:

Almighty and Everlasting God, Grant us grace so to pass through this holy time of our Lord's Passion, that we may obtain pardon of our sins; through the same, Thy Son....

The prayer may seem bland (Luther Reed noted "In the terse Latin of the original the prayer has more strength and meaning than the colorless English translation indicates.") Paul Strodach pondered the meaning, "The Collect turns our hearts to the true use of these hours—the most fruitful use—contemplation. This means quiet, devout meditation... and then if contemplation has borne its fruit, comes consecration... [I]n the fullness of communion with our dear Lord one finds what it means when the heart knows the forgiveness of sins!"[35]

The Prayer Book appoints a collect from the 1928 Proposed English Prayer Book for Holy Cross Day.

O God, by the passion of your blessed Son you made an instrument of shameful death to be for us the means of life: Grant us so to glory in the cross of Christ, that we may gladly suffer shame and loss for the sake of your Son our Savior Jesus Christ; who lives and reigns....

The petition echoes Gal. 6:14, the antiphon of the historic Introit, retaining its theme, even though the Introits were never included in the Prayer Book.

The Revised Common Lectionary appoints one set of lessons for all three years of the lectionary cycle.

Isa. 49:1-7. The mission of the Servant of God
Psalm 71:1-14. You are my hope
1 Cor. 1:18-31. We proclaim Christ crucified, the power of God
John 12:20-36. "The hour has come for the Son of Man to be glorified."

In the later medieval period, the Gospel was the reading of St. Mark's Passion (chapters 14-15).

Wednesday in Holy Week

On Wednesday in Holy Week, according to one way of reading the Synoptic chronology ("two days before the Passover" Mark 14:1; Matt. 26:2), Judas "went to the chief priests in order to betray" Jesus to them and receive their promise of money (Mark 14:10-12; Matt. 26:14-16; Luke 22:3-6). Because Judas became a clandestine agent for the governing authorities, Wednesday in Holy Week became known as "Spy Wednesday." The tradition that gave rise to the nickname is preserved in the Gospel appointed in the Roman Catholic lectionary and in the alternative Gospel in the Book of Common Prayer (Matt. 26:1-5, 14-25, "Judas Iscariot went to the chief priests and said, 'What will you give me if I betray him to you?' They paid him thirty pieces of silver.")

The traditional Introit (*In Nomine Jesu*), as if to answer those who are plotting against Jesus, declares his supreme authority. The antiphon is drawn from the glorious Epistle of the Sunday of the Passion, Phil. 2:10, 8b, 11b.

Antiphon. At the Name of Jesus every knee should bend, in heaven and on earth and under the earth, for he became obedient to the point of death—even death on a cross; wherefore he is Lord, to the glory of God the Father.

> *Psalm 102:1.* Hear my prayer, O Lord; let my cry come to you.
> *Gloria Patri.*

The antiphon is repeated: At the Name...God the Father.

In the liturgy, the passion is never proclaimed without at least an undercurrent of triumph. Jesus's death is in fact his victory.

The Collect in the Roman and Lutheran rites is Gregorian. In the translation made for the 1868 Lutheran *Church Book* it is

> Grant, we beseech thee, Almighty God, that we, who for our evil deeds are continually afflicted, may mercifully be relieved [better, "set free"] by the Passion of thine Only-begotten Son, who liveth and reigneth....

"One cannot help but note the utter simplicity and restraint of the Collect. There are so many things crowding in, so many things to pray for, but this simple little prayer 'collects' and carries all our ills to the One and Only Source of healing. Its lesson is most salutary. Sin is SIN—the sin that crucified our Lord; the sin that condemned the soul, that sin that always carries its penalty.... The reality of this pleading seeks the merciful relief: the rescue, the healing, the salvation of His Passion."[36]

The Book of Common Prayer appoints the collect proposed for the 1892 Book of Common Prayer and included in the 1928 book on Tuesday in Holy Week.

> Lord God, whose blessed Son our Savior gave his body to be whipped and his face to be spit upon: Give us grace to accept joyfully the sufferings of the present time, confident of the glory that shall be revealed; through Jesus Christ your Son our Lord, who lives and reigns....

The prayer recalls Isa. 50:6 (see the First Lesson); Isa. 53; Rom. 8:18. Its author is unknown.

The Revised Common Lectionary appoints one set of readings for all three years of the lectionary cycle.

> Isa. 50:4-9a. The Servant's humiliation and vindication
> Psalm 70. A cry of distress
> Heb. 12:1-3. Jesus disregarded the shame of the cross
> John 13:21-32. Jesus foretells his betrayal.

In the medieval period, the Gospel was the reading of St. Luke's passion account (chapters 22-23).

In previous Roman Catholic use, still preserved in some Anglican and Lutheran parishes, the service of Tenebrae ("shadows" or darkness) began on Wednesday night and continued on Thursday and Friday evenings. It was a special form of Matins and Lauds, taken as one office, for the last three days of Holy Week, until 1955 in the Roman Church sung in anticipation (that is, earlier than the appointed morning time) on the three preceding evenings. Such anticipation was common when the Liturgy of the Hours had broken loose from its ties to particular times throughout the day. The service itself was quite dramatic,[37] involving the extinguishing of the lights in the church one by one. Fifteen candles were placed in a stand called a "hearse" set before the altar; one candle was extinguished at the end of the singing of each Psalm until only the one at the apex of the triangular hearse remained. This candle was then hidden behind the altar at the end of the Benedictus (the Gospel canticle at Lauds, Morning Praise), signifying Jesus's death. After a time of silence, a loud noise was made (often with a wooden clapper) suggesting the rending of the tomb, and the candle was returned in silence to its place on the hearse. After the reforms of the Holy Week liturgy the hours were no longer anticipated, and modifications to Tenebrae were introduced. Several texts from the service remain in the 1971 Liturgy of the Hours for Good Friday and Holy Saturday.

The extra-liturgical devotion, the Stations of the Cross, or the Way of the Cross, is frequently prayed during Holy Week. See chapter 5, p. 152.

Maundy Thursday

Thursday in Holy Week, as the day was called in the English-speaking Lutheran tradition until 1978, has been known by many names. It has carried the title *Dies natalis Eucharistae,* the birthday of the Eucharist; *Natalis calixis,* the birthday of the chalice; *Dies panis,* the day of the Bread; *Dies Mysteriorum,* the day of the [sacred] Mysteries; *Dies Pedilavii,* the day of the foot-washing. Since the time of St. Augustine it has been *Coena Domini,* [the day of] the Lord's Supper. It has also been called Holy Thursday, a name sometimes also given to Ascension Day. In increasing ecumenical use, the day is known, as it has been since the seventh century, as Maundy Thursday, from *mandatum,* commandment, mandate, from Jesus's saying at the Supper, *Mandatum novum do vobis,* "I give you a new commandment, love one another" (John 13:34).

It is a complex day. In Rome in the seventh century, as evidenced by the Gelasian sacramentary, there were three masses: one for the reconciliation of penitents, another for the consecration of holy oils, and a third for the commemoration of the institution of the Eucharist. In the morning, then, and in present-day practice in Roman Catholic and Anglican cathedrals, there is the blessing of the oils for use at Baptisms at the Easter Vigil and also the reaffirmation of priestly vows.[38] During the day the penitents who had been expelled from the church on Ash Wednesday were reconciled to the community. The day was therefore called in German *Gründonnerstag*, "green Thursday," the green vestments worn on this day and the green branches given to the penitents alluding to vegetation that had withered because it had no root and lacked life-giving water now restored to life and health and growth as living green branches (see John 15:1ff).[39] In Dante's *Purgatorio* both the robes and the wings of the two guardian angels sent in response to the Compline hymn ("To you before the close of day") are "Green as a leaf at its first unfurling."[40] In the evening the Mass of the Lord's Supper is celebrated, commemorating the institution of the Eucharist.

Thursday was the first weekday in Holy Week to have a Eucharist. In fact, in Jerusalem, Egeria observes, there were two. This was also the case in North Africa in Augustine's time. Later the washing of feet, perhaps originally done on Holy Saturday, was added to the Thursday evening Mass.

The Triduum Begins

The evening Mass (Thursday evening being understood as the beginning of Friday) is the beginning of the *Triduum sacrum*, the sacred three days: three days treated as one, "one day made of three," the climax of the Great Week and the central celebration of the entire Church year proclaiming the heart and center of the Christian faith. These three days are the high holy days of Christianity. In them the essence of the faith is distilled in swiftly moving, dramatic events: supper, arrest, trial, judgment, crucifixion, burial, resurrection. Since Advent, everything has been moving toward the "hour," as Jesus called it; the remainder of the liturgical year flows from these central events. The cross and resurrection, understood together, stand at the center of the year and of all time. From now until the Great Vigil the voice of the bells and the sound of the organ are silenced, representing the final fast of Lent, the "fast of the ears." The celebration emphasizes the primacy of the community and its intimacy: mutual forgiveness, absolution, reconciliation and peace, the service of one another. And the service of one another is led by the clergy, from the pope to the humblest parish priest.

At the Mass of the Lord's Supper, as it is called in the Roman sacramentary, the Introit is the same as the one used on Tuesday. The three rites each have a different Collect. The Book of Common Prayer has:

Almighty Father, whose dear Son, on the night before he suffered, instituted the Sacrament of his Body and Blood: Mercifully grant that we may receive it thankfully in remembrance of Jesus Christ our Lord, who in these holy mysteries gives us a pledge of eternal life; and who now lives and reigns....

The prayer was composed for the 1928 American Prayer Book incorporating phrases from the 1892 proposal, Cranmer's post-Communion collect (Rite I, p. 339), and the exhortation (p. 316) preparatory to the Eucharist.[41]

> The Roman sacramentary has a newly-composed prayer.
> O God, who have called us to participate in this most sacred Supper, in which your Only Begotten Son, when about to hand himself over to death, entrusted to the Church a sacrifice new for all eternity, the banquet of his love, grant, we pray, that we may draw from so great a mystery the fullness of charity and of life....

The style of the prayer, with its prolonged preamble and abbreviated petition, marks this as a recent composition.

The Lutheran rite uses the Collect that Thomas Aquinas wrote for the Feast of Corpus Christi. The prayer is addressed to Christ:

> O Lord God, who hast left unto us in a wonderful Sacrament a memorial of thy Passion: Grant, we beseech thee, that we may so use this Sacrament of thy Body and Blood, that the fruits of thy redemption may continually be manifest in us; who livest and reignest....

The translation was made for the 1868 *Church Book*. In the 1958 *Service Book and Hymnal* the verb "use" was replaced by "partake of."

The Revised Common Lectionary appoints one set of readings for all three years of the lectionary cycle.

> Exod. 12:1-4 (5-10), 11-14. The institution of the Passover
> Psalm 116:1-2, 12-19. Thanksgiving for deliverance from death
> 1 Cor. 11:23-26. The institution of the Lord's Supper
> John 13:1-17, 31b-35. The new commandment dramatized in the washing of feet.

After the Gospel is proclaimed, the washing of feet follows, acting out what has just been described. It is a powerful dramatization of humble and loving service, made more striking by its oddity in most modern cultures. In the previous Roman Missal and in present Anglican and Lutheran practice the action is accompanied by the singing of a ninth-century antiphon *Ubi caritas et amor, Deus ibi est,* translated by Omer Westendorf (pseudonym: J. Clifford Evers) as a hymn, "Where charity and love prevail" (*Lutheran Book of Worship* no. 126; *Hymnal 1982* no. 581) and by Joyce MacDonald Glover as "Where true charity and love dwell" (*Hymnal 1982* no. 606). The antiphon reflects the Epistle (1 Cor. 11:23-26), reminding us that we are to be united in love, especially at the celebration of the Holy Supper, and it reflects also Jesus's directive given in the Gospel, "I give you a new commandment, that you love one another. Just as I have loved you, you also should love one another. By this everyone will know that you are my disciples, if you have love for one another" (John 13:34-35).

> Where charity and love are, there is God.
>> The love of Christ has gathered us together.
>> Let us rejoice in him and be glad.
>> Let us fear and love the living God
>> and love one another with a sincere heart.
> Where charity and love are, there is God.
>> When therefore we are assembled,
>> let us take heed that we be not divided in mind.
>> Let malicious quarrels and contentions cease,
>> and let Christ our God dwell among us.
> Where charity and love are, there is God.
>> Let us also with the blessed see your face in glory,
>> O Christ our God,
>> there to possess an immense and happy joy
>> for infinite ages of ages. Amen

The present Roman sacramentary has reassigned the antiphon from the foot washing to the offertory of the Mass. There remain seven antiphons from the 1570 Roman Missal, rearranged and abbreviated, that may be sung during the foot washing. (1) "After the Lord had risen from supper he poured water into a basin and began to wash his disciples' feet: he left them this example" [see John 13:4, 5, 15]; (2) "The Lord Jesus, after eating supper with his disciples washed their feet and said to them, Know what I, your Lord and Master, have done for you: I have given you an example that you should do as I have done for you" [see John 13:12, 13, 15]; (3) "Lord, are you to wash my feet? Jesus answered and said to him, If I do not wash your feet you have no part in me. V. He came to Simon Peter who said to him, Lord, are you to wash my feet? V. You do not know now what I am doing, but later you will understand.

Lord, are you to wash my feet?" [John 13:6-8]; (4) "If I, your Lord and Master, have washed your feet, you also ought to wash one another's feet" [John 13:14]; (5) "By this everyone will know that you are my disciples, if you have love for one another. V. Jesus said to his disciples By this everyone will know that you are my disciples: if you have love for one another" [John 13:35]; (6) "I give you a new commandment, that you love one another as I have loved you, says the Lord" [John 13:34]; (7) "Let these three abide in you: faith, hope, and love; but the greatest of these is love" [1 Cor. 13:13].

In the Eucharistic prayer it is customary in some places to insert into the words of institution, following "in the night in which he was betrayed" a phrase indicating the contemporaneous character of the commemoration, "even this night." It is an anticipation of a similar understanding of the nature of ritual that will be proclaimed repeatedly in the Exsultet at the Easter Vigil, "This is the night."

As early as the time of Tertullian (ca. 160-ca. 225), some as a sign of their fasting refrained from exchanging the kiss of peace. (Tertullian condemned the omission of "the seal of prayer.")[42] Later, the Peace came to be omitted on Thursday, Friday, and Saturday[43] out of repugnance at Judas's treacherous kiss that betrayed Jesus to his enemies.[44]

At the Mass, sufficient Eucharistic elements are consecrated to serve for the Communion on Good Friday.

Following the celebration of the evening Mass, there is another dramatic action, the stripping of the altar. The custom had a practical origin. The altar was stripped of all its adornment so it could be washed in preparation for the Easter liturgies. The action inevitably took on a symbolic interpretation: the altar was stripped and left bare even as Jesus was stripped of his followers and led away under arrest for trial and judgment. A Psalm of desolation (Psalm 22 "My God, why have you forsaken me" or Psalm 88 "Darkness is my only companion") is sung as the altar is stripped of flower vases, candles, moveable crosses, linens, and paraments; lights in the church are dimmed. Indeed, everything moveable in the chancel is taken away. Not only are we to see Jesus alone and in darkness; we are to see the destruction of the church. At the conclusion of the demolition, everything that pertains to the life of the Church, even the Blessed Sacrament, has been removed and the building rendered empty and lifeless. It is no longer, in a liturgical sense, a church.[45] The Lamentations of Jeremiah, a traditional reading for Holy Week, takes on additional power as the destruction and desolation of the church makes the building like Jerusalem after it had been sacked and razed. Christians share with Jews the grief at the overwhelming emptiness. With sundown on Thursday, Good Friday has begun.

There is, therefore, no final hymn. The celebration of this evening does not conclude; it merely pauses for a time and will resume on Friday, for the liturgies of Thursday evening, Good Friday, and the Great Vigil of Easter are to be understood as one. The Church is celebrating one day made of three. An interesting expanding antiphon, derived from Phil. 2:8-9 and sung in place of the responsory, ties the Triduum together. At Maundy Thursday vespers it is

> For our sake Christ was obedient, accepting even death.[46]

On Good Friday at both Morning and Evening Prayer it becomes,

> For our sake Christ was obedient, accepting even death,
> death on a cross.[47]

And at Holy Saturday Morning Prayer it has become,

> For our sake Christ was obedient, accepting even death,
> death on a cross.
> Therefore God has highly exalted him,
> and bestowed on him the Name that is above every name.[48]

Good Friday

"Good Friday" is a peculiarly English and Dutch expression. It is "God's Friday," as "Good-bye" is derived from "God be with you." In early times the day was called *Pascha staurosimon*, the Pascha of the crucifixion, as Easter was *Pascha anastasimon*, the Pascha of resurrection. It was *Dies Domini Passionis*, the day of the Lord's passion. In German it is *Karfreitag*, Friday of mourning; it is Long Friday in Norway, Holy Friday in Latin nations, Great Friday among the Eastern Orthodox. In the Roman books it was simply *Feria sexta in Parasceve*, weekday six in the Preparation [Week], derived from the Greek *Parasceve*, from the Jewish Preparation for the Sabbath, as in Matt. 27:62; Mark 15:42; Luke 23:54; John 19:31, 42. In the present Roman Sacramentary it is Friday of the Lord's passion.

The central theme of this most solemn day is the cross, a word that in the New Testament reverberates with rich and manifold meaning. It is the instrument of death as well as the death itself, but the cross also speaks of sacrifice and self-giving love and perfect obedience and redemption and atonement. The cross also speaks of victory for it includes the resurrection; indeed it would be robbed of meaning without it. The cross is the essential content of Christian preaching (1 Cor. 1:17-18) and it stands at the heart of the Christian story (Gal. 6:12, 14). The complex meanings—death and life, defeat and victory—are perhaps no more compellingly set forth than in the passion according to St. John, which since ancient times has been appointed as the Gospel for Good Friday. It is fitting that this passion is read or chanted on this day every year. Its selection is more than a mechanical taking of the four Gospels in order as they were in medieval times (Matthew on Palm Sunday, Mark on Tuesday in Holy Week, Luke on Wednesday, John on Friday). John's Gospel, with its emphasis on the glory of the Son of God who moves majestically through these events, is another indication that the appropriate mood for Good Friday, God's Friday, is restrained celebration. In the judgment hall, Pilate is the prisoner and Jesus the judge. Jesus carries his own cross to the execution site as one who has power to lay down his life (John 10:17-18). Jesus dies on the cross, but as John tells the story, he dies with a shout of triumph on his lips, "It is finished"; his work is completed, consummated.[49] The redemption of the world has been accomplished, although at a fearsome cost.

The earliest witness to a fast on Friday as well as on Saturday is from the second-century Gospel according to the Hebrews and also Irenaeus of Lyons, who died ca. 202. In the third century the unitive understanding of Pascha was dividing into two parts: Pascha of Crucifixion and the Pascha of Resurrection. Friday eventually detached altogether from Pascha and became a commemoration of the death of Jesus. In the later fourth century in Jerusalem, Holy Week developed and Friday became the principal fast in the calendar.

The Roman Catholic and Lutheran rubrics are similar, noting the traditional time of the Good Friday Liturgy, about 3 in the afternoon, the traditional hour of Jesus's death. The setting is austere: the altar is bare, without cloths, candles, or cross. The color of the vestments is red/crimson. The Lutheran rubrics preserve a recognition of the fast of the ears by limiting the use of the organ.[50]

The Liturgy of the Passion and Death of the Lord, as the service is called in the Roman sacramentary, is a uniquely austere liturgy. The passion hymns associated with the day are profound and deeply moving.

The liturgy itself is characterized by a stark opening: silent entrance, prostration before the altar, and the praying of the opening collect. It is in fact a drastically simplified liturgy, close to the practice of the early days of Christianity. The Good Friday liturgy has three parts: the Mass of the Catechumens, the adoration of the crucified, and the Mass of the presanctified gifts.

The Mass of the Catechumens

The Mass of the Catechumens begins directly with the Collect. The Anglican and Lutheran rites use a Gregorian prayer:

> Almighty God, we pray you graciously to behold this your family, for whom our Lord Jesus Christ was willing to be betrayed, and given into the hands of sinners, and to suffer death upon the cross; who now lives and reigns....

In the Gregorian and Sarum sacramentaries it was a prayer over the people on Wednesday in Holy Week, hence the reference to betrayal. The Sarum rite also uses the prayer as the post-Communion for Good Friday.

The Roman sacramentary provides two opening prayers from the Gelasian sacramentary. Both appeared in William Bright's *Ancient Collects*, where they are translated:

> Remember your compassions, O Lord, and sanctify with eternal protection your servants, for whom Christ your Son by his blood appointed unto us the Paschal mystery; through the same Jesus Christ our Lord.

> O God, who by the Passion of your Christ our Lord dissolved that hereditary death of the ancient sin, to which the whole race of Adam's posterity had succeeded; grant that having been made conformable to him, as we by necessity of nature have borne the image of the earthly, so by the sanctification of grace we may bear the image of the Heavenly, even of Christ our Lord.[51]

Note the simplified termination as the liturgy is reduced to a minimum on this day.

The Revised Common Lectionary proves one set of lessons for all three years.

> Isa. 52:13-53:12. The suffering Servant
> Psalm 22. The psalm of the passion
> Heb. 10:16-25. Confidence to enter the sanctuary
>   or Heb. 4:14-16; 5:7-9. Jesus the Great High Priest
> [Before the Gospel the *Lutheran Book of Worship* appoints Paul
>   Gerhard's hymn "O sacred Head, now wounded."]
> John 18:1-19:42. The Passion according to St. John.

The choice of John is significant for two reasons. First, John in the traditional view was an eyewitness of the crucifixion, the one evangelist who was there.[52] Second, John understands the crucifixion as triumph: Jesus reigns from the cross as the King on his throne. Such was the ancient understanding of this day. One did not need to wait until Easter morning to see the victory. John Chrysostom preached,

> Have you seen the wonderful victory? Have you seen the splendid deeds of the Cross? Shall I tell you something still more marvelous? Learn in what way the victory was gained, and you will be even more astonished. For by the very means by which the devil had conquered, by these Christ conquered him; and taking up the weapons with which he had fought, he defeated him. Listen to how it was done.
>
> A virgin, a tree, and a death were the symbols of our defeat. The virgin was Eve; she had not yet known man; the tree was the tree of the knowledge of good and evil; and the death was Adam's penalty. But behold again a Virgin and a tree and a death, those symbols of defeat, become the symbols of his victory. For in place of Eve there is Mary; in place of the tree of the knowledge of good and evil, the tree of the Cross; in place of the death of Adam, the death of Christ.
>
> Do you see him defeated by the very things through which he had conquered? At the foot of the tree the devil overcame Adam; at the foot of the tree of the Cross Christ vanquished the devil. And that first tree sent men to Hades; this second one calls back even those who had already gone down there. Again, the former tree concealed man already despoiled and stripped; the second tree shows a naked victor on high for all to see. And that earlier death condemned those who were born after it; this second death gives life again to those who were born before it. Who can tell the Lord's mighty deeds? By death we were made immortal: these are the glorious deeds of the Cross.
>
> ...The Cross is the Father's will, the glory of the Only-begotten, the Spirit's exultation, the beauty of the angels, the guardian of the Church. Paul glories in the Cross; it is the rampart of the saints, it is the light of the whole world.[53]

The chanting of St. John's Passion on Good Friday had become traditional in the Church by the time of Egeria's visit to Jerusalem in the late fourth century; its use has been nearly universal since then. It is the most triumphant account of the crucifixion: the hour of Christ's death is the hour of his glorification. He dies with a cry of victory, *Consummatum est*, "It is accomplished!" That understanding and insight is reflected in the custom in the Western Church of genuflecting during the Nicene Creed. The knee is bent at the incarnation, "And was made man"; the people stand upright as they declare belief in the crucifixion. They genuflect to honor Christ's humility; they stand to praise his triumph.

The Mass of the Catechumens concludes with the intercessions in the form of the Solemn Bidding Prayers that date from the time of Leo the Great in the fifth century; the earliest extant form is found in the Gelasian sacramentary. The pattern is a bid by the deacon, a time of kneeling in silence, and then standing for the prayer that gathers and gives expression to the silent prayers and intentions of the people. The form was preserved in Lutheran books after the Reformation as the Bidding Prayer. "By ancient usage this Prayer was specially appointed for Good Friday. It may also be used on Wednesdays and Fridays in Lent."[54]

There is nothing in the Solemn Prayers that relates specifically to Good Friday, but their comprehensiveness and generous spirit are a response to Jesus's open arms on the cross to draw all peoples to himself. In the Roman sacramentary there are ten general intercessions; in the Lutheran form there are nine, omitting the one for the Pope[55]; in the form in the Book of Common Prayer there are five solemn collects but with expanded bids. The Roman and Lutheran form of the prayers is notable for its compassionate progression. The first prayer is for the Church; then for the pastors and people of God; then those not yet members of the Church but who are preparing for baptism; then the unity of Christians; next for the Jewish people; then for those who do not believe in Christ; then those who do not believe in God; next for all in public office; and finally for those in special need. The order of prayers in the 1570 Roman Missal, after prayer for the Church and its leaders, for Christian rulers, for catechumens, and for all in special need, was for heretics and schismatics, then for the Jews, and finally for the pagans. Especially noteworthy in the present form is the changed attitude toward the Jews. The 1570 Roman Missal invited the people, "Let us pray also for the perfidious Jews: that our God and Lord would withdraw the veil from their heart, that they also may acknowledge our Lord Jesus Christ." The veil imagery derives from St. Paul, 2 Cor. 3:14-16, although there it refers to the hearing of Moses, "the old covenant," not the New Testament Gospel. The especially offensive slur, "the perfidious Jews" was repeated in the collect. The 1970 Roman sacramentary invites the people, "Let us pray for the Jewish people, the first to hear the Word of God, that they may receive the fulfillment of the covenant's promises," and then the prayer is offered, "Almighty and eternal God, long ago you gave your promise to Abraham and his posterity. Hear the prayers of your Church that the people you first made your own may arrive with us at the fullness of redemption." The prayer is no longer for the conversion of the Jews but for their increased faithfulness, a prayer that they become more faithful Jews. The respect accorded the Jewish people acknowledges their priority in the biblical faith; they were the "first to hear the Word of God." The next prayer, after the prayer for the Jews, significantly is for those who do not believe in Christ and then, moving outward, for those who do not believe in God. The view underlying the order of these prayers is to be understood as more than an increased tolerance necessitated by a pluralistic society. It represents a changed theology. The older triumphalist confidence in the exclusive truth of Christian doctrine is gone, and has been replaced by a new appreciation of the honesty and validity of the positions of many who are outside the Church and an acknowledgment of the role of the Church in turning many away from the faith. In these Good Friday prayers may be found evidence of Christianity adapting itself to its minority role in the modern world, done not with a sense of loss but with a clear sense of gain.[56] The attitude expressed in these prayers is moreover especially appropriate for the end of Lent.

The Veneration of the Cross

The second part of the Good Friday liturgy is the veneration of the cross, what the Taizé community calls the adoration of the Crucified. The practice was perhaps introduced by Cyril of Jerusalem. Egeria describes the unveiling (on the morning of Good Friday) of the true cross discovered by St. Helena and the threefold veneration by the devout who touched the cross with their forehead, then their eyes, and then their lips, and also provides a vivid account of the care taken in Jerusalem to prevent worshippers from biting out pieces of the wood of the cross to take away for use as talismans.[57] Relics of the cross spread throughout Europe; they were known in Rome at the end of the seventh century.

In the modern form of the veneration a wooden cross is brought into the church and successively unveiled (first the upper part, then the right arm, then the entire cross) as the procession pauses three times and an antiphon is sung, "This is the wood of the cross, on which was hung the Savior of the world." The antiphon is probably derived from Wis. 14:7, a verse thought in earlier times to adumbrate the crucifixion, "Blessed is the wood by which righteousness comes." The people reply, "Come, let us adore." The cross is then held before the people who come one by one to make their devotion to the instrument of death transformed into the source of forgiveness, life, and salvation. During the veneration Psalm 67 with a Byzantine antiphon is sung. In the Book of Common Prayer it is set so that it may be read responsively.

> We glory in your cross, O Lord,
> *and praise and glorify your holy resurrection;*
> *for by virtue of your cross*
> *joy has come to the whole world.*

> May God be merciful to us and bless us,
> show us the light of his countenance, and come to us.

> *Let your ways be known upon earth,*
> *your saving health among all nations.*

> Let the peoples praise you, O God;
> let all the peoples praise you.

> *We glory in your cross, O Lord,*
> *and praise and glorify your holy resurrection;*

> *for by virtue of your cross*
> *joy has come to the whole world.*

The antiphon sums up the entire meaning of Good Friday: death and life, conflict and victory. Other antiphons are also used that are found in late medieval rites.

> We adore you, O Christ, and we bless you,
> *because by your holy cross you have redeemed the world.*[58]

and

> O Savior of the world,
> who by thy cross and precious blood hast redeemed us:
> *Save us and help us, we humbly beseech thee, O Lord.*[59]

Most impressive of all are the Reproaches, *Improperia* or complaints, of Christ against his people, sung during the veneration of the cross; they are extraordinarily powerful and moving. Their technique has been employed by exasperated parents, we may imagine, through the ages. The idea and the language are traceable to Micah 6:3ff and 2 Esdras 1:12ff. Components of the verses, especially the ancient Greek and Latin Trisagion (Holy God, holy and mighty, holy and immortal, have mercy on us) are found in the seventh century; the first three verses appear in documents of the ninth and early tenth centuries. The pattern is contrast: an event in the history of Israel is set against an incident in the passion.

In the first three verses of the Reproaches, introduced by a quotation from Micah 6:3, each verse is followed by a refrain, the ancient Trisagion ("thrice holy") sung in both Greek and the vernacular.

> O my people, what have I done to you,
> or how have I wearied you, says the Lord?
>   Testify against me.
> I brought you forth from the land of Egypt:
> You prepared a cross for your Savior.
>   Hagios o Theós. Holy God,
>   Hagios íschyros. Holy and mighty,
>   Hagios athánatos. Holy and immortal,
>   Eléison imas. Have mercy on us.

> I led you through the desert forty years
> and fed you with manna
> and brought you into a land exceedingly good:
> You have prepared a cross for your Savior.
>   Holy God,
>   Holy and mighty,
>   Holy and immortal,
>   Have mercy on us.

> What more could I have done for you
> that I have not done?
> I planted you, O my vineyard, exceedingly fair,
> and you became very bitter to me:
> You gave me vinegar to quench my thirst;
> you pierced with a spear the side of your Savior.
>   Holy God,
>   Holy and mighty,
>   Holy and immortal,
>   Have mercy on us.

The second part of the hymn is not found until the eleventh century. It consists of nine verses, each beginning with "I," arranged in groups of three each followed by a refrain (Micah 6:3), echoing the opening of the Reproaches.

> I scourged Egypt with her first-born for your sake,
>   and you scourged me.
> I led you out of Egypt through the Red Sea,
>   and you delivered me to the chief priests.
> I opened the sea before you,
>   and you have opened my side with a spear.
>   O my people, what have I done to you
>   or how have I wearied you, says the Lord?
>   Testify against me.
>
> I went before you in the pillar of cloud,
>   and you brought me into the judgment hall of Pilate.
> I fed you with manna in the desert,
>   and you have struck me with blows and scourges.
> I gave you the water of life from the rock to drink,
>   and you gave me gall and vinegar to drink.
>   O my people, what have I done to you
>   or how have I wearied you, says the Lord?
>   Testify against me.
>
> I smote kings for your sake,
>   and you have smitten my head with a reed.
> I gave you a royal scepter,
>   and you put a crown of thorns on my head.
> I raised you on high with great power,
>   and you hung me on the gibbet of the cross.
>   O my people, what have I done to you
>   or how have I wearied you, says the Lord?
>   Testify against me.

Some have seen what they perceive as an underlying anti-Semitism in these verses,[60] but the objection is unfounded, especially in view of the altered attitude toward the Jewish people revealed in the Solemn Bidding Prayers. The use of the Reproaches in various medieval English lyrics demonstrates that they were even at that time heard not as directed against the Jews but against all humanity. One such lyric, while including an unpleasant three-line reference to the Jews rebuking, grimacing, spitting on Jesus and despising him, directs the words of Jesus to the whole human race with the intent of arousing contrition and grateful obedience. The lyric's refrain, spoken by the Savior, is

> Wofully araide [afflicted],
> My blode, man,
> For thee ran.
> It may not be naide [denied],
> My body blo and wanne [black and blue],
> Wofully araide.

Jesus is heard to say as the poem continues,

> Beholde me, I pray thee.. .
> That I for thy saule [soul's] sake was slaine....
> Thus naked I am nailed, O man, for thy sake.
> I love thee: thenne love me....

Then a direct quotation from the Reproaches,

> What might I suffer more
> Than I have suffered, man, for thee?

The final stanza extends the appeal

> Dere brother, non other thing I desire
> But geve me thy hert free, to reward mine hire [service].[61]

This lyric is a key to understanding the Reproaches. It emphasizes the tenderness of the ancient verses and underscores their intent to induce repentance. Such, indeed, is an essential aspect of the Good Friday liturgy.

The *Lutheran Book of Worship*, in place of the Reproaches, appoints a classic hymn by Johann Heermann (1585-1647), "Ah, holy Jesus, how hast thou offended." The hymn is a paraphrase of a passage from chapter seven of the fifteenth-century *Meditationes*, attributed erroneously to St. Augustine, which derives from the twelfth-century *Orationes* attributed to St. Anselm of Canterbury. The passage used by Heermann was drawn by Anselm from the writings of Jean de Fécamp (d. 1078). The intensely powerful hymn is, therefore, like the medieval lyrics, another expression of that devotional tradition that gave rise to the Reproaches. In the hymn, the "I" who speaks is the individual; in the Reproaches, the "I" is God in Christ. The hymn, like the lyrics, gives voice to the individual response to the accusation of the Reproaches: "I crucified thee." The deeply moving hymn begins with a wondering question: What has Jesus done that caused mortals to pretend to judge him who is himself the Judge of the living and the dead?

> Ah, holy Jesus, how hast thou offended,
> That man to judge thee hath in hate pretended?
> By foes derided, by thine own rejected,
> O most afflicted.

One might be tempted to deflect the force of these lines by assuming that the "foes" were the Roman soldiers who mocked him and that "thine own" who rejected him were his own people the Jews, especially Simon Peter who explicitly denied knowing Jesus. The next stanza asks the still more probing question and will not allow any evasive answer or transfer of responsibility. The blame falls squarely not on Judas or Peter or the Jewish people or the Roman soldiers but on each one who sings the hymn.

> Who was the guilty? Who brought this upon thee?
> Alas, my treason, Jesus, hath undone thee.
> 'Twas I, Lord Jesus, I it was denied thee:
> I crucified thee.

All who sing the hymn are led in three steps to confront their shame and to make an honest and full confession. The double question of the first line, the second question intensifying the first, receives a triple answer: the first is a hesitant and ashamed " 'Twas I"; the second answer intensifies the admission, I, not Peter, denied thee; and the third is the unambiguous confession, I, not the Roman soldiers who were but the instruments of the execution, crucified thee. The wonderful and paradoxical mysteries of the redemption abound, even in the face of human indifference.

> Lo, the good Shepherd for the sheep is offered;
> The slave hath sinnèd, and the Son hath suffered;
> For man's atonement, while he nothing heedeth,
> God intercedeth.

It is all to be received individually in each person as, continuing the pattern of the hymn, an objective stanza is followed by a personal one.

> For me, kind Jesus, was thine Incarnation,
> Thy mortal sorrow, and thy life's oblation;
> Thy death of anguish and thy bitter Passion,
> For my salvation.

The translation is by Robert Bridges (1844-1930), whose careful avoidance of exact rhyme once in each previous stanza is abandoned in the final stanza in which the rhymes of lines 1-2 and 3-4 are at last exact, emphasizing the concluding resolve to adore and plead for mercy. The last lingering words of the hymn are an admission of unworthiness that evokes a gratitude too deep for words.

> Therefore, kind Jesus, since I cannot pay thee,
> I do adore thee, and will ever pray thee,
> Think on thy pity and thy love unswerving,
> Not my deserving.[62]

The hymn is always sung to the grave and solemn tune *Herzliebster Jesu* by Johann Crüger (1598-1662), Cantor at St. Nicholas' Church in Berlin.

The Reproaches and Heermann's hymn both provide the wilderness experience of rebellion and denial of God's gifts and promises as the Church becomes one with Israel wandering in the desert and with the mob denouncing Jesus and demanding his execution. It is an essential element in the Christian celebration of the Passover. The Reproaches and the hymn, it is to be noted, leave room for repentance.

The sixth-century hymn by Venantius Fortunatus, *Pange, lingua, gloriosi proelium certaminis*, is appointed in the Roman, Anglican, and Lutheran rites to be sung during the adoration of the crucified. It is a hymn of victory and praise, again showing the ancient character of Good Friday. The mighty conflict between death and life, Satan and Christ, was glorious because it was the victim who was the victor in the battle. The hymn is well-suited for use during the people's adoration of the one who triumphed on the cross, offering their tribute one by one.

> Sing, my tongue, the glorious battle;
> Of the mighty conflict sing;
> Tell the triumph of the victim,
> To his cross thy tribute bring.

Jesus Christ, the world's Redeemer
From that cross now reigns as King.

The victorious passion was the end for which the Savior, the Passover Lamb,
had willingly come into the world

Thirty years among us dwelling,
His appointed time fulfilled,
Born for this he, he meets his passion,
This the Savior freely willed:
On the cross the Lamb is lifted,
Where his precious blood is spilled.

Then, in an extraordinary assertion explicating Romans 8:20-23 the cosmic
effects of that purifying sacrifice are detailed. Not only humanity but everything in the natural world has been made clean and new.

He endures the nails, the spitting,
Vinegar, and spear, and reed;
From that holy body broken
Blood and water forth proceed:
Earth, and stars, and sky, and ocean,
By that flood from stain are freed.

Even the brutality of crucifixion is transformed and the instruments of execution themselves become desirable, sanctified by him who hangs on the tree.

Faithful cross! Above all other,
One and only noble tree!
None in foliage, none in blossom,
None in fruit thy peer may be:
Sweetest wood and sweetest iron!
Sweetest weight is hung on thee.

The tree that brought death into the world not only becomes the tree of life;
the tree is asked to suspend its inherent properties and be transformed into
the nurturing mother of the Redeemer.

Bend thy boughs, O tree of glory!
Thy relaxing sinews bend;

> For a while the ancient rigor
> That thy birth bestowed, suspend;
> And the King of heavenly beauty
> Gently on thine arms extend.

The earlier version of the translation was even bolder in the last line which read, "On thy bosom gently tend." The traditional doxology concludes the hymn.

> Praise and honor to the Father,
> Praise and honor to the Son,
> Praise and honor to the Spirit,
> Ever Three and ever One:
> One in might and one in glory
> While eternal ages run.[63]

The effects of the sacrifice roll through all ages of ages as the hymn extols not the gloom of the later Middle Ages but the heroic faith of the passion.

A second hymn by Fortunatus, *Vexilla Regis prodeunt*, like "Sing, my tongue" written for the procession on November 19, 569, when the relics of the cross that Queen Rhadegunda had obtained from Emperor Justinian were brought from Tours to her new monastery of St. Croix at Poitiers, also expresses the victorious spirit of Good Friday. John Mason Neale, the translator, called this hymn "one of the grandest in the treasury of the Latin Church." The "banners" (*vexilla*) of the king were the old Roman cavalry standards that, after Constantine, were surmounted by the cross instead of the Roman eagle. The cross is the place of victory, as Christ "through whom all things were made" as the Nicene Creed confesses, put on our human nature and came among us to do battle on our behalf.

> The royal banners forward go,
> The cross shines forth with mystic glow
> Where he through whom our flesh was made,
> In that same flesh our ransom paid.

The original Latin of the last two lines is *Quo carne carnis conditor/suspensus est patibulo*, translated "Where he, as man, who gave man breath/Now bows beneath the yoke of death."[64] The cross is pictured here as a *patibulum*, a Y-shaped yoke to which the hands of criminals were tied, here becoming not only a yoke but also a balance on which the ransom of the world was weighed out.[65] (A common design of the back of a chasuble shows such a Y-shaped yoke.) The payment of that ransom is described.

> Where deep for us the spear was dyed,
> Life's torrent rushing from his side,
> To wash us in that precious flood,
> Where mingled water flowed, and blood.

Reference is made to Psalm 96:10, "reign in triumph from a tree" (*reganbit a lingo deus*), an addition to the Hebrew text in some Old Latin and Septuagint manuscripts. Tertullian refers to the verse,[66] and Justin Martyr in *Against Trypho* 73 accuses the Jews of having erased it from the Hebrew.

> Fulfilled is all that David told
> In true prophetic song of old;
> How God the nations' King should be,
> For God is reigning from the tree.

The first three stanzas focus on the victor in the vigorous spiritual warfare; the next three stanzas address the cross. The transformation wrought by the cross is praised, the crimson of the blood becoming the purple of royalty.

> O tree of beauty, tree most fair,
> Ordained those holy limbs to bear
> Gone is thy shame, each crimsoned bough
> Proclaims the King of glory now.

As the tree of the knowledge of good and evil bore the forbidden fruit, so the tree of the cross bears a more precious burden.

> Blest tree, whose chosen branches bore
> The wealth that did the world restore,
> The price which none but he could pay
> To spoil the spoiler of his prey.

> O cross, our one reliance hail!
> Still may thy power with us prevail
> To save us sinners from our sin,
> God's righteousness for all to win.[67]

The doxology concludes the hymn in which the cross is still the tree that grew in the forests foredoomed to its terrible destiny, the inspiration of those "who later made their cathedral aisles in the pattern of forest rides...."[68]

Holy Communion

The concluding part of the Good Friday liturgy is the simple reception of Holy Communion from elements consecrated the previous evening. Because there is no consecration, the Good Friday Communion is liturgically one with Maundy Thursday. After the Communion, there is no blessing or dismissal; the three-day liturgy pauses temporarily until it resumes in the Easter Vigil.

In the second century, on weekdays when no Mass was celebrated, the people communicated from the sacrament reserved in their homes. By the beginning of the seventh century in Constantinople, the custom had been transferred to the church. It is the present practice of the Eastern churches to celebrate a liturgy of the Pre-sanctified every Wednesday and Friday in Lent. The early Roman practice apparently was a fast from Communion on the two days before Pascha (Friday and Saturday). The first unambiguous evidence of a Good Friday Communion in the Roman tradition is an eighth-century manuscript of the old Gelasian sacramentary. After the Reformation, in some Lutheran and Anglican circles there was a celebration of the Holy Communion on Good Friday. Although some respected Lutheran scholars have supported and even seem to encourage the practice,[69] others dismiss it as arising in places that came under Calvinist influence in which the Holy Communion was understood primarily as a memorial of the death of Jesus.[70]

The Three Hours Devotion

The Three-Hour (Tre-ore) service, an extra-liturgical (that is, outside the liturgical tradition) service, held to mark the hours of Jesus's passion from noon until three in the afternoon, was instituted by the Jesuits on the occasion of an earthquake in Lima, Peru, in 1687. The service was introduced into the Church of England in the 1860s and was for a time widely observed in Anglican and Lutheran and some Roman Catholic churches. A prominent feature was preaching on the "Seven Last Words" of Jesus from the cross, a conflation of the accounts in the four Gospels.[71]

The Great Sabbath

Holy Saturday, the Great Sabbath, is marked liturgically by a sense of emptiness, a great void, as Jesus rests in the tomb as God rested on the Sabbath from the work of creation. Originally the day was observed by a total fast and absolute silence. The sense of desolation continued in seventeenth-century Germany, powerfully expressed in the one-stanza hymn by Friedrich von Spee (1591-1635). In Catherine Winkworth's translation it is:

> O darkest woe!
> Ye tears, forth flow!
> Has earth so sad a wonder?
> God the Father's only Son
> Now lies buried yonder.[72]

A second stanza, added by Johann Rist (1607-1667), is, especially in the original German, even more shocking. "O grosse Not! Gott selbst liegt tot," "O sorrow dread:/Our God lies dead" (literally, "O great calamity! God himself lies dead.)"

There is no traditional liturgy for the daylight hours of Holy Saturday; it was a completely aliturgical day. Christ is dead; the world experiences this day as a day devoid of his presence, without his life.

The 1979 American Book of Common Prayer provides Propers for a Liturgy of the Word on Holy Saturday. The collect, newly composed, tempers the desolation and emphasizes expectant waiting.

> O God, Creator of heaven and earth: Grant that, as the crucified body of your dear Son was laid in the tomb and rested on this holy Sabbath, so we may await with him the coming of the third day, and rise with him to newness of life, who now lives and reigns....

The Liturgy of the Hours provides a collect for Holy Saturday.

> Almighty and everlasting God, your only-begotten Son went down among the dead and rose again in glory: In your mercy raise up your faithful people, buried with him in baptism, to be one with him in the eternal life of heaven; where he lives and reigns....

It is similar to the collect, probably by John Cosin, provided in the Book of Common Prayer from 1662 through the 1928 American book for Easter Even.

> Grant, O Lord, that as we are baptized into the death of thy blessed Son, our Saviour Jesus Christ, so by continual mortifying our corrupt affections we may be buried with him; and that through the grave, and gate of death, we may pass to our joyful resurrection; for his merits, who died, and was buried, and rose again for us, the same thy Son Jesus Christ our Lord.

Both prayers are freely based on Rom. 6:3ff and join us through our baptism to the death and resurrection of our Lord.

The Responsory in the Office of Readings begins in desolation but promptly turns to the theme of victory.

> Our Shepherd, the fountain of living water, has died.
> At his passing the sun was darkened;
> but now humanity's captor is made captive.
>   Today our Savior broke through the gates of death.
> He has demolished the ramparts of hell,
> and overthrown the devil's might
>   Today our Savior broke through the gates of death.[73]

The responsory reminds us that what Christ was doing on Holy Saturday was descending into hell, "harrowing hell" in the medieval English phrase, going to the place of the dead to set free those who under the earlier covenant had been waiting for his salvation. (See Matt. 27:52f; Luke 23:43; 1 Peter 3:18-20; the Apostles' Creed, "he descended to the dead" or "he descended into hell.") He descended to the place of the dead not as one deserving punishment but as victor in the first movement of the resurrection, "for he penetrated to those depths in order to vanquish death in its own domain."[74] It was there that the decisive battle took place. "Hell seized a body, and met God face to face," John Chrysostom declared in his Paschal sermon. As a result of that decisive battle, as the Te Deum sings, the kingdom of heaven was opened to all believers.

The antiphon to the Benedictus at Lauds is, "Save us, O Savior of the world. On the cross you redeemed us by the shedding of your blood; we cry out for your help, O God."[75] If the liturgical year were purely chronological history, one would not pray to the Savior in the tomb. In the Eastern Orthodox churches the previous Saturday was Lazarus Saturday, anticipating the resurrection from a human point of view; Lazarus was brought back from the dead, but he had to die again. Easter Eve proclaims the resurrection from God's point of view; Christ was raised, never to die again.

The Great Vigil of Easter

With sundown on Holy Saturday the Great Sabbath ends and Easter begins. It is as if the natural processes of nature were reversed. "Sunset to sunrise changes now," a hymn by Clement of Alexandria (170?-220?) declares.[76] The transition is marked by the Great Vigil of Easter, *Vigilia Paschalis,* the vigil of Pascha. In Latin, Pascha has two meanings. One is passion (*passio*) as St. Paul (1 Cor. 5:7) has interpreted Exodus 12, "Christ our Passover [our paschal lamb] is sacrificed for us." The other meaning is passage (*transitus*), Israel's passage through the Red Sea (Exod. 14:15-31) and Jesus's passage through death to life. St. Augustine, commenting on John 13:1, brings the two together, affirming that Christ in his passion passes from this world to the Father and that through faith and the sacraments Christians join him in that passage.[77] Pascha (Easter in English) is therefore the center of the Christian faith and thus the center of the liturgical year. The fullness of the faith is found in this great liturgy, and the fullness of Judaism is there as well, for this is the Christian Passover. This magnificent ritual, packed with deep and ancient symbols, gathers into one celebration the essence of Christianity. The whole history of salvation is told in symbol and words and actions: the striking of the new fire, bringing light into the darkness; praising the Easter candle that shows Passover and resurrection and the hope of all creation; reading from the biblical record, interspersed with interpretative song and prayer; making new Christians in the font; eating and drinking the new life in the risen Christ. Christians have been doing such things on this night at least from the fourth century, and millennia of universal religious impulses lie behind the Christian use. In the Great Vigil we participate in events beyond our understanding: death and resurrection in a wide context, brought to a focus on a hill and in a tomb outside Jerusalem; Passover and the moon, the natural world and human worship bound in ways so deep that their full comprehension is now hidden from us.[78]

Anciently, the celebration of Pascha began with a lengthy vigil, "the mother of all vigils" Augustine called it, in which the whole history of salvation was rehearsed in readings and song culminating in the joyous celebration of the Eucharist. It was a night of hope and expectation, oriented, as is the whole developed liturgical year, toward the future. The Advent theme is renewed as the celebrants of the vigil wait in expectation not only for the annual commemoration of the resurrection but for the return of the conqueror of death.[79] The Church lives in hope of the time when each of us with our own eyes will see the living Lord in all his life-giving splendor.

To the relatively simple structure of the vigil liturgy other features were added in the West: the blessing of the new fire, stemming from the Jewish blessing of the lamp on the eve of the Sabbath; the blessing and lighting of the Paschal candle spreading in the fourth and fifth centuries from Africa to Spain, Gaul, and Italy; the baptism of catechumens as the Great Vigil became the preferred time for the administration of the sacrament of Christian initiation.

The Service of Fire

The vigil begins in the darkness and desolation of Holy Saturday. Fire is kindled, a flame leaps up, a great candle is lighted, and by its light lessons from the Bible are read. The introductory service of light is extraordinarily powerful. Since Good Friday all the lamps and candles in the church have been put out; the sacrament has been entirely consumed. The liturgy begins in the darkness of the tomb. The striking of the new fire (the historic method, striking flint and steel can be dated to seventh-century Spain) dramatizes the mystery of Jesus's resurrection. But the symbolism is more profound than that. As the fire is struck and brought into the dark and desolate church that was liturgically demolished on Maundy Thursday evening, we understand a still greater mystery. We are present at the moment of creation. In the darkness we have returned to the moment before time began. The fire that comes into the darkness is the voice of God commanding, "Let there be light." The faces of those around the fire emerge from the darkness, their number can be counted, objects come forth from the shadows of the church as the candle is brought into the dark building. We are witnesses to what no one has seen, creation itself. It is, however, the new creation that is the center of the celebration, and the candle is its focus. The great candle is inscribed, marked, and blessed; it is treated and honored as if it were Christ himself. It is marked with his cross and his name, Alpha and Omega; it receives the five wounds, the trophies of his passion; it is addressed in the procession, three times so there can be no mistake, "Light of Christ." (The acclamation is not a didactic instruction, "This candle as a sign reminds us that Jesus called himself the Light of the world," but is a direct address spoken to the Living One.) The One seated on the throne who bears the title Alpha and Omega (Rev. 1:8; 1:6; 1 Peter 5:11), the eternal Pantocrator, is in the midst of his gathered people, the Church.

When the candle has been lighted, the celebrant says, "May the light of Christ gloriously rising dispel the darkness of our hearts and minds." The lighting of the candle is an enactment of this very rising; yet the one rising continues to display "his holy and glorious wounds" even as the burning candle evokes sacrifice by consuming itself in order to give light.[80]

A procession brings the candle into the darkened church. It is a dramatization of the triumph of the resurrection, Christ the light, the pillar of fire, leading the dead into the land of life. The light is spread from the candle to the hand-candles of the worshippers, giving increasing joy to those who hold in their hands the light of life.

The candle is set in its place before the altar, and the proclamation of Easter (*praeconium Paschale*), called from its first word the *Exsultet*, is sung by its light. It is the most extraordinary passage in the liturgy of the Church. The prologue is an elaborate invitation that moves through the cosmos in ever-decreasing circles and then declares the actual praise of the candle and the proclamation of Easter in the remarkable and repeated announcement, "This is the night." Again, the declaration is not, "This is the anniversary of the night long ago" or "Many centuries, even millennia ago, on a night like this." The declaration is the straightforward assertion, "This is the night." It is the night before creation began, the night of exodus from slavery, the night of resurrection all rolled into one event that is happening here and now, an event in which the worshippers are actual participants. Each congregant sees worlds upon worlds leap into being, walks through the Red Sea on dry land, emerges from the darkness of the tomb. Creation, exodus, resurrection are made contemporary experiences and proclaim the same mystery: creation takes place before our very eyes, the world is renewed, and life begins again.

The "happy fault," the "necessary sin of Adam" is praised, for if our ancestor had not fallen into sin by disobeying the explicit command of God, we would not have had the demonstration to the extent of God's love for his creation shown in Christ. The fifteenth-century English lyric "Adam lay ybounden" declares,

> Blessed be the time
> That apple taken was.
> Therefore we moun [may] singen,
> Deo gracias![81]

In the light of the resurrection, the original sin that condemned the whole human race and the world with it to death is transformed into a happy fault, *felix culpa.* This passage is not in the version of the Exsultet in the Book of Common Prayer, nor is the passage that proclaims the mystery of endless division, "We sing the glories of this pillar of fire, the brightness of which is not diminished, even when its light is divided and borrowed." The next sentence, preserved in the Lutheran version of the great Easter proclamation and restored in the revision of the present Roman sacramentary, praises "the melting wax, which the bees, your servants, have made for the substance of this candle." All creation participates in this first service of Easter, even the bees rendering their part selflessly, teaching us to imitate their generous service.

The concluding eschatological supplication of the Exsultet "asks in effect that the marvelous reality coming into existence liturgically expand and endure until he who now makes himself present in sign comes in person."[82]

The Service of Readings

The second part of the Easter Vigil is the service of readings in which we listen to the history of salvation. The list in the *Lutheran Book of Worship*, reflecting the eighth-century lectionary, the *Comes* of Murbach and the 1570 Roman Missal, is the fullest listing. The readings marked with an asterisk are common to all three rites.

1. *Creation (Gen 1:1-2:2) *or* Creation and Fall (Gen. 1:1-3:24)
2. The Flood (Gen. 7:1-5, 11-18; 8:6-18; 9:8-13)
3. *Abraham's willingness to sacrifice Isaac (Gen. 22:1-18)
4. *Israel's deliverance through the Red Sea (Exod.14:10-15:1a *or* Exod. 13:17-15:1a)
5. *Salvation freely offered to all (Isa. 55:1-11)
6. In praise of Wisdom (Baruch 3:9-37)
7. The valley of the dry bones (Ezek. 37:1-14)
8. The future glory of a purified Jerusalem (Isa. 4:2-6)
9. The institution of the Passover (Exod. 12:1-14 *or* Exod. 12:1-24)
10. The conversion of Nineveh (Jonah 3:1-10)
11. The Song of Moses (Deut. 31:19-30)
12. Deliverance from the fiery furnace (Dan. 3:1-29).

The Book of Common Prayer provides nine lessons.

1. *Creation (Gen. 1:1-2:2)
2. The Flood (Gen 7:1-5, 11-18; 8:6-18; 9:8-13)
3. *Abraham's willingness to sacrifice Isaac (Gen 22:1-18)

4. *Israel's deliverance through the Red Sea (Exod. 14:10-15:1)
5. God's presence in a renewed Israel (Isa. 4:2-6)
6. *Salvation freely offered to all (Isa. 55:1-11)
7. A new heart and a new spirit (Ezek. 36:24-28)
8. The valley of dry bones (Ezek. 37:1-14)
9. The gathering of God's people (Zeph. 3:12-20)

The Roman sacramentary provides seven readings.

1. *Creation (Gen 1:1-2:2)
2. *Abraham's willingness to sacrifice Isaac (Gen. 22:1-18)
3. *Israel's deliverance through the Red Sea (Exod. 14:15-15:1)
4. The loving kindness of God (Isa. 54:5-14)
5. *Salvation freely offered to all (Isa. 55:1-11)
6. In praise of Wisdom (Baruch 3:9-15, 32:4-4:4)
7. A new heart and a new spirit (Ezek. 36:16-17a, 18-28).

Each reading is followed by a psalm or canticle and a prayer. The readings serve as final instruction for those who are about to be baptized and as a review of the history of the salvation that those who have been baptized are expected to be living. The readings are all from the Hebrew Bible, God's promises that will be fulfilled in Christ. As in Advent, so in the Easter Vigil: God's people of the Church now wait with God's ancient people for the fullness of the divine promises.

The Service of Holy Baptism

The third part of the Easter Vigil is the service of Holy Baptism: the womb of the Church gives birth to new Christians. The Vigil liturgy has been preparing for this since the striking of the new fire. Baptism in the ancient Church was referred to as illumination (Eph. 5:14) and enlightenment (Heb. 6:4). The Thanksgiving is said over the water, and, through the power of the Holy Spirit invoked upon it, the water is made capable of doing what of itself it cannot do—contain and impart the Spirit—"so that all who enter it are 'born of water and spirit' (John 3:5) and so made adopted children of the Father."[83] The divine image in which they were created is restored, the gates of heaven are thrown open and behind them are the open arms of the Father. Satan and all his works and all his ways are renounced, the threefold profession of faith in the Father, Son, and Holy Spirit as formulated in the Apostles' Creed is made, the catechumens receive the sacrament of new birth and the faithful are sprinkled with baptismal water. The Litany of the Saints is sung as the procession moves from the font to the altar as the newly baptized are introduced to their new family, the holy people of God of all times and all places.

The First Eucharist of Easter

The final part of the Great Vigil of Easter is the service of the Holy Eucharist: the risen Lord makes himself known in the Breaking of Bread. After its Lenten absence, the Gloria in excelsis returns to its accustomed place in the festive Mass accompanied by the organ and bells of many kinds; the fast of the ears is ended. Veils fall from the crosses and images; the fast of the eyes is broken. The whole congregation, newly baptized and long-baptized together, share in a foretaste of heaven; the Lenten fast of the mouth is over. The time of feasting has begun.

The transition from the discipline of Lent to the abounding joy of Easter was sometimes dramatic. John Mason Neale in his *Hymns of the Eastern Church* quotes an unnamed "modern [i.e., nineteenth-century] author" describing the scene at Athens.

As midnight approached, the Archbishop, with his priests, accompanied by the King and Queen, left the Church, and stationed themselves on the platform, which was raised considerably from the ground, so that they were distinctly seen by the people. Everyone now remained in breathless expectation, holding their unlighted tapers in readiness when the glad moment should arrive, while the priests still continued murmuring their melancholy chant in a low half-whisper. Suddenly a single report of a cannon announced that twelve o'clock had struck, and that Easter day had begun; then the old Archbishop elevating the cross, exclaimed in a loud exulting tone, "Christos anesti, Christ is risen!" and instantly every single individual of all that host took up the cry, and the vast multitude broke through and dispelled for ever the intense and mournful silence which they had maintained so long, with one spontaneous shout of indescribable joy and triumph, "Christ is risen!" "Christ is risen!" At the same moment, the oppressive darkness was succeeded by a blaze of light from thousands of tapers, which communicating one from another, seemed to send streams of fire in all directions, rendering the minutest objects distinctly visible, and casting the most vivid glow on the expressive faces, full of exultation, of the rejoicing crowd; bands of music struck up their gayest strains; the roll of the drum through the town, and further on the pealing of the cannon announced far and near these "glad tidings of great joy;" while from hill and plain, from the sea-shore and the far olive grove, rocket after rocket ascending to the clear sky, answered back with their mute eloquence, that Christ is risen indeed, and told of other tongues that were repeating those blessed words, and other hearts that leapt for joy...and all the while, rising above the mingling of many sounds, each one of which was a sound of gladness, the aged priests were distinctly heard chanting forth a glorious old hymn of victory in tones so loud and clear, that they seemed to have regained their youth and strength to tell the world how "Christ is risen from the dead, having trampled death beneath His feet, and henceforth the entombed have everlasting life."[84]

Then follows Neale's translation of the eighth-century "Canon for Easter Day called the Golden Canon or The Queen of Canons" by St. John of Damascus.[85] The first stanza shows why Neale prefaced it with the long description of the manifold expressions of joy that erupted in nineteenth-century Athens. We have passed over with Christ from death to life, from earth to heaven.

> The day of resurrection!
>   Earth, tell it out abroad;
> The Passover of gladness,
>   The Passover of God!
> From death to life eternal,
>   From earth unto the sky,
> Our Christ hath brought us over
>   With hymns of victory.

The second stanza is marked with "the brilliant interpolation of the sudden '*All Hail*' (so printed) [which] captures wonderfully the excitement of the Eastern Church at the beginning of Easter Day."[86] The "All hail" is the King James translation of Matt. 28:9, from the ancient Gospel for the Vigil of Easter, a greeting rendered excessively pedestrian in modern translations.[87] Neale's original punctuation emphasizes the sudden surprise of hearing Jesus's actual greeting directed to us. We trust that we may see and that we also may hear the Lord.

> Our hearts be pure from evil,
>   That we may see aright
> The Lord in rays eternal
>   Of resurrection light:

> And, listening to his accents,
>   May hear, so calm and plain,
> His own—All Hail!—and hearing,
>   May raise the victor strain!

The concluding stanza returns to the opening invitation to heaven and earth to unite in praise.

> Now let the heavens be joyful,
>   Let earth her song begin,
> The round world keep high triumph,
>   And all that is therein;
> Let all things seen and unseen
>   Their notes together blend,
> For Christ the Lord is risen,
>   Our joy that hath no end.[88]

Jesus's unexpected and thrilling greeting was addressed to the two Marys; their worshipping response is subtly suggested in the feminine pronoun describing the earth.

The Eucharist of the Vigil begins with the Collect, from the Gelasian, Gregorian, and Sarum sacramentaries, common to all three rites.

> O God, who made this most holy night to shine with the glory of the Lord's resurrection: Stir up in your Church that Spirit of adoption which is given to us in Baptism, that we, being renewed both in body and mind, may worship you in sincerity and truth; through Jesus Christ our Lord, who lives and reigns....

The concluding reference is to St. Paul's statement "Christ our Passover is sacrificed for us; therefore let us keep the feast... with the unleavened bread of sincerity and truth" (1 Cor. 5:7-8, the ancient Epistle for Easter Day).

There are but two readings at the Mass, Epistle and Gospel, both from the New Testament, the Old Testament having provided all the readings earlier in the Vigil.

> Rom. 6:3-11. Dying and rising with Christ in baptism
> Psalm 114. The wonders of the Exodus
> Matt. 28:1-10. The risen Jesus meets the two Marys.

The Gospel has been used at the Vigil since the earliest Roman lectionaries. Between the Epistle and the Gospel, the song of heaven, Alleluia, which was put away on the Sunday before Lent, is returned to the liturgy with great festivity and elaboration. The Church now stands safely in the promised land.

In Orthodox and Byzantine churches this night part of a powerful Paschal sermon by St. John Chrysostom is read as part of the Vigil liturgy. The passage is remarkable for its broad and generous spirit, inviting all, no matter how well or how indifferently they have kept the Lenten fast, to join the gladness of whole Christian community. The Paschal feast is not a time for judgment or superiority; it is a time only for joy. John's words leap out from the fourth century, bound across the ages to those who celebrate this night, and proclaim a vigorous understanding of this night and of the resurrection. This sermon is an example of why Bishop John of Constantinople is called "Golden mouth."

If any are devout and love God, let them enjoy this fair and radiant triumphal feast. If any are wise servants, let them enter into the joy of their Lord. If any have labored long in fasting, let them now receive their recompense. If any have worked from the first hour, let them today receive their just reward. If any have come at the third hour, let them with thankfulness keep the feast. If any have arrived at the sixth hour, let them have no misgivings; because they shall in no way be deprived because of it. If any have delayed until the ninth hour, let them draw near, fearing nothing. If any have tarried even until the eleventh hour, let them also be not alarmed at their tardiness; for the Lord, who is jealous of his honor, will accept the last even as the first; he gives rest to those who come at the eleventh hour even as to those who have worked from the first hour. And he shows mercy on the last and cares for the first; to the one he gives, and on the other he bestows gifts. And he both accepts the deeds and welcomes the intention, and honors the acts and praises the offering.

Wherefore, enter all of you into the joy of your Lord; and receive your reward, both the first, and likewise the second. You rich and poor together, hold high festival. You sober and you heedless, honor the day. Rejoice today, both you who have fasted and you who have disregarded the fast. The table is full-laden; all of you feast sumptuously. The calf is fatted; let no one go hungry away. All of you enjoy the feast of faith: Receive all of you the riches of loving-kindness. Let none bewail their poverty, for the universal kingdom has been revealed. Let none weep for their iniquities, for pardon has shone forth from the grave. Let none fear death, for the Savior's death has set us free. He who was held prisoner by it, has annihilated it. By descending into Hell, he made Hell captive. He embittered it when it tasted his flesh. And Isaiah [38:18], foretelling this, cried: Hell, said he, was embittered when it encountered you in the lower regions. It was embittered, for it was abolished. It was embittered, for it was mocked. It was embittered, for it was slain. It was embittered, for it was overthrown. It was embittered, for it was fettered in chains. Hell seized a body, and met God face to face. It seized earth, and encountered heaven. It seized that which was seen, and fell upon the unseen. O Death, where is your sting? O Hell, where is your victory? Christ is risen, and you are overthrown. Christ is risen, and the demons are fallen. Christ is risen, and the angels rejoice. Christ is risen, and life reigns. Christ is risen, and not one dead remains in the grave. For Christ, being risen from the dead, is become the first-fruits of those who have fallen asleep. To him be glory and dominion unto ages of ages. Amen.

The destruction of death has fascinated poets as well as preachers and theologians. Richard Crashaw imagined that although all creatures have life by the light that comes from the place of resurrection,

> Death only by this Day's just doom is forc'd to die;
> Nor is Death forc'd; for may he lie
> Throned in thy grave;
> Death will on this condition be content to die.[89]

Death may still pretend royal power, for Death is reigning in the tomb over himself.

The proper Preface for Easter in all three rites dates from the Gelasian and Gregorian sacramentaries, and the Gallican Bobbio Missal. In the Prayer Book translation it is

But chiefly are we bound to praise you for the glorious resurrection of your Son Jesus Christ our Lord; for he is the true Paschal Lamb, who was sacrificed for us, and has taken away the sin of the world. By his death he has destroyed death, and by his rising to life again he has won for us everlasting life.

Christ as the victorious Lamb of God recalls the proclamation of John the Baptist heard at the beginning of the liturgical year during Advent and whose proclamation can now be understood in its fullness.

The post-Communion prayer at the Vigil in the Roman sacramentary also appears as one of the prayers after communion in the Lutheran rite.

> Pour out upon us the Spirit of your love, O Lord, and unite the wills of those whom you have fed with one bread from heaven, your Son Jesus Christ our Lord.

It is remarkably simple, yet it recalls the teaching of the Maundy Thursday foot washing and anticipates the high priestly prayer of Jesus that will be the Gospel for the concluding Sundays of Eastertide and looks forward to the gift of the Holy Spirit.

The Roman sacramentary enriches the dismissal at the conclusion of the Mass by adding a double Alleluia to the dismissal by the deacon and to the congregation's response. The Prayer Book permits the same. The singing of Alleluia, returned with joyful energy in the verse before the Gospel in the Vigil Eucharist, is characteristic of the liturgy for these glad fifty days of rejoicing, made the more joyous because of the discontinuance of Alleluia during Lent. The Church, now standing in the promised land, sings repeatedly and with great joy throughout these glad days the song of heaven. St. Augustine said it clearly, "We are Easter people, and Alleluia is our song."

7

Easter. Pascha

EASTER IS THE central feast of the liturgical year, honored as the greatest of all festivals, celebrated as the Queen of Feasts. The name Easter seems to come from Old English "east," the direction of sunrise: the Venerable Bede says that it comes from an Anglo-Saxon spring goddess, Eastre; others suggest a Germanic dawn goddess, Austron, whose feast was celebrated on the vernal equinox. The name Easter is limited to the Germanic languages and English; in other tongues the feast is called Pascha, from the Greek for Passover.

This chapter might well have begun with Maundy Thursday, for originally, as we have seen, Jesus's Passion-Death-Resurrection was understood to be one event and was perhaps celebrated as such. That unity is still useful to keep in mind, and the Triduum is meant to be celebrated as one continuous, although interrupted, commemoration. It is difficult if not impossible to comprehend this vast event all at once, and therefore there is devotional and spiritual value in dividing the days. Maundy Thursday, Good Friday, Holy Saturday, and Easter Day, being the progressive commemoration of the saving Act, should be understood as one event although observed in its several stages. There is wisdom also in dividing the days that follow Easter Day as the mystery of the resurrection and the new life gradually unfolds. Easter Day is resplendent with the full light of the resurrection; Easter Week presents various appearances of the risen Lord; as the Sundays of Easter succeed one another they begin to turn toward the Ascension and the end of the resurrection appearances; Ascension Day commemorates Jesus's triumphant return to the place he left in order to do his great work on earth and his coronation as King; and finally the Day of Pentecost as the completion of the fifty days of abounding joy brings the gift of the Holy Spirit as the fulfillment of the Easter promise as well as bestowal of the energy and power that moved the Church outward from Jerusalem into all the earth.

Nature's Participation in the Celebration

When Jesus died, the natural world shuddered and went into mourning. Darkness descended (Matt. 27:45; Mark 15:33; Luke 23:44); Matthew reports an earthquake that split the rocks and opened tombs (27:51-52). A hymn by Gregory the Great (540-604), *Rex Christe, factor omnium*, declares,

> When thou didst hang upon the tree
> The quaking earth acknowledged thee;
> When thou didst there yield up thy breath
> The earth grew dark as shades of death.[1]

One of the most striking aspects of the celebration of Easter is the joyful response of nature to the resurrection, answering the hiding of its face at the dreadful events of Good Friday. Now at Easter the whole created world is involved in expressing its joy. A versicle and response in the Divine Office reminds us how large is the chorus of praise.

> Over your resurrection, O Christ, alleluia.
> Let heaven and earth rejoice, alleluia.[2]

"Earth" is understood here in the broadest sense. Nature bears its testimony to the risen life. It is as if the world is new-born, and it eloquently contributes to the praise. Spring, the awakening, is at hand. Some of the testimony of the natural world is silent—the lengthening of daylight, the increasing warmth of the sun, the appearing of flowers. Other testimony is audible—the song of birds, the flowing of water, the energy of awakening life in bees and animals. Even to those who know nothing of Christianity, the coming of spring gladdens the heart. Gregory of Nazianzus (329/330-389/390) in his "Homily on the New Sunday" notes how in the spring nature adorns itself for the grand celebration of Easter.

> Everything contributes to the beauty and joy of the feast. The queen of the seasons prepares a feast for the queen of days, and presents to her all the beautiful and delightful things she possesses. The sky is transparent, the sun radiant, the moon brilliant, and the choir of stars bright. The springs of water are clear and the rivers full, for these are now freed from the fetters of ice. The fields emit sweet scents, green plants sprout, and lambs bound in green pasture.[3]

The great hymns of Easter also describe how the natural world rejoices in the resurrection, celebrating its own redemption. *Salve festa dies* by Venantius Fortunatus (540?-600?) in John Ellerton's translation observes not only that age after age will welcome the glad morning, but that all God's works participate in the praise.

> "Welcome, happy morning!" age to age shall say,
> "Hell today is vanquished, heaven is won today!"
> Lo! the dead is living, God for evermore!
> Him, their true Creator, all his works adore.
> "Welcome, happy morning!" age to age shall say.

The first two lines of the hymn become, in the version preserved by the Lutherans, the alternating refrain of the successive stanzas: the first, third, and fifth stanzas welcoming the glad morning; the second, fourth, and sixth completing the thought by providing the reason for the joyful greeting. Building on the reference in the first stanza to "all his works," the second stanza describes the joy of the earth.

> Earth with joy confesses, clothing her for spring,
> All good gifts return with her returning King;
> Bloom in every meadow, leaves on every bough,
> Speak his sorrows ended, hail his triumph now.
> "Hell today is vanquished, heaven is won today!"

The passage of time has its part to play.

> Months in due succession, days of lengthening light,
> Hours and passing moments praise thee in their flight;
> Brightness of the morning, sky and fields and sea,
> Vanquisher of darkness, bring their praise to thee:
> "Welcome, happy morning," age to age shall say.

This great victory was the purpose and goal of the incarnation of the Son of God, whose names are Faithful and True (Rev. 19:11).

> Maker and Redeemer, life and health of all,
> Thou from heaven beholding man's abasing fall,
> Of the eternal Father true and only Son,

Manhood to deliver, manhood didst put on:
"Hell today is vanquished, heaven is won today!"

Thou, of life the author, death didst undergo,
Tread the path of darkness, saving strength to show;
Come then, true and faithful, now fulfill thy word;
'Tis thine own third morning; rise, O buried Lord!
"Welcome, happy morning," age to age shall say.

The prayer is for freedom for the human race bound by its sin, for life for all creation that has been in bondage to decay (Rom. 8:21), and for light for the nations to enable them to see and recognize and do the truth.

Loose the souls long-prisoned, bound with Satan's chain;
All that now is fallen raise to life again;
Show thy face in brightness, bid the nations see;
Bring again our daylight, day returns with thee;
"Hell today is vanquished, heaven is won today!"[4]

With the rising of the Son the night of ignorance and fear in which humanity has been groping since the entrance of sin into the world is ended.

John of Damascus's (eighth century) first ode of the canon for the Sunday of St. Thomas (the Second Sunday of Easter) also recognizes the participation of the natural world in the joy of Pascha. In the amusing fastidiousness of John Mason Neale's translation, the biblical "dry-shod" (Isa. 11:15 AV) becoming Neale's "unmoistened," the first stanza makes the connection with the Passover and Exodus.

Come, ye faithful, raise the strain of triumphant gladness!
God hath brought his Israel into joy from sadness:
Loosed from Pharaoh's bitter yoke Jacob's sons and daughters,
Led them with unmoistened foot through the Red Sea waters.

In the Christian Passover, Christ's resurrection has brought about a change of seasons.

'Tis the spring of souls today: Christ hath burst his prison,
And from three days' sleep in death as a sun hath risen;
All the winter of our sins, long and dark, is flying
From his light, to whom we give laud and praise undying.

> Now the queen of seasons, bright with the day of splendor,
> With the royal feast of feasts, comes its joy to render;
> Comes to glad Jerusalem, who with true affection
> Welcomes in unwearied strains Jesus' resurrection.

Human precautions and defenses and understandable fear in the face of the unknown could not prevent the fulfillment of God's work of peace.

> Neither might the gates of death, nor the tomb's dark portal,
> Nor the watchers, nor the seal, hold thee as a mortal:
> But today amid the Twelve thou didst stand, bestowing
> That thy peace which evermore passeth human knowing.[5]

With the resurrection we stand at the limits of understanding and enter upon a new and disconcerting world. The mystery will only deepen as the weeks of Easter and the years of our lives and the centuries of the Church pass, and we are drawn more and more into its wonder and its life.

The Pentecost, the great Fifty Days, is the oldest season of the Church year. Its ancient roots are lost in distant antiquity back behind Passover and its celebration at the vernal equinox and full moon. The mystery of the moon fascinated and induced deep awe in ancient peoples. Its cycle approximating the menstrual cycle, its light softer than the harsh sun, the moon was widely regarded as female. In the Hebrew Bible the new moon sometimes appears to be a greater festival than the Sabbath. In Isa. 1:13 and 66:23 the new moon is mentioned first, then the Sabbath. See also Numb. 28:11 (the offering "at the beginnings of your months"); 1 Sam. 20:5 18, 24 ("When the new moon came the king sat at the feast"); 2 Kings 4:23 ("It is neither new moon nor Sabbath"); Isa. 1:13-14 ("new moon and Sabbath"); Ezek. 46:1, 3 (the gate of the inner court of the temple is opened "on the sabbath day and on the day of the new moon"); Hos. 2:11 ("her festivals, her new moons, her sabbaths"); Amos 8:5 ("When will the new moon be over...and the sabbath").[6] Passover was originally a spring new moon festival, its date determined by the vernal equinox and the first full moon of the spring. We cannot now know all that the moon meant for the origins of Passover, but that ignorance is reason enough to leave the date of Easter as it is and allow it to vary from year to year. Ancient intuitions embedded in the mystery of the moon, three days dark, are fulfilled and perfected in Christ, three days in the darkness of the tomb. The moving date of Easter, varying as does Passover, preserves the Christian connection with the tradition from which it came. That connection with Judaism, Christianity's elder brother and first to hear the Word of God, is essential for an understanding of who Christians are and what the Church is.

In addition to its origins as a new moon festival, Passover also has roots in the soil. The ancient Hebrews counted seven weeks from the Feast of Unleavened Bread to the Feast of First Fruits. These were two agricultural festivals, the first the consecration of the grain harvest by waving a freshly cut sheaf of barley (Lev. 23:9-11), the second, the Feast of Weeks, fifty days later, ended the harvest. After the destruction of the temple and the exile in Babylonia, a new awareness of the work of God in human history developed, and the festivals of the ancient Hebrew calendar were reinterpreted and associated with great historical events of past ages. Events thus had meaning for the generation in which they occurred but also for all who followed afterward. Every devout Hebrew was thus a participant in the formative events.[7] Passover became the anniversary of deliverance from slavery and thus had meaning for all who were in any kind of bondage. The Feast of Weeks (Pentecost), once a spring festival associated with the barley harvest, became the anniversary of Moses's reception of the Law on Mount Sinai and a reminder of God's will and human obedience to it. Among Greek-speaking Jews, the Feast of Weeks was called Pentecost ("fifty"), as it is in the New Testament (Acts 2:1; 20:16; 1 Cor. 16:18.) Among Christians, the period from Passover-Easter to the Feast of Weeks (Pentecost) was celebrated as a fifty-day-long Sunday. Athanasius called it *magna dominica*, the Great Sunday. It was a "week of weeks" celebrated as one extended feast day, an unbroken celebration of the victory of the risen Lord. During these glad days there was no fasting, no kneeling.

In the present time, throughout these Fifty Days, the Paschal candle, the sign of the presence of the risen Lord and honored as Christ himself, stands before the people. It is no longer required, as it was previously, to be at the Gospel side of the altar. (That custom was doubtless for convenience: the candle was extinguished after reading the Gospel on Ascension Day.)

Easter Day: The Queen of Feasts

At the beginning of the Eucharist, since at least the ninth century, Easter water, a reminder of baptism, is sprinkled on the people while an antiphon, *vidi aquam* drawn from Ezekiel 47:1-2, is sung.

> *Antiphon.* I saw water flowing from the right side of the temple, alleluia; and all to whom that water came were saved, and they shall say, alleluia, alleluia.
>
> *Psalm 118:1.* O give thanks to the Lord, for he is good; his steadfast love endures forever! *Gloria Patri.*
>
> *The antiphon is repeated.* I saw water … alleluia, alleluia.

After its desolation on Maundy Thursday, the temple of the church has been restored to its accustomed dignity and splendor. The mystical, life-giving, and ever-increasing river that flowed from the Jerusalem temple is a figure of baptism, the water of life that makes the earth a new Paradise (Gen. 2:10-14; Ps. 46:4). As Lent prepared candidates for baptism, so the days of Easter explore its implications in everyday life. In the lectionary, the biblical books that are emphasized are the Acts of the Apostles, read as the first Lesson throughout the weeks of Easter, because it tells of the work of the risen Christ through the Church, and the Gospel of St. John for whom the crucifixion is the moment of victory and for whom Easter, Ascension, and the gift of the Spirit are one event.

In the historic Introit (*Resurrexi*) the voice of Christ is heard, but what he says all his followers, because of his resurrection victory, may now also declare.

> *Antiphon.* I awake [or I arose] and I am still with you, alleluia. You lay your hand upon me, alleluia. Such knowledge is too wonderful for me; it is so high that I cannot attain it, alleluia, alleluia.
>
> > *Psalm 139:1,2.* O Lord, you have searched me and known me. You know when I sit down and when I rise up. *Gloria Patri.*
>
> *The antiphon is repeated:* I awake...attain it, alleluia, alleluia.

The antiphon is drawn from Ps. 139:18b, 5b, 6. The translation of verse 18b is uncertain; the NRSV has "I come to the end" with a textual footnote allowing "*or* I awake." The RSV following the Authorized Version had "When I awake, I am still with thee." The Latin is "Resurrexi," "I arose." Robert Alter, who translates the line "I awake, and am still with You," comments, "The effort of many modern interpreters to link the verb with *qets*, 'end,' is dubious, because *heqitsoti* elsewhere always means 'I awake.' "[8] After his sleep in death, Jesus wakes and finds that he is still in the presence of God. Such is also the confidence of those who belong to him by baptism.

The Gloria in excelsis, absent during Lent, returns to its accustomed place in the Eucharist. The Lutheran rite since 1978 provides instead of the greater Gloria a new hymn of praise for Eastertide, drawn from Rev. 5:12-13, "Worthy is Christ" sometimes known by its Antiphon, "This is the feast."[9]

The Collect for Easter Day in the Roman Missal (1570), north European missals (Bamberg, Constance, Nuremberg, Sarum), the Book of Common Prayer through 1928, and Lutheran books is from the Gregorian sacramentary. In the Lutheran version of the Prayer Book translation it is:

Almighty God, who through thine only-begotten Son Jesus Christ hast overcome death and opened unto us the gate of everlasting life: We humbly beseech thee, that as thou dost put into our minds good desires, so by thy continual help we may bring the same to good effect; through the same, Jesus Christ our Lord, who liveth and reigneth with thee and the Holy Ghost, ever one God, world without end.

Luther Reed, quoting Charles Neil and J. M. Willoughby, editors of *The Tutorial Prayer Book* (1913), observes, "We agree that the petition of this Collect 'has the merit of associating a consistent Christian life with the Resurrection, but seems inadequate to the greatest festival of the Christian year.' "[10] Paul Strodach, however, understands the prayer differently. The Collect "teaches that simply because Christ in his victorious power *is* risen for us does not guarantee our rising 'in the likeness of his resurrection' to the enjoyment of those eternal blessings; something is required of the believer...."[11] Massey Shepherd, noting the form of the petition in the earlier Gelasian sacramentary, "Grant, we beseech thee, that we who celebrate the solemnities of the Lord's resurrection, may through the renewal of thy Spirit arise from the death of the soul," a prayer included in the Lutheran *Church Book* (p. 59); the *Common Service Book* (p. 81), and the *Service Book and Hymnal* (p. 90) as one of two "other Easter Collects," comments,

> The change made by the Gregorian reviser is indicative of the impact upon the Church's thought of the struggle with the Pelagian heresy in the fifth and sixth centuries. The Pelagian heresy maintained that man was not a fallen creature, but only weak, who could of his own free will and power turn to God and obey Him without the necessity of any special assistance of grace. The Church, however, held steadfast to its faith that every good desire and work we can claim are due to God's prevenient and sustaining grace, and that through the victory wrought by Christ's perfect offering and obedience He has done for us what we could never do in and through and of ourselves. The Easter Collect is the key that unlocks the meaning of all our other Collects, for they but explain and comment upon it.[12]

The reservations of Reed-Neil-Willoughby concerning the petition seem not entirely convincing. The old prayer in the understated way of the Latin collects encourages the movement from acclamation of the risen Lord to participation in his risen life. The idea will be repeated many times in the prayers of the Easter season. The continuing prayer may also be understood as a response to the generosity of John Chrysostom's Paschal Sermon, quoted toward the end of the previous chapter, inviting both those who have kept the preparatory fast and also those who have disregarded it to join in the celebration of the Paschal feast: those who have been careless in their preparation are given a second opportunity to demonstrate their seriousness by living the new life. Nonetheless, the 1970 Roman sacramentary and the 1979 Prayer Book replaced the petition of the Gregorian collect with the earlier one found in the Missale Gallicanum vetus and the Gelasian sacramentary. The 1979 Prayer Book translates it:

> Almighty God, who through your only-begotten Son Jesus Christ overcame death and opened to us the gate of everlasting life: Grant that we, who celebrate with joy the day of the Lord's resurrection, may be raised from the death of sin by your life-giving Spirit; through Jesus Christ our Lord, who lives and reigns....

The reference to opening the "gate of everlasting life" is echoed in the Psalm (118:19-20), "Open for me the gates of righteousness..." It is probably an allusion to the opening of Jesus's side, an idea drawn from St. Augustine: " 'One of the soldiers laid open his side, and forthwith came thereout blood and water.' A suggestive word was made use of by the evangelist, in not saying pierced or wounded his side, or anything else, but 'opened'; that thereby, in a sense, the gate of life might be thrown open, from whence have flowed forth the sacraments of the Church, without which there is no entrance to the life which is true life."[13] The Te Deum praises Christ for having "opened the kingdom of heaven to all believers."

The Revised Common Lectionary appoints these readings for Easter Day. The First Reading and the Psalm are the same for all three years; the Epistle and Gospel are different in each of the three years.

> Acts 10:34-43. Peter summarizes the Good News
> Psalm 118:1-2, 14-24. This is the day the Lord has made
> > Year A. Col. 3:1-4. The new life in Christ
> > Year B. 1 Cor. 15:1-11. The resurrection of Christ
> > Year C. 1 Cor. 15:19-26. The resurrection of the dead
> John 20:1-18. Mary Magdalene testifies to the resurrection
> > Year A or Matt. 28:1-10 [from the Vigil]. In Galilee they will see me
> > Year C or Luke 24:1-12. The empty tomb.

After the Epistle, to prepare for and welcome the Holy Gospel it became customary to sing a Sequence. These hymns are said to have been the invention of Notker Balbulus (ca. 840-912), a monk of the Benedictine abbey of St. Gall in Switzerland. The Gradual, verses sung between the Epistle and Gospel at Mass, concluded, except in Lent, with "alleluia." On festive occasions the final syllable "-ia" was prolonged through varied cadences forty or fifty or even a hundred notes to give time for the deacon to go from the altar to the place, often distant (sometimes even as far as the rood loft), where the Gospel was to be chanted. Notker's contribution was to put words in place of the prolonged "-ia"; the words were called *sequences,* because they followed the gradual and continued the alleluia, or *proses,* compositions in rhythmical prose without a regular meter.[14] Hundreds of such sequences are known; in the present Roman rite the number has been reduced to five: Easter, Pentecost, Corpus Christi, *Dies irae* on All Souls' Day (November 2), and *Stabat Mater* (on Our Lady of Sorrows, September 15, but better known for its association with the Stations of the Cross.). Of these five only two are required, Easter and Pentecost, the first and the last days of the Easter season. The Easter sequence is *Victimae Paschali laudes,* perhaps by Wigbert [Wipo] of Burgundy, who died ca. 1050, a priest and chaplain to the Holy Roman emperors Conrad II (reigned 1024-1039) and Heinrich III (1039-1056). It is sung to a melody attributed to him. The traditional sequence is appointed in the Roman sacramentary and in the *Lutheran Book of Worship.*[15]

> Christians, to the Paschal Victim offer your thankful praises!
>
> A Lamb the sheep redeemeth: Christ, who only is sinless,
> Reconcileth sinners to the Father.
>
> Death and life have contended in that combat stupendous:
> The Prince of Life, who died, reigns immortal.
>
> Speak, Mary, declaring what thou sawest, wayfaring:
>
> "The tomb of Christ, who is living, the glory of Jesus' resurrection;
> Bright angels attesting, the shroud and napkin resting.
>
> Yea, Christ my hope is arisen; to Galilee he will go before you."
>
> Christ indeed from death is risen, our new life obtaining;
> Have mercy, victor King, ever reigning. Amen. Alleluia![16]

The hymn presents a rudimentary drama. There is an invitation to praise and a statement of the cause of the Paschal joy. Then Mary Magdalene is addressed, who in response, as the apostle to the Apostles, gives her testimony to what she has seen and experienced at the tomb. The little drama concludes with a ringing affirmation of her testimony. *Victimae Paschali* is an example of the gradual emergence of fully formed drama from the liturgical action of the Church during these years.[17] In addition to its use as the sequence sung on Easter Day and sometimes during Easter Week, in many places it was also sung at Matins on Easter Day between the third lesson and the singing of the Te Deum as a drama connected with the Easter Sepulcher, a representation of Jesus's tomb set up in the church. After the third responsory, two boys vested in white, representing the angels at the tomb, took their places to the right and to the left of the high altar. Three deacons in white dalmatics, representing the three Marys, came in from the right side and stood before the altar. The angels ask whom they sought; they answer, and the angels, taking a white cloth from the altar to represent the grave clothes, declare, "He is not here." The Marys respond, "Alleluia. The Lord is risen" and pass through the choir singing the *Victimae Paschali*. Then the Te Deum is sung.[18] From the *Victimae Paschali* the German vernacular spiritual folksong of ca. 1100 *Christ ist erstanden* ("Christ is arisen from the grave's dark prison"[19]) is derived. (The hymn makes its appearance in Goethe's *Faust*.[20]) Luther admired the hymn and incorporated its vivid picture of the conflict between Death and Life in his *Christ lag im Todesbanden* ("Christ Jesus lay in death's strong bands"[21]) to which he gave the title, "The song of praise, Christ is risen, improved."[22] Luther's second stanza in Richard Massie's translation reads:

> It was a strange and dreadful strife
>   When Life and Death contended;
> The victory remained with Life,
>   The reign of death was ended;
> Stripped of his power, no more he reigns,
> An empty form alone remains;
>   His sting is lost for ever!
>   Alleluia!

Jane Eliza Leeson (1807-1882) made a translation of *Victimae Paschali*, "Christ the Lord is ris'n today,"[23] which replaced the dialogue of the sequence with abounding praise. Her third stanza is

> Christ, the Victim undefiled, Alleluia!
> God and man hath reconciled; Alleluia!
> Whilst in strange and awful strife, Alleluia!
> Met together death and life. Alleluia!

Each line of the hymn lends itself to antiphonal singing, one group of voices singing the first part of each line and a second group responding with the Alleluia.

The solemn blessing for the Easter Season, derived from the Leofric Missal,[24] employs the three images of redemption, baptism, and freedom.

> May Almighty God, who has redeemed us and made us his children
> through the resurrection of his Son our Lord,
> bestow upon you the riches of his blessing. *Amen.*

> May God, who through the water of baptism has raised us from sin
> into newness of life, make you holy and worthy to be united with
> Christ for ever. *Amen.*

> May God, who has brought us out of bondage to sin into true and lasting
> freedom in the Redeemer, bring you to your eternal inheritance. *Amen.*

>   *or this*

> The God of peace, who brought again from the dead our Lord Jesus
> Christ, the great Shepherd of the sheep, through the blood of the ever-
> lasting covenant, make you perfect in every good work to do his will,
> working in you that which is well-pleasing in his sight; and the blessing
> of God Almighty, the Father, the Son, and the Holy Spirit, be among
> you, and remain with you always. *Amen.*

The second form is from Heb. 13:20-21.

Bright Week

Easter Week, called Bright Week in the Eastern churches, was given prominence very early; until the eighth century it was the only customary octave
in the Church's calendar. Surely one influence on the observance of Easter
Week was the Jewish weeklong celebration of Passover (Exod. 12:14-20). In
Egeria's time in Jerusalem there was a daily Eucharist that week, and it was
the occasion for the bishop's mystagogical lectures to the newly baptized to
continue their instruction and incorporation into the body of believers. In
Rome, the neophytes were brought together on successive days to each of the
great churches of the city for a celebration of the Eucharist and instruction in
the faith: The Easter Vigil was celebrated in the cathedral of Rome, St. John

Lateran; Easter Day at Saint Mary Major; Easter Monday at St. Peter's; Easter Tuesday at St. Paul's outside the walls; Easter Wednesday at St. Lawrence's outside the walls; Easter Thursday at the Church of the Twelve Apostles; Easter Friday at the Pantheon dedicated in the seventh century to St. Mary of the Martyrs; and Easter Saturday back at St. John Lateran. The week was given over to acts of Christian love. Bounteous meals were provided for the poor. The Emperor Theodosius closed the theaters and the circus during this week, and all labor ceased so that everyone might gather in the churches every day in praise of the joyful time, to encourage the newly baptized, and to review their own Christian responsibilities.

In later medieval times the week was shortened to three days (Monday, Tuesday, Wednesday), balancing the Triduum of Maundy Thursday, Good Friday, and Holy Saturday, by that time separated as three distinct days; and in 1094 the week was further shortened to two days, Monday and Tuesday. That custom, Easter Monday and Easter Tuesday, was continued in the Book of Common Prayer until 1979 and *The Lutheran Hymnal* (1941); in the Lutheran *Church Book* (1868), the *Common Service Book* (1917), and the *Service Book and Hymnal* (1958) provision was made for but one day, Monday after Easter. In general parish practice, Holy Week is given considerable attention, especially the last three days, but Easter Week is passed over as if the clergy and other ministers are exhausted by the time of Easter evening. It is nonetheless desirable to balance the austerity of Holy Week by finding ways to celebrate each of the days of Easter Week, by praying for and supporting and encouraging the newly baptized in the parish and beyond, by instruction in the faith, and by acts of love and care.

Easter Monday

Monday in Easter Week is Bright Monday. The antiphon of the Introit (*Introduxit vos*), given in Roman Catholic books and in *The Lutheran Hymnal*, is from Exod. 13:5, 9, "The Lord has brought you into a land flowing with milk and honey, alleluia, so that the teaching of the Lord may be on your lips, alleluia." In its original context the words are addressed to the Israelites upon their entrance into the Promised Land. In Christian use the image of the rich land "flowing with milk and honey" is a standard description of heaven, as in the twelfth-century hymn *Urbs Sion aurea* by Bernard of Cluny, "Jerusalem the golden, with milk and honey blest."[25] At their baptism new Christians were given a taste of milk and honey as a foretaste of the land that is now theirs. By Christ's passion and resurrection, Paradise has been restored. Already we stand in the heavenly country. But the antiphon and the psalm verse that follows, "O give thanks to the Lord, call upon his Name, make known his deeds among the peoples" (Ps. 105:1), remind the celebrants of the joyful Eastertide of the reason for their deliverance and their resulting responsibility: obedience to the Law of God and a missionary fervor. The collect in the Roman sacramentary, from the Gelasian sacramentary, reflects the Introit and prays for the newly baptized. It is translated in the Episcopal *Lesser Feasts and Fasts*:

> O God, you continually increase your Church by the birth of new sons and daughters in Baptism: Grant that they may be obedient all their days of their life to the rule of faith which they received in that Sacrament; through Jesus Christ your Son our Lord, who lives and reigns....[26]

The collect for Easter Monday in the Book of Common Prayer is from the Gregorian sacramentary, the Missale Gallicanum vetus, and the Missale Gothicum and is a more general prayer, having in its view all Christian people.

> Grant, we pray, Almighty God, that we who celebrate with awe the Paschal feast may be found worthy to attain everlasting joys; through Jesus Christ our Lord, who lives and reigns....

The Revised Common Lectionary does not provide readings for the days of Easter Week. The readings appointed in the Prayer Book and the Roman lectionary are

> Acts 2:14, 22-32. Peter testifies to the resurrection
> Psalm 16:8-11. The path of life
> Matt. 28:9-15 [Roman lectionary: 8-15]. The guards are bribed to lie about the resurrection.

On weekdays only two lessons are read, an Epistle (or Old Testament reading) and the Gospel.

Easter Tuesday

Tuesday in Easter Week is Bright Tuesday. The Introit (*Aqua sapientiae*) in Roman Catholic books and *The Lutheran Hymnal* is from Sirach (Ecclesiasticus) 15: 3, 4. The reference is to Wisdom: "She gave them the water of wisdom to drink, alleluia; she shall be made strong and shall not be moved, alleluia, and she shall exalt them forever, alleluia, alleluia." The Psalm is the same as on

Monday, Ps. 105:1. The reference to Wisdom in connection with the baptized is a reference to the Holy Spirit whose enlightenment was bestowed in baptism. The collect in the Roman Sacramentary is from the Gregorian sacramentary; it is translated in *Lesser Feasts and Fasts:*.

> O Lord, you have saved us through the Paschal mystery of Christ: Continue to support your people with heavenly gifts, that we may attain true liberty, and enjoy the happiness of heaven which we have begun to taste on earth; through Jesus Christ our Lord, who lives and reigns....[27]

The prayer is for the newly baptized, but it is also applicable to the whole body of believers. An accurate, straightforward, and suggestive translation would be "in the Paschal mystery you have healed the world." *The Daily Missal* of Dom Gaspar Lefebvre (1930) translates, "O God, who in the Paschal solemnity hast bestowed Thy saving remedies on the world...." *The Lutheran Hymnal* (1941) provides two collects for Easter Monday; curiously, they are both versions of the same translation. The first has "bestowed restoration upon the world" and the second "didst bestow life and freedom upon the world." The Book of Common Prayer provides for Easter Tuesday a collect from *Parish Prayers* edited by Frank Colquhoun (1967).

> O God, who by the glorious resurrection of your Son Jesus Christ destroyed death and brought life and immortality to light: Grant that we, who have been raised with him, may abide in his presence and rejoice in the hope of eternal glory; through Jesus Christ our Lord, to whom, with you and the Holy Spirit, be dominion and praise for ever and ever.

The biblical quotation is 2 Tim. 1:10; the conclusion alludes to Col. 1:27.
The readings appointed in the Prayer Book and the Roman lectionary are

Acts 2:36-41. The first converts to Christianity
Psalm 33:18-22. The Lord delivers from death
John 20:11-18. Jesus appears to Mary Magdalene.

Easter Wednesday

Wednesday in Easter Week is Bright Wednesday. The antiphon of the Introit (*Venite, benedicti*) extends Jesus's invitation, "Come, you that are blessed by my Father, receive the kingdom, alleluia, which was prepared for you from the foundation of the world, alleluia, alleluia, alleluia" (Matt. 25:34). Those who have been baptized are now heirs and citizens of heaven. The Psalm verse is 96:1, "Sing to the Lord a new song; sing to the Lord, all the earth." The new song is the song of heaven, the Church's perpetual hymn, Alleluia.

The collect in the Roman sacramentary for Easter Wednesday is appointed in the *Lutheran Book of Worship* for Easter evening. It is from the Gelasian sacramentary.

> O God, you gladden our hearts by the annual celebration of the resur-
> rection of our Lord: In your mercy grant that we, who now celebrate
> these joyous days on earth, may at length attain to the eternal Easter
> in heaven; through your Son Jesus Christ our Lord, who lives and
> reigns....[28]

If a congregation sang "Alleluia song of gladness" at the farewell to Alleluia before Lent began, this collect will echo the concluding stanza:

> Therefore in our hymns we pray thee
> Grant us, blessed Trinity,
> At the last to keep thine Easter
> In our home beyond the sky,
> There to thee forever singing
> Alleluia joyfully.[29]

Here Christians say with the Jews, "Next year in Jerusalem!"

The Prayer Book appoints a revision of a prayer by John W. Suter that in the 1928 Prayer Book was assigned to Easter Monday (the appointed Gospel was Luke 24:13-35)[30]; it is in the 1979 book also appointed for the Third Sunday of Easter.

> O God, whose blessed Son made himself known to his disciples in the
> breaking of bread: Open the eyes of our faith, that we may behold him
> in all his redeeming work; who lives and reigns....

The reference here is to the Gospel account of the supper at Emmaus.

The readings appointed in the Prayer Book and the Roman lectionary are

> Acts 3:1-10. Peter heals a crippled beggar
> Psalm 105:1-8. Praise of God's faithfulness
> Luke 24:13-35. The supper at Emmaus.

Easter Thursday

Thursday in Easter Week is Bright Thursday. The antiphon of the Introit is from the Wisdom of Solomon (10:20, 21), *Victricem manum tua*, "They praised with one accord your defending hand, O Lord, alleluia; for wisdom opened the mouths of those who were mute, and made the tongues of infants speak clearly, alleluia, alleluia, alleluia." The thanksgiving continues for the great things that have been done to the catechumens who have been enlightened by the Holy Spirit in their baptismal incorporation into the Church. The Psalm verse is 98:1, "O sing to the Lord a new song, for he has done marvelous things." The new song is preeminently the Alleluia. Clement of Alexandria, who died ca. 215, in his *Protreptikos* (Exhortation) made an eloquent appeal to the Greeks to listen to and abide by the New Song that is rising triumphantly over the fading voices of the past.[31]

The Roman sacramentary appoints a Gregorian collect.

> O God, you have made many nations, peoples, and races one in the confession of your Name: Grant that all who have been born again in the waters of Baptism may be united in faith and in holiness of life; through your Son Jesus Christ our Lord, who lives and reigns....[32]

Contrary to what one hears these days in praise of diversity, the prayer makes it clear that in the Church diversity is not of primary importance. What is important is that God has made a diversity of peoples one in the confession of his Name. It is their unity that is significant, reversing the chaos of Babel (Gen. 11:1-9), anticipating the perfect unity of heaven, and demanding ever more strenuous efforts toward the unity of the Church on earth.

The Book of Common Prayer appoints the Gregorian collect for Easter Friday. The translation is by William Bright.

> Almighty and everlasting God, who in the Paschal mystery established the new covenant of reconciliation: Grant that all who have been reborn into the fellowship of Christ's Body may show forth in their lives what they profess by their faith; through Jesus Christ our Lord, who lives and reigns....

The readings appointed in the Prayer Book and in the Roman lectionary are

> Acts 3:11-26. The power of the risen Jesus
> Psalm 8. The majesty of God and the dignity of humanity

or Psalm 114. God's wonders at the Exodus
Luke 24:36b-48 [Roman: 35-48]. Jesus appears to his disciples.

Easter Friday

Friday in Easter Week is Bright Friday. The antiphon of the Introit (*Eduxit eos*) is from Psalm 78:53, "He led them to safety, alleluia, but the sea overwhelmed their enemies, alleluia, alleluia, alleluia." The reference is to the passage through the Red Sea, understood as a type of baptism, and echoing a key reading at the Easter Vigil. The Psalm is the first verse of Ps. 78, "Give ear, O my people, to my teaching; incline your ears to the word of my mouth." It reminds all the baptized of their responsibility to obey the Law of God and its teachings, and corresponds to the Book of Deuteronomy in the experience of the Hebrews after their deliverance from Egypt through the sea.

The Roman sacramentary appoints the Gregorian collect given above, used by the Prayer Book on Easter Thursday. It echoes the request of the collect for Easter Day, asking that our faith in Jesus's resurrection be apparent in the way we live. The 1979 Book of Common Prayer appoints a Collect that Archbishop Cranmer composed for the 1549 Prayer Book for the second Communion on Easter Day, for Easter Tuesday, and for the First Sunday after Easter.

> Almighty Father, who gave your only Son to die for our sins and to rise for our justification: Give us grace so to put away the leaven of malice and wickedness, that we may always serve you in pureness of living and truth; through Jesus Christ your Son our Lord, who lives and reigns....

The biblical references are John 3:16; Rom. 4:25; 1 Cor. 5:7-8. (In the previous lectionary the Epistle for Easter Day was 1 Cor. 5:6-8.) "Put away the leaven" recalls the Jewish practice of removing all traces of leavened bread from the house at the time of the Passover celebration. "Leaven, because of its infectious quality, was a symbol of defilement and sin (except in Matt. xiii.33); unleavened bread was a sign of a new start, without the need of the sour dough from a previous baking."[33] The striking prayer extends the transformative process of fasting begun in Lent into the proper celebration of the resurrection.

The readings appointed in the Prayer Book and in the Roman lectionary are

Acts 4:1-12. Peter and John before the Council
Psalm 116:1-8. God's restoration of life
John 21:1-14. Jesus shows himself to seven disciples.

Easter Saturday

Saturday in Easter Week is Bright Saturday. The antiphon of the Introit (*Eduxit Dominus populum*) is from Ps. 105:43, "The Lord brought out his people with joy, alleluia; his chosen ones with singing, alleluia, alleluia, alleluia." The Psalm verse is Ps. 105:1, "O give thanks to the Lord, call on his Name, make known his deeds among the peoples." The joy of the baptized breaks into songs of praise and thanksgiving.

The Roman sacramentary uses a collect from the Gelasian and the Gregorian sacramentaries as the opening prayer. It is primarily a prayer for the newly baptized who are soon to lay aside their baptismal robes, but it is also a prayer for us all.

> O God, in the abundance of your grace you increase and multiply the number of those who believe in you: Mercifully look upon your chosen people, so that, having been reborn in the sacrament of Holy Baptism, they may be clothed in the garments of immortality; through your Son Jesus Christ our Lord, who lives and reigns....[34]

The Book of Common Prayer has revised a collect from the Mozarabic sacramentary, translated by William Bright in *Ancient Collects*.

> We thank you, heavenly Father, that you have delivered us from the dominion of sin and death and brought us into the kingdom of your Son; and we pray that, as by his death he has recalled us to life, so by his love he may raise us to eternal joys; who lives and reigns....

The biblical allusions are to Col. 1:13 and Rom. 6:9-14.

The readings appointed in the Prayer Book and the Roman lectionary are

> Acts 4:13-21. Peter and John cannot keep silent about the resurrection
> Psalm 118:14-18. The gate of the Lord
> Mark 16:9-15 [BCP adds v. 20]. The longer ending of Mark.

The Octave of Easter

The Sundays following Easter Day, which used to be counted "after Easter," are now counted as Sundays "of Easter," because Easter is to be understood as one long and great Sunday, a week of weeks, comprising the fifty days of rejoicing. The Second Sunday of Easter is now one of the two octaves remaining on the present calendar (the other being the octave of Christmas, January 1). In the old medieval Latin Missal and Breviary the Sunday bore the name *Dominica in albis [depositis]*, "the Sunday of [putting off] the white robes" by the newly baptized who had been so clothed throughout Easter Week. The octave acquired the name "Low Sunday," apparently derived from the first word of the sequence assigned to this day, *Laudes Salvatori vice modulemur* by Notker of St. Gall; less likely is the suggestion that the spirit of the Sunday is "low" compared to the high festivity of Easter Day. The Gospel in all three years of the lectionary cycle is the account of St. Thomas's insistence on visible and tangible proof of the resurrection. The narrative is in its proper chronological place, the resolution coming on the Sunday following the first appearance of Jesus to the ten Apostles (Thomas then being absent and Judas having killed himself), but the historical sequence, as always in the liturgical year, is only of secondary importance. The selection of the Gospel for the Sunday of St. Thomas is a consolation and encouragement of those thoughtful people who find the resurrection difficult or impossible to comprehend. Throughout these days of Easter the Church itself struggles with the fact and the meaning of the raising of Jesus from the dead and encourages all those who, like Thomas, struggle to believe the impossible. That Gospel continues to be part of the instruction that members of the Church all need to hear, Jesus's blessing of those who have not seen and yet have believed.

The Introit for the Octave of Easter (*Quasi modo geniti*) is from 1 Peter 2:2.

Antiphon. Like newborn infants, long for the pure, spiritual milk, alleluia, alleluia, alleluia.

   Ps. 81:1. Sing aloud to God our strength;
   shout for joy to the God of Jacob. *Gloria Patri.*
The antiphon is repeated: Like newborn infants...alleluia.

The antiphon presents an interesting image. The Church as a mother provides for her children the nourishing milk of the Word of Christ that leads to spiritual growth. (Julian of Norwich declared that Jesus is our Mother.[35]) The psalm verse quietly reminds Christians of their Hebrew ancestry, "God of Jacob."

The Octave once marked the close of Easter, and therefore the Gregorian collect appointed in the northern European missals (Bamberg, Constance, Nuremberg), the Roman Missal, and Lutheran orders for what was called the First Sunday after Easter could say by way of closure, we "have celebrated the solemnities of the Lord's resurrection." In the present calendar, however, this Sunday is the second of seven Sundays "of Easter." The mystery of the resurrection continues to unfold throughout the great Fifty Days.

The collect in the present Roman sacramentary, from the Missale Gothicum, responds to the struggle to believe with a presentation of the larger picture of the meaning of the declaration that Jesus, who was dead, is now alive for evermore.

> God of everlasting mercy, you renew the faith of your holy people by the yearly return of the paschal feast: Increase in us the grace you have bestowed, that we may comprehend more fully in whose font we have been cleansed, through whose Spirit we have been reborn, and by whose blood we have been redeemed; even your Son Jesus Christ our Lord, who lives and reigns....[36]

The prayer combines in an impressive way the font and the cross, our cleansing, rebirth, and redemption as evidences of God's mercy and grace.

The Book of Common Prayer appoints the Gregorian Collect it used on Thursday in Easter Week (used in the Roman rite on Easter Friday) and also after the seventh lesson at the Easter Vigil.

> Almighty and everlasting God, who in the Paschal mystery established the new covenant of reconciliation: Grant that all who have been reborn into the fellowship of Christ's Body may show forth in their lives what they profess by their faith; through Jesus Christ our Lord....

Faith is only the beginning; those who profess the Christian faith must show in their lives the reconciled fellowship into which they have been reborn.

The Revised Common Lectionary appoints these readings for the three years of the lectionary cycle.

Year A
>> Acts 2:14a, 22-32. Peter's Pentecost sermon
>>> (the beginning of a semi-continuous reading of Acts during Easter)
>> Psalm 16. You show me the path of life
>> 1 Peter 1:3-9. A living hope
>>> (the beginning of the continuous reading of 1 Peter)
>> John 20:19-31. My Lord and my God

Year B
>> Acts 4:32-35. The common life of believers
>>> (continuous reading of Acts from this point on)

Psalm 133. The blessings of unity
1 John 1:1-2:2. Eternal life revealed to us
    (beginning of the continuous reading of 1 John)
John 20:19-31. My Lord and My God
Year C
    Acts 5:27-32. We are witnesses
        (continuous reading of Acts from this point on)
    Psalm 118:14-29. Song of victory
    Rev. 1:4-8. Every eye will see him
        (beginning of a continuous reading of the Apocalypse)
    John 20:19-31. My Lord and my God.

The two Responsories in the Office of Readings in the *Liturgy of the Hours* both continue the emphasis of the old Collect for Easter Day: there is an ethical and moral dimension to the celebration of Easter. It is not sufficient to sing glad hymns and to rejoice in the celebration of the resurrection; we must change our lives and live the new life.

> Since you have been raised to life with Christ,
> set your hearts on the things of heaven
> where Christ is seated at God's right hand.
> > Seek the things that are above
> > and not the things of earth, alleluia.
> You have died,
> and your life is hidden with Christ in God.
> > Seek the things that are above
> > and not the things of earth, alleluia. [Col. 3:1-3]

The second Responsory emerges from the first.

> You have died,
> and your life is hidden with Christ in God.
> > When Christ who is your life appears,
> > you will appear with him in glory, alleluia.
> You must consider yourselves dead to sin,
> but alive to God in Jesus Christ our Lord.
> > When Christ who is your life appears,
> > You will appear with him in glory, alleluia.
> > > > [Col. 3:3-4; Rom. 6:11]

We are reminded that Easter is not the end. The liturgy maintains its forward look, waiting for the appearing of the risen Lord at the end of time. Then we, too, with St. Thomas, will see him with our own eyes.

The Third Sunday of Easter

This Sunday presents various appearances of the risen Lord. The antiphon of the Introit for the Third Sunday of Easter (*Misericordia*[37] *Domini*) is from Ps. 33:5, 6, "The earth is full of the steadfast love of the Lord, alleluia. By the word of the Lord were the heavens made, alleluia, alleluia." With eyes opened by faith, everywhere we look we see signs of God's goodness and mercy. The very existence of the world is evidence of his power and his love. Therefore, the psalm verse (33:1) directs, "Rejoice in the Lord, O you righteous. Praise befits the upright."

The collects for the Third Sunday of Easter all move in different directions. The opening Prayer in the Roman sacramentary recalls baptism and looks ahead to the resurrection at the last day. The prayer is a combination of collects in the Leonine and Gelasian sacramentaries, reflecting the Introit's childlike wonder at the glories of creation and redemption.

> Let your people ever exult, O God, in a renewed and youthful spirit, that we who now rejoice to be your adopted children may look forward with certain hope to the day of resurrection; through Jesus Christ our Lord....[38]

The biblical references include Ps. 103:5 and Isa. 40:31.

The Book of Common Prayer repeats the collect assigned to Easter Wednesday, a revision of the Collect for Easter Monday in the 1928 Prayer Book, written by John W. Suter, Sr.

> O God, whose blessed Son made himself known to his disciples in the breaking of bread: Open the eyes of our faith, that we may behold him in all his redeeming work; who lives and reigns....

The Collect was selected to go with the Gospel in Year A, the risen Lord's revelation of himself in the breaking of bread at Emmaus. The Roman Missal (1570) and previous Lutheran books used a Collect from the Gelasian and Gregorian sacramentaries, in the present Roman sacramentary appointed for Monday after Easter 4 and for the Fourteenth Sunday in Ordinary Time.

God, who by the humiliation of your Son raised up the fallen world: Grant to your faithful people perpetual gladness, and make those whom you have delivered from the danger of everlasting death partakers of eternal joys; through your Son Jesus Christ our Lord, who lives and reigns....

The proper celebration of the resurrection never leaves behind the crucifixion, for the two are two sides of one picture. The collect quietly reminds us once again that the effect of the humiliation of Christ was the restoration not just of fallen humanity but the restoration of the fallen world. "Earth, and stars, and skies, and ocean by that flood from stain are freed." The translation in Lutheran use from the *Church Book* through the *Service Book and Hymnal* is unusual in its one-word address, "God" (rather than "O God"), although the simple "*Deus*" is a not uncommon address in the Latin collects.

The Revised Common Lectionary appoints these readings.
Year A
>> Acts 2:14a, 36-41. The first converts
>> Psalm 116:1-4, 12-19. Deliverance from death
>> 1 Peter 1:17-23. Ransomed and born anew
>> Luke 24:13-35. Supper at Emmaus

Year B
>> Acts 3:12-19. The healing power of Jesus
>> Psalm 4. Prayer of thanksgiving
>> 1 John 3:1-7. Children of God
>> Luke 24:36b-48. Jesus appears to his disciples

Year C
>> Acts 9:1-6 (7-20). The conversion of Saul
>> Psalm 30. Thanksgiving after mortal danger
>> Rev. 5:11-14. Worthy is the Lamb
>> John 21:1-19. Jesus appears to seven disciples.

The Gospel in Year C notes that this was the third time that Jesus appeared to his disciples, hence its appointment on the Third Sunday of Easter.

The Fourth Sunday of Easter

The Fourth Sunday of Easter is the Sunday of the Good Shepherd, an image that distills the essence of the rescuing work wrought by Jesus. In many of the ancient baptisteries the figure of the Good Shepherd was a popular adornment, reinforcing its connection with Easter. Because we are under the watchful eye of the Good Shepherd, the antiphon of the Introit (*Jubilate Deo*), from Ps. 66:1-2, declares, "Make a joyful noise to God, all the earth, alleluia; sing the glory of his Name, alleluia; give to him glorious praise, alleluia, alleluia, alleluia." Again, as throughout Easter, all the earth rejoices in the restoration of life and joy; the people of God, standing in the light of the resurrection during these glad days, are unwearied in their praise of the mighty act of God. The Psalm verse is 66:3, "Say to God, 'How awesome are your deeds! Because of your great power, your enemies cringe before you.'"

The Collect common to the previous books of all three rites, was from the Leonine sacramentary. The Prayer Book translation was borrowed by the Lutherans.

> Almighty God, who showest to them that be in error the light of thy truth, to the intent that they may return into the way of righteousness: Grant unto all them that are admitted into the fellowship of Christ's religion that they may eschew those things that are contrary to their profession, and follow all such things as are agreeable to the same; through Jesus Christ, thy Son, our Lord, who liveth and reigneth....

The 1928 Prayer Book lamely replaced "eschew" with "avoid," but the original English translation of *respuere* was much more exact. "Eschew" means "spit out" (cf. Rev. 3:16, "because you are lukewarm...I am about to spit you out of my mouth"), and the use of the word here recalls the ancient baptismal practice, as part of the renunciation of Satan and all his works and all his ways, of spitting in the direction of the setting sun and then, turning toward the east and the rising sun, making the threefold profession of faith in the Father, the Son, and the Holy Spirit, following the three articles of the Apostles' Creed. The Collect is baptismal throughout, making reference to the enlightenment that baptism provides. Paul Strodach observes, "The Collect is of more than passing interest. It first of all admirably describes the life of the believer..." who is brought out of past error, converted by the guidance of the light of truth, returned into the Way, received into the Church for life in God's service. "Think of the countless throngs who have prayed it year after year these *centuries*! Think of the great multitude...*for* whom it has been prayed! What priceless, inspiring treasures these little prayers are!"[39]

The Roman sacramentary has replaced that superb collect with a prayer from the Gelasian sacramentary appropriate to the Good Shepherd and anticipating the ascension.

Almighty, everlasting God, guide us toward the joyful company of heaven, so that your lowly flock may follow where Christ, the great Shepherd, has gone before.[40]

The Book of Common Prayer appoints a new collect by Massey H. Shepherd, Jr., which is not unlike the Roman collect.

> O God, whose Son Jesus is the good shepherd of your people: Grant that when we hear his voice we may know him who calls us each by name, and follow where he leads; who, with you and the Holy Spirit, lives and reigns....

These two prayers fit with the Gospel for all three years, especially in Year A. The Good Shepherd (John 10:3-4) "goes ahead of them, and the sheep follow him because they know his voice." He calls his own sheep by name and leads them out of the safety and comfort of the fold and into the world.

The Revised Common Lectionary appoints these readings.

Year A
> Acts 2:42-47. Life of the believers
> Psalm 23. The Good Shepherd
> 1 Peter 2:19-25. The example of Christ's suffering
> John 10:1-10. The Good Shepherd

Year B
> Acts 4:5-12. Salvation only in Jesus
> Psalm 23. The Good Shepherd
> 1 John 3:16-24. Love in truth and action
> John 10:11-18. The Good Shepherd

Year C
> Acts 9:36-43. Peter raises Dorcas from the dead
> Psalm 23. The Good Shepherd
> Rev. 7:9-17. The ransomed from every nation
> John 10:22-30. The Good Shepherd.

This Sunday teaches that the Lamb who was slain is one with the Shepherd who lays down his life for the sheep. Moreover, as the Fourth Gospel presents the image, when Jesus calls himself the Good Shepherd he is making a divine claim, appropriating an image that in the Hebrew Bible was applied to God himself. In Ezek. 34:11-16, God condemns those who should have served as the shepherds of the people for abandoning their task and declares that he himself will do what they should have done.

The Fifth Sunday of Easter

All the days of Easter are to be understood as one feast, but their unity and coherence is not static. Rather, week by week the mystery deepens. Easter Day and the Second and Third Sundays of Easter present appearances of the risen Jesus. The Fourth Sunday presents the image of the Good Shepherd, who goes in search of his lost sheep and lays down his life for them. Beginning with Fifth Sunday of Easter the attention of the Church turns toward the Ascension and the deeper communion between the Lord and the faithful that the end of the resurrection appearances was understood to have brought about. The antiphon of the Introit (*Cantate Domino*), from Ps. 98:1a, 2, begins the subtle shift of focus from the resurrection to yet more wonderful things that flow from it: the ascension and the gift of the Holy Spirit. "O sing to the Lord a new song, for he has done marvelous things, alleluia. He has revealed his vindication in the sight of the nations, alleluia, alleluia, alleluia." The Psalm verse is 98:1b, "His right hand and his holy arm have gotten him victory." The Father has shown his power and his love by raising his Son from the dead. God has done marvelous things indeed, and here we praise his victory, its declaration, its application, its perpetuation through the centuries even to our own day.

The Roman sacramentary appoints a Gelasian collect as the opening prayer for this Sunday.

> O God, through whom redemption comes to us and our adoption
> is accomplished: Look in mercy on your children, and bestow upon
> all who believe in Christ perfect freedom and an eternal inheritance;
> through your Son Jesus Christ our Lord, who lives and reigns....[41]

The baptismal theme of Lent comes to its fruition in Easter. Not only are sinners redeemed by Christ's sacrifice on the cross; in Holy Baptism they are brought into God's family and adopted as his sons and daughters. The prayer is also used in the Roman rite on the Twenty-third Sunday in Ordinary Time and also on the Saturday of the second week of Easter. The Anglican and Lutheran rites avoid such duplication of use. The Book of Common Prayer appoints a revision of the collect written (1549) and revised (1662) for the Feast of SS. Philip and James.

> Almighty God, whom truly to know is everlasting life: Grant us so perfectly to know your Son Jesus Christ to be the way, the truth, and the life, that we may steadfastly follow his steps in the way that leads to eternal life; through Jesus Christ your Son our Lord, who lives and reigns....

It was chosen because of the specific allusion to the Gospel for Year A. The *Lutheran Book of Worship* retained the Gelasian collect, formerly shared by all three liturgical traditions. The original translation read:

> O God, who makest the minds of the faithful to be of one will: Grant unto thy people that they may love what thou commandest, and desire what thou dost promise; that, among the manifold changes of this world, our hearts may there be fixed where true joys are to be found; through thy Son, Jesus Christ our Lord....

The 1662 Prayer Book altered the antecedent clause to "who alone canst order the unruly wills and affections of sinful men." It is a prayer for the transformation of our lives, for a change so complete that we will love what we are required to do, that we obey God's Law and commands not out of constraint nor a sense of duty but out of a spontaneous desire. "To live from love and not from obligation is to exist in the precise place 'where true joys are to be found.' "[42]

The Revised Common Lectionary appoints these readings.
Year A
Acts 7:55-60. The death of the first martyr
Psalm 31:1-5, 15-16. Confident prayer in distress
1 Peter 2:2-10. A royal priesthood, a holy nation
John 14:1-14. Jesus is the Way to the Father, the Truth and Life
Year B
Acts 8:26-40. Philip and the eunuch
Psalm 22:25-31. God's universal dominion
1 John 4:7-21. God is love
John 15:1-8. Jesus the true vine

Year C

> Acts 11:1-18. Inclusion of the Gentiles
> Psalm 148. Cosmic Praise
> Rev. 21:1-6. A new heaven and a new earth
> John 13:31-35. The new commandment.

The Sixth Sunday of Easter

With this Sunday the Church looks ahead to the coming of the Holy Spirit of love. The antiphon of the Introit for the Sixth Sunday of Easter (*Vocem jucunditatis*) is from Isa. 48:20. "Declare this with a shout of joy, proclaim it, send it forth to the end of the earth: The Lord has redeemed his people, alleluia, alleluia." The Psalm verse is adapted from Ps. 100:1-2, "Make a joyful noise to God, all the earth; sing forth the honor of his Name; make his praise glorious." Again, the Church is reminded that the glad news of the resurrection is for all the world.

For this Sunday the Roman sacramentary has a new collect combined from the Leonine and the Gelasian sacramentaries.

> Enable us, almighty God, to celebrate with appropriate joy these days of gladness in the resurrection of our Lord, that we may proclaim in our lives the events we commemorate; through Jesus Christ our Lord....[43]

The request, often repeated during these days of Easter, is that we show in the way we live the life we celebrate with such joy.

The Book of Common Prayer appoints the Collect from the Gallican and Gelasian sacramentaries that in previous Prayer Books was appointed for the Sixth Sunday after Trinity, for the Fifth Sunday after Trinity in Lutheran use, and for the Fifth Sunday after Pentecost in the Roman Missal.

> O God, you have prepared for those who love you such good things as surpass our understanding: Pour into our hearts such love towards you, that we, loving you in all things and above all things, may obtain your promises, which exceed all that we can desire; through Jesus Christ our Lord, who lives and reigns....

"The Collect," Luther Reed comments, "is one of the finest in the Church's use, a prayer of rare spiritual beauty, perfect form, and fine diction. The original is Gelasian. The invocation is based on 1 Corinthians 2:9: 'Eye hath not seen, nor ear heard, neither have entered into the heart of man,' etc. The original chose the phrase, 'The things which eye hath not seen' (*invisibilia*); the 1549 translation, 'The things which have not entered into man's heart'; and the final form incorporated the phrase from Philippians 4:7, 'which passeth all understanding,' and became 'such good things as pass man's understanding.' The opening phrase 'for them that love thee' brings to mind our Lord's question addressed to Peter: 'Lovest thou me?' "[44] In its new context in the Easter season, the collect looks ahead to the coming of the promised Holy Spirit and beyond life in this world to the ultimate goal of life with the blessed in the heavenly kingdom.

The Revised Common Lectionary appoints these readings.

Year A

       Acts 17:22-31. Paul preaches in Athens

       Psalm 66:8-20. Corporate thanksgiving

       1 Peter 3:13-22. Baptism and new life

       John 14:15-21. The promise of the Advocate

Year B

       Acts 10:44-48. Gentiles receive the Holy Spirit

       Psalm 98. God, ruler of the world

       1 John 5:1-6. Love and obedience

       John 15:9-17. Love one another

Year C

       Acts 16:9-15. Baptism of Lydia

       Psalm 67. The nations called to praise God

       Rev. 21:10, 22-22:5. The new Jerusalem

       John 14:23-29. The promise of the Holy Spirit

       or John 5:1-9. Jesus heals a paralyzed man.

Rogationtide

In the year 470 Bishop Mammertus of Vienne in France ordered fasting, processions, and praying of litanies on the Monday, Tuesday, and Wednesday before Ascension Day. The occasion seems to have been earthquakes and poor harvests. The practice spread and took on the aspect of prayer asking God's blessing on the fields so that there would be a fruitful harvest, although the original penitential character remained and the liturgical color continued to be the Lenten violet for these "rogation days" (days of asking, from the Latin *rogare*, to ask, pray). The Sunday preceding these three days was sometimes called Rogation Sunday; a Latin name, still preserved among some Lutherans, was *Rogate*, "ask." Some sixteenth-century Lutheran church orders retained the rogation days; more commonly they were replaced by penitential days declared by proclamation as the need arose. A widespread European Lutheran custom was to observe a Day of Humiliation and Prayer yearly on the Wednesday before the last Sunday after Trinity, the last Sunday of the Church year. (The Episcopal *Book of Occasional Services* provides assistance for those parishes seeking to continue the traditional Rogationtide procession.) The present Prayer Book, followed by the Lutheran liturgy, expands these Rogation Days from their agricultural concern to include farming and fishing, commerce and industry, and the stewardship of creation. Although some may regard these days as irrelevant to an increasingly urban civilization, it may be countered that in such a situation the preservation and observance of days that remind city-dwellers of the origin of food supplies and their dependence on the moderate forces of nature are even more essential. Even for urban congregations, one is tempted to say *especially* for urban congregations, Rogationtide is an important contribution reminding us of what we can so easily ignore or forget: we are not independent creatures and need to remember our dependence on the natural world of which we are but a part.

The present Roman calendar now joins the rogation days to the ember days as times to pray for human needs, especially for the productivity of the earth and for human labor. Since the Roman Catholic Church includes dioceses in temperate and equatorial latitudes, in the northern and in the southern hemisphere, the time and the manner of the observance of these agricultural days are left to the episcopal conferences.

The rogation days are, however, of more than agricultural interest. The observance of these days can also foster and express gratitude for the world of nature. A familiar hymn by the Anglican layman Folliott Sandford Pierpoint (1835-1917) provides a comprehensive view of the beauty and wonder of nature.

> For the beauty of the earth,
>   For the beauty of the skies,
> For the love which from our birth
>   Over and around us lies:
> Christ our God, to thee we raise
>   This our sacrifice of praise.[45]

It is not the mere enjoyment of nature. The beauty that surrounds us is perceived as an expression of the all-encompassing love of the Creator for his creatures, love that was there when we were born, before we were aware of the beauty over us in the skies and around us on the earth or of the love of which the natural splendor is an expression. From our entrance into the world, the beautiful love has been there for us to discover and enjoy.

The biblical Psalm 19 has its primary focus on the testimony of the sun. Joseph Addison (1672-1719) in his remarkable paraphrase of the Psalm gives the day and the night equal attention. The "Ode" as he calls it in his periodical *The Spectator* No. 465, Saturday, August 23, 1712, begins in daylight.

> The spacious firmament on high,
> With all the blue ethereal sky,
>   And spangled heavens, a shining frame,
>   Their great Original proclaim.
> The unwearied sun, from day to day,
> Does his Creator's power display,
>   And publishes to every land
>   The work of an Almighty hand.

The splendor of the vault of heaven and the progress of the sun day after day display to all below the skies the handiwork of God. Then the glory of the night sky continues the proclamation and instruction. The waxing of the moon rehearses for the earth in their silent conversation the story of creation, emerging from darkness and increasing in fullness day after day.

> Soon as the evening shades prevail,
> The moon takes up the wondrous tale,
>   And nightly to the listening earth
>   Repeats the story of her birth;
> Whilst all the stars that round her burn,
> And all the planets in their turn,
>   Confirm the tidings as they roll,
>   And spread the truth from pole to pole.[46]

The feminine pronoun "her" refers equally well to the moon and to the earth. The moon repeats its own creation and at the same time shows the earth how it, too, emerged from the primal darkness.

Nature has a distinctive voice to praise its Maker, so the canticle *Benedicite, omnia opera* exults, "All you works of the Lord, bless the Lord—praise him and magnify him forever."[47]

Ascension Day

The observance of the Ascension of our Lord was originally kept on Easter Day or on the Fiftieth Day as a component of the unitive celebration of Easter and in accordance with the chronology of St. John's Gospel in which Jesus's Resurrection, Ascension, and sending of the Holy Spirit all occurred on the same day as one event. In fourth-century Jerusalem the pilgrim Egeria says nothing about the Ascension, but in the late fourth century in Asia Minor the Ascension was being separated from the Pentecost and celebrated as an historical event in accordance with Luke's chronology on the fortieth day after Easter Day. The emerging interest in chronological commemoration led to the division of the original fifty-day Pentecost into a forty-day Eastertide and a nine-day Ascensiontide. The emerging feast of the Ascension did more than mark the taking up of Jesus into heaven. It was an enthronement festival, the celebration of the exaltation of Christ as Lord of heaven and earth and his coronation as King of the universe. The Ascensiontide section of the great hymn by Fortunatus, who died ca. 600, has the continuing flowering of nature praise the continuation of the exaltation of Christ.

> He who was nailed to the cross is Lord and the ruler of nature;
> All things created on earth sing to the glory of God:
> Daily the loveliness grows, adorned with the glory of blossom;
> Heaven her gates unbars, flinging her increase of light.[48]

At Easter, the renewal of the earth is frequently in its early stages. Forty days later, at Ascension and ten days after that, at Pentecost, the renewal is in full flower.

The antiphon of the Introit for Ascension Day (Holy Thursday in Old English usage), *Viri Galilaei*, is the words of the angel to the apostles as they saw Jesus taken up into heaven from the first reading, Acts 1:11. "Men of Galilee, why do you stand looking up toward heaven? Alleluia. He who has been taken up from you into heaven will come in the same way as you saw him go into heaven, alleluia, alleluia, alleluia." The feast marks the completion of our Lord's redemptive work, and yet the story is not finished, for as the angel reminds the Eleven and us of the ever-present assurance, the risen Lord, whose earthly appearances have ended, will come again. The Psalm verse is 47:1, "Clap your hands, all you peoples; shout to God with loud songs of joy." God's people acclaim his victory and declare their sure and certain hope.

The Collect for Ascension Day in previous Roman, Lutheran, and Anglican books was drawn from the Gelasian sacramentary with a clear allusion to Col. 3:1-2. It continues to be appointed as an alternative prayer in the 1979 Prayer Book.

Grant, we pray, Almighty God, that as we believe your only-begotten Son to have ascended into heaven, so we may also in heart and mind there ascend, and with him continually dwell; who lives and reigns....

Paul Strodach comments, "The Collect brings a new element into our prayers. It is a petition based on a direct, simple, confession of faith, and much as in the Lord's Prayer our seeking forgiveness is based upon our own forgiving spirit, so the longed for inspiration for our life of service, our communion with our Lord, will reveal [and] be the measure of our faith in our ascended Lord and His blessed promises."[49]

The other collect provided for Ascension Day in the Book of Common Prayer derives from the Leonine sacramentary and recalls Eph. 4:10 and Matt. 28:20.

Almighty God, whose blessed Son our Savior Jesus Christ ascended far above all heavens that he might fill all things: Mercifully give us faith to perceive that, according to his promise, he abides with his Church on earth, even to the end of the ages; through Jesus Christ our Lord, who lives and reigns....

The prayer sets forth the mystery that the end of Jesus's resurrection appearances and his being taken from the earth into heaven does not imply his absence from his Church. In fact, because he is now beyond the bounds of time and space and free of their confinement, he is able to be present everywhere at once. The Roman sacramentary appoints a prayer drawn from a sermon (73,4) by Leo the Great.

Almighty God, on this day you took your only-begotten Son beyond our sight into heaven, exalting our human nature and promising us a share in your eternal splendor: Confirm our hope and lead us after him into the new creation, where he lives and reigns....[50]

In the ascension of Christ, the Church sees a promise of where his followers will be. Indeed, St. Augustine preached in a sermon on the ascension, we "are already in heaven with him, even though what is promised us has not yet been fulfilled in our bodies."[51]

The Revised Common Lectionary appoints one set of readings for Ascension Day.

Acts 1:1-11. Jesus ascends into heaven
Psalm 47. God, King of the world
  or 93. The splendor of God
Eph. 1:15-23. The riches of our inheritance
Luke 24:44-53. The ascension of Jesus.

In previous practice, to dramatize what was being celebrated, the Paschal candle was extinguished at the conclusion of the reading of the Gospel to show that the resurrection appearances had ended. In present practice with its emphasis on the unity of the Fifty Days of Easter, the candle remains lighted throughout the fifty days and is extinguished without ceremony after the final service on the Day of Pentecost.

The proper preface for the Ascension is from the Gregorian sacramentary and is used by all three rites. The translation that has been in Lutheran use since 1917 (*Common Service Book*) is in the *Lutheran Book of Worship*

> ...through Christ our Lord, who, after his resurrection openly appeared
> to his disciples and, in their sight was taken up into heaven, that he
> might make us partakers of his divine nature.

The translation is careful to say, instead of "ascended," "was taken up" reflecting the New Testament description of the action (Mark 16:19; Luke 24:51). Moreover, the preface expresses the Church's understanding of the Ascension as an enthronement festival, not only of Christ the King but in him of all humanity as well. John Chrysostom declared, "Our very nature...is enthroned today high above all cherubim."[52] Christopher Wordsworth (1807-1885) in his hymn "See the Conqueror mounts in triumph" sets forth clearly the same understanding of the meaning of the Ascension.

> Thou hast raised our human nature
> On the clouds to God's right hand:
> There we sit in heavenly places,
> There with thee in glory stand.
> Jesus reigns, adored by angels;
> Man with God is on the throne;
> Mighty Lord, in thine ascension,
> We by faith behold our own.[53]

The faith and teaching of the Church is that as we, like the Apostles, "stand looking up toward heaven" (Acts 1:11), so we will at the last be taken up with him and find our place at his side. Moreover, as always throughout the liturgy and liturgical year, the hope is directed toward the consummation of Christ's redeeming work. The "two men in white robes" who stood beside the Eleven, directed their eyes not up but ahead. "This Jesus, who has been taken up from you into heaven, will come in the same way as you saw him go into heaven" (Acts 1:11). In the Divine Office, the Responsory for Ascension Day points in the same direction.

> The Lord in all his beauty has been raised above the stars,
> and his splendor shines forth among the clouds of heaven,
>> where his Name shall be praised for ever, alleluia.
> From the heights of heaven he has come forth,
> and to those heights he returns,
>> where his Name shall be praised for ever, alleluia.
> Glory to the Father and to the Son and to the Holy Spirit,
>> where his Name shall be praised for ever, alleluia.[54]

Jesus, who left the Father's throne to be born as one of us, now, his work done, returns to the place from which he came. The circle is now complete.

A function of Ascension Day, coming toward the end of the Fifty Days, is to prepare us for the gift of the Holy Spirit, and its message is not complete until the days of the Pentecost have been fulfilled. The antiphon on the Magnificat at second vespers on Ascension Day is the moving plea,

> Victorious King, Lord of power and might,
>> today you have ascended in glory above the heavens.
> Do not leave us orphaned,
>> but send us the Father's promised gift,
>> the Spirit of truth, alleluia.[55]

As the Church, one with the Virgin Mary and the Apostles, waits during the nine days between the Ascension and Pentecost, the time is appropriately spent as a novena of prayer for the Holy Spirit that the Church and the world might be prepared to receive the promised gift.[56] Johannes Tauler (1300-1361) preached, "The Holy Spirit...comes according to our preparedness, and the more receptive we are, the more perfectly He will be received."[57] Isidore of Seville (d. 636), assuming that the joy of Easter was now past, encouraged fasting during these days: "We fast after Ascension Day and before Pentecost, the days in which the Bridegroom is taken away" (Matt. 9:15).

The Seventh Sunday of Easter

The Seventh Sunday of Easter focuses on the work of Christ the eternal High Priest and Intercessor on our behalf, praying to the Father for the welfare and unity of the Church. The antiphon of the Introit for this Sunday (*Exaudi Domine*) is from Ps. 27:7-9. "Hear, O Lord, when I cry aloud, alleluia; 'Come,' my heart says, 'seek his face!' Your face, Lord, do I seek. Do not hide your face from me, alleluia, alleluia, alleluia." The Psalm verse is 27:1, "The Lord is my light and my salvation; whom shall I fear?" We hear the waiting, expectant Church, then between the Ascension and Pentecost, now between Pentecost and the Parousia, struggling to come to terms with the end of the resurrection appearances, pleading to God still to show his face, assured of his continuing presence and protection.

The collect in the Book of Common Prayer, introduced in the 1549 Prayer Book, derives from the antiphon to the Magnificat at vespers on Ascension Day.

> O God, the King of glory, you have exalted your only Son Jesus Christ with great triumph to your kingdom in heaven: Do not leave us comfortless, but send us your Holy Spirit to strengthen us and exalt us to that place where our Savior Christ has gone before; who lives and reigns...

Drawing on many passages in Jesus's long farewell discourse reported in John 14-16, the collect is an appeal to the Father to remember his Son's promise of a Comforter (or Advocate in modern translations, John 14:16, 18), one who will strengthen and defend his followers. There is a tradition that the Venerable Bede prayed this antiphon on his deathbed.

The Roman sacramentary and the Lutheran rite appoint the Leonine collect used in the Book of Common Prayer on Ascension Day, given above, "Almighty God, whose blessed Son our Savior Jesus Christ ascended far above all heavens that he might fill all things: Mercifully grant that, according to his promise, he abides with his Church on earth, even to the end of the ages; through Jesus Christ our Lord...."

The Revised Common Lectionary gives these readings.
> Year A
>> Acts 1:6-14. The ascension of Jesus
>> Psalm 68:1-10, 32-35. Exalt him who rides upon the heavens
>> 1 Peter 4:12-14; 5:6-11. The inevitability of suffering
>> John 17:1-11. The high priest prays for his people

Year B

> Acts 1:15-17, 21-26. Matthias chosen to replace Judas
>
> Psalm 1. The two ways
>
> 1 John 5:9-13. Whoever has the Son has life
>
> John 17:6-19. The high priest prays for his people

Year C

> Acts 16:16-34. Paul and Silas in prison
>
> Psalm 97. Earth rejoices in its King
>
> Rev. 22:12-14, 16-17, 20-21. Surely I am coming soon
>
> John 17:20-26. The high priest prays for his people.

The Day of Pentecost: the Fiftieth Day of Easter

The Day of Pentecost, from the Greek *pentakoste*, fifty, marks the completion of Easter, the gift of the Holy Spirit on the fiftieth day. The feast has been celebrated as a Christian festival at least since the third century. It also bears the name Whitsunday, that is, "white Sunday" perhaps from the white robes worn by the newly baptized (baptism, because of the climate, being delayed until Pentecost in northern Europe), although it may perhaps come from "Wit-Sunday" from the early Anglo-Saxon "wit" meaning wisdom, since the Spirit, the Counselor, teaches the Church and leads into all truth.[58] One of the names for the Holy Spirit is Wisdom and readings from the Wisdom literature of the Hebrew Bible are traditional in connection with the Spirit. Roses, whose bloom looks something like tongues of fire, are a traditional adornment of the altar on Pentecost. In some places it was customary to scatter roses from the roofs of the churches to recall the descent of the Holy Spirit, and hence the name arose *Pascha rosatum*, the Paschal day of roses. In other places the blowing of trumpets during the services brought to ear and mind the Pentecostal sound of the "rushing, mighty wind."

In German lands, Pentecost, *Pfingsten*, involves a celebration of the arrival of spring and the resurrection of the life of the natural world corresponding to the celebration of Rogationtide in England. The yearly renewal of nature, which, as we have seen, is a feature of the celebration of Easter, took longer to arrive in northern Europe.

The increasing separation of Pentecost from Easter and its emergence as a separate festival, the Festival of the Holy Spirit, following Christmas as the Festival of God the Father and Easter as the festival of God the Son, is perhaps related to the developing of a theology of the Holy Spirit, especially by the Cappadocians in the latter fourth century. As a separate feast, Pentecost was given a Vigil and became the occasion for the baptism of those who could not be baptized at the Great Vigil of Easter. (Acts 2:41 reports that on the first Christian Pentecost three thousand were baptized.) A rubric in the 1979 Prayer Book (p. 227) outlines such a Vigil service. Later, in Rome by the seventh century (in the Gelasian sacramentary), Pentecost was given an octave, destroying the coherence of the Fifty Days and establishing Pentecost as a distinctly separate festival. The observance of Whitsun Week happened quite early. The *Apostolic Constitutions* (ca. 350-380) directs, "After you have kept the festival of Pentecost, keep one more week of festival, and, after that, fast."[59] In the Gregorian sacramentary a second and even a third day of celebration was added to the Sunday, as had happened with Christmas and Easter.[60] The present calendars of the Roman, Anglican, and Lutheran rites all restore the Day of Pentecost as the conclusion of the single festival of the risen Christ. The next day, Monday after Pentecost, ordinary time begins.

The antiphon of the Introit (*Spiritus Domini*) is from the Wisdom of Solomon 1:7. "The Spirit of the Lord has filled the world, alleluia; and that which holds all things together knows what is said, alleluia, alleluia, alleluia." The Lutheran rite replaced the second and obscure part of the antiphon with Ps. 68:3, "Let the righteous be joyful; let them exult before God; let them be jubilant with joy, alleluia, alleluia." The Psalm verse is 68:1, "Let God rise up, let his enemies be scattered; let those who hate him flee before him." This day is a feast of consummate triumph.

The collect in the Roman sacramentary and the Book of Common Prayer is from the Gelasian sacramentary and is a new appointment in both books. It is translated in the Prayer Book:

> Almighty God, on this day you opened the way of eternal life to every race and nation by the promised gift of your Holy Spirit: Shed abroad this gift throughout the world by the preaching of the Gospel, that it may reach the ends of the earth; through Jesus Christ our Lord, who lives and reigns with you, in the unity of the Holy Spirit, one God, for ever and ever.

The Book of the Acts of the Apostles, the first reading throughout the Fifty Days, has detailed the extension of the growing Church beyond the boundaries of the Holy Land into the lands of the Mediterranean. The collect asks for the continuation in our own time of that expansion into all the earth.

The Book of Common Prayer also provides an alternative Collect for Pentecost. It is from the Gregorian sacramentary and was the collect appointed in the 1570 Roman Missal, previous Lutheran orders, and previous Prayer Books. It is a splendid prayer, suitable to many occasions in the life of the Church.

> O God, who on this day taught the hearts of your faithful people by sending to them the light of your Holy Spirit: Grant us by the same Spirit to have a right judgment in all things, and evermore to rejoice in his holy comfort; through Jesus Christ your Son our Lord, who lives and reigns....

The prayer is built on Jesus's promise, "I still have many things to say to you, but you cannot bear them now. When the Spirit of truth comes, he will guide you into all the truth" (John 16:12-13, from the Gospel in Year B). The word "comfort," from the Authorized Version translation "Comforter," means "strength" as well as "consolation." (John 14:16-17, 26). In the Prayer Book, the Collect for Easter 7 in the traditional form has "send to us thine Holy Ghost to comfort us"; in the contemporary form it becomes "send us your Holy Spirit to strengthen us." In his translation Thomas Cranmer brought the already admirable Latin prayer to perfection with the addition of "in all things," "evermore," and "holy."

The Revised Common Lectionary appoints these readings. The first reading that tells the story of the day and also the responsorial Psalm are the same in all three years.

Year A
    Acts 2:1-21. The coming of the Holy Spirit
    Psalm 104:24-34, 35b. The glories of creation
    1 Cor. 12:3b-13. Varieties of gifts
    John 20:19-33. Jesus breathes his Spirit upon the Church
Year B
    Acts 2:1-21. The coming of the Holy Spirit
    Psalm 104:24-34, 35b. The glories of creation
    Rom. 8:22-27. The Spirit intercedes for the saints
    John 15:26-27; 16:4b-15. The work of the Spirit
Year C
    Acts 2:1-21. The coming of the Holy Spirit
    Psalm 104:24-24, 35b. The glories of creation
    Rom. 8:14-17. The Spirit of adoption
    John 14:8-17 (25-27). The promise of the Holy Spirit.

The alleluia verse sung after the Epistle to welcome the Gospel is an eleventh-century antiphon "Alleluia. Come, Holy Spirit, fill the hearts of the faithful and kindle in them the fire of thy love, alleluia" The hymn "Come down, O Love divine" by Bianco da Siena (d. 1434?)[61] expands on the thought of this antiphon. Luther based his hymn "Komm, heiliger Geist, Herre Gott" ("Come, Holy Ghost, God and Lord"[62]) on a German stanza that had developed from the Latin antiphon.

The traditional sequence hymn that follows the alleluia is the twelfth-century *Veni, Sancte Spiritus*, called "the Golden Sequence." It is a masterpiece of Latin hymnody and has been described as the first in loveliness as the *Dies irae* is the first in terror.[63] It is a remarkable and moving gathering of images in praise of the Holy Spirit. The translation in *Hymns Ancient and Modern* is a revision of the work of Edward Caswall.[64] The translation reproduces the rhyme scheme of the original Latin, aabccb.

> Come, thou Holy Spirit, come,
> And from thy celestial home
>   Shed a ray of light divine;
> Come, thou Father of the poor,
> Come, thou source of all our store,
>   Come, within our bosoms shine:

The hymn is saturated with the spirit and language of the wisdom litera-ture of the Bible. In the first stanza the first line echoes Wis. 7:7; the sec-ond line Wis. 7:25; 9:4, 10; the third line Wis. 6:12; 7:26; the fourth line Ps. 68:5; Job 29:16; Sirach 4:10 (see also Luke 6:20); the fifth line Prov. 8:18-21, 35; Sirach 1:17; the sixth line Prov. 2:10. Thus, biblical language informs the entire hymn.

> Thou of comforters the best,
> Thou the soul's most welcome guest,
>   Sweet refreshment here below;
> In our labor rest most sweet,
> Grateful coolness in the heat,
>   Solace in the midst of woe.
>
> O most blessèd Light divine,
> Shine within these hearts of thine,
>   And our inmost being fill;
> Where thou art not, man hath naught,

Nothing good in deed or thought,
  Nothing free from taint of ill.

Heal our wounds; our strength renew;
On our dryness pour thy dew;
  Wash the stains of guilt away;
Bend the stubborn heart and will;
Melt the frozen, warm the chill;
  Guide the steps that go astray.

On the faithful, who adore
And confess thee, evermore
  In thy sevenfold gifts descend:
Give them virtue's sure reward,
Give them thy salvation, Lord,
  Give them joys that never end.[65]

The torrent of images and prayers suggests both the depth of human need and the abundance of the Spirit's gifts.

The Gospel for Pentecost, especially in Year A with its echo of Genesis 2:7, God breathing the Spirit of life into mortals at the creation and also breathing the Holy Spirit into believers at the creation of the Church, suggests the striking description by Pius XII of the Holy Spirit as "the soul of the Church." It is the Holy Spirit dwelling in Christians that gives life and vitality to the people of God.

The proper preface for Pentecost in the Gelasian and Gregorian sacramentaries, the Sarum rite, the Roman Missal, and the Lutheran orders is

through Jesus Christ our Lord, who, ascending above the heavens and sitting at your right hand, poured out on this day the Holy Spirit, as he had promised, upon the chosen disciples, at which the whole earth rejoices with exceeding joy.

The redemption of the world, begun before the foundation of the world, inaugurated in Bethlehem, accomplished on the cross, confirmed in the ascension and enthronement of Christ is fulfilled in the sending of the Spirit, and all the components of the great work are at last in place. This finality causes the whole world to rejoice with surpassing joy. The Preface of Pentecost in the Roman sacramentary emphasizes the unity given by the Holy Spirit.

> ...bringing your Paschal Mystery to completion,
> you bestowed the Holy Spirit today
> on those you made your adopted children
> by uniting them to your Only-Begotten Son.
> This same Spirit, as the Church came to birth,
> opened to all peoples the knowledge of God
> and brought together the many languages of earth
> in profession of the one faith.

The 1979 Prayer Book focuses on several graces that are the work of the Spirit: guidance into truth; unity in the one faith, the priesthood of the laity, and the "Great Commission" to preach the Gospel to all nations.[66]

> Through Jesus Christ our Lord. In fulfillment of his true promise, the Holy Spirit came down [on this day] from heaven, lighting upon the disciples, to teach them and to lead them into all truth; uniting peoples of many tongues in the confession of one faith, and giving to your Church the power to serve you as a royal priesthood, and to preach the Gospel to all nations.

The solemn blessing for the Day of Pentecost in the Episcopal *Book of Occasional Services* is based on the blessing in the Roman sacramentary.

> May Almighty God, who enlightened the minds of the disciples by pouring out upon them the Holy Spirit, make you rich with his blessing, that you may abound more and more in that Spirit for ever. *Amen.*

> May God, who sent the Holy Spirit as a flame that rested upon the heads of the disciples, burn out all evil from your hearts, and make them shine with the pure light of his presence. *Amen.*

> May God, who by the Holy Spirit caused those of many tongues to proclaim Jesus as Lord, strengthen your faith and send you out to bear witness to him in word and deed. *Amen.*

> And the blessing of God Almighty, the Father, the Son, and the Holy Spirit, be upon you and remain with you for ever. *Amen.*

> *or this*

May the Spirit of truth lead you into all truth, giving you grace to confess that Jesus Christ is Lord, and to proclaim the wonderful works of God; and the blessing of God Almighty, the Father, the Son, and the Holy Spirit, be among you and remain with you always. *Amen.*

In the Daily Office the antiphon on the Magnificat at first vespers anticipates the events of the day of Pentecost as well as the antiphon in the Alleluia Verse before the Gospel.

> Come, Holy Spirit, fill the hearts of the faithful
> and kindle in them the fire of your love.
> > Though they spoke many different languages,
> > you made the nations one in professing the same faith.[67]

The Holy Spirit is the Spirit and bond of unity among Christians. The repeated invocation of the Holy Spirit, "Come," echoes the insistent Advent pleading, "Come, Lord Jesus." Christians, since the ascension without the visible presence of Christ, have the continuing presence of his Spirit to guide them into all the world and into all truth.

The antiphon on the Magnificat at second vespers brings not just the services of the day to a close but also the celebration of Easter, the Pentecost, to its conclusion.

> Today the fifty days have been completed, alleluia.
> The Holy Spirit gave the apostles spiritual gifts
> > and sent them out to preach to the whole world
> > and to proclaim that all who believe and are baptized
> > > shall be saved. Alleluia.[68]

The Paschal candle is extinguished after the last service on Pentecost, marking the completion of the Great Fifty Days.

The traditional summer ember days were the Wednesday, Friday, and Saturday after Pentecost, signifying the return to the regular round of fasting that had been forbidden during the Great Fifty Days of Easter.

Popular Customs

Corresponding to the Christmas Crèche, the Easter garden, an arrangement of plants and flowers around a representation of a tomb, was set up in many churches (and in some churches still), making vivid the verse from the Gospel,

"Now there was a garden in the place where he was crucified, and in the garden there was a new tomb in which no one had ever been laid" (John 19:41). The origins are doubtless pre-Christian, rooted in celebrations of the renewal of the earth, but the custom can still speak to a congregation (at least in the northern hemisphere) of the celebration of the resurrection by the natural world, bringing nature into the church and allowing it to show its joyful praise not only outside the building but inside as well. On Good Friday a crucifix was placed in the undecorated tomb to dramatize the death and burial. The crucifix would be quietly removed from the tomb before the Easter Vigil in preparation for the services of Easter Day. The annual awakening of nature is transformed by the representation of the empty tomb, and the natural rhythm of the seasons becomes a celebration of the great once-for-all event of the victory of Life over the forces of death. Moreover, the Easter garden teaches that as nature is renewed and produces new life, so must each Christian be renewed to live the new life as several Easter collects pray.

The decoration and blessing of eggs, from pre-Christian fertility celebrations, was incorporated into the life of the Church, East and West, as a sign and celebration of the resurrection.

The blessing of lambs at Easter is recorded as early as the seventh-century Bobbio missal. Lamb was long a favorite food at Easter because of its association with the Passover (Exodus 12:8) and the sacrificial Lamb of God. Lamb is surely to be preferred to the Easter ham, which seems to have its origins in a blatant rejection of the Jewish dietary laws.

A once-popular custom, the blessing of food at Easter seems to have originated as a check on overindulgence after the Lenten fast. In a time of general excessive consumption, the remembrance of such a custom can again be useful, healthful, and instructive. We are to use responsibly our restored freedom to eat, and we ought to keep in mind Luther's remarkably broad understanding of "daily bread" in his explanation of the Our Father in the *Small Catechism,* "Everything included in the necessities and nourishment for our bodies, such as food, drink, clothing, shoes, house, farm, fields, livestock, money, property, an upright spouse, upright children, upright members of the household, upright and faithful rulers, good government, good weather, peace, health, decency, honor, good friends, faithful neighbors, and the like."[69] Food is only one part of God's gifts of daily bread that we are to use with responsible care.

8

Ordinary [Ordered] Time

THE TIME BETWEEN the Epiphany and Ash Wednesday and between the Day of Pentecost and the beginning of Advent are two "green seasons," so called from their liturgical color. There is a slight divergence in understanding and observance between the Roman Catholic Church on the one hand and the Anglicans and Lutherans on the other. In Roman Catholic use, immediately after the Epiphany what is called in the Roman calendar "ordinary," that is to say, ordered or numbered, time begins. Sundays during these two periods are counted as simply "Sundays of the Year." The old Epiphany season loses its distinctive character.

The Time after the Epiphany

In Anglican and Lutheran use, the season following the Epiphany retains something of its former character. Although the liturgical color is usually the neutral green, the proper preface throughout the season is the preface of the Epiphany. Especially among Lutherans, the time after the Epiphany, the Epiphany season, often focused on (mostly foreign) missions as an extension of the manifestation of Christ to the Gentiles. On January 6, the Magi come and worship. The Gospel for the First Sunday after the Epiphany was Luke 2:41-52, the boy Jesus in the temple exploring his station as Son of God. The Gospel for the Second Sunday, John 2:1-11, described Jesus at the marriage at Cana in Galilee as the Lord of gladness. The Gospel for the Third Sunday, Matt. 8:1-13, the healing of the Roman centurion's servant, showed Jesus to be the Savior of the Gentiles. The Gospel for the Fourth Sunday, Matt. 8:23-27 in which Jesus calms the storm on the Sea of Galilee revealed Jesus as the Lord of nature. On the Fifth Sunday, the Gospel was Matt. 13:24-30, the parable of the wheat and the weeds, in which Jesus is manifested as the Lord of time and history.[1] The Epistles for the first four Sundays after the Epiphany were from the concluding hortatory section of Romans and are evidently survivals of a *lectio continua* in the early Church.[2]

The Baptism of Our Lord

In Lutheran practice, the time after the Epiphany begins and ends with a festival, the color of which is white. The voice of the Father is heard at the beginning and at the end of the season, over the Jordan and above the mount of transfiguration, and the declaration is the same: "This is my Son." The First Sunday after the Epiphany in all three traditions is the celebration of the Baptism of Our Lord. The liturgical commemoration of the event originated in the East. Since the eighth century the West remembered the Baptism of Our Lord on the octave of the Epiphany (January 13) with a collect and Gospel (John 1:29-34); the rest of the Mass was a repetition of the Mass for the Epiphany. The feast of the Baptism of Christ was formally introduced into the Roman calendar in 1960 and since the reforms of the Second Vatican Council has been set on the Sunday following the Epiphany to bring the Christmas cycle to a close, the figure of John the Baptist tying together the first seasons of the liturgical year, Advent through the Epiphany. The Anglicans and Lutherans quickly accepted the festival of the Baptism of the Lord into their calendars.

In the Graduale Romanum as in the Gregorian missal, the Introit antiphon for the Feast of the Baptism of the Lord is Ps. 45:7, "You love righteousness and hate wickedness. Therefore God, your God, has anointed you with the oil of gladness beyond your companions." The Psalm verse is 45:1, "My heart overflows with a goodly theme; I address my verses to the king." In the Roman sacramentary the entrance antiphon for the Baptism of the Lord is from Matt. 3:16-17, "After the Lord was baptized, the heavens were opened, and the Spirit descended upon him, and the voice of the Father thundered, 'This is my beloved Son, with whom I am well pleased.'"

The newly composed collect derives from the antiphon.

> Almighty and everlasting God, when Christ was baptized in the River Jordan, the Holy Spirit came upon him and your voice declared him your beloved Son: Grant that your adopted children, who have been born anew of water and the Spirit, may continue always to do your will; through Jesus Christ our Lord....

The Roman book also provides as an alternative prayer the Gelasian and Gregorian collect that in the 1570 Missal had been appointed for January 13, the octave of the Epiphany (now also appointed for Tuesday between the Epiphany and the Baptism).

> O God, your only-begotten Son has appeared in the substance of our human flesh: Grant that he, whose outward form is like our own, may reshape us inwardly by his grace; through the same....[3]

The Book of Common Prayer has a collect drafted by Charles Mortimer Guilbert based on the two Roman prayers.

> Father in heaven, who at the baptism of Jesus in the River Jordan proclaimed him your beloved Son and anointed him with the Holy Spirit: Grant that all who are baptized into his Name may keep the covenant they have made, and boldly confess him as Lord and Savior; who with you and the Holy Spirit lives and reigns, one God, in glory everlasting.

The *Lutheran Book of Worship* slightly revised the Prayer Book collect to avoid any implication that the baptismal covenant is something that mortals can make and safeguarding the biblical understanding of God's unilateral covenant with his people.

> Father in heaven, at the baptism of Jesus in the River Jordan you proclaimed him your beloved Son and anointed him with the Holy Spirit. Make all who are baptized into Christ faithful in their calling to be your children and inheritors with him of everlasting life; through your Son, Jesus Christ our Lord....

The Revised Common Lectionary appoints these readings for the Baptism of Our Lord.

Year A
> Isa. 42:1-9. Here is my servant
> Psalm 29. The voice of the Lord over the waters
> Acts 10:34-43. God anointed Jesus with the Holy Spirit
> Matt. 3:13-17. John baptizes Jesus

Year B
> Gen. 1:1-5. God's Spirit moves over the waters at creation
> Psalm 29. The voice of the Lord over the waters
> Acts 19:1-7. The Holy Spirit came upon them
> Mark 1:4-11. John baptizes Jesus

Year C

Isa. 43:1-7. I have called you by name
Psalm 29. The voice of the Lord over the waters
Acts 8:14-17. They received the Holy Spirit
Luke 3:15-17, 21-22. The baptism of Jesus.

An office hymn from the eleventh century or earlier, sung at Lauds during the Epiphany octave in some breviaries, *A Patre Unigenitus*, neatly weaves together the themes of Advent, Christmas, the Epiphany, and the baptism of Jesus. The translation is by John Mason Neale, revised in current Lutheran books.[4]

> From God the Father, virgin-born,
> To us the only Son came down;
> By death the font to consecrate,
> The faithful to regenerate.

The consecration of the baptismal font reflects the understanding that Jesus was baptized in order to baptize the waters of the earth so they could effect the rebirth of those who were washed in Holy Baptism. "Christ is baptized, not to be made holy by the water, but to make the water holy," Bishop Maximus of Turin preached.[5] The second stanza speaks more clearly of the restoration of creation achieved by the passion and the bestowal of new joy in a world that because of the fall had been bereft of gladness.

> Beginning from his home on high
> In human flesh he came to die;
> Creation by his death restored,
> And shed new joys of life abroad.

The themes of light and healing derive not only from Mal. 4:2 ("the sun of righteousness shall rise, with healing in its wings") but from the emphases of the Epiphany season.

> Glide on, O glorious Sun, and bring
> The gift of healing on your wing;
> To every dull and clouded sense
> The clearness of your light dispense.

> Abide with us, O Lord, we pray;
> The gloom of darkness chase away;

> Your work of healing, Lord, begin,
> And take away the stain of sin.

The Advent promise of the Lord's return is never far away in the liturgy, and that confidence in his final appearing is the strength of those who engage in the struggles of life now. Moreover, a vigorous antiphon in the Liturgy of the Hours declares the victory of Christ in combat with Satan in the Jordan: "In the Jordan river our Savior crushed the serpent's head and wrested us free from his grasp."[6] In the Gospel accounts, the next event in Jesus's life after his baptism was his temptation. Already, the antiphon asserts, the victory has been won, and the promise of Gen. 3:15 is accomplished. The hymn prays that he who was victor in his contest with Satan will defend his people in theirs.

> Lord, once you came to earth's domain
> And, we believe, shall come again;
> Be with us on the battlefield,
> From every harm your people shield.
>
> To you, O Lord, all glory be
> For this your blest epiphany;
> To God whom all his hosts adore,
> And Holy Spirit evermore.

"Epiphany" in the final stanza refers not simply to the themes of the January 6 feast and the Sunday following but to the whole revelation of the love of God in the birth, passion, death, resurrection, and return of Christ.

The Last Sunday after the Epiphany: Transfiguration

In the Lutheran calendar, the last Sunday after the Epiphany is observed as the Transfiguration of Our Lord. The reformers Veit Dietrich (1506-1549) and Johann Bugenhagen (1485-1558) chose the Transfiguration as the theme for sermons on the Sixth Sunday after the Epiphany, and eventually this became the general Lutheran use. The 1868 *Church Book*, remembering that Jesus after descending from the mount of transfiguration "set his face to go to Jerusalem" (Luke 9:53), appointed the Transfiguration for the Last Sunday after the Epiphany every year, except when there was only one Sunday after the Epiphany.[7] It was a happy innovation. The festival provides a conclusion to the time after the Epiphany, commemorating a stunning manifestation of the glory of Christ and at the same time serving as a bridge to Lent, a glimpse of glory before descending into the shadowed valley of the great fast. The 1979 Book of Common Prayer on this Sunday shares everything the Lutherans had introduced except for the title, Transfiguration. The 1570 Roman Missal commemorated the Transfiguration on the Second Sunday in Lent as an introduction to the Paschal mystery, and the ancient custom was continued in the 1970 Roman sacramentary. Thus, all three Western liturgical traditions observe the Transfiguration twice in the year: on August 6[8] and also on a Sunday after the Epiphany or in Lent. In the Roman rite, the Sunday before Ash Wednesday is simply a Sunday in Ordinary Time; the liturgical color is green. In Lutheran use the color is white for the feast; in Episcopal use white is optional.

The Collect for the Last Sunday after the Epiphany appointed in the Book of Common Prayer is from the 1928 proposed revision of the English Prayer Book. It is an apt description of the purpose of the day as the last Sunday before Ash Wednesday.

> O God, who before the passion of your only-begotten Son revealed his glory upon the holy mountain: Grant to us that we, beholding by faith the light of his countenance, may be strengthened to bear our cross, and be changed into his likeness from glory to glory; through Jesus Christ our Lord, who lives and reigns....

The Lutheran rite generally uses the collect written for the Feast of the Transfiguration on August 6, 1456-7, perhaps composed by Pope Calixtus for the celebration of which he extended to the whole Western Church.[9] The English translation was made for the *Church Book* (1868).

> O God, who in the glorious Transfiguration of thy only-begotten Son hast confirmed the mysteries of the faith by the testimony of the fathers, and who, in the voice that came from the bright cloud, didst in a wonderful manner foreshow the adoption of sons: Mercifully vouchsafe to make us co-heirs with the King of his glory, and bring us to the enjoyment of the same; through the same Jesus Christ, thy Son, our Lord, who liveth and reigneth....

It is a fine collect, despite its unusual length and complex structure with double antecedent clauses and parallel construction throughout indicating that it is not an early Latin composition. It recites the event being commemorated and looks backward and forward: back to the testimony of the eyewitnesses (see 2 Peter 1:16-19), confirming the truth of Moses the lawgiver and Elijah the first of the prophets, and forward to the fulfillment of the purpose of the coming of the Son of God that all humanity become participants in the divine nature (2 Peter 1:4). The voice from the cloud declared, "You are my Son," but through him and in him it comes to us also, saying, "Now you are co-heirs with the King."[10]

The Revised Common Lectionary appoints these readings for the Last Sunday after the Epiphany, which make use of the Transfiguration theme.

Year A
>Exod. 24:12-18. Moses ascends Mount Sinai
>Psalm 2. The Messiah: King and Conqueror
>>*or* 99. The power and holiness of God
>2 Peter 1:16-21. Eyewitnesses of Christ's glory
>Matt. 17:1-9. The mountain of transfiguration

Year B
>2 Kings 2:1-12. Elijah ascends to heaven
>Psalm 50:1-6. God reveals himself in glory
>2 Cor. 4:3-6. The glory of God in Jesus
>Mark 9:2-9. The transfiguration

Year C
>Exod. 34:29-35. Moses' face shines
>Psalm 99. The power and holiness of God
>2 Cor. 3:12-4:2. Moses' veil
>Luke 9:28-36 (37-43). Moses and Elijah speak of Jesus' departure.

A fifteenth-century Latin hymn, *Caelestis formam gloriae,* written by an unknown author for the then new Feast of the Transfiguration, provides an interpretation of the event. It generally appears in English in John Mason Neale's translation. In devotional language a "type" is a foreshadowing, an image that will be brought to fulfillment at a later time. So in the Transfiguration of Christ we see an anticipation of the glory that the Church will enjoy at the consummation. Christ, on the mountain between heaven and earth, shows today what the blessed here will one day enjoy there.

>O wondrous type! O vision fair
>Of glory that the Church may share,
>Which Christ upon the mountain shows,
>Where brighter than the sun he glows!
>
>With Moses and Elijah nigh
>The incarnate Lord holds converse high;

And from the cloud, the Holy One
Bears record to the only Son.

With shining face and bright array,
Christ deigns to manifest today
What glory shall be theirs above
Who joy in God with perfect love.

And faithful hearts are raised on high
By this great vision's mystery;
For which in joyful strains we raise
The voice of prayer, the hymn of praise.

O Father, with the eternal Son,
And Holy Spirit, ever One,
Vouchsafe to bring us by thy grace
To see thy glory face to face.[11]

Behind the hymn one may perhaps discern the insight of Irenaeus of Lyons (d. ca. 202), "Now the glory of God is humanity fully alive, for the life of humanity is the vision of God. If the revelation of God through creation gives life to all who live on the earth, much more does the revelation of the Father by the Word give perfect being to those who see God."[12]

In the Western Church Alleluia is not sung or said during Lent. In the medieval period its discontinuance developed into a ceremony of farewell to the word and even its burial, until its resurrection at Easter. The Ambrosian rite created an anthem to accompany the saying goodbye to an old friend:

Alleluia, enclose and seal up the world, alleluia;
let it remain in the secret of your heart, alleluia,
until the appointed time.
You shall say it with great joy when that day comes:
Alleluia, alleluia, alleluia.[13]

A Latin hymn of the eleventh century expresses more fully the conflicted emotions at the putting away of Alleluia.

Alleluia, song of gladness,
   Voice of joy that cannot die;
Alleluia is the anthem
   Ever raised by choirs on high;

In the house of God abiding
Thus they sing eternally.

Alleluia thou resoundest,
True Jerusalem and free;
Alleluia, joyful mother,
All thy children sing with thee;
But by Babylon's sad waters
Mourning exiles now are we.

Alleluia though we cherish
And would chant for evermore
Alleluia in our singing
Let us for a while give o'er,
As our Savior in his fasting
Pleasures of the world forebore.

Therefore in our hymns we pray thee,
Grant us, blessèd Trinity,
At the last to keep thine Easter
With thy faithful saints on high;
There to thee for ever singing
Alleluia joyfully.[14]

Toward the end of the second stanza the word "But" marks a sharp transition as the reality of a fallen world intrudes on the picture of the joys of heaven. (The biblical allusions in the second stanza are Gal. 4:26, Rev. 19:4-7, and Psalm 137:1-4.) "Alleluia" that has been repeated at the beginning of the first and third lines of the first three stanzas is delayed in the final stanza until the last line, anticipating its absence from the Lenten liturgy but concluding the hymn with the hope of heaven and its unending joyful praise.

In the previous Roman breviary and also other office books in that tradition,[15] the word "Alleluia" after the Gloria Patri at the beginning of the office was replaced with "Praise to you, O Lord, King of eternal glory." In the present rites the word "Alleluia" is simply omitted, and the effect of its omission is the more striking.

The Intervening Weeks after the Epiphany

The intervening Sundays between the Baptism and the Transfiguration retain in Anglican and Lutheran use something of the general shape they had in the previous calendar and lectionary. Even in the previous books, however, the historic Introits bore only a tenuous connection with the teaching of the day, and gave "a general Festival tone to the Church's worship, inspired by no *single* Event, but by the great all-revealing glory of the Epiphany."[16] Their function was to serve as a general call to worship and to offer an ascription of praise. They will therefore be passed over in this study.

In the Roman calendar the Monday following the Baptism of the Lord begins the first week on Ordinary Time. The liturgical color is green. The collect for the first week in ordinary time is from the Gregorian sacramentary, assigned in previous Roman, Sarum, Anglican, and Lutheran books to the First Sunday after the Epiphany. It was originally translated in the 1549 Book of Common Prayer:

> O Lord, we beseech thee mercifully to receive the prayers of thy people who call upon thee, and grant that they may both perceive and know what things they ought to do, and also have grace and power faithfully to fulfill the same.

The prayer to know what to do and also to be able to do it coordinated well with the appointed Gospel in the previous lectionary, Luke 2:41-52, the twelve-year-old Jesus in the Temple inquiring of the learned in the Law concerning, we imagine, just those things; and also correlated with the Epistle then appointed, Rom. 12:1-5, "present your bodies as a living sacrifice." The 1979 Book of Common Prayer assigns this collect to Proper 10, where it is understood to be a general teaching about prayer. Further comment may be found below, p. 314.

The collect for the Second Sunday after the Epiphany in the previous Roman, Lutheran, and Anglican books is from the Gregorian sacramentary and continues to be assigned to this Sunday, called the Second Sunday in Ordinary Time, in the Roman sacramentary. In the 1979 Prayer Book translation:

> Almighty and everlasting God, you govern all things both in heaven and on earth: Mercifully hear the supplications of your people, and in our time grant us your peace; through Jesus Christ our Lord, who lives and reigns....

The Latin collect is a prayer for outward peace, "peace in our time" (the reference is to Sirach 50:23, "peace in our days"); Cranmer's original translation, "grant us thy peace all the days of our life," turned it toward inner and spiritual peace. The prayer is a distant echo of Christmas with its petition for peace, which the world cannot give, and it is always a relevant prayer in a fallen and combative world.

The 1979 Prayer Book has moved the collect to the Fourth Sunday after the Epiphany and has inserted here a new collect based on the collect for the Twentieth Sunday after Pentecost in the *Book of Common Worship* of the Church of South India.[7]

> Almighty God, whose Son our Savior Jesus Christ is the light of the world: Grant that your people, illumined by your Word and Sacraments, may shine with the radiance of Christ's glory, that he may be known, worshiped, and obeyed to the ends of the earth; through Jesus Christ our Lord, who with you and the Holy Spirit lives and reigns....

The collect summarizes the traditional themes of the Epiphany season, the kingdom and glory of Christ. It is also an anticipation of the themes that will be heard in the Transfiguration and in the Ascension.

The Gospels for the Second Sunday after the Epiphany in all three years of the lectionary cycle are from the beginning of Jesus's ministry as reported by St. John.

> Year A. John 1:29-42. The Lamb of God and his first disciples
> Year B. John 1:43-51. The call of Philip and Nathanael
> Year C. John 2:1-11. The wedding at Cana.

A hymn by Ephrem of Edessa (fourth century) similarly gathers many of the themes of the time after the Epiphany, the paradoxes of the ministry of Jesus.

> From God Christ's deity came forth, his manhood from humanity;
> His priesthood from Melchizedek, his royalty from David's tree:
>> Praised be his Oneness.
>
> He joined with guests at wedding feast, yet in the wilderness did fast;
> He taught within the temple's gates; his people saw him die at last:
>> Praised be his teaching.
>
> The dissolute he did not scorn, nor turn from those who were in sin;
> He for the righteous did rejoice, but bade the fallen to come in:
>> Praised be his mercy.
>
> He did not disregard the sick; to simple ones his word was given;

And he descended to the earth, and, his work done, went up to heaven:
> Praised be his coming.

Who then, my Lord, compares to you? The Watcher slept, the Great was
> [small,
The Pure baptized, the Life who died, the King abased to honor all:
> Praised be your glory.[18]

The collect in the Book of Common Prayer for the Third Sunday after the Epiphany is a new composition by Massey H. Shepherd, Jr. It is related to the Gospel in each of the three years, and like the collect for the previous Sunday, it also builds on the missionary theme of the season.

> Give us grace, O Lord, to answer readily the call of our Savior Jesus Christ and proclaim to all people the Good News of his salvation, that we and the whole world may perceive the glory of his marvelous works; who lives and reigns....

The Roman sacramentary appoints as the collect for this Third Sunday in Ordinary Time a prayer from the Gregorian sacramentary that in the 1570 Roman Missal and previous Lutheran books had been assigned to the First Sunday after Christmas Day.

> Almighty and everlasting God, direct our actions according to your gracious will, that we may abound in doing good in the Name of your beloved Son, Jesus Christ our Lord; who lives and reigns....[19]

In the Gregorian sacramentary it was the collect for a Mass for redemption from the worship of idols. One may recall Luther's definition of an idol as anything that takes the place of God. "To have a god is nothing else than to trust and believe in that one with your whole heart. As I have often said, it is the trust and faith of the heart alone that makes both God and an idol.... Anything on which your heart relies and depends, I say, that is really your God."[20] The prayer asks that we, who have been baptized into his Name, may be like Jesus of Nazareth, who "went about doing good" (Acts 10:38).

The Gospels for the Third Sunday after the Epiphany in the Revised Common Lectionary resume the continuous reading of each of the synoptic accounts.

> Year A. Matt. 4:12-23. Jesus begins his ministry
> Year B. Mark 1:14-20. The beginning of the Galilean ministry
> Year C. Luke 4:14-21. Jesus' ministry begins.

The Week of Prayer for Christian Unity is observed in many places, but the Evangelical Lutheran Church in America and the Evangelical Lutheran Church in Canada are the only denominations to have put the week on their calendar.[21] The Week begins on January 18, the Confession of St. Peter, and concludes on the Conversion of St. Paul, January 25. The practice began in 1908 at Graymoor, just north of Peekskill, in the Hudson Valley of New York, when an Episcopal priest, Paul James Francis Wattson (1863-1940) and Mother Lurana (1870-1935) founded the Franciscan religious congregations comprising the Society of the Atonement at Graymoor. Both leaders were vigorous advocates of Anglican and Roman Catholic reunion. One of their supporters suggested that a day of prayer for Christian unity should be observed throughout the world each year. The day soon expanded to a week, from January 18 to January 25. The first observances were confined to the tiny chapel at Graymoor. The next year, Father Wattson and other members of the community were received into the Roman Catholic Church, and in time what came to be known as the Church Unity Octave was widely observed by Roman Catholics. Other Christians took up the idea, but because they could not support reunion with Rome, they developed other observances. The Faith and Order movement that in the early years of the twentieth century drew together Orthodox, Anglicans, and some Protestant groups, had from its earliest days stressed prayer for unity. In 1913 an Episcopal group suggested a day of prayer for unity to be observed on the day of Pentecost, the birthday of the Church. In 1926 at a Geneva conference of Faith and Order, an official appeal was extended for a weeklong observance around the time of Pentecost. The Faith and Order movement supplied materials to promote the observance. In 1935 Abbé Paul Courturier (1881-1953) invited all Christians to pray for the unity of the Church; the call was endorsed by the Commission on Faith and Order of the World Council of Churches.

In praying for the unity of the Church, Christians join the high priestly prayer of Jesus for his disciples and for all who through the centuries will believe because of their testimony, "that they may all be one" (John 17:21). The purpose of such prayer and work is for the sake of the world (John 17:21, 23) that all nations may see in the Church the love of God for the world, believe, and find life. The Week of Prayer for Unity is thus appropriately observed during the Epiphany season.

On the Fourth Sunday after the Epiphany/Fourth Sunday in Ordinary Time the 1570 Roman Missal, previous Prayer Books, and the Lutheran books have a Gregorian collect that had been assigned to Ember Saturday in Lent. The "many and great dangers" in the historical context of the original prayer can be heard as a reference to the troubled times of Gregory's pontificate, although they also describe the situation of God's people at any time in history. Our spiritual infirmity is described in physical terms: we need God's help to support us as we walk (that is, live) and sometimes even to carry us when we are weak.

> Almighty God, you know that we are set in the midst of so many and great dangers, that by reason of the weakness of our nature we cannot always stand upright: Grant to us such strength and protection as may support us in all dangers and carry us through all temptations; through your Son Jesus Christ our Lord, who lives and reigns.... [22]

The *Lutheran Book of Worship* radically revised the collect. The 1979 Prayer Book replaced it with the one previously appointed for the Second Sunday after the Epiphany given above. The 1970 Roman sacramentary appoints a simple and straightforward collect from the Leonine sacramentary.

> Teach us, Lord God, to worship you with undivided hearts and to cherish all people with true and faithful love.

The prayer can be related to the Gospels appointed in the three-year lectionary.

> Year A. Matt. 5:1-12. The Beatitudes
> Year B. Mark 1:21-28. Jesus expels an unclean spirit
> Year C. Luke 4:21-30. Jesus is rejected in Nazareth, his hometown.

On the Fifth Sunday in Ordinary Time (the Fifth Sunday after the Epiphany) the Roman sacramentary retains the Gregorian collect that had been previously appointed in the 1570 Missal, the Book of Common Prayer, and the Lutheran books.

> Lord God, we ask you to keep your Church and household continually in your true religion, that those who lean only on the hope of your heavenly grace may evermore be defended by your mighty power; through your Son Jesus Christ our Lord, who lives and reigns....

"Church and household" is Cranmer's contribution. Literally the Latin collect prays for God's "family"; *pietas* (here rendered "religion") in the Latin petition, *continua pietate custodi* "is used of God's sentiment towards us, not of ours towards Him. The thought behind the Collect is that of a household (*familia*) dependent upon its head for sustenance and protection."[23]

The 1979 Prayer Book has replaced the collect with a new composition by Massey H. Shepherd, Jr.

Set us free, O God, from the bondage of our sins, and give us the liberty of that abundant life which you have made known to us in your Son our Savior Jesus Christ; who lives and reigns. . . .

The collect rests on several biblical passages: Gal. 4:3-5; Rom. 8:15, 19-21; John 10:10; Luke 4:16-21.

The Revised Common Lectionary appoints these Gospels:

Year A. Matt. 5:13-20. The sermon on the mount continued
Year B. Mark 1:29-39. Jesus' healing and preaching
Year C. Luke 5:1-11. Jesus calls the first disciples.

On the Sixth Sunday in Ordinary Time the Roman sacramentary appoints a Leonine collect. Dirk van Dissel has translated it:

O God, you have promised to dwell in true and upright hearts: Abide with us in your grace and mercy, and make us a dwelling worthy of you; through your Son Jesus Christ our Lord, who lives and reigns. . . .[24]

The prayer is rich with biblical echoes and allusions. The promise is heard in such passages as Isa. 66:2; John 14:15-17; Eph. 4:17. The worthy dwelling recalls the confession of the centurion, "I am not worthy to have you come under my roof" (Matt. 8:8). The translation "Abide with us" recalls the plea of the two disciples on their way to Emmaus Easter evening (Luke 24:29 AV).

For the Sixth Sunday after the Epiphany the 1979 Book of Common Prayer assigns the Gelasian collect previously appointed in all three rites, as it was in the Gregorian sacramentary, for the First Sunday after Trinity (the Second Sunday after Pentecost).

O God, the strength of all who put their trust in you: Mercifully accept our prayers; and because in our weakness we can do nothing good without you, give us the help of your grace, that in keeping your commandments we may please you both in will and deed; through your Son Jesus Christ our Lord. . . .

God's strength is contrasted with our weakness. Only with God's grace can we please him both in will and action. The Roman sacramentary has moved this collect to the Eleventh Sunday of the Year.

The Revised Common Lectionary appoints these Gospel readings for the Sixth Sunday after the Epiphany:

> Year A. Matt. 5:21-37. The sermon on the mount continued
> Year B. Mark 1:40-45. Jesus cleanses a leper
> Year C. Luke 6:17-26. The beginning of the sermon on the plain.

On the Seventh Sunday of Ordinary Time the Roman sacramentary appoints a collect from the Gelasian and Gregorian sacramentaries that in the 1570 Missal was assigned to the Sixth Sunday after the Epiphany.

> Almighty God, fix our hearts on what is right and true, that we may please you always by doing your will in word and deed; through your Son Jesus Christ our Lord, who lives and reigns....[25]

It is a prayer for conformity to the will of God by focusing on the Source of all truth.

For the Seventh Sunday after the Epiphany the 1979 Book of Common Prayer uses the collect composed for Quinquagesima in the 1549 Prayer Book, based on the Epistle for that Sunday, 1 Cor. 13:1-13. It is thus a remnant of pre-Lent.

> O Lord, you have taught us that without love whatever we do is worth nothing: Send your Holy Spirit and pour into our hearts your greatest gift, which is love, the true bond of peace and of all virtue, without which whoever lives is accounted dead before you. Grant this for the sake of your only Son Jesus Christ, who lives and reigns....

It may be noted that this prayer departs from the received collect form, providing instruction in the nature and necessity of love, which is the principal gift of the Holy Spirit (Gal. 5:22, "The fruit of the Spirit is love, joy, peace....") Without love whoever lives is accounted dead before God, as St. John teaches, "whoever does not love abides in death" (1 John 3:14).

The Revised Common Lectionary appoints these Gospels:

> Year A. Matt. 5:38-48. The sermon on the mount continued
> Year B. Mark 2:1-12. Jesus heals a paralytic

Year C. Luke 6:27-38. The sermon on the plain continued.

On the Eighth Sunday of Ordinary Time the Roman sacramentary assigns the Leonine collect given below at Proper 3 (pp. 310–311). On the Eighth Sunday after the Epiphany the 1979 Book of Common Prayer appoints an original prayer by William Bright from his collection *Ancient Collects* that the 1928 American Prayer Book had included among additional family prayers (p. 596).

> Most loving Father, whose will it is for us to give thanks for all things, to fear nothing but the loss of you, and to cast all our care on you who care for us: Preserve us from faithless fears and worldly anxieties, that no clouds of this mortal life may hide from us the light of that love which is immortal, and which you have manifested to us in your Son Jesus Christ our Lord; who lives and reigns with you, in the unity of the Holy Spirit, one God, now and for ever.

The biblical allusions are 1 Tim. 2:1; Phil. 3:8; 1 Peter 5:7. The phrase "give thanks for all things" may be problematic, less effective than the comparable phrase in the Liturgy of St. John Chrysostom, give thanks "for all and on behalf of all." Marion Hatchett notes, "in the Gospels the antithesis of faith is not doubt but fear, for faith is essentially trust in God's love and care."[26] Such trust may enable us to "give thanks for all things."

The Revised Common Lectionary assigns these Gospels to this Sunday.

> Year A. Matt. 6:24-34. The sermon on the mount continued
> Year B. Mark 2:13-22. The call of Levi; the requirement of fasting
> Year C. Luke 6:39-49. Conclusion of the sermon on the plain.

The Revised Common Lectionary also provides readings for a Ninth Sunday after the Epiphany for those congregations that do not observe the Transfiguration on the last Sunday of Epiphanytide.

The Time after Pentecost

Because the Day of Pentecost is the final day of Easter and the conclusion of the Fifty Days, the time after Pentecost is not to be understood as the "Pentecost season." It is, for all the traditions, in character if not in name, ordinary time.

Trinity Sunday

Like the time after the Epiphany, the time after Pentecost is bracketed by two festivals. The first is Trinity Sunday. (In the East, this Sunday following Pentecost is the Feast of All Saints, teaching that sanctity is the work of the Holy Spirit.) The feast of the Most Holy Trinity is a late Western introduction to the liturgical calendar. The observance of a day in honor of the Holy Trinity passed from one section of the Church to another very slowly through many centuries, and only in 1334 obtained papal authorization.[27] In the fourth and fifth centuries the Arian controversies in Spain and Gaul emphasized the Holy Trinity. About the year 800 the votive Mass of the Holy Trinity was used on those Sundays that did not have another appointment. The early medieval centuries witness local diocesan celebrations in the West in honor of the Holy Trinity. Pope Alexander II (d. 1077) and Alexander III (d. 1181) regarded the practice as unnecessary and discouraged the observance, contending that the Holy Trinity was acclaimed in every liturgy in the Gloria Patri, in other doxologies, in the termination of the collects. Finally, however, Pope John XXII (d. 1334) ordered the feast to be observed by the universal Church and that it be observed on the Sunday following Pentecost.[28] The Sunday had been a "vacant" day without propers because the ordinations of Ember Saturday continued into the following day.

The Festival of the Holy Trinity is sometimes referred to dismissively as "a feast of a doctrine," comparing it unfavorably to feasts of events or persons. But, it is to be observed, every feast has a significant doctrinal component: Christmas celebrates the doctrine of the Incarnation, Epiphany the person and dual nature of Christ, Pascha the Atonement and Redemption, Ascension the taking of our human nature to the throne of God, Pentecost the person and work of the Holy Spirit leading into all truth, Corpus Christi the doctrine of the real presence of the body and blood of Christ in the Holy Sacrament.[29] Although a late introduction to the calendar, Trinity Sunday has become integral to the Western liturgical year. It can be understood as the culmination of the three great festivals of the year: Christmas, the feast of God the Father; Easter, the feast of God the Son; Pentecost, the feast of God the Holy Spirit. Trinity Sunday, although not a commemoration of an historical event, is a celebration of the experience of the God of the Bible as the human mind has reflected on that experience. It is, in a simple phrase, a celebration of the mystery of God. A splendid hymn by Frederick William Faber sets forth the idea.

> Most ancient of all mysteries,
> Before thy throne we lie;

Have mercy now, most merciful,
　Most holy Trinity.

When heaven and earth were yet unmade,
　And time was yet unknown,
Thou in thy bliss and majesty
　Didst live and love alone.

Thou wert not born; there was no fount
　From which thy Being flowed;
There is no end which thou canst reach;
　But thou art simply God.

How wonderful creation is,
　The work which thou didst bless,
And O, what then must thou be like,
　Eternal loveliness!

O listen, then, most pitiful,
　To thy poor creature's heart:
It blesses thee that thou art God,
　That thou art what thou art.

Most ancient of all mysteries,
　Still at thy throne we lie;
Have mercy, now, most merciful,
　Most holy Trinity.[30]

The first three stanzas describe, as best as human thought and words can, the ancient mystery. Before creation was begun, before there was such a thing as time, the Holy Trinity in sovereign majesty, without beginning, without end, lived and loved in awesome solitude. The central description in the hymn is that the most Holy Trinity is "simply God," not simple so as to be easily understood or comprehended, but in plain and straightforward language, just "God" with all the wonder and mystery and incomprehensibility inherent in the name. Then the hymn turns to nature to assist in appreciating the wonder and mystery. If creation is so marvelous in its beauty, how much more wonderful and lovely must its creator be. In the face of such mystery, language fails, and without words the heart must in silence rejoice that God is God. In the concluding stanza the singers remind God that "still at thy throne we lie."

They remain in the same posture as at the beginning of the hymn: prostrate before the awesome and ancient Mystery. "Still" also has another meaning and serves further to describe the adoring suppliant's posture: silent and motionless before the throne of the Most High awaiting his mercy. (Martin Luther's last words are reported to have been, "We are all beggars; that is true.")

A second excellent exposition of the Holy Trinity is the familiar hymn by Reginald Heber (1783-1826). Advancing largely by an accumulation of epithets, it attempts, borrowing its imagery from the Revelation of St. John the Divine (chapters 4 and 5), to capture in vivid language the glory of God the blessed Trinity.

> Holy, holy, holy, Lord God Almighty!   [Rev. 4:8]
>   Early in the morning our song shall rise to thee;   [Isa. 26:9 AV]
> Holy, holy, holy, merciful and mighty,
>   God in three Persons, blessed Trinity.
>
> Holy, holy, holy! all the saints adore thee,   [Rev. 4:6, 10]
>   Casting down their golden crowns around the glassy sea,
> Cherubim and seraphim falling down before thee,
>   Which, wert, and art, and evermore shalt be.   [Rev. 4:8b]
>
> Holy, holy, holy! though the darkness hide thee,   [Exod. 20:21]
>   Though the eye made blind by sin thy glory may not see,
> Only thou art holy; there is none beside thee,
>   Perfect in power, in love, and purity.
>
> Holy, holy, holy, Lord God Almighty!
>   All thy works shall praise thy Name in earth and sky and sea;
> Holy, holy, holy, merciful and mighty,   [Rev. 5:13]
>   God in three persons, blessed Trinity![31]

Bishop Heber's mastery of the language involves the repetition of the Sanctus at the beginning of each stanza, suggesting the endless worship of the whole company of heaven (stanza 2), and combines it with a confession of the imperfection of earthly praise (stanza 3). Triple combinations emphasize the Triune being of the Lord God Almighty reflected throughout creation: the saints, cherubim, seraphim; wert (were), art (are), shalt be; power, love, purity; earth, sky, sea; the last, "sea," returning the earthly worship to the starting point in heaven.[32] We who sing this hymn with understanding should not be fearful of God's majestic grandeur, nor should we be tempted to presume upon his merciful love.[33]

The antiphon of the Introit for Trinity Sunday (*Benedicta sit*) is a liturgical composition deriving from such biblical texts as Tobit 8:15-16, "Blessed be the Holy Trinity and the undivided Unity. Let us give glory to him because he has shown his mercy to us." The Psalm verse is 8:1, "O Lord our Sovereign, how majestic is your Name in all the earth!" The two themes of the mercy and the majesty of God are the foundation of adoration and worship.

The collect appointed for the Feast of the Most Holy Trinity dates from late medieval missals; its length and complexity show its lack of antiquity. In the translation in the 1979 Prayer Book it is:

> Almighty and everlasting God, you have given to us your servants grace, by the confession of a true faith, to acknowledge the glory of the eternal Trinity, and in the power of your divine Majesty to worship the Unity: Keep us steadfast in this faith and worship, and bring us at last to see you in your one and eternal glory, O Father; who with the Son and the Holy Spirit live and reign, one God, for ever and ever.

In our confession, that is, our declaration of belief, we acknowledge the Trinity; under the influence of the divine Majesty we worship the unity of the one God. The Church worships not the doctrine nor even the mystery, but God.

The Revised Common Lectionary appoints these readings for Trinity Sunday. The Gospel in Year A is the one reference in the Gospels to the Trinity; the Gospels for Years B and C reflect the older observance on this Sunday of the octave of Pentecost.

Year A
> Gen. 1:1-2:4a. The beginning of creation
> Psalm 8. The majesty of the Creator
> 2 Cor. 13:11-13. A Trinitarian blessing
> Matt. 28:16-20. Baptism into the Triune Name

Year B
> Isa. 6:1-8. A vision of God in the temple
> Psalm 29. The voice of God in a storm
> Rom. 8:12-17. The Spirit joins us to the Father and the Son
> John 3:1-17. Born of water and Spirit

Year C
> Prov. 8:1-4, 22-31. Wisdom's share in creation
> Psalm 8. The majesty of the Creator
> Rom. 5:1-5. Peace with God through Christ

John 16:12-15. The Spirit will guide you into all truth.

The proper preface for Trinity Sunday in the Roman sacramentary and the Lutheran rite is from the Gelasian sacramentary of the mid-eighth century.

> It is indeed right and salutary that we should at all times and in all places offer thanks and praise to you, O Lord, holy Father, almighty and everliving God. You have revealed your glory as the glory also of your Son and of the Holy Spirit: three persons, equal in majesty, undivided in splendor, yet one Lord, one God, ever to be adored in your everlasting glory.

The preface appointed in the Book of Common Prayer, from the Mozarabic, Gelasian, and Gregorian sacramentaries, is similar.

> For with your co-eternal Son and the Holy Spirit, you are one God, one Lord, in Trinity of Persons and in Unity of Being; and we celebrate the one and equal glory of you, O Father, and of the Son, and of the Holy Spirit.

The focus of the celebration of the Holy Trinity is not on doctrine but on worshipful adoration, as indeed is the focus of the Athanasian Creed: "Now this is the catholic faith: we worship one God in trinity and the Trinity in unity...and so we must worship the Trinity in unity and the one God in three persons."[34]

The use of the Athanasian Creed (*Quicunque vult*) as a canticle in the daily office was once frequent in the use of the Western Church. (It is a Western composition, perhaps of the fifth century.) It was used daily in the Sarum breviary; the 1549 Prayer Book printed it after Evensong and directed its use on the six greater festivals after the Benedictus at Mattins. Continental Lutheran practice was similar.[35] John Henry Newman praised the *Quicunque vult* as

> the war-song of faith, with which we warn first ourselves, then each other, and then all those who are within its hearing, and the hearing of the Truth, who our God is, and how we must worship Him, and how vast our responsibility will be, if we know what to believe, and yet believe not.... For myself, I have ever felt it as the most simple and sublime, the most devotional formulary to which Christianity has given birth....[36]

The creed has now fallen out of use, except in certain Lutheran quarters. (*The Book of Concord*, the collection of the Confessions of the Evangelical Lutheran

Church, begins with The Three Chief Creeds (Symbols): the Apostles' Creed, the Nicene Creed, and the Athanasian Creed.) The *Quicunque vult* is included in the *Lutheran Book of Worship* (1978) and in the *Lutheran Service Book* (2006), as well as in *The Daily Prayer of the Church*.[37]

The Roman sacramentary does not provide a solemn blessing for Trinity Sunday. The solemn blessing for the feast in the Episcopal *Book of Occasional Services* is the Aaronic benediction (Numb. 6:22-26).

> The Lord bless you and keep you. *Amen.*
> The Lord make his face to shine upon you and be gracious to you. *Amen.*
> The Lord lift up his countenance upon you, and give you peace. *Amen.*

> The Lord God Almighty, Father, Son, and Holy Spirit, the holy and undivided Trinity, guard you, save you, and bring you to that heavenly City, where he lives and reigns for ever and ever. *Amen.*
> > *or this*

> May God the Holy Trinity make you strong in faith and love, defend you on every side, and guide you in truth and peace; and the blessing of God Almighty, the Father, the Son, and the Holy Spirit, be among you, and remain with you always.
> *Amen.*

The Feast of the Holy Trinity was enormously popular in Northern Europe and England as evidenced in the large number of churches dedicated to the Trinity, and the Sundays succeeding the Feast were numbered not "after Pentecost" as in the Roman rite but "after Trinity."

Corpus Christi

The Thursday after Trinity Sunday, the sixtieth day after Easter Day, is the Feast of Corpus Christi. The observance began in the diocese of Liège in Belgium when devotion to the sacrament and to the real presence was burgeoning. The feast was established in Liège in 1247; it was extended to the whole Western Church in 1264 but was generally ignored.[38] Pope John XXII promulgated it more successfully in 1317. Because Maundy Thursday is under the shadow of Good Friday and therefore is not conducive to joyful celebration of the institution of the Eucharist, the new feast was set on the next free Thursday after Eastertide (Pentecost then continuing through an octave), the Thursday after Trinity Sunday. The Reformers rejected the relatively new feast. Their objections seemed to center on the popular processions in which the blessed sacrament in the form of a consecrated host was carried through towns and cities. The processions were not part of the original celebration of the feast and in fact were often opposed by those who were promulgating the observance. Among the Lutherans at least, the doctrine of the real presence celebrated in the feast was never at issue. Many later twentieth-century Anglican calendars (England 1980, Scotland 1982, Wales 1984, South Africa 1989, New Zealand 1989, Australia 1995) include a celebration of "Thanksgiving for Holy Communion." The 1970 Roman sacramentary gives to the feast the name The Body and Blood of Christ (no longer the Body alone, *Corpus Christi*). In the United States the celebration of the feast is moved to the following Sunday.

The propers for the feast were composed by Thomas Aquinas and are remarkably coherent and unified, unusually rich biblically and theologically. At first vespers the antiphon on the Magnificat is drawn from Wis. 16:20-21 and Luke 1:52:

> How sweet, O Lord, is your Spirit;
> For you have shown your sweetness to your children:
> You have given them most wondrous Bread from heaven:
> You fill the hungry with good things and the rich you have sent away empty.

The antiphon on the Benedictus at Lauds is John 6:51, "I am the living bread that came down from heaven; whoever eats this bread will live for ever." The collect, addressed to God the Son, was borrowed by the Lutherans for use on Maundy Thursday, for which it is also remarkably appropriate.

> O God, in this wonderful sacrament you have left us a memorial of your Passion: Grant us, we pray, so to revere the sacred mysteries of your Body and Blood that we may ever perceive within ourselves the fruit of your redemption; who live and reign with the Father....

The Epistle is 1 Cor. 11:23-29 (Paul's report of the institution of the Supper); the sequence hymn (now optional) is *Lauda, Sion, Salvatorem*;[39] the Gospel is John 6:56-59 (Jesus, the living bread from heaven). The communion verse is the warning from 1 Cor. 11:26-27, repeated from the Epistle, "As often as you eat this bread and drink the cup, you proclaim the Lord's death until he comes. Whoever, therefore, eats the bread or drinks the cup of the Lord in an unworthy manner will be answerable for the body and blood of the Lord." At second vespers, to bring the feast to a close, the antiphon on the Magnificat is the glorious *O sacrum convivium* with its fourfold praise, "O sacred banquet, in which Christ is received, the memory of his passion is renewed, the soul is filled with grace, and a pledge of future glory is given to us. Alleluia."

Anniversary of the Dedication of a Church

In 1536 the English Convocations ordered that the Feast of the Dedication of each parish church should be kept on the first Sunday in October "throughout the realm." It was a practice commonly followed in England and on the continent when the actual date of the dedication was not known. The annual commemoration of the dedication on the actual date or in October is a custom that deserves to be continued for it provides occasion for a yearly consideration of the nature of the Church and of its house as more than merely a convenient shelter ("to keep the rain off the Bible," Bishop William Lazareth used to say). Despite the order of King Henry VIII and the Convocation, no liturgical Propers were provided in the Prayer Book until the Scottish Book of 1912. The Lutherans included the collect from the Gregorian, Roman, and Sarum missals for the dedication anniversary in this translation:

> O God, who year after year dost return to us the day of the dedication of this thy holy temple, and ever dost bring us again into the presence of thy holy mysteries: Hear the prayers of thy people, and grant that whosoever shall enter this temple about to seek blessings may rejoice to have had his desires wholly fulfilled; through Jesus Christ our Lord.[40]

The collect in the 1928 American Book of Common Prayer, based on the Scottish Book of 1912, is a simplified version of this collect: "O God, whom year by year we praise for the dedication of this church; Hear, we beseech thee, the prayers of thy people, and grant that whosoever shall worship before thee in this place, may obtain thy merciful aid and protection." The Anglican and Lutheran books assign these readings for the anniversary of the consecration.

1 Kings 8:22-30. Solomon's prayer at the dedication of the Temple
     or Gen. 28:10-17. The house of God and gate of heaven
Psalm 84. Longing for the joy of the temple
1 Peter 2:1-9 [BCP 2:1-5, 9-10]. A house built of living stones
Matthew 21:12-16. Jesus cleanses the temple.

The proper preface for the dedication given in the Prayer Book makes use of the reading from 1 Peter: "Through Jesus Christ our great High Priest; in whom we are built up as living stones of a holy temple, that we might offer before you a sacrifice of praise and prayer which is holy and pleasing in your sight."

The Roman calendar includes on November 9 the Dedication of St. John Lateran, the cathedral of the diocese of Rome and the mother church of the (Western) world. In 324 the bishop of Rome consecrated the church under the name of the Basilica of St. Savior (i.e., the Holy Savior), the first public consecration of a church. The anniversary has been observed since the twelfth century, when the church was dedicated to St. John the Baptist; the anniversary of the dedication is kept throughout the Latin Church. The thought of the Gregorian collect is spread over the three presidential prayers of the Mass in the Roman sacramentary and focus on the Church not as building but as people. The two collects declare, "God, of living and elect stones you fashion for yourself an eternal dwelling place...." and "God, you call your people the Church...." The prayer over the offerings asks, "Grant that all who seek your help may be strengthened by the sacraments and receive an answer to their prayers"; the prayer after communion asks "you foreshadow in your Church on earth the new and heavenly Jerusalem; through our sharing in these holy mysteries make us into a temple of your grace."

The commemoration of the date of the dedication of the other principal Roman basilicas is optional in the present Roman Catholic calendar: St. Peter in the Vatican and St. Paul's Outside the Walls together on November 18; Santa Maria Maggiore (St. Mary Major) on August 5.

The Sunday of Christ the King

The time after Pentecost, ordinary time, concludes with the Feast of Christ the King. This feast was instituted by Pope Pius XI in 1925 to combat what he considered the destructive forces of the age: the rise of the Bolsheviks in Russia, Fascism in Italy, the confiscation of the Papal States, materialism generally (such as the "roaring twenties" in the United States). The new feast was intended to reassure the faithful that Christ the King was still in control. It was set on the last Sunday in October ("before celebrating the triumph of all the Saints, we proclaim and extoll the glory of him who triumphs in all the Saints"), although some say the date was chosen to counter the popularity of Reformation Sunday among the Protestants. The reforms of the Second Vatican Council moved the observance to the last Sunday of the liturgical year, replacing the terrifying theme of the Last Judgment (the Gospel was Matt. 24:15-35) with which the year then concluded. It was a happy innovation quickly adopted by Anglican and Lutheran churches. Christ the King had already become a popular title for churches in both those traditions.

There had been objections to the introduction of the Feast of the Holy Trinity because the Trinity was celebrated at every service of the Church. Likewise, there were objections to the introduction of a Feast of Christ the King. Such a feast, some said, was unnecessary, noting that there already was such a feast celebrating the kingship of Christ: Ascension Day, the coronation of Christ as King. Moreover, such an understanding was announced in the Easter Vigil at the marking of the Paschal candle: "Christ yesterday and today, the beginning and the ending, Alpha and Omega, all time belongs to him and all ages." These words, originating in the Bible, "project on the wide screen of the universe the image of Christ the Pantocrator. By his resurrection Jesus Christ has gained dominion over the entire universe."[41]

More recent is the objection to the masculine imagery of the King, but a common substitute, "The Reign of Christ," is neither accurate nor effective. The British sovereign reigns, but the people rule. In Christianity the authority rests not with a constitutional monarch with carefully circumscribed powers but with an absolute King, the only absolute monarch, Jesus Christ the Lord, a king mortals did not crown and whom they cannot depose.[42] That reliable stability undergirds the faith of the Church.

The entrance antiphon in the Roman sacramentary is Rev. 5:12 and 1:6, "Worthy is the Lamb that was slaughtered to receive power and wealth and wisdom and might and honor; to him be glory and dominion forever and ever." The verse had been introduced to Lutheran use in a canticle included in the *Church Book* (1868), the *Common Service Book* (1917), and *The Lutheran Hymnal* (1941), the *Dignus est Agnus* (Rev. 5:12, 13; 15:3-4; 19:6). The antiphon is the song of the heavenly choir of "myriads of myriads and thousands of thousands" of angels who surround the throne of God. Their praise of the Redeemer of all is taken up by "every creature in heaven and on earth and under the earth and in the sea, and all that is in them" (v. 13), declaring the one seated on the throne and the Lamb as equal in majesty. It is a thrilling, indeed stunning picture of the universal praise described in Reginald Heber's hymn to the thrice-holy, "All thy works shall praise thy Name in earth and sky and sea."

The collect, written for the new feast in 1925, is translated in the Book of Common Prayer:

> Almighty and everlasting God, whose will it is to restore all things in your well-beloved Son, the King of kings and Lord of lords: Mercifully grant that the peoples of the earth, divided and enslaved by sin, may be freed and brought together under his most gracious rule; who lives and reigns with you and the Holy Spirit, one God, now and for ever.

The preamble of the collect in its declaration that it is the Father's will to restore all things in Christ, is a grand conception. All creation is to be redeemed and restored to its original perfection so that once again the Creator can look at all that has been remade, the whole universe, and as the beginning (Gen. 1:31) declare it "very good."

The way of the restoration requires of us a radical submission. Christ the King, unlike earthly despots who divide and enslave (one of those despots is Sin), sets free and unites those who paradoxically submit to his rule "in whose service is perfect freedom." It is the mystery that George Matheson (1842-1906) explored in his hymn

> Make me a captive, Lord,
> And then I shall be free;
> Force me to render up my sword,
> And I shall conqueror be.
> I sink in life's alarms
> When by myself I stand;
> Imprison me within thine arms,
> And strong shall be my hand.
>
> My heart is weak and poor
> Until it master find;
> It has no spring of action sure,
> It varies with the wind.
> It cannot freely move
> Till thou hast wrought its chain;
> Enslave it with thy matchless love,
> And deathless it shall reign.

My power is faint and low
Till I have learned to serve;
It wants the needed fire to glow,
It wants the breeze to nerve;
It cannot drive the world
Until itself be driven;
Its flag can only be unfurled
When thou shalt breathe from heaven.

My will is not my own
Till thou hast made it thine;
If it would reach a monarch's throne
It must its crown resign;
It only stands unbent
Amid the clashing strife,
When on thy boson it has leant
And found in thee its life.[43]

It is the road traveled in Lent and Holy Week, the way of the cross that paradoxically, as the Prayer Book collect for Monday in Holy Week describes it, is "none other than the way of life and peace."

The Revised Common Lectionary appoints these readings.

Year A
Ezek. 34:11-16, 20-24. God the true shepherd
Psalm 95:1-7a. Call to praise and obedience
or 100. God, Creator and Shepherd
Eph. 1:15-23. The exaltation of Christ
Matt. 25:31-46. The judgment of the nations

Year B
Dan. 7:9-10, 13-14. A vision of eternal kingship
Psalm 93. The splendor of God the creator
Semi-continuous series. 2 Sam. 23:1-7. A just king
Psalm 132:1-12 (13-18). The house of David
Rev. 1:4b-8. Jesus Christ the ruler of the kings of the earth
John 18:33-37. My kingdom is not from this world

Year C
Jer. 23:1-6. The righteous Branch of David [RC: 2 Sam. 5:1-3]
Psalm. Luke 1:68-79. The Song of Zechariah
or Psalm 46. God, a mighty fortress

Col. 1:11-20. The kingdom of Christ
Luke 23:33-43. Remember me in your kingdom.

It is significant that not Palm Sunday with its triumphal procession, not the enthronement festival of Ascension Day, but Good Friday supplies two of the Gospels for this feast. Jesus the King upsets all expectations and reigns from the throne of the cross.

Thomas Kelly (1769-1855) views Christ's final triumph through the necessary remembrance of his passion.

> The head that once was crowned with thorns
>   Is crowned with glory now;
> A royal diadem adorns
>   The mighty Victor's brow.
>
> The highest place that heaven affords
>   Is his, is his by right,
> The King of kings and Lord of lords,
>   And heaven's eternal light,
>
> The joy of all who dwell above,
>   The joy of all below
> To whom he manifests his love
>   And grants his Name to know.
>
> To them the cross, with all its shame,
>   With all its grace, is given,
> Their name an everlasting name,
>   Their joy the joy of heaven.
>
> They suffer with their Lord below,
>   They reign with him above,   [2 Tim. 2:12]
> Their profit and their joy to know
>   The mystery of his love.
>
> The cross he bore is life and health,
>   Though shame and death to him;
> His people's hope, his people's wealth,
>   Their everlasting theme.

To the text of the hymn Kelly attached Heb. 2:10 in the Authorized Version, "For it became him, for whom are all things, and by whom are all things, in bringing many sons unto glory, to make the Captain of their salvation perfect through sufferings." The hymn works by powerful and carefully controlled contrasts: the derisive crown of thorns replaced with a royal diadem, the shame of the cross replaced by the joy of heaven, suffering then but reigning now, earth and heaven, shame and death replaced by life and health. The perfection through suffering that Christ endured also is the experience of those who belong to him.

The feast of Christ the King that concludes the liturgical year leads seamlessly into Advent, with its promise of the return of the King who comes to his people. The image of Christ the King continues throughout Advent. The references to his coming are more prominent in the Daily Office than in the revised lectionary. At first vespers of the First Sunday a psalm antiphon declares,

> New city of Zion, let your heart sing for joy;
> see how humbly your King comes to you.[44]

The invitatory at Lauds:

> Behold, the King is coming:
> O come, let us worship him.[45]

A psalm antiphon at Lauds:

> This is our heavenly King;
> he comes with power and might to save the nations.[46]

Another psalm antiphon:

> Behold, your King comes, the Ruler of the earth;
> he will shatter the yoke of our slavery.[47]

The antiphon on the Benedictus on the first Monday:

> Lift up your eyes, Jerusalem, and see the great power of
>   your King;
> your Savior comes to set you free.[48]

The antiphon on the Benedictus on the First Friday:

> Our God comes, born of David's line,
> enthroned as King for ever.[49]

A psalm antiphon at second vespers on the First Sunday:

> Daughter of Jerusalem, rejoice and be glad; your King
> comes to you.
> Zion, do not fear: your Savior hastens on his way.[50]

A psalm antiphon on the Second Sunday:

> Christ our King will come to us:
> the Lamb of God foretold by John.[51]

Another psalm antiphon:

> The Lord, our King and lawgiver,
> will come to save us.[52]

An antiphon at second vespers on the Fourth Sunday:

> Ever wider will his kingdom spread,
> eternally at peace.[53]

An antiphon for the final week of Advent:

> The Lord, the ruler of the kings of the earth, will come;
> blessed are they who are ready to welcome him.[54]

This is but a sampling of the texts.

The Intervening Weeks after Pentecost.
Propers 1-28; 6th-34th Weeks

The Sundays between Trinity Sunday and the end of the Church's year have always seemed a long and featureless stretch, only occasionally interrupted by a festival. John Meade Falkner's poem of 1910 spoke for many.

> We have done with dogma and divinity,
> Easter and Whitsun past,
> The long, long Sundays after Trinity
> Are with us at last;
> The passionless Sundays after Trinity,
> Neither feast-day nor fast.[55]

(It was partly for this reason that Lutheran and Anglican books directed that, during the time after Trinity, Lesser Festivals occurring on Sunday displace the Sunday propers.[56]) In the medieval calendar, however, the time counted "after Pentecost" or "after Trinity" had, to those who looked carefully, a suggestion of a shape. "An ancient scheme of four cycles, or groupings of material, is still evident after the many substitutions and dislocations which the Propers in this half of the year have suffered," Luther Reed observed.[57] Paul Strodach was even more insistent. The time after Trinity, he said, "appears as well-ordered and purposeful in its development."[58] Four sections or cycles were identified. (1) The first was from the First Sunday after Trinity Sunday to June 29, the Feast of SS. Peter and Paul, five Sundays, Trinity 1-5. The common theme was the invitation to the kingdom of grace.[59] The Propers for the Fifth Sunday after Trinity were originally appointed for the Sunday immediately preceding the Feast of SS. Peter and Paul; the Epistle was 1 Peter 3:8-15a and the Gospel was Luke 5:1-11, the miraculous haul of fish and the call of Peter to be an Apostle. The first section of the season presented a general exhortation to fearless Christian living: "who will harm you if you are eager to do what is good?" [1 Peter 3:13] (2) The second cycle consisted of the next six Sundays, to the Feast of St. Lawrence, August 10, the sixth through the eleventh Sundays after Trinity. Their theme was the new life of righteousness as a mark of those who have entered the kingdom of grace and who are "alive unto God."[60] (3) The third cycle was the next seven Sundays to the Feast of St. Michael, September 29, the twelfth through the eighteenth Sundays after Trinity. Their focus was on practical aspects of Christian faith and life manifested in works of love and service.[61] (4) The final cycle stretched from the nineteenth Sunday after Trinity to the Last Sunday after Trinity, which was the twenty-second, twenty-third, twenty-fourth, twenty-fifth, twenty-sixth, or twenty-seventh Sunday after Trinity, depending on the date of Easter. The general theme was the completion of the kingdom of righteousness, its fulfillment and its rewards.[62]

To conclude the time after Pentecost, the Roman Missal repeated the choir anthems (Introit, Gradual, Offertory, and Communion) from Pentecost XXII until the last Sunday of the year and supplied these Sundays with the Collect, Epistle, and Gospel from the Sundays after Epiphany that were omitted that year (in this order: sixth, fifth, fourth, third). It always used the Propers for Pentecost 24 (Col. 1:9-14; Matt. 24:15-35) on the Sunday before Advent. The Book of Common Prayer provided collects, Epistles, and Gospels for twenty-five Sundays, those for the last Sunday (Jer. 23:5-8; John 6:5-14) always being used on "the Sunday next before Advent." If there were twenty-six or twenty-seven Sundays, the Propers for Epiphany 6 and 5 were used as required.

The Lutheran liturgy was unique in providing Propers for twenty-seven Sundays after Trinity. The *Service Book and Hymnal* (p. 105) suggested the use of the Propers for the twenty-fifth, twenty-sixth, and twenty-seventh Sundays at the conclusion of every year to focus on Christ's return to judgment and to prepare the Church for Advent. The readings for Trinity 25 were

> 1 Thess. 4:13-18 The coming of the Lord
>   and
> Matt. 24:15-28 The desolating sacrilege;

for Trinity 26 were

> 1 Thess. 5:1-11 The day will come like a thief in the night
>   and
> Matt. 25:31-46 The judgment of the nations;

and for Trinity 27, the Last Sunday after Trinity

> 2 Peter 3:8-14 The Lord is not slow but patient
>   and
> Matt. 25:1-13 The wise and foolish maidens,[63] which inspired the stirring Advent hymn "Wake, awake, for night is flying."

A longing for heaven emerges in these last three Sundays of the Church's year. A remarkable hymn by the rector of the University of Erfurt, Johann Matthaeus Meyfart (1590-1642), *Jerusalem, du hochgebaute Stadt*, expresses the homesickness.

> Jerusalem, blest city fair and high,
>   Your towers I yearn to see!
> My longing heart to you would gladly fly;
>   It will not stay with me.
>   Far over vale and mountain,
>   Far over field and plain,
>   It hastes to seek its fountain
>   And your bright courts attain.
>
> O happy day, and yet far happier hour,
>   When will you come at last?
> When fearless to my Father's love and power,
>   Whose Word continues fast,
>   My soul I gladly render;
>   For surely will his hand
>   Lead her, with guidance tender,
>   To heaven, her fatherland.

The poet imagines the soul (traditionally pictured as feminine) carried from the earth in the chariots of Israel (2 Kings 2:9-12) and being met by descending hosts of angels and saints.

> A moment's space, most wonderful to view,
>   Released from earthly ties,
> Elijah's chariot bears her up to you,
>   Through all these lower skies
> To yonder shining regions,
>   While down to meet her come
> The blessed angel legions
>   And bid her welcome home.

At the gates of the holy city, the point of view has changed. Heaven is no longer, as in the previous stanza, "yonder," but it is the earth that is now distant.

> O Zion, hail! Bright city, now unfold
>   The gates of grace to me.
> How many times I longed for you of old
>   Ere yet I was set free
> From yon grim life of sadness,
>   The world of shadowy nought,
> And God had given the gladness,
>   The heritage, I sought.

The soul, drawing closer to the gate of heaven, is met by a welcoming company of saints and martyrs, patriarchs, and prophets.

> What glorious throng and what resplendent host
>   Comes sweeping swiftly down?
> The chosen ones, on earth who wrought the most,
>   The Church's brightest crown,
> Our Lord has sent to meet me,
>   As in the far-off years
> Their words oft came to greet me
>   In yonder land of tears.
>
> The patriarchs' and prophets, noble train,
>   With all Christ's followers true,

Who bore the cross and could the worst disdain
That tyrants dared to do,
I see them shine for ever,
All-glorious as the sun,
'Mid light that fades not ever,
Their perfect freedom won.

Encouraged by the vision, the soul, confident in the hope of heaven and sure of her place in paradise, returns to the earth to await her time of departure to join the great choir.

And when, within that lovely paradise
At last I safely dwell,
From out my soul what songs of bliss shall rise,
What joy my lips shall tell,
While holy saints are singing
Hosannas o'er and o'er,
Pure hallelujahs ringing
Around me evermore.

Unnumbered choirs before the shining throne
Their joyful anthem raise
Till heaven's glad halls are echoing with the tone
Of that grand hymn of praise;
And all its host rejoices,
And all its blessed throng
Unite their myriad voices
In one eternal song.[64]

The conclusion of the spiritual expedition is a vision of the unity of all creation joining in one harmonious song of praise.

In addition to the fourfold shape of the Trinity season, with its progression from the declaration of the kingdom of grace, to the description of the kingdom, to the life demanded of its citizens, to the fulfillment and rewards of the kingdom, on any of the Sundays after Trinity it was often possible to find a common theme in the Propers. To take but one example, the Third Sunday after Trinity (Lutheran orders)/Third Sunday after Pentecost (Roman Missal).[65] The appointed Introit was Psalm 25:16, 18, 1-2a:

Turn thee unto me, and have mercy upon me: for I am desolate and afflicted.
Look upon mine affliction and my pain: and forgive all my sins.
>   Unto thee, O Lord, do I lift up my soul:
>   O my God, I trust in thee, let me not be ashamed.

The Epistle was 1 Peter 5:6-11 (discipline yourselves; keep alert); the Gospel Luke 15:1-10. "Between the Introit and the Gospel there is a very rich harmony. The cry of the Introit is that of the desolation and affliction of sin, of the world-torn soul hungering for God. To this the Gospel answers in the Voice which spake the Parables of the Lost Sheep and the Lost Coin to that thronging group of publicans and sinners, a message of comfort, welcome, joy.... 'The Son of Man is come to seek and to save that which was lost.'.... The Epistle leads us to the rest of the flock. Perhaps there was some thought when the Epistle was first chosen that it would be wise in this connection to warn the 'Ninety and Nine' of the dangers which are constantly threatening them, and just where they are—that no false sense of security engender carelessness. 'Your adversary, the devil, as a roaring lion, walketh about, seeking whom he may devour,' is an exceedingly pertinent warning to the ninety-nine sheep left in the wilderness...[of] the forms of danger that may result in *their* becoming the lost.... And the Collect addresses [God] as the Protector of all that trust in him (compare the last verse of the Introit) without whom nothing is strong, nothing is holy, and asks humbly for that shepherding care, guardianship and direction through the perils of the present that we finally...lose not the things eternal."[66]

In the present reconstruction of the calendar, "ordinary time" is a shapeless season, stretching on and on, the only pattern found in reading through various books of the Bible. The intended correlation between the Old Testament and the Gospel is not always apparent, and if the semi-continuous pattern of the Revised Common Lectionary is followed, each of the three readings goes its own way. Here, it may be said, the tyranny of the lectionary takes over the imagination of the Church,[67] and for all the commendable intentions of putting more of the Bible before the people, one may wonder how much will be followed by the listeners. *Lectio continua,* George Muenich was fond of observing, requires *audito continua,* continuous reading requires continuous attendance and listening with care, and that continuity is much more difficult to achieve.

The original common lectionary, like the Roman Catholic lectionary from which it was derived, was based on a continuous reading of New Testament Epistles and Gospels, and the Old Testament reading was chosen to harmonize in some way with the Gospel selection. Because there arose some opposition to this approach on the (laudable) grounds that the Hebrew Bible ought to stand on its own as Scripture and not be used simply to support the New Testament, the Revised Common Lectionary provides, for the time after Pentecost, two methods of reading the Hebrew Scriptures: one in which the lection is chosen as a companion to the Gospel reading and the other in which a semi-continuous reading progresses through selected books of the Old Testament.[68] Here is how the various books are read.

Year A. First Lesson, semi-continuous series

Genesis	through Proper 15
Exodus	Proper 16-24
Deuteronomy	Proper 25
Joshua	Proper 26-27
Judges	Proper 28

Second Lesson

Romans	through Proper 15
Philippians	Proper 20-23
1 Thessalonians	Proper 24-28

Gospel

 continuous reading of Matthew

Year B. First Lesson, semi-continuous series

1 Samuel	through Proper 7
2 Samuel	Proper 8-14
1 Kings	Proper 15-16
Song of Solomon	Proper 17
Proverbs	Proper 18-20
Esther	Proper 21
Job	Proper 22-25
Ruth	Proper 26-27
1 Samuel	Proper 28

Second Lesson

2 Corinthians	through Proper 9
Ephesians	Proper 10-16
James	Proper 17-21
Hebrews	Proper 22-28

Gospel

 continuous reading of Mark interspersed with John

Year C. First Lesson, semi-continuous series

1 Kings	through Proper 7

2 Kings	Proper 8-9
Amos	Proper 10-11
Hosea	Proper 12-13
Isaiah	Proper 14-15
Jeremiah	Proper 16-21, 23-24
Lamentations	Proper 22
Joel	Proper 25
Habakkuk	Proper 26
Haggai	Proper 27
Isaiah	Proper 28

Second Lesson

Galatians	through Proper 9
Colossians	Proper 10-13
Hebrews	Proper 14-17
Philemon	Proper 18
1 Timothy	Proper 19-21
2 Timothy	Proper 22-25
2 Thessalonians	Proper 26-28

Gospel

continuous reading of Luke.

Formerly, the Sundays were numbered "after Pentecost" in Roman Catholic use and "after Trinity" in northern European (Anglican and Lutheran) use. In the revised calendar the Sundays continue to be counted "after Pentecost," which, although correct, is no longer a helpful designation. What matters in finding the appropriate readings and prayers is not the number of the Sunday after Pentecost but the number of the Sunday in Ordinary Time (the Sunday of the Year) in Roman Catholic use and the number of what the Book of Common Prayer and the Revised Common Lectionary designate the "Proper," determined by the date of the Sunday. Propers not required in a particular year are omitted from the beginning of the time after Pentecost.

Many of the classic collects from the previous books have been preserved in the current calendar, but they have often been reassigned. Such reassignment continues what has been practiced in the Church from time to time through the centuries, moving collects and other Propers to what were thought to be more (or at least equally) suitable occasions. The collects especially, because of their depth and richness, work equally well in various places.

Proper 1 is used on weekdays following Whitsunday, when Easter occurs very early and there are twenty-eight Sundays after Pentecost; hence it is described in the Prayer Book as "Week of the Sunday closest to May 11" (i.e., between May 10 and 14 inclusive).

Proper 1 in the Book of Common Prayer corresponds to the Sixth Sunday in Ordinary Time on the Roman calendar. The collect for this Sunday in the Roman sacramentary was considered above in connection with the Sixth Sunday after the Epiphany (see p. 285). The Prayer Book appoints a Leonine collect: "Remember, O Lord, what you have wrought in us and not what we deserve; and, as you have called us to your service, make us worthy of our calling; through..." The prayer makes the connection between what God has done for us by the events commemorated in the first half of the liturgical year and the response that is expected of us, which in the final analysis is also God's work in us. Advent through Pentecost has been a summons, our calling; now in the long time after Pentecost we are to become what God has made us. St. Augustine charged the newly baptized, "Become what you already are."

Proper 2 is used on weekdays following Trinity Sunday, when there are twenty-eight Sundays after Pentecost, Proper 1 having been used on weekdays following Whitsunday. When there are twenty-seven weeks after Pentecost, Proper 2 is used on weekdays following Whitsunday.

Proper 2, "Week of the Sunday closest to May 18" (between May 17 and 21), corresponds to the Seventh Sunday in Ordinary Time. The Roman sacramentary appoints the prayer given above under the Seventh Sunday after the Epiphany (see p. 286). The Prayer Book appoints a collect from the Gelasian and Gregorian sacramentaries that in previous books had been assigned to the Twentieth Sunday after Trinity (Nineteenth Sunday after Trinity in Lutheran books; the Nineteenth Sunday after Pentecost in the Roman Missal): "Almighty and merciful God, in your goodness, keep us, we pray, from all things that may hurt us, that we, being ready both in mind and body, may accomplish with free hearts those things which belong to your purpose; through..." The contrast between "the things that may hurt us" and the things that belong to God's good will for his creation is basic to this prayer. Sin enslaves; God gives freedom for his service.

Because Proper 3 is the first of the "Propers" that can be used on a Sunday, the description in the Prayer Book of Propers 3 and following changes from "Week of the Sunday..." to "The Sunday closest to...."

Proper 3, "the Sunday closest to May 25" (between May 24 and 28), which in the Roman calendar is the Eighth Sunday in Ordinary Time, has in both the Roman and Episcopal books a Leonine Collect that in previous books had been assigned to the Fourth Sunday after Pentecost in the Roman Missal, the Fifth Sunday after Trinity in the Prayer Book, the Fourth Sunday after Trinity in Lutheran books: "Grant, O Lord, that the course of this world may be peaceably ordered by your providence; and that your Church may joyfully serve you in confidence and serenity; through..." William Bright remarks that the collect from the time of Leo the Great (d. 461) "seems to have been suggested...by the disasters of the dying Western Empire."[69] The word *nobis* in the original text, "May be peaceably ordered *for us*," may support this observation.

Proper 4, "the Sunday closest to June 1" (between May 29 and June 4), the Ninth Sunday in Ordinary Time, has in both the Roman and the Episcopal rites a Gelasian collect that had in previous books been assigned to the Seventh Sunday after Pentecost, the Seventh Sunday after Trinity in Lutheran books: "O God, your never-failing providence sets in order all things both in heaven and on earth: Put away from us, we entreat you, all hurtful things, and give us those things which are profitable for us; through..." The 1549 translation, replaced in 1662 with the paraphrase above, was closer to the original Latin, "whose providence is never deceived." Luther Reed says that "this fine collect" still falls short of the original invocation, "God, whose providence is not deceived in the management of its own" (*Deus, cuius providentia in sui dispositione non fallitur*).[70] The present English translation of the Roman sacramentary has "whose providence never fails in its design."

Proper 5, "the Sunday closest to June 8" (between June 5 and 11), the Tenth Sunday in Ordinary Time, in both the Roman and Episcopal books, has a collect from the Gelasian and Gregorian sacramentaries that in previous Roman, Anglican, and Lutheran books was appointed for the Fifth Sunday after Easter. Because it was not clearly related to the themes of Easter, it was assigned to this Sunday in Ordinary Time. "O God, from whom all good proceeds: Grant that by your inspiration we may think those things that are right, and by your merciful guiding may do them; through..." God must put into our minds good and right thoughts (we cannot think them on our own), and then God must also guide us to carry them out. The translation is that of the Prayer Book.

Proper 6, "the Sunday closest to June 15" (between June 12 and 18), the Eleventh Sunday in Ordinary Time, in the Roman sacramentary has a Gelasian and Gregorian collect that in the Roman Missal of 1570 was appointed for the First Sunday after Pentecost (where it was said after the collect for Trinity Sunday to commemorate the older celebration of the Sunday after Pentecost) and in Anglican and Lutheran books for the First Sunday after Trinity. "O God, the strength of all who put their trust in you: Mercifully accept our prayers; and because in our weakness we can do nothing good without you, give us the help of your grace, that in keeping your commandments we may please you both in will and deed; through..." Those who put their hope and trust in God can be sure of his strength and support. Like the prayer of the previous

Sunday (Proper 5), we acknowledge our dependence on God in order for us to do anything that is good.

The 1979 Book of Common Prayer assigns the collect to the Sixth Sunday after the Epiphany and introduces on this Sunday a new composition by Massey H. Shepherd, Jr., which more explicitly suggests our responsibility to others. "Keep, O Lord, your household the Church in your steadfast faith and love, that through your grace we may proclaim your truth with boldness, and minister your justice with compassion; for the sake of our Savior...." The prayer makes use of Gal. 6:10 and Eph. 2:19 and phrases from the collects previously assigned to Epiphany 5, Trinity 22, and Trinity 2 in the previous Prayer Book. The twin ideals of truth and justice are joined with courage and compassion as the fullness of Christian duty and service.

Proper 7, "the Sunday closest to June 22" (between June 19 and 25), the Twelfth Sunday in Ordinary Time, has a collect that in the Gelasian sacramentary was assigned to the Sunday after the Ascension, in the Gregorian for the second Sunday after the Pentecost octave (reassigning collects has a long history in the Church), in the Roman Missal for the Second Sunday after Pentecost (the Sunday within the octave of Corpus Christi), and in Anglican and Lutheran use for the Second Sunday after Trinity. It is translated in the 1979 Prayer Book: "O Lord, make us have perpetual love and reverence for your holy Name, for you never fail to help and govern those whom you have set upon the sure foundation of your loving-kindness; through..." Marion Hatchett, noting the Latin original *timorem partier et amorem*, suggests the translation "make us perpetually to have fear, and no less, love of your holy Name." (The previous translation had "fear and love of thy holy Name.") He further notes that "Name" carries the idea of God's self-revelation.[71] It is for this reason that in the Prayer Book and in previous Lutheran books, until 1978, "Name" when referring to God's strength and revelation was always capitalized. The word is redolent with the very power of God. Massey Shepherd notes that the Prayer Book translation obscures the image of the helmsman (*gubernator*). Our safety is in his hands, and so we may fear or at least respect him, and we may love him, for he does not abandon us in heavy weather.[72]

Proper 8 and the Thirteenth Sunday in Ordinary Time diverge in their appointed collects. The Roman sacramentary has a newly appointed prayer from the Bergamo sacramentary: "In your loving-kindness, O God, you have adopted us into your family as children of light: Grant that we may not become entangled in the darkness of error and lies, but may always live in the brightness of your truth; through..."[73] The light of truth is contrasted with the darkness that leads first to error and then to lies to cover up the misdeeds. The biblical source of "children of light" is Eph. 5:8 and 1 Thess. 5:5.

The 1979 Book of Common Prayer for this "Sunday closest to June 29" (between June 26 and July 2) uses the collect written for the 1549 Prayer Book for the festival of SS. Simon and Jude (October 28): "Almighty God, you have built your Church upon the foundation of the apostles and prophets, Jesus Christ himself being the chief cornerstone: Grant us so to be joined together in unity of spirit by their teaching, that we may be made a holy temple acceptable to you; through..." Cranmer's "congregation" was changed in 1662 to "Church" because of the Puritan connotation of "congregation." The 1979 version changed "head" to "chief" in the description of the cornerstone, closer to modern usage but losing the allusion to the headship of the Church, which is the body of Christ. The biblical reference is Eph. 2:20-21. Because of its reference to the Apostles, the collect was assigned to this "Sunday closest to June 29," the Feast of SS. Peter and Paul, the two greatest apostles.

Proper 9, "the Sunday closest to July 6" (between July 3 and 9) and the Fourteenth Sunday in Ordinary Time, diverge in the appointed collects. The Roman sacramentary appoints the Gelasian and Gregorian collect formerly appointed for the Second Sunday after Easter, which it also uses on Monday in the Fourth Week of Easter: "God, who by the humiliation of your Son raised up the fallen world: Grant to your faithful people perpetual gladness, and make those whom you have delivered from the danger of everlasting death partakers of eternal joys." (See chapter 7, pp. 248–249.)

The 1979 Book of Common Prayer appoints a Leonine collect: "O God, you have taught us to keep all your commandments by loving you and our neighbor: Grant us the grace of your Holy Spirit, that we may be devoted to you with our whole heart, and united to one another with pure affection; through..." The translation is by William Bright in his *Ancient Collects*. Anglicans will remember the Summary of the Law (Matt. 22:37-40) in the Penitential Order of the Prayer Book (p. 319): "Hear what our Lord Jesus Christ saith: Thou shalt love the Lord thy God with all thy heart, and with all thy soul, and with all thy mind. This is the first and great commandment. And the second is like unto it: Thou shalt love thy neighbor as thyself. On these two commandments hang all the Law and the Prophets."

Proper 10 and the Fifteenth Sunday in Ordinary Time diverge in the appointed collects. The Roman sacramentary uses the impressive Leonine collect formerly assigned to what was then accounted the Third Sunday after Easter: "Almighty God, you show to those who are in error the light of your truth, so that they may return into the way of righteousness: Grant to all those who are admitted into the fellowship of Christ's religion that they may resolutely reject those things that contradict the faith they profess and follow all those things that are in agreement with it; through..." (See the comments on p. 250).

The 1979 Prayer Book for this "Sunday closest to July 13" (between 10 and 16) uses a collect that has wandered a great deal. In the Gregorian sacramentary it was appointed for a Sunday after Christmas; in the supplement to the Gregorian for the First Sunday after the Epiphany; in the Sarum Missal for the Sunday after the octave of the Epiphany; in the 1549 Prayer Book, the observance of the Epiphany octave being omitted, for the First Sunday after the Epiphany; in the 1979 Book, because Epiphany 1 is the Baptism of the Lord, for Proper 10. "O Lord, mercifully receive the prayers of your people who call upon you, and grant that they may know and understand what things they ought to do, and also may have grace and power faithfully to accomplish them; through..." The collect, based on Jas. 4:17, John 13:17, and Luke 12:47, "summarizes succinctly the twofold meaning and purpose of prayer: to perceive God's will, and to seek the strength which is necessary for the accomplishment of it."[74] Luther Reed remarks, "The original of the Collect is of such excellence that Dr. [Edward Traill] Horn was moved to say, 'Such a collect makes one wish that we always said our prayers in Latin.' The translators have not preserved the terseness and crispness of its balanced phraseology, though they have contributed smoothness."[75] We pray that we not only know what we ought to do but that we understand why it is right, and then, knowing our need, we ask for the gift of strength to do the right thing.

Proper 11 and the Sixteenth Sunday in Ordinary Time also diverge in their prayers. The Roman sacramentary appoints a collect from the Bergamo and Ambrosian sacramentaries. "Look in mercy, O Lord, upon your family and pour out upon us the gifts of your grace, so that, aflame with faith, hope, and love, we may always watch and pray, and walk in the path of your commandments; through..."[76] We pray for the three theological virtues so that in faith and hope we may watch and pray and in love walk in the way of God's commandments. (Compare the Leonine collect given below at Proper 25.)

The 1979 Book of Common Prayer for this "Sunday closest to July 20" (between July 17 and 23) appoints from the 1549 Prayer Book one of the six "Collects to be said after the Offertory when there is no Communion." (The same collect appears in another form as no. 4 of The Collect at the Prayers [pp. 394-395] in the 1979 Book.) "Almighty God, the fountain of all wisdom, you know our necessities before we ask and our ignorance in asking: Have compassion on our weakness, and mercifully give us those things which for our unworthiness we dare not, and for our blindness we cannot ask; through the worthiness of your Son..." The biblical sources of the prayer include Sirach 1:5; Matt. 8:8; Rom. 8:26. See also below, the collect assigned to Proper

22 in the Prayer Book, and also the prayer For Those We Love: "Almighty God, we entrust all who are dear to us to thy never-failing care and love, for this life and the life to come, knowing that thou art doing for them better things than we can desire or pray for; through Jesus Christ our Lord." In its earliest form it appears in 1876 and entered the American Prayer Book in 1928 and continues in the 1979 book (p. 831).

Proper 12, "the Sunday closest to July 27" (between July 24 and 30), the Seventeenth Sunday in Ordinary Time, appoints a collect from the Gregorian sacramentary previously used on the Third Sunday after Pentecost in the Roman Missal, the Fourth Sunday after Trinity in Anglican use, and the Third Sunday after Trinity in the Lutheran books. "O God, the protector of all who trust in you, without whom nothing is strong, nothing is holy: Increase and multiply upon us your mercy, that, with you as our ruler and guide, we may so pass through things temporal, that we lose not the things eternal; through..." It is a fine collect given in a free translation in the Prayer Book. It encourages us to make the necessary distinction between what is passing and what abides. The "things temporal" are what the Latin calls "the good things of time" (*bona temporalia*) reminding us, as Barbee and Zahl note, that we are in danger not only from temporal adversity, but also from temporal prosperity.[77]

Proper 13 and the Eighteenth Sunday in Ordinary Time diverge in the collect each appoints. The Roman sacramentary appoints a collect from the Leonine sacramentary: "Be present, Lord, with your family and bless them with your unfailing kindness, so that in those who glory in having you as their author and guide, you may restore what you have given and keep intact what you have restored; through..."[78] It is a prayer of intimacy, the baptized constituting God's family, and of total dependence on God. The Father of the family must restore what we have lost through our disobedience and sin and then must preserve what he has restored, for we cannot save ourselves nor on our own live in obedience. Our need of divine help pervades our whole life and being.

For this "Sunday closest to August 3" (between July 31 and August 6), the Book of Common Prayer assigns the Gelasian and Gregorian collect previously appointed in the Roman Missal to the Fifteenth Sunday after Pentecost, in previous Prayer Books to the Sixteenth Sunday after Trinity, and in Lutheran books to the Fifteenth Sunday after Trinity. "Let your continual mercy, O Lord, cleanse and defend your Church; and, because it cannot continue in safety without your help, protect and govern it always by your goodness; through..." Because the Church is made of sinful people, its cleansing is not a one-time or even occasional requirement but a perpetual condition. So also is the Church's need of God's defense and protection against its many enemies both within and outside its borders. The Church is forever fragile, yet with God's cleansing and guidance all the forces arrayed against it will fail in their attempts to destroy it. As is the case with the collect the Prayer Book appoints for Proper 8, the 1662 Book replaced Cranmer's "congregation" with "Church" because of the Puritan connotation of "congregation."

Proper 14 and the Nineteenth Sunday in Ordinary Time diverge in the appointed collect. The Roman sacramentary appoints a collect from the Bergamo and Ambrosian missals. "Almighty and everlasting God, with boldness and confidence we dare to call you Father: Fulfill and make perfect in our hearts the work of your Holy Spirit, through whom we have become your adopted children, so that we may be found worthy to enter upon the glorious inheritance you have promised to us in Jesus Christ our Lord; who..."[79] The prayer reminds us of the boldness of presuming to call God our Father, as in the introduction to the Lord's Prayer in the Eucharist: "And now, as our Savior Christ has taught us, we are bold to say," (Prayer Book) or "Commanded by his saving precepts and informed by his divine instruction, we are bold to say" (Roman Catholic).

The 1979 Book of Common Prayer for this "Sunday closest to August 10" (between 7 and 13) appoints a collect from the Leonine, Gelasian, and Gregorian sacramentaries formerly assigned in the Roman Missal to the Eighth Sunday after Pentecost, in Anglican books to the Ninth Sunday after Trinity, and in Lutheran use to the Eighth Sunday after Trinity: "Grant to us, Lord, we pray, the spirit to think and do always those things that are right, that we, who cannot exist without you, may by you be enabled to live according to your will; through..." The prayer, Massey Shepherd says, "expresses as succinctly as possible the whole doctrine of grace."[80] Without God we would not even be; such is our dependence upon God's strength and guidance. "The hindrances are many, great and constant; they also are attractive, seductive. The false spirits would lead away; and, while seemingly attractive and harmless, will only *prove themselves* to be hard masters of a slavery that leads to destruction!"[81]

Proper 15 and the Twentieth Sunday in Ordinary Time diverge in the appointed collect. The Roman sacramentary appoints a Gelasian prayer, inspired by 1 Cor. 2:9 (itself perhaps a paraphrase of Isa. 64:4) and 1 John 4:19, previously assigned in the Roman Missal to the Fifth Sunday after Pentecost, in Anglican books to the Sixth Sunday after Trinity, and in Lutheran use to the Fifth Sunday after Trinity, and in the 1979 Book of Common Prayer to the Sixth Sunday of Easter. "O God, you have prepared for those who love you such good things as surpass our understanding: Pour into our hearts such love towards you, that we, loving you in all things and above all things, may obtain your promises, which exceed all that we can desire; through..." Our love for God is itself a gift from God.[82] We pray that we may keep things in proper perspective, finding God in all things and yet loving the Creator above all created things. "Do you love me more than these?" Jesus asked Peter (John 21:15).

The Prayer Book appoints for this "Sunday closest to August 17" (between August 14 and 20) a collect written for the 1549 book and appointed in all previous Prayer Books for the Second Sunday after Easter: "Almighty God, you have given your only Son to be for us a sacrifice for sin and also an example of godly life: Give us grace to receive thankfully the fruits of his redeeming work, and to follow daily in the blessed steps of his most holy life; through..." Redemption, forgiveness, and life are the results of his sacrifice, which we are to receive with thanksgiving and are to imitate in our own lives. The collect was included in the Lutheran *Service Book and Hymnal* (1958) as a post-Communion prayer.

Proper 16 and the Twenty-first Sunday in Ordinary Time diverge in their appointed prayers. The Roman rite has a collect from the Gelasian sacramentary previously assigned to the Fourth Sunday after Easter in Roman, Lutheran, and Anglican books and in the 1979 Prayer Book assigned to the Fifth Sunday in Lent. "O God, you make the minds of the faithful to be of one will: Grant that your people may love what you command and desire what you promise; that, among the manifold changes of this word, our hearts may there be fixed where true joys are to be found; through..." We ask that we be made one not just with each other but, together, one with the will of God. "His will is our peace," the blessed Piccarda says in Dante's *Paradiso*,[83] and in that will and peace is true joy. The unity of the Church is to be found in loving God's commands, desiring the promises, and fixing the heart on Christ, in whom is the fullness and the perfection of joy.

The Book of Common Prayer appoints for Proper 16, "the Sunday closest to August 24" (between August 21 and 27), a collect for unity that was introduced in the 1928 American Prayer Book for Tuesday in Whitsun Week: "Grant, O merciful God, that your Church, being gathered together in unity by your Holy Spirit, may show forth your power among all peoples, to the glory of your Name; through..." The opening phrase is from the collect for Friday after Pentecost in the Sarum and Roman missals.

Proper 17, "the Sunday closest to August 31" (between August 28 and September 3), the Twenty-second Sunday in Ordinary Time, has this collect from the Gelasian sacramentary previously appointed in the Roman Missal for the Sixth Sunday after Pentecost, in Lutheran use to the Sixth Sunday after Trinity, and in Anglican books to the Seventh Sunday after Trinity: "Lord of all power and might, the author and giver of all good things: Graft in our hearts

the love of your Name; increase in us true religion; nourish us with all goodness; and bring forth in us the fruit of good works; through..." The biblical
allusion is Jas. 1:17. The address in Latin, "Deus virtutum," may be translated
"God of hosts." The collect is a forceful prayer, enriched by the 1549 translation.[84] Life in the kingdom of grace has a new motive: no longer fear-driven
obedience but grace-inspired love.[85]

Proper 18, "the Sunday closest to September 7" (between September
4 and 10), and the Twenty-third Sunday in Ordinary Time diverge. The
Roman sacramentary for this ordinary Sunday repeats the prayer used on
the Fifth Sunday of Easter: "O God, through whom redemption comes to
us and our adoption is accomplished: Look in mercy on your children, and
bestow upon all who believe in Christ perfect freedom and an eternal inheritance; through your Son..." The Book of Common Prayer appoints a collect from the Leonine sacramentary, translated in William Bright's *Ancient
Collects*: "Grant to us, O Lord, to trust in you with all our hearts; for, as you
always resist the proud who confide in their own strength, so you never
forsake those who make their boast of your mercy; through..." The biblical
allusion is Jas. 4:6 and recalls St. Paul's paradoxical boasting of his weakness
(2 Cor. 11:16-30).

Proper 19, "the Sunday closest to September 14" (between September 11 and
17), and the Twenty-fourth Sunday in Ordinary Time diverge in their prayers.
The Roman sacramentary uses a Leonine collect: "O God, creator and ruler
of all that exists: Look kindly on the prayers of your servants, and grant that
we may serve you with undivided hearts, and so experience the power of your
mercy; through..."[86] In its biblical and liturgical context, mercy is neither
weak nor sentimental. It is in fact the power to oppose blind and unthinking
justice and to overcome. God's answer to this prayer is proof of the power
inherent in God's mercy, which is never the mere ignoring of wrongdoing but
the eradication of sin, the abolition of punishment, and the strength to live
the new life.

The Book of Common Prayer appoints a collect from the Gelasian and
Gregorian sacramentaries previously assigned in the Roman Missal to the
Eighteenth Sunday after Pentecost, in Anglican books to the Nineteenth
Sunday after Trinity, and in Lutheran use to the Eighteenth Sunday after Trinity.
"O God, because without you we are not able to please you, mercifully grant
that your Holy Spirit may in all things direct and rule our hearts; through..."
A more literal translation, supplied by Marion Hatchett, is, "Direct our hearts,
O Lord, we beseech you, by the working of your mercy, for without you we are
not able to please you."[87] Cranmer's translation reverses the order of the Latin
collect so that the acknowledgment of our inability to please God comes first

as it does in our experience, and after "direct" added "and rule," asking that God both guide and govern all we do.

Proper 20 and the Twenty-fifth Sunday in Ordinary Time diverge in their appointed prayers. The Roman sacramentary has the Leonine collect appointed in the Prayer Book for Proper 9 ("O God, you taught us to keep all your commandments by loving you and our neighbor: Grant us the grace of your Holy Spirit, that we may be devoted to you with our whole heart, and united to one another with pure affection"). The Prayer Book introduces for Proper 20, "the Sunday closest to September 21" (between 18 and 24), a collect from the Leonine sacramentary, reflecting the tumultuous times of barbarian invasions, evocatively translated in Bright's *Ancient Collects*: "Grant us, Lord, not to be anxious about earthly things, but to love things heavenly; and even now, while we are placed among things that are passing away, to hold fast to those that shall endure; through..." The biblical allusion is Col. 3:2. The prayer already anticipates the theme of the final Sunday in the liturgical year and of Advent, reminding us that all we now see is temporary and is in the process of "passing away." A mark of spiritual maturity is the ability to distinguish between what is passing and what abides.

Proper 21, "the Sunday closest to September 28" (between September 25 and October 1), the Twenty-sixth Sunday in Ordinary Time, uses a collect from Gallican Missale Gothicum, the Gelasian sacramentary, and the Gregorian supplement, used previously in the Roman Missal on the Tenth Sunday after Pentecost, in the Sarum rite and previous prayer books on the Eleventh Sunday after Trinity, and in Lutheran use on the Tenth Sunday after Trinity. "O God, you declare your almighty power chiefly in showing mercy and pity: Grant us the fullness of your grace, that we, running to obtain your promises, may become partakers of your heavenly treasure; through..." God's almighty power is shown most clearly in his self-restraint. Marion Hatchett suggests that "mercy and pity" would be more literally rendered "sparing and showing compassion" and "Grant us the fullness of your grace" might be more literally "multiply upon us your grace."[88] The Pauline image of running occurs again in the collect for Proper 26.

Proper 22, "the Sunday closest to October 5" (between October 2 and 8), the Twenty-seventh Sunday in Ordinary Time, uses a collect the germ of which is Leonine for the autumn ember days; it was greatly revised in the Gallican Missale Francorum to conclude the intercessions at a Sunday Mass. It was appointed in the Gelasian sacramentary for the seventh of the sixteen Sunday Masses; the Roman Missal appointed it for the Eleventh Sunday after Pentecost; the Sarum missal and previous Prayer Books appointed it for the Twelfth Sunday after Trinity; Lutheran use for the Eleventh Sunday after

Trinity. "Almighty and everlasting God, you are always more ready to hear than we to pray, and to give more than we either desire or deserve: Pour upon us the abundance of your mercy, forgiving us those things of which our conscience is afraid, and giving us those good things for which we are not worthy to ask, except through the merits and mediation of Jesus Christ our Savior; who..." With its honesty in describing prayer and the spirit of humility, it is a remarkably fine and indeed glorious prayer.[89] Behind it and giving it power is the experience of the prodigal son (Luke 15:11-32).

Proper 23, "the Sunday closest to October 12" (between October 9 and 15), the Twenty-eighth Sunday in Ordinary Time, uses a collect from among the Gregorian prayers for morning and evening. In the Roman Missal it was assigned to the Sixteenth Sunday after Pentecost, in the Sarum rite and previous Prayer Books to the Seventeenth Sunday after Trinity, and in Lutheran use to the Sixteenth Sunday after Trinity. "Lord, we pray that your grace may always precede and follow us, that we may be continually given to good works; through..." The prayer is for both "prevenient" and "cooperating" grace: grace that precedes and anticipates us and grace that accompanies us. The prayer is a recognition of and thanksgiving for God's grace, which goes before us to prepare the way for us and to encourage us to follow and which also follows us, correcting and making good the things we have done.

Proper 24 and the Twenty-ninth Sunday in Ordinary Time diverge in their prayers. The Roman sacramentary appoints a Gelasian collect that in previous Roman and Lutheran books was assigned to the Sunday after the Ascension: "Almighty and everlasting God, make us always to have a will that is devoted to you and to serve your Majesty with a pure heart; through..." The end of the liturgical year is now not far away, and the simple prayer, addressing God with the royal reference "your Majesty," recalls the promise of Jesus, "Blessed are the pure in heart, for they will see God" (Matt. 5:8).

For this "Sunday closest to October 19" (between October 16 and 22), the Book of Common Prayer appoints what in the Gelasian and later sacramentaries, including the 1570 Roman Missal, the 1970 Roman sacramentary, and the *Lutheran Book of Worship,* is the first of the solemn prayers for Good Friday: "Almighty and everlasting God, in Christ you have revealed your glory among the nations: Preserve the works of your mercy, that your Church throughout the world may persevere with steadfast faith in the confession of your Name; through..." The translation is by William Bright. The bidding in the Good Friday liturgy invites prayer "for the holy Church of God throughout the world, that God will guide it and gather it together, so that we may worship the Father in tranquility and peace." The collect that follows is a prayer for the peace, unity, and protection of the Church. The "works of your mercy" are God's revelation to the nations (see Rom. 9:17); what he has done in the past and what he continues to do to establish, protect, and sustain the Church so that through peaceful and through troubled times it may continue steadfast in the proclamation of the mighty works of God (Acts 2:11). It is more than a prayer that the Church may be able to go about its business without persecution by its opponents; it is a prayer that in times of persecution it may be so confident in God's care that it will persevere through whatever troubles it may be called to endure (see Acts 9:15-16).

Proper 25, "the Sunday closest to October 26" (between October 30 and November 5), the Thirtieth Sunday in Ordinary Time, appoints a collect from the Leonine sacramentary where it was assigned to vespers; in the Roman Missal it was appointed for the Thirteenth Sunday after Pentecost, in the Sarum rite and previous Prayer Books for the Fourteenth Sunday after Trinity, and in Lutheran books for the Thirteenth Sunday after Trinity. "Almighty and everlasting God, increase in us the gifts of faith, hope, and charity; and, that we may obtain what you promise, make us love what you command; through..." The Latin has "that we may deserve to obtain what you promise," but Cranmer eliminated any idea of merit from the collect by omitting "deserve to."[90] We pray that when we inherit God's promises we may be made worthy of them. Meanwhile, we are to be so transformed in attitude that we will learn to love what God commands us to do.

Proper 26, "the Sunday closest to November 2" (between October 30 and November 5), the Thirty-first Sunday in Ordinary Time, uses a Leonine collect that in the Roman Missal was appointed for the Twelfth Sunday after Pentecost, in the Sarum rite and previous Prayer Books for the Thirteenth Sunday after Trinity; and in Lutheran use for the Twelfth Sunday after Trinity. "Almighty and merciful God, it is only by your gift that your faithful people offer you true and laudable service: Grant that we may run without stumbling to obtain your heavenly promises; through..." In the prayer, "true" is used in the sense of "worthy" (Latin *digne*). The imagery of physical exertion, running, here and in the collect for Proper 21, is drawn from St. Paul's encouragement of such energetic action in 1 Cor. 9:24-27, Gal. 2:2; 5:7; Phil. 2:16; 2 Tim. 4:7; also Heb. 12:1-2.

Proper 27 and the Thirty-second Sunday in Ordinary Time diverge. The Roman sacramentary uses the collect that in the Book of Common Prayer is appointed for the Seventh Sunday after the Epiphany, which is the equivalent of Proper 2 ("Almighty and merciful God, in your goodness, keep us, we pray, from all things that may hurt us, that we, being ready in both mind and body, may accomplish with free hearts those things which belong to your purpose").

For this "Sunday closest to November 9" (between November 6 and 12), the Prayer Book uses the prayer composed perhaps by John Cosin for the 1662

Prayer Book for the Sixth Sunday after the Epiphany based on the Epistle for that Sunday, 1 John 3:1-9. "O God, whose blessed Son came into the world that he might destroy the works of the devil and make us children of God and heirs of eternal life: Grant that, having this hope, we may purify ourselves as he is pure; that, when he comes again with power and great glory, we may be made like him in his eternal and glorious kingdom; where he lives and reigns..." The present location of the prayer, the third Sunday before Advent, turns the attention of the Church toward the eschatological fulfillment, which is a theme of the final Sundays of the liturgical year and of Advent as well.

Proper 28 and the Thirty-third Sunday in Ordinary Time diverge. The Roman sacramentary uses a collect from the Leonine sacramentary: "Grant to us, O Lord our God, we pray, that we may always find joy in your service, for it is only through our faithfulness to you, the author of every good, that full and lasting happiness will be ours; through..."[91]

For this "Sunday closest to November 16" (between November 13 and 19) the Book of Common Prayer uses the collect written for the 1549 Book, inspired by Rom. 15:4, the initial verse of the Epistle then appointed for the Second Sunday in Advent. "Blessed Lord, who caused all holy Scriptures to be written for our learning: Grant us so to hear them, read, mark, learn, and inwardly digest them, that we may embrace and ever hold fast the blessed hope of everlasting life, which you have given us in our Savior Jesus Christ; who lives and reigns..." The address, "Blessed Lord," is to the Father. The word "all" in the opening of the prayer stresses the importance of the whole Bible, not simply selected passages. The daily lectionary since the Reformation has arranged a reading of nearly the entire Bible over the course of a year or, in the present Prayer Book, over two years. And now the Eucharistic lectionary also has been expanded over a course of three years to put much of the Bible before the preachers and before the people.

A collect from the 1639 *Evangeliebok* of the Church of Sweden was appointed for the Twenty-sixth Sunday after Trinity in the Lutheran *Church Book* (1868), *Common Service Book* (1917), *Service Book and Hymnal* (1958), and for the Twenty-sixth Sunday after Pentecost in the *Lutheran Book of Worship* (1978): "O God, so rule and govern our hearts and minds by your Holy Spirit, that being ever mindful of the end of all things and the day of your just judgment, we may be stirred up to holiness of living here, and dwell with you forever hereafter; through..." The prayer avoids the fear associated in the medieval period with "the four last things" (death, judgment, heaven, hell) and provides a more encouraging understanding of the last things, asking that we may face them without fear and always keep them in mind as an encouragement to holy living.

Proper 29, "the Sunday closest to November 23" (between November 20 and 26), is the Sunday of Christ the King, discussed on pp. 296–302.

For the weekdays that follow the festival, the Thirty-Fourth Week in Ordinary Time, the Roman sacramentary provides a Gregorian collect that in the Roman Missal had been appointed for the Twenty-fourth Sunday after Pentecost and in Lutheran use for the Twenty-fourth Sunday after Trinity: "Stir up, O Lord, the wills of your faithful people, that they, more earnestly seeking to do good, may receive more abundant help from your mercy; through..." The opening words, "Stir up," anticipate the opening words of three of the four traditional Advent Collects now preserved only in certain Lutheran uses. The petition of the collect asks that being stirred up to greater effort to do what is right, we may enjoy the support that only God can give. As St. Paul learned, "My grace is sufficient for you, for power is made perfect in weakness" (2 Cor. 12:9).

The collects of the Eucharist, most of them tested and sifted for more than a thousand years, continue to speak to those who attend to their richly condensed meaning and week by week ponder what has been prayed at the Sunday Eucharist.

9

The Sanctoral Cycle

INTERWOVEN WITH THE days and seasons of the liturgical year is another, related calendar, the calendar of saints. Thomas Cranmer described the elect as "knit together...in the mystical body." The saints are not simply joined closely to each other in family fellowship. Their unity comes from their intimate life in their one Lord, a truth understood by Lancelot Andrewes in his prayer,

> Have mercy on your Church, divided in your service; and grant that we, seeking unity in Christ and in the truth of your holy Word, and united by our baptism in one Spirit, may with one mind and one mouth glorify you.[1]

With a similar understanding William Temple prayed,

> Draw us to yourself, that in love and obedience to you we may be united to one another by the one Spirit....[2]

The sanctoral calendar therefore is not to be understood as a separate listing and celebration of worthies and exemplars. We are to understand that as the teaching of Christianity becomes concrete in the liturgical celebration of the events of Christ's life, rehearsed in the Church year, so it is made real to us in individual lives, the lives of holy people, the saints. There, in people like us, we can see what Christianity is and what it can do. The lives of the saints take us to the rich core of the Christian Gospel.

The Paschal Focus

The center of the Christian year, as of the Christian faith and life, is Pascha: Christ's triumphant passage through death to life. Jesus Christ recapitulates the experience of his ancestors in their deliverance from Egypt and their passage through the Red Sea from slavery to freedom. By opening the gates of everlasting life, Christ's Paschal victory also anticipates the victory in which his followers participate, a victory that is not a distant goal but is even now a present possession. St. John puts it plainly: "Very truly, I tell you, anyone who hears my word and believes him who sent me has eternal life, and does not come under judgment, but has passed from death to life" (John 5:24). And again, "God gave us eternal life, and this life is in his Son. Whoever has the Son has life; whoever does not have the Son of God does not have life. I write these things to you who believe in the name of the Son of God, so that you may know that you have eternal life" (1 John 5:11-13). This Johannine understanding is reflected in the formula provided in the 1979 Book of Common Prayer at the distribution of Holy Communion, "The Body (Blood) of our Lord Jesus Christ keep you in everlasting life" as well as in the concluding words of the absolution: "Almighty God have mercy on you, forgive you all your sins through our Lord Jesus Christ, strengthen you in all goodness, and by the power of the Holy Spirit keep you in eternal life." Baptism gives each Christian a share in the transforming grace of God, and in the passage from death to life: Christ's resurrection becomes theirs. The saints, therefore, are those in whom the paschal victory of Christ is clearly manifest, those in whom the holy and life-giving Spirit is clearly at work.

The New Testament understanding of sanctity is richer and more demanding than the simple assertion, "All believers are saints." We are, St. Paul says carefully, "called to be saints" (Rom. 1:7; 1 Cor. 1:2). Sanctity, therefore, is a goal toward which we are to progress. Martin Luther affirmed the same understanding: "This life, therefore, is not righteousness but growth in righteousness; not health, but healing; not being, but becoming; not rest, but exercise. We are not yet what we shall be, but we are growing toward it."[3] One finds even in the New Testament a developing understanding and complexity regarding the saints, the holy people of God. In the world of the New Testament Church, Christians were few in number, tested and purified by opposition, hostility, and soon outright persecution. That entire brave band of courageous believers could truly be called saints, holy people, in and through whom the Holy Spirit was alive and active. Many passages do exactly that and refer to the entire body of believers as "saints" (Acts 9:13, 32, 41; Rom. 16:2; 1 Cor. 6:1; 16:1; Eph. 2:19; 5:3; 1 Tim. 5:10). But as the Church grew and became more diverse, and especially after it received legal recognition in the Roman Empire, some of its members stood out from the rest by their exemplary witness, and they were therefore deserving of special honor.

Today, with church membership easy to be had without rigorous require-ments, to call everyone who claims church membership a "saint" is dangerous and misleading. It is a kind of "cheap grace"[4] as Bonhöffer called it, honor without cost, contributing to human pride and ultimately destructive of the fullness of the Gospel of the passion, death, and resurrection of Christ. In our time, the description "saint" is better reserved for those in whom the grace of God is clearly revealed, those who have earned the distinction by taking the faith seriously and at great cost, who heroically live their baptismal adoption into the family of God and who as good examples to us all are worthy of emu-lation. They show the world what all who would follow Christ are called to be. The call extended by the proclamation of the Gospel is to join the others on the pilgrims' way.

The Communion of Saints

Entering a Byzantine church, one is confronted by an encompassing army of holy men and women represented on every wall and, in a strictly ordered pattern, on the iconostasis that guards the altar. The abundance of icons make visible to the physical eye what the eyes of faith see and what the faith-ful heart knows: the great cloud of witnesses that surrounds us (Heb. 12:1), those holy people who reveal that the life proclaimed in the liturgy is pos-sible, even for us. The saints are people like us who by the power of the Holy Spirit have lived the new life here and who now support and encourage us in our present struggle to be faithful to our baptismal calling to become what we already are.

Evelyn Underhill, a master of the spiritual life, reminds us of what it means to be members together of the body of Christ.

> Christian worship is never a solitary undertaking. Both on its visible and invisible sides, it has a thoroughly social and organic character. The worshipper, however lonely in appearance, comes before God as a member of a great family; part of the Communion of Saints, living and dead. His own small effort at adoration is offered "in and for all." The first words of the Lord's Prayer are always there to remind him of his corporate status and responsibility, in its double aspect.... [H]e shares the great life and action of the Church, the Divine Society; however he may define that difficult term, or wher-ever he conceives its frontiers to be drawn. He is immersed in that life, nourished by its traditions, taught, humbled, and upheld by its saints.

> The custom of invoking those saints, found from primitive times
> in the Eastern and Western Church, is a special aspect of this spiritual
> solidarity; an appeal as it were from the struggling individual for family
> support....[I]t deepens family feeling, upholds the family standard,
> and bridges the gap between the living and the dead.[5]

Unity is basic to Christian worship and doctrine. It is the purpose of the
Preface in the Eucharist to join together the whole Church so that heaven and
earth speak with one voice and sing one song. "Therefore we praise you, joining our voices with angels and archangels and with all the company of heaven,
who for ever sing this hymn to proclaim the glory of your Name: Holy, holy,
holy."[6] The daily prayer of the Church involves its participants in another and
larger unity assisting them to enter the ancient cycle of prayer, with roots deep
in the Hebrew consciousness, by which day by day and even hour by hour the
people of God in the name of all creation adore and implore the eternal and
Holy One. "Catholic worship is...thoroughly social and organic; for all its outward rites and symbols declare a hidden supernatural order, where all things
are united in God. Here the individual, entering this order, always worships as
part of the Church; and in his personal action is always implied the surrounding action of the Communion of Saints—the total adoring movement of all
Christian souls living and dead."[7]

The Apostles' Creed declares belief in "the communion of saints." The
phrase has been variously interpreted. Some say that it is to be understood
in connection with the preceding phrase, "the holy Catholic Church" as an
explanation or definition of the Church, and so the last article of the Creed
ought to be so punctuated: "I believe in the Holy Spirit; the holy Catholic
Church, the communion of saints; the forgiveness of sins; the resurrection of
the body; and the life everlasting." The Latin word translated "saints," *sanctorum,* can be either masculine or neuter, and so some have suggested that the
phrase ought to be translated "the communion in holy things," that is, the
Holy Communion, the Eucharist. Robert Louis Wilken in a careful study of
the history and development of the phrase *communio sanctorum,* suggests that
the primary meaning of *sanctorum* is those who have gone before and has to
do with the close bond that exists between the Church militant and the saints
who have preceded us. He notes that all the ancient liturgies included prayers
remembering the faithful departed. As early as the second century Christians
had begun to honor the dead by gathering at their tombs for worship and
prayer as described in the *Martyrdom of Polycarp* (d. 156). Communion with
the saints was tangible as well as spiritual as people came to the tombs of the
saints to see and touch their relics. The best translation of the Creed, Wilken

suggests, is "fellowship with the saints" or "communion with the saints." It is unlikely that the phrase is a synonym for the Church. It is rather an affirmation of an essential characteristic of the Church. "The church is a community that enjoys fellowship with the saints through prayer, veneration of their relics, pilgrimage to the shrines of the saints, telling the stories of their lives, painting their pictures and sculpting their statues, and, of course, by imitating their holy lives."[8]

The preservation and veneration of relics of the saints has long been part of popular devotion.[9] Rome, always conservative, was unwilling to divide and disperse relics of its saints. (There were aberrations: Charles VI distributed the ribs of his ancestor St. Louis at a banquet.) The Eastern church was less particular. The gathering and honoring of relics, which was sometimes carried to bizarre lengths,[10] is easily understood. A relic provides a physical connection with the past, provides a sense of the reality of departed people, a tangible sign of their continuing presence.

The saints help us to remember, to keep memory rooted in reality. They help us remember our long family history. The practice of singing of the Litany of the Saints at Holy Baptism at the Easter Vigil is a way of saying to the newly baptized, "This is your new family; these people are your relatives." So it is for us all who are living the baptized life. Some of the names of the saints are known, others are remembered in their "holy anonymity." The border between the saints and other Christians, the known and the obscure is not always sharp or clear. Gregory Dix in one of those glorious and memorable passages that enliven *The Shape of the Liturgy* ponders the unity of Christians of all times and places.

> To those who know a little of christian history probably the most moving of all the reflections it brings is not the thought of the great events and the well-remembered saints, but of those innumerable millions of entirely obscure faithful men and women, every one with his or her own individual hopes and fears and joys and sorrows and loves—and sins and temptations and prayers—once every whit as vivid and alive as mine are now. They have left no slightest trace in this world, not even a name, but have passed to God utterly forgotten by men. Yet each of them once believed and prayed as I believe and pray, and found it hard and grew slack and sinned and repented and fell again. Each of them worshipped at the eucharist, and found their thoughts wandering and tried again, and felt heavy and unresponsive and yet knew—just as really and pathetically as I do these things. There is a little ill-spelled ill-carved rustic epitaph of the fourth century from Asia Minor:—"Here

sleeps the blessed Chione, who has found Jerusalem for she prayed much." Not another word is known of Chione, some peasant woman who lived in that vanished world of christian Anatolia. But how lovely if all that should survive after sixteen centuries were that one had prayed much, so that the neighbours who saw all one's life were sure one must have found Jerusalem! What did the Sunday eucharist in her village church every week for a life-time mean to the blessed Chione—and to the millions like her then, and every year since? The sheer stupendous *quantity* of the love of God which this ever repeated action has drawn from the obscure christian multitudes through the centuries is in itself an overwhelming thought.[11]

Such is a glimpse into that "great multitude that no one could count, from every nation, from all tribes and peoples and languages, standing before the throne and before the Lamb, robed in white, with palm branches in their hands" (Rev. 7:9). The antiphon on the Magnificat at second vespers on All Saints' Day in the Roman *Liturgy of the Hours,* once familiar also to Lutherans from its use in the burial office, exclaims, "O how glorious is that kingdom, where all the saints rejoice with Christ. Clothed with white robes, they follow the Lamb wherever he goes."[12] Their perfect unity is with one another and with God.

The Variety of Gifts

A wide-ranging calendar of saints teaches us an important insight of the New Testament: the variety of gifts that enrich the Church. We do not all possess the same gifts, and that is a good thing. The body of Christ, St. Paul says, has "many members, and not all the members have the same function....We have gifts that differ according to the grace that is given to us," and he lists, as examples of the various gifts, prophecy, ministering, teaching, exhortation, generosity, leadership, and cheerful compassion. (Rom. 12:4-8) Paul says again to the Corinthians, "Now there are varieties of gifts, but the same Spirit; and there are varieties of services, but the same Lord; and there are varieties of activities, but it is the same God who activates all of them in everyone" (1 Cor. 12:4-6).

The saints are a diverse collection, even (at least from the point of view of the world, of those outside the Church) a motley crew. It is not difficult to see why the Pharisees were offended by Jesus having any dealings with "outcasts and sinners," those unsavory types whom society finds it easy to reject, condemn, or ignore. Yet here they are, gathered and forgiven and made new in the image of God.

A calendar of saints ought to remind us of the manifold gifts of God by commemorating a wide variety of people and bridging the gulfs that separate classes and occupations and denominations. It ought to confront us with new and unaccustomed voices, even alien voices, who challenge us to grow with a broader and deeper understanding of the size and extent of the Church of God. But with it all, we must be careful to listen to St. Paul's primary concern, especially clear in 1 Corinthians. Paul insists that the Church understand its unity. One Spirit, one Lord, one God bestows and activates all these good gifts. Christians are gathered from the ends of the earth from all races and nations and people and languages and are made into the one body of Christ through Holy Baptism. Diversity is transformed into unity.

Thomas Cranmer's superb collect for All Saints' Day expresses in a beautiful way the essential unity of all those called to be saints, undivided even by death.

> Almighty God, you have knit together your elect in one communion and fellowship in the mystical body of your Son Christ our Lord: Give us grace to follow your blessed saints in all virtuous and godly living, that we may come to those ineffable joys that you have prepared for those who truly love you; through Jesus Christ our Lord...[13]

It is a grand vision of the living and the dead not simply joined but interwoven, "knit together," each stitch interlocked with every other in such a way that if one is dropped, the whole line unravels. The archbishop may have had in mind Rom. 12:5, "We, who are many, are one body in Christ, and individually we are members one of another" and perhaps also the phrase from Eph. 3:9 in the Authorized Version, "the fellowship of the mystery." The result clause of the collect derives from the unidentified quotation in 1 Cor. 2:9 "What no eye has seen, nor ear heard, nor the human heart conceived, what God has prepared for those who love him." Charles Wesley, surely inspired by Archbishop Cranmer's collect, expressed the same theme in a striking hymn. In its original form the hymn begins

> Come, let us join our friends above
> That have obtained the prize,
> And on the eagle wings of love
> To joys celestial rise:
> Let all the saints terrestrial sing

With those to glory gone;
For all the servants of our King,
In earth and heaven, are one.

One family, we dwell in him,
One Church, above, beneath,
Though now divided by the stream,
The narrow stream of death;
One army of the living God,
To his command we bow;
Part of his host have crossed the flood,
And part are crossing now...[14]

The river of death, which seems so broad, deep, and fearsome, is in fact but a "narrow stream" that barely separates those who have already crossed from those who wait on this side. Indeed, it is so narrow that "All the servants of our King/In heaven and earth are one."

Enlarging Our Vision

The liturgical year, as we have seen, has a way of upsetting our commonplace ideas and confounding our expectations, enriching and enhancing our spiritual life. So, too, the Church's remembrance of saints enlarges our vision. The saints are remembered not on the day of their birth into this world but on their "heavenly birthday"; the day of their death is understood as their birth into heaven.[15]

Luther called death "the completion of baptism" as the Christian is lifted out of the water of this life into life that has no end. "The significance of baptism is a blessed dying unto sin and a resurrection in the grace of God....This significance of baptism—the dying or drowning of sin—is not fulfilled completely in this life....[T]he lifting up out of the baptismal water is quickly done, but the thing it signifies—the spiritual birth and the increase of grace and righteousness—even though it begins in baptism, lasts until death, indeed, until the Last Day. Only then will that be finished which the lifting up out of baptism signifies."[16] In such a profound understanding, Baptism breaks out of its liturgical boundaries to embrace and involve the whole life, past, present, and future, of each one who is baptized. Baptism is thus the beginning of a pilgrimage for those who are thus set on "the Way" (Acts 9:2). It is the initiation of a process that continues throughout life.

Again, to confound the world, a principal common characteristic of the saints is their suffering. To those who would be righteous, Luther says, "Now there is no shorter way or manner than through baptism and the work of baptism, which is suffering and death....For in the easy life no one learns to suffer, to die with gladness, to get rid of sin, and to live in harmony with baptism....[I]n baptism we all make one and the same vow: to slay sin and to become holy through the work and grace of God, to whom we yield and offer ourselves."[17] For Luther and for the movement that bears his name, the holy cross, that is, suffering, is one of the seven "marks of the Church." (The other six are the holy Word of God, the holy sacrament of baptism, the holy sacrament of the altar, the office of the keys or absolution, the ministry that administers the four foregoing marks, and prayer, praise, and thanksgiving.) "These," he said, "are the true seven principal parts of the great holy possession whereby the Holy Spirit effects in us a daily sanctification and vivification in Christ."[18]

Thus, in the development of the calendar of saints, the first to be remembered were the martyrs, who by their witness ("martyr" is from the Greek *martus,* "witness") were bound to the life and death of Christ, who was himself the primary witness: "Jesus Christ, the faithful witness" (Rev. 1:5) and "the words of the Amen, the faithful and true witness" (Rev. 3:14). His title was soon applied to those who proved the seriousness of their witness by suffering death for the sake of Christ. It is not the martyrs' own achievement; Christ suffers and triumphs in his martyrs. The Passion of Procopius in the *Acta Martyrum* says that the martyr goes directly to heaven "by the shortest way."[19] Moreover, those who lived and died closest to Christ here on earth are thought to be closest to him there in paradise.

The first to follow in the train of Christ was Stephen, called the protomartyr. St. Paul gives his testimony to the event: "While the blood of your witness Stephen was shed, I myself was standing by, approving" (Acts 22:20). In his death, the Book of the Acts of the Apostles emphasizes, Stephen emulated Christ in attitude, words, and action. He is depicted as being clearly and consciously like Christ. His dying words echo those of the dying Jesus. Jesus commended himself to the Father; Stephen, seeing heaven opened and Jesus standing at the right hand of God, commended himself to Jesus: "Lord Jesus receive my spirit." Jesus asked forgiveness for those who put him to death, and Stephen did the same in almost identical words, "Lord, do not hold this sin against them" (Acts 7:59-60). In life, but especially in death, Stephen was like Christ. As Jesus said, "A disciple is not above the teacher, nor a slave above the master; it is enough for the disciple to be like the teacher and the slave like the master" (Matt. 10:24-25).

As Stephen emulated Christ in his martyrdom, so some sixty years later, about the year 115, Ignatius, Bishop of Antioch was brought to Rome to suffer martyrdom. In his steadfast determination to die he consciously emulates Paul's radical commitment described in the Acts of the Apostles. "I am on my way to Jerusalem, not knowing what will happen to me there, except that the Holy Spirit testifies to me in every city that imprisonment and persecutions are waiting for me. But I do not count my life of any value to myself, if only I may finish my course and the ministry that I have received from the Lord Jesus...." (Acts 20:22-24). Paul's intention to go to Jerusalem was unshakeable, and the people were not to dare to interfere with his decision. The people, hearing Agabus's prophesy of Paul's captivity, "urged him not to go up to Jerusalem. Then Paul answered, 'What are you doing, weeping and breaking my heart? For I am ready not only to be bound but even to die in Jerusalem for the name of the Lord Jesus'" (Acts 21:12-13). Ignatius wrote to the Roman Christians (Romans 1), "I hope to greet you in chains for Christ Jesus, if it is his will for me to be reckoned worthy to reach the goal. For the beginning is auspicious, provided that I attain to the grace to receive my fate without interference. For I am afraid of your love, in that it may do me wrong; for it is easy for you to do what you want, but it is difficult for me to reach God, unless you spare me." Spare him, that is, by allowing him to attain the crown of martyrdom. He continues his forceful plea,

> For I do not want you to please people, but to please God, as you in fact are doing. For I will never again have an opportunity such as this to reach God, nor can you, if you remain silent, be credited with a greater accomplishment. For if you remain silent and leave me alone, I will be a word of God, but if you love my flesh, then I will again be a mere voice. Grant me nothing more than to be poured out as an offering to God while there is still an altar ready, so that in love you may form a chorus and sing to the Father in Jesus Christ, because God has judged the bishop from Syria worthy to be found in the west, having summoned him from the east. It is good to be setting from the world to God in order that I may rise to him. (Letter to the Romans 2)[20]

Ignatius's words and intent turn the expectation of the world upside down. We may think of keeping silent as being complicit in evil, but here Ignatius pleads for the people's silence so that the intended execution by the Empire can be carried out. Their silence so that he can attain martyrdom will transform his human voice into a word of God. He has been summoned from the rising of the sun, from Antioch in Syria, to the west where the sun sets, so that he may rise from the gathering darkness of the world into the light of life that has no end. He no doubt has in mind such passages as Ps. 50:1; Isa. 41:25b ("from the rising of the sun he was summoned by name"); 59:19 ("So those in the west shall fear the Name of the Lord"); and most of all, Mal. 1:11 ("from the rising of the sun to its setting my Name is great among the nations, and in every place incense is offered to my Name, and a pure offering; for my Name is great among the nations, says the Lord of hosts"). The people, Ignatius allows, do have a part to play in the impending event. "Just pray that I will have strength both outwardly and inwardly so that I may not just talk about it but want to do it, so that I may not merely be called a Christian but actually prove to be one.... Pray for me, that I may reach the goal. I write to you not according to human perspective but in accordance with the mind of God." (To the Romans 3:2; 8:3)

Ignatius connects the Eucharist with his martyrdom as one great action. The Eucharist is the great feast of divine love, *agape,* a feast of unity making us one in Christ, one with the Father and one with each other. It makes Christ live in us. The terminology used for the Eucharist is transferred to martyrdom: the martyr is offering sacrifice. Ignatius is himself the wheat of God, a living bread.[21] "I am God's wheat and am being ground by the teeth of the wild beasts, so that I may prove to be pure bread," he declared (To the Romans 4:1).

"The white-robed army of martyrs" established the pattern for all who followed them. A hymn by Joseph the Hymnographer (ninth century) extends to the whole Church the challenge to emulate the martyrs' courage. It is a hymn for Lauds, morning praise, that makes the breaking of the day celebrate the triumph of the martyrs.

> Let us now our voices raise,
> Wake the day with gladness;
> God himself to joy and praise
> Turns our human sadness;
> Joy that martyrs won their crown
> Opened heaven's portal,
> When they laid the mortal down
> For the life immortal.

The martyrs with clear eye saw, like Stephen, the land of life. "I see the heavens opened and the Son of Man standing at the right hand of God!" (Acts 7:56)

> Never flinched they from the flame,
> From the torment never;
> Vain the tyrant's sharpest aim,
> Vain each fierce endeavor:

For by faith they saw the land
Decked in all its glory,
Where triumphant now they stand
With the victor's story.

Up and follow, Christians all:
Press through toil and sorrow;
Turn from fear, and heed the call
To a glorious morrow!
Who will venture on the strife;
Who will first begin it?
Who will grasp the land of Life?
Christians, up and win it![22]

It is not sufficient to remember the bravery of the martyrs. We are expected to be like them.

With the end of active persecution, the definition of martyr was broadened to include confessors, those who suffered imprisonment and torture but not actual death for the Name of Christ. The ascetics were added to the list, those who in reaction to the popularity of legalized Christianity and its inevitable weakening, fled into the desert. Uncompromising ascetics, "athletes of Christ," were accorded honors reserved for martyrs and confessors: their austerities seemed equal to the torments of the original witnesses.

After the Council of Ephesus in 431, which confirmed the status of the Theotokos as the birth-giver of God, feasts related to the Virgin Mary were introduced to the calendar, although devotion to her antedated the council.[23] The feast of her Nativity, September 8, and her Dormition (falling asleep in the Lord) on August 15 evolved from the dedication of basilicas in Jerusalem. The Roman church celebrates the Conception of Mary on December 8, exactly nine months before her birth. There is a feast of the Presentation of Mary on November 21, that is in the East an important day, the Entry of the Mother of God in the Temple.

Bishops, especially of Rome, were added to the calendar, as were pastors of souls and theologians, but the calendar came to include also missionaries who laid down their bones in their adopted lands, evangelists (Philip the Deacon), kings and queens, mothers of emperors (Helena) and of theologians (Monica), women who in their own right taught and strengthened the Church, workers for justice and compassion in the social order, hymn writers, nurses caring for the needs of the sick and injured.

The beginnings of a cult of saints of the old covenant can be traced to the time of Jesus, who charged, "Woe to you, scribes and Pharisees, hypocrites! For you build the tombs of the prophets and decorate the graves of the righteous...." (Matt. 23:29). The eleventh chapter of Hebrews gives a catalogue of heroes: Abel, Enoch, Noah, Abraham, Isaac, Jacob, Joseph, Moses, Gideon, Barak, Samson, Jephthah, David, Samuel and the prophets. The great cloud of witnesses includes not only the memorable heroes but countless others who "were tortured, refusing to accept release, in order to obtain a better resurrection. Others suffered mocking and flogging, and even chains and imprisonment. They were stoned to death, they were sawn in two, they were killed by the sword; they went about in skins of sheep and goats, destitute, persecuted, tormented—of whom the world was not worthy. They wandered in deserts and mountains, and in caves and holes in the ground" (Heb. 11:35-38). Among those included in this general catalog of suffering were the faithful heroes of the Maccabean rising (2 Macc. 5:27; 6:12-7:42). The list of exemplars of faith that begins with righteous Abel culminates in Jesus, "the pioneer and perfecter of our faith, who for the sake of the joy that was set before him endured the cross, disregarding its shame, and has taken his seat at the right hand of the throne of God." (Heb 12:2). The focus is consistently on Jesus, the primary witness-martyr who gathered into himself the experience of his people and brought it to perfection. An influx of pilgrims to the Holy Land gave fresh impetus to the remembrance of Old Testament persons, especially in the East, where they were in a sense, local figures. The influence was less strong in the West, although there was a Gallican Feast of Elijah. In Rome there was the inclusion of the names of Abraham and Melchizedek in the canon of the Mass but little else. The seven Maccabean brothers who were brutally put to death under Antiochus IV Epiphanes ca. 168 (their story is told in 2 Maccabees 7), found their way onto the calendar of the Church (both East and West) as forerunners of the Christian martyrs, their commemoration observed on August 1; the commemoration is now celebrated only in the East.

The Eastern churches, with a broader view of sanctity than obtained in the West, continue to commemorate Old Testament figures. January 3, for example, is the day of the Holy Prophet Malachi; February 8, Prophet Jeremiah; March 12, Righteous Aaron. The broad inclusion of Old Testament people in the calendar of saints was introduced in the West by the Bavarian Lutheran pastor Wilhelm Löhe in his calendar (1868). Some days were taken from the calendar of the Eastern Church and others were his own invention.[24] The practice is continued in the *Lutheran Service Book* (2006) of the Lutheran

Church—Missouri Synod; Löhe's emissaries had a significant role in the development of that part of the Lutheran Church.

In addition to holy men and women the sanctoral calendar includes the company of angels, whose commemoration enlarges our conception of the fellowship of the faithful. The existence and work of the angels direct our attention to the vastness and richness of creation. "The panorama of creation must be far more breathtaking than we can guess in our corner of the cosmos, for there must be many higher orders of beings whose service is joined with ours under God."[25] More than that, the ministry of the angels may turn us again to the wonders of the natural world. John Henry Newman, giving credit to "the Alexandrian school and the early Church," describes his awakening to the scope of the service of the angels:

> I viewed them, not only as the ministers employed by the Creator in the Jewish and Christian dispensations, as we find on the face of Scripture, but as carrying on, as Scripture also implies, the economy of the visible world. I considered them as the real causes of motion, light, and life, and of those elementary principles of the physical universe, which, when offered in their developments to our senses, suggest to us the notion of cause and effect, and of what are called the laws of nature. I have drawn out this doctrine in my sermon for Michaelmas day, written not later than 1834. I say of the angels, "Every breath of air and ray of light and heat, every beautiful prospect is, as it were, the skirts of their garments, the waving of the robes of those whose faces see God." Again, I ask what would be the thoughts of a man who, "when examining a flower, or a herb, or a pebble, or a ray of light, which he treats as something so beneath him in the scale of existence, suddenly discovered that he was in the presence of some powerful being who was hidden behind the visible things he was inspecting, who, though concealing his wise hand, was giving them their beauty, grace, and perfection, as being God's instrument for the purpose, nay, whose robe and ornaments those objects were, which he was so eager to analyse?" and I therefore remark that 'we may say with grateful and simple hearts with the Three Holy Children, "O all ye works of the Lord, etc., etc., bless ye the Lord, praise him and magnify him for ever.' ""[26]

The angels enable us to see nature in a new and more reverent way. Once again we find the Church's calendar pushing back the horizon, expanding the range of our view, enabling us to penetrate beneath the appearance and surface of things to behold their marvelous essence.

The Way to Heaven

Thomas Traherne (1637-1674) pondered the significance of the remembrance of the saints.

> To delight in the Saints of God is the way to Heaven....

> With all their eyes behold our Saviour, with all their hearts adore Him, with all their tongues and affection praise Him. See how in all closets, and in all temples; in all cities and in all fields; in all nations and in all generations, they are lifting up their hands and eyes unto His cross; and delight in all their adorations. This will enlarge your Soul and make you dwell in all kingdoms and ages: strengthen your faith and enrich your affections: fill you with their joys and make you a lively partaker in communion with them. It will make you a possessor greater than the world. Men do mightily wrong themselves when they refuse to be present in all ages: and neglect to see the beauty in all kingdoms, and despise the resentments of every soul, and busy themselves only with pots and cups and things at home, or shops and trades and things in the street: but do not live to God manifesting Himself in all the world, nor care to see (and be present with Him in) all the glory of His Eternal Kingdom. By seeing the Saints of all Ages we are present with them: by being present with them become too great for our own age, and near to our Saviour.[27]

It is an exhilarating vision, breathtaking in its scope.

Such a vision elicits a desire to join the blessed in the heavenly kingdom and to share in their perfection. Peter Abelard's *O quanta qualia sunt illa Sabbata,* "O what their joy and their glory must be,"[28] expresses the longing of those on earth to share in the joys of those already in the blessed place where wish and fulfillment are one and where what is prayed for never falls short of the request.

> Now in the meanwhile, with hearts raised on high,
> We for that country must yearn and must sigh,
> Seeking Jerusalem, dear native land,
> Through our long exile on Babylon's strand.

A similar longing was expressed in a sermon by Abelard's contemporary, Bernard of Clairvaux (1090-1153). "The saints have no need of honor from us.... Clearly, if we venerate their memory, it serves us, not them.... Calling the saints to mind inspires, or rather arouses in us, above all else, a longing to enjoy their company, so desirable in itself.... When we commemorate the saints we are inflamed with another yearning: that Christ our life may also appear to us as he appeared to them that we may one day share in his glory."[29]

Isaac Watts (1674-1748) in a bold hymn is more daring than simply to long to join the company of heaven. He demands from God such a faith that he may look into the heavenly home of the saints and question them about their condition.

> Give me the wings of faith to rise
>   Within the veil, and see   [Heb. 6:19-20]
> The saints above, how great their joys,
>   How bright their glories be.
>
> Once they were mourners here below,
>   And poured out sighs and tears;
> They wrestled hard, as we do now,
>   With sins and doubts and fears.
>
> I ask them whence their victory came;
>   They, with united breath,
> Ascribe their conquest to the Lamb,
>   Their triumph to his death.
>
> They marked the footsteps that he trod,
>   His zeal inspired their breast;
> And, following their incarnate God,
>   Possess the promised rest.
>
> Our glorious Leader claims our praise
>   For his own pattern given;
> While the long cloud of witnesses [Heb. 12:1]
>   Show the same path to heaven.[30]

Such energetic desire be shown the whole truth of Christianity, its path of suffering that is the only way to triumph and joy, is characteristic of the faithful of all times and ages. The concluding two lines of Watts's hymn echo Traherne's assertion, "To delight in the Saints of God is the way to heaven." They are our companions on the pilgrims' way, which leads to the heart of God.

10

Into the Heart of God

THE LITURGICAL YEAR is a most peculiar construct that can drive logical fundamentalists crazy. What was said in a different context may apply equally well to the Church's year. "Those who attempt to dominate poetic language by fixing its senses are doomed to madness."[1] That is true of poetry because it is true of the world. G. K. Chesterton in his delightfully profound book *Orthodoxy* observes,

> The real trouble with this world of ours is not that it is an unreasonable world, nor even that it is a reasonable one. The commonest kind of trouble is that it is nearly reasonable, but not quite. Life is not an illogicality; yet it is a trap for logicians. It looks just a little more mathematical and regular than it is; its exactitude is obvious, but its inexactitude is hidden; its wildness lies in wait.
>
> It is this silent swerving from accuracy by an inch that is the uncanny element in everything. It seems a sort of secret treason in the universe. An apple or an orange is round enough to get itself called round, and yet is not round after all. The earth itself is shaped like an orange to lure some simple astronomer into calling it a globe. A blade of grass is called after the blade of a sword, because it comes to a point; but it doesn't. Everywhere in things there is this element of the quiet and incalculable. It escapes the rationalists, but it never escapes till the last moment.
>
> ...Whenever we feel there is something odd in Christian theology, we shall generally find that there is something odd in the truth.[2]

Thus, because it is a representation of human experience, the liturgical year has its quirks and oddities that cannot be flattened out and harmonized in every particular without serious loss, even betrayal of its central affirmations.

Peculiarities of the Liturgical Year

The Church year has its own peculiar beginning, generally understood (in the West) to be the First Sunday in Advent, but there are other days that also serve equally well as a beginning, such as Septuagesima on the medieval calendar when in the Daily Office the reading of Genesis commenced, beginning the preparation for the spring festival of rebirth and renewal, a new year; or March 25, the Annunciation, the beginning movement of the Incarnation; or, especially in the present calendar, Ash Wednesday, coming as an unexpected intrusion and abrupt reminder of our mortality, inviting us to take up the new life. The liturgical year has many beginnings, many continually renewed invitations to turn around, to return to the right way, and to begin again.

The date of Easter, like the date of its ancestor Passover, varies from year to year depending on the appearance of the first full moon after the vernal equinox, and that variation is disturbing to some who would prefer to control Easter and make it easily predictable, always falling on the same Sunday of each year. And the calendar provides little help in determining the date of Easter, for Christianity has its own way of computing when the first full moon of spring reaches its fullness; the determination is made not by looking at the night sky nor by asking Jewish neighbors but by consulting books and tables and making complex computations.[3] The "ecclesiastical full moon" does not correspond to the astronomical full moon.

The central celebration of Christianity, Jesus's passage through death to life for the redemption of the world, is observed as the holy Triduum, three days understood as just one day. And when Easter, the day of resurrection, dawns, we find that it is not just a day or a season but a feast celebrated for a week that is composed not of seven days but of seven weeks; Easter is "a week of weeks" and an octave not of days but of eight Sundays.

Hemispheric differences accentuate the oddities. Christianity had its beginnings in the northern hemisphere, and its elaboration has made a great many poetic and emotional connections between its two most significant festivals and the condition of the natural world when each is celebrated. For many, Christmas is a winter holiday, celebrated amid the snows at the depth of the year, bringing the light of hope into the long dark nights. Easter is a spring festival, welcomed by the rebirth and renewal of nature with flowers pushing up from the earth and new leaves appearing on the trees. But as missionaries carried the faith into the southern hemisphere, Christmas is celebrated there in the summer and Easter in the autumn. And in the tropics, the change of seasons is not evident except for rainfall.[4]

If we embrace this fluidity and apparent contradiction that are inherent in the liturgical year—some of it deliberate, some the product of the merging of competing, even conflicting, traditions—we may learn to welcome its surprise and delight, not simply as entertainment or a pleasant pastime, but as teaching, instruction in the ways of God and the world. Such an attitude is not to be taken as an invitation to or confirmation of a free-wheeling carelessness, but rather as a sober invitation to exploration and disciplined search for new insight in the old words and odd ways.

"Do not call it fixity,/Where past and future are gathered," observed T. S. Eliot.[5] It is not possible to express in language the full impact of this encounter with the living God that is the Church year. Eliot again: "Words strain,/Crack and sometimes break, under the burden,/...will not stay in place,/Will not stay still...."[6] Common ideas and assumptions about the nature of time are overturned, ordinary thinking about the meaning of the events of Christ's life is upset, for we have entered into a different realm and may be disoriented.

> The end is where we start from....
>
> And the end of all our exploring
> Will be to arrive where we started
> And know the place for the first time.[7]

There is repetition in many areas of our life, and we find that familiarity comfortable, but in that repetition there is always room for discovery and surprise and reward and satisfaction. John Keble (1792-1866) wrote of such discovery of the new in what is familiar and expected.

> New every morning is the love
> Our waking and uprising prove;...
>
> New mercies, each returning day,
> Hover around us while we pray;
> New perils past, new sins forgiven,
> New thoughts of God, new hopes of heaven....
>
> Old friends, old scenes will lovelier be,
> As more of heaven in each we see....[8]

Discovery awaits, even in the routine.

The Shape of the Year: A Circle with a Destination

The liturgical year is an annual round, but its shape is yet another of its per-plexing oddities. It is a circle with a destination. The matter is not, as a com-mon simplification holds, that the view of archaic people, and Eastern thought still, is circular, while Jewish and Christian experience is linear. The Church year is a circle, but it is not a mere repetition year after year. When we begin the year once more, we are not the same people as we were when we began the cycle the year before. The world has changed, and we have changed with it. New experiences must be incorporated in the recurring cycle. We do not know whether we will live through another year of grace. But the way opens before us through the valley of the shadow to the green pastures and the still waters.[9]

The Church's year is a circle, but it is not an endless round. It has a goal, an end, a purpose as we move from slavery to the Promised Land, from exile to return, "from this world to that which is to come" as the fuller title of John Bunyan's *Pilgrim's Progress* describes it. As the Church progresses through the circle year after year, it leads ever higher, spiraling ever up the mountain, for this journey is going somewhere, moving always to a higher level, toward the final goal. It is not unlike Dante's *Purgatorio,* the mountain of Purgatory up which the departed climb by going round and round until they reach Paradise. Dante's path through Hell and Purgatory is one continuous spiral movement through the world of matter toward the perfect circularity of the closing lines of the whole *Divine Comedy.*

> High phantasy lost power and here broke off;
>   Yet, as a wheel moves smoothly, free from jars,
>   My will and my desire were turned by love,
>
> The love that moves the sun and the other stars.[10]

The very rhyme scheme of the great poem, *terza rima* (aba bcb cdc etc.), may be less an act of homage to the Trinity and more a movement through time in which the forward propulsion has also a retrospective dimension, a spi-ral.[11] M. H. Abrams in his study of Romantic Literature describes "Progress by reversion: the Romantic Spiral":

> [I]n the most representative Romantic version of emanation and return, when the process reverts to its beginning the recovered unity is not, as in the school of Plotinus, the simple, undifferentiated unity of its origin, but a unity which is higher, because it incorporates the intervening differentiations. "We have now returned," as Hegel said

in a comment which was added to the conclusion of his shorter *Logic,* "to the notion of the Idea with which we began," but "this return to the beginning is also an advance." The self-moving circle, in other words, rotates along a third, a vertical dimension, to close where it had begun, but on a higher plane of value. It thus fuses the idea of the circular return with the idea of linear progress, to describe a distinctive figure of Romantic thought and imagination—the ascending circle, or spiral.[12]

The ecclesiastical year continually retraces the circle but on successively higher levels. It thus preserves two equally valid insights: we repeat the past by making it contemporary, and we have somewhere to go. The figure of the spiral corrects, informs, and interprets the symbol of the circle. The liturgical year is not endless repetition, for time has a goal, a destination. In addition to the round of Daily Prayer, the Church year is another way in which time, which, we are encouraged to remember, is a creature, something created by God, is made to serve the proclamation of the Gospel and enrich the Church's central and everlasting activity, the worship of God.

The Year Is Jesus Christ

In his encyclical letter *Mediator Dei* Pope Pius XII provided a remarkable description of the liturgical year. It is, he declares, "Christ himself who is ever living in his Church."[13] That is to say, the Church's year is not simply a calendar of festivals and seasons to remind us of the basics of the faith. It is in fact none other than the Lord of the Church living in his people, walking with them in their pilgrimage through this world. The seasons and feasts of the liturgical year unfold step by step the mystery of Christ from his coming into the world, to his passion, death, and resurrection, to his promised return in glory. He lives not in majestic splendor apart from his Church, but lives and works with and in and through his gathered baptized people who are the body, his body, of which he is the head.

> When we consider the church and its existence, we can only describe it as God's great venture among us.... The church of Jesus Christ and its history, Calvin once said, is nothing but a chain of resurrections from the dead. It is also a passion history of the incarnate Son of God. In everything that is taught and believed, loved and suffered, planned and thought in this church, Jesus Christ is venturing himself, daily repeating the washing of the feet of this church which have daily been soiled on its journey. And he must follow up everything that people do

in this church, even the most shining deeds, and in some way set them straight and make something good out of them.[14]

The Church lives by this ministry of Jesus Christ.

In the life of Jesus as recorded in the Gospels one finds that same peculiarity that characterizes the liturgical year. In the view of Matthew, Mark, and Luke the ministry of Jesus lasted one year; in the tradition followed by St. John it continued for three years. Indeed, the whole chronology of the events in Christ's life is strikingly different in John's Gospel when compared with the three synoptic accounts. Christians have learned not simply to accept these differences and contradictions but in fact to treasure them for the richness of insight and interpretation that they offer. A one-year ministry is like an historical line moving inexorably toward the climax of Golgotha and the tomb and triumph. A three-year ministry is something of a circle, moving in recurring patterns as it makes its way forward to the triumphant climax of the Cross and the cry of victory, "It is finished!"

The Emmaus experience confounds our understanding: in the instant that Jesus is recognized by the disciples at the table, he vanishes (Luke 24:13-35).[15] Nonetheless, that story set the basic pattern for Christian worship. The exposition of the Scriptures given by Jesus as he walks with the two disciples, teaching them how they all point to him, is followed by the holy meal in which he reveals himself to them and is made known in the breaking of the bread. Since that evening, it is Christ who walks with his people and unfolds to them the mysteries of his mission and his ministry and his being and feeds them with himself. The liturgical year is an important part of the recapitulation of that long and rich and ever-new experience, which continues to surprise those who live it.

A Work of Art

The Church's year is a consummate work of art, built up through the centuries by many hands and shaped by many forces, secular as well as spiritual. It is a creation of rich and inexhaustible beauty. A key to its beauty and purpose may be found in an event that is celebrated twice in the year, the Transfiguration. Jesus takes three of his disciples, Peter, James, and John, with him to the top of a mountain to pray. As he is praying, he is changed. A vision is granted to the three disciples to reveal what he will become when, in obedience, he endures betrayal and undergoes death. In his obedience he will fulfill the Law, and therefore Moses stands beside him. He is himself that future of righteousness for which the prophets yearned, and so Elijah joins him. By his death and by his rising, God's Son will become God's Christ, God's agent and bearer of God's glory. In his obedience and through his suffering he will reveal the unimaginable depth of God's love; in his rising he will make known God's victory and ultimate defeat of all that opposes him.

As St. Paul understands the revelation of God's glory, he sees in it a spiritual and mystical meaning that is at the heart of all Christian life. "And all of us, with unveiled faces, seeing the glory of the Lord as though reflected in a mirror, are being transformed into the same image from one degree of glory to another." (2 Cor. 3:18). St. John makes it even clearer: "Beloved, we are God's children now; what we will be has not yet been revealed. What we do know is this: when he is revealed, we will be like him, for we will see him as he is." (1 John 3:2). The vision of God transforms us. We are transfigured; the beauty of his glory makes us become glorious and beautiful. By his grace we become what we see. The liturgical year is a dramatized response to the call to transformation that St. Paul urges: "present your bodies as a living sacrifice....Do not be conformed to this world, but be transformed by the renewing of your minds, so that you may discern what is the will of God—what is good and acceptable and perfect" (Rom. 12:1-2). The Venerable Bede preached concerning the call of Matthew, "'Follow' meant 'imitate'—not by the movement of his feet, but rather by a change of life. For whoever says he is following Christ ought himself to walk as Christ walked."[16] In biblical idiom, "walk" means "live," the way one conducts one's life.

There is a moral dimension to glory, and beauty makes its demands. We cannot remain as we are; we must turn around and repent. Rainer Maria Rilke, who loved art and in his own way spoke to the world about God and the beautiful, in his sonnet *Archäischer Torso Apollos,* "Archaic Torso of Apollo," describes the sublime and transcendent beauty of an ancient Greek statue of Apollo, only the torso of which remains, which lives for those who see it with a life even greater than physical life. He describes the elegance, the sensuality, the power of the statue, and then, abruptly, he stops and addresses the reader in the last line of the poem: *Du mußt dein Leben ändern,* "You must change your life."

The vision of glory demands that we turn around and reject whatever is not glorious. Beauty's requirement is that we become beautiful. It is only by allowing ourselves to be changed that we can enter the kingdom into which we are invited.[17] The only entrance to that glorious kingdom is through the gate of Pascha, the portal that opens on to limitless life in God. Bishop Anastasius of Sinai preached on the Feast of the Transfiguration, "Jesus goes before us to show us the way, both up the mountain and into heaven, and—I speak boldly—it is for us now to follow him with all speed, yearning for the heavenly vision that will give us a share in his radiance, renew our spiritual nature, and transform us into his likeness, making us for ever sharers in his Godhead and raising us to heights as yet undreamed of."[18] To be a pilgrim is to commit one-self to change, to being changed. Charles Wesley concludes his familiar hymn "Love divine, all loves excelling,"

> Finish then thy new creation,
>   Pure and spotless let us be;
> Let us see thy great salvation
>   Perfectly restored in thee!
> Changed from glory into glory,
>   Till in heaven we take our place,
> Till we cast our crowns before thee,
>   Lost in wonder, love, and praise.[19]

The impressive point is that the new creation will be complete when we have been transformed into the full glory of heaven.[20]

The Purpose Is Perfection

The purpose and goal of the work of God in Christ set forth in the Church's year is to bring us and all the world to perfection. Because the purpose is per-fection, all that is unworthy is to be rejected in the worship of God, and there is rightly an impatience with carelessness and casualness in the doing of the liturgy. But there is a further and more glorious promise in this perfection. St. Augustine preached in metrical prose,

> Thus believing, you will be touching.
> Thus touching, you will be bonded.
> Thus bonded, you will never be separated,
> For you will remain in his divinity,
> who died for us in our infirmity.[21]

This being bonded into and remaining in the divinity of Christ is the great and indeed stunning transformation that is called *theosis*, deification, divinization, making human beings God. The teaching has always been remembered in the Eastern Churches. In recent decades it has begun to be rediscovered and explored by Western Christians as well. In the Garden the tempter promised in his duplicitous way, "You will be like God" (Gen 3:5). It was in fact, whether he was aware of it or not, not a lie. In the Gospel according to St. John (10:34),

Jesus reminded his opponents of the declaration in Psalm 82:6, "Is it not written in your law, 'I said, you are gods'?" Those who in faith receive the grace of God partake of his divine nature as in 2 Peter 1:4 ("that...ye might be partakers of the divine nature" [AV]), quoted also in the proper preface for the Ascension, "through Jesus Christ our Lord, who after his resurrection appeared openly to his disciples and in their sight was taken up into heaven, that he might make us partakers of his divine nature."[22] The profound expression of 2 Peter[23] repays extended reflection and contemplation.

Theosis, deification, does not mean that human beings will become divine by nature and participate in God's essence, thus abolishing the distinction between God and humanity. Such abolition of the distinction between the Creator and the creation is not possible. Deification is the process of re-creation, renewal in God's image and likeness through his grace and divine energies. Being joined to Christ, who has assumed human flesh in the incarnation, means experiencing the fulfillment of the image God has of each of us, the image in which and for which we have been made, the destiny God has prepared for us.[24] The idea can be found throughout Western theology, even in surprising places.[25] Salvation is described as union with Christ, and humanity finds its true identity in communion with each other and together in union with God. Such union constitutes the ultimate good for all human beings: the fulfillment of God's loving desire for union with each person he has made. In Christ, human nature is perfected, renewed, reconstructed, created anew. In him human destiny reaches its goal, and henceforth human life is, in the words of the Apostle, "hidden with Christ in God" (Col. 3:3).[26]

Despite what inferior hymns may suggest, deification is not an individualistic process, as if at the last we can be alone with our divine Lover in cozy twilight.[27] We find that we are being re-created not alone by ourselves but together with our family, the people of God of all times and all places. Despite the modern preoccupation with the self and individual fulfillment, the journey traced in the liturgical year is always corporate. (Samuel Johnson in his famous Dictionary dismissed "enthusiasm" as "A vain belief of private revelation.") In *Pilgrim's Progress*, Christian, the central character, is seldom alone; he has companions on the way. And the great book is not complete until in Part 2 his wife and children follow him "from this world to that which is to come." The Christian pilgrimage is a communal action. Moreover, the community extends beyond recreated humanity; all creation will be made new, paradise will be regained, and the original harmony of humanity and the natural world, as God intends, will be restored.

In the new creation, our sight is granted "a longer range and a new precision."[28] As our vision expands, it becomes apparent that the journey is not our undertaking. The completion is not due to our bravery, persistence, or endurance. It is entirely the work of God, who has called us and lifted us and carried us throughout the pilgrimage. We, together with our vast family, are brought into a great and broad place bathed with brilliant light, pulsing with life that can never end, for time is no more.

The journey of the liturgical year leads us at last into the very heart of God.

Notes

INTRODUCTION

1. Joseph Sittler quoted in *Circle* (Lutheran Council in the USA/Department of Campus Ministry) May 1972; from an article in *The Environmental Journal* of the National Parks and Conservation Department.

2. John Barton, "Earth as Temple," *TLS* December 24 & 31, 2010, p. 30.

3. *The Jewish Study Bible* ed. Adele Berlin and Marc Zvi Brettler (New York: Oxford University Press, 2004), p.14. See Theodore Hiebert, "Reclaiming the World: Biblical Resources for the Ecological Crisis," Interpretation. A Journal of Bible and Theology 66:4 (October 2011).

4. See Richard Bauckham, *The Bible and Ecology: Rediscovering the Community of Creation.* Waco, Texas: Baylor UP, 2010; Jack Kilcrease, "Creation's Praise: A Short Liturgical Reading of Genesis 1-2 and the Book of Revelation," Pro Ecclesia 21:3 (Summer 2012), 314-325.

5. *Service Book and Hymnal* (1958) no. 542; unfortunately altered and distorted in the *Lutheran Book of Worship* no. 364 and in *Evangelical Lutheran Worship* no. 655.

6. Walter M. Abbott ed., *The Documents of Vatican II* (New York: Guild Press, America Press, Association Press, 1966), p. 141.

7. Abbott 19–20; see also George H. Tavard, *The Pilgrim Church* (New York: Herder and Herder, 1967). Chapter VII of the Constitution on the Church is entitled, "The Eschatological Nature of the Pilgrim Church and Her Union with the Heavenly Church."

8. *Hymnal 1982* no. 255.

9. Martin Luther, *"Lectures on Galatians 1519,"* *Luther's Works* vol. 27 (St. Louis: Concordia, 1964), p. 289, expounding Gal. 4:4–5. The reference to "the prophet" may be to Jer. 8:11.

10. See C. K. Williams, "The Music of Poetry and the Music of the Mind," Literary Imagination: The Review of the Association of Literary Scholars and Critics 7:1 (2005), pp. 19–29.

11. *Common Service Book of the Lutheran Church* (1917, 1918), p. 290.

12. Robert Payne, *The Holy Fire* (New York: Harper & Bros., 1957), p. 86.

13. From the hymn *Alleluia dulce carmen*, see the *Service Book and Hymnal* no. 58, stanza 3; *Hymns Ancient and Modern revised*, no. 82, stanza 3.

14. Book of Common Prayer, p. 270, Collect at the Liturgy of the Palms on the Sunday of the Passion; the collect for Wednesday in Holy Week added to the 1928 American Book of Common Prayer.

15. Northrup Frye, *Anatomy of Criticism* (Princeton, N.J.: Princeton UP, 1967), p. 56.

16. John Ruskin, *Sesame and Lilies. Lecture I. Sesame. Of King's Treasuries.* Section 13. Originally a lecture delivered at Manchester in 1864; published in 1871. Half a century later T. S. Eliot in his essay *Tradition and the Individual Talent* (1919, 1920) would declare that the poet "must be aware of the mind of Europe—the mind of his own country—a mind which he learns in time to be much more important than his own private mind." A similar awareness is required to those who would know and represent "the mind of the Church." See Luther Reed, *The Lutheran Liturgy* rev.ed. (Philadelphia: Muhlenberg, 1960) "Introduction: The Mind of the Church," pp. 1–23. Behind that lies what St. Paul calls "the mind of Christ" (1 Cor. 2:16).

CHAPTER 1

1. *Quas Primas*, December 11, 1925.

2. Heraclitus, Fragment 91; cf. 12; quoted by Plato, *Cratylus* 401, a and 401, d.

3. J[ohn] B[oynton] Priestly, *Man and Time* (New York: Dell, 1968 [1964]), pp. 130–131.

4. *The General Instruction on the Liturgy of the Hours* 2.II.37.

5. *Hymnal 1982* no. 11; *Lutheran Book of Worship* no. 269; *Lutheran Service Book* no. 868; *Evangelical Lutheran Worship* no. 557.

6. *Hymnal 1982* no. 10; *Service Book and Hymnal* no. 201.

7. "The Whisper," *New York Times*, April 27, 1969. From the *New York Times* April 27 © 1969 the *New York Times*. All rights reserved. Used by permission and protected by the Copyright Laws of the United States. The printing, copying, redistribution, or retransmission of this Content without express written permission is prohibited.

8. Translation by Athelstan Riley in *The English Hymnal* (1906, with tunes 1933), no. 195.

9. See the editorial by Hal Borland, "New Year," *New York Times*, December 30, 1973.

10. For this description I am indebted to Ruth Bosch Becker.

11. See Paul F. Bradshaw and Maxwell E. Johnson, *The Origins of Feasts, Fasts, and Seasons in Early Christianity* (Collegeville: Liturgical Press, 2011), p. 21.

12. Translated by John Ellerton and Fenton J. A. Hort; *Service Book and Hymnal* no. 219, *Hymns Ancient and Modern Revised* no. 17, *The English Hymnal* no. 271.

13. Tertullian, *de Cor.* 3.4.

14. Anscar J. Chupungco, "The Liturgical Year: The Gospel Encountering Culture," Studia Liturgica 40:1–2 (2010), 61. "Sunday came to be known as *dies dominica,* the day of the eucharist or, alternatively, the day of the Lord."

15. Ignatius, *To the Magnesians* 9.1. Translation by Michael W. Holmes.

16. Justin Martyr, *1 Apology* 67. Translation by Michael W. Holmes.

17. *The English Hymnal* 50; translation from the *Yattendon Hymnal* ed. Robert Bridges.

18. Translated by Henry Williams Baker, *Hymns Ancient and Modern* 39; the *Hymnal 1982* 47; appointed in the old Breviary for Sunday Nocturns from Pentecost to Advent.

19. *Service Book and Hymnal* 182; altered in the *Hymnal 1982* (48) to "O day of radiant gladness": Sunday is no longer generally regarded as a day of rest.

20. *Hymnal 1982* no. 52.

21. Bradshaw and Johnson, p. 13.

22. *Epistle of Barnabas* 15.8.

23. Basil, *de Spiritu Sancto,* 27

24. Mark Searle, *"Sunday: The Heart of the Liturgical Year,"* in Maxwell E. Johnson ed., *Between Memory and Hope* (Collegeville: Liturgical Press, 2000), p. 76.

25. *Didache* 8.1.

26. See Bradshaw and Johnson, pp. 29–36.

27. Edward T. Horn III, *The Christian Year* (Philadelphia: Muhlenberg Press, 1957), p. 19.

28. Adolf Adam, *The Liturgical Year: Its History and Its Meaning after the Reform of the Liturgy* trans. Matthew J. O'Connell (New York: Pueblo, 1981), p. 52.

29. Chupungco, *Studia Liturgica,* 50.

30. See Evelyn Underhill, *Worship* (New York: Harper, 1936), pp. 73–77.

31. Horn, p. 12.

32. Paul Zeller Strodach, *The Church Year. Studies in the Introits, Collects, Epistles, and Gospels* (Philadelphia: United Lutheran Publication House, 1924), p. 7.

33. Adrian Nocent, *The Liturgical Year: Advent, Christmas, Epiphany* trans. Matthew J. O'Connell (Collegeville, Minn.: Liturgical Press, 1977), p. 293.

34. Melito of Sardis, "Homily on the Pasch," *From the Fathers to the Churches* ed. Brother Kenneth CGA (London: Collins Liturgical Publications, 1983), pp. 294–295.

35. Nocent, p. 326; see also p. 305, "The journey into the mystery."

36. Strodach, 24–25, 26–27.

37. *Hymnal 1982* no. 131; *Lutheran Book of Worship* no. 85.

CHAPTER 2

1. For a detailed consideration of the evidence see Paul F. Bradshaw and Maxwell E. Johnson, *The Origins of Feasts, Fasts, and Seasons in Early Christianity* (Collegeville: Liturgical Press, 2011), pp. 158–168.

2. Adolf Adam, *The Liturgical Year: Its History and Its Meaning after the Reform of the Liturgy* trans. Matthew J. O'Connell (New York: Pueblo, 1981), p. 131.

3. Although a date of four thousand years before Christ was generally accepted throughout the Middle Ages and the Reformation period, John Lightfoot, vice chancellor of the University of Cambridge and eminent Hebrew scholar, calculated that creation began in 3929 B.C. and that "man was created by the Trinity about the third hour of the day, or nine o'clock in the morning." James Ussher, Archbishop of Armagh, in his *Annales Veteris et Novi Testamenti* (1650-1654) calculated the date of the beginning of creation precisely as Sunday, October 23, 4004 B.C. The dates he calculated were inserted in editions of the King James Bible printed by Thomas Guy from 1675 and in Church of England Bibles from 1701 onward.

4. Translated by Martin L. Seltz (1909-1967) in *The Lutheran Book of Worship* (1978), no. 38. Text © 1969 Concordia Publishing House. Used with Permission. www.cph.org.

5. Cyril of Jerusalem, *Catechetical Lectures* 15.1. The reference to "rain on fleece" derives from the sign given to Gideon in Judges 6:37.

6. Mircea Eliade, *Cosmos and History. The Myth of the Eternal Return* trans. Willard R. Trask (New York: Harper & Row, 1954), pp. 55, 76, 83, 85, 91, 105–106, 112, 121, 129. "At that time" was the formula used to introduce many of the Gospels in the lectionary that accompanied the Lutheran *Service Book and Hymnal* (1958), *Epistles and Gospels Together with Lessons from the Old Testament from the Service Book and Hymnal of the Lutheran Church in America* (1959).

7. Paul Zeller Strodach, *The Church Year* (Philadelphia: United Lutheran Publication House, 1924), p. 27.

8. Book of Common Prayer (1928), p. l; the Lutheran *Service Book and Hymnal* (1958), p. 277; both follow the Roman Catholic description of the beginning of Advent.

9. Book of Common Prayer (1979), p. 15; *Lutheran Book of Worship Ministers Edition*, p. 13.

10. The *Lutheran Service Book* (2006) appears to be the sole exception, retaining the designation "in Advent." The former Anglican and Lutheran practice was careful to identify the Sundays falling within the two preparatory seasons as Sundays "in Advent" and "in Lent." The Lenten Sundays, not being fast days, were explained as being "in" although not "of" Lent and were therefore excluded from the counting of the forty days. It was presumably this understanding that caused the drafters of the 1979 Book of Common Prayer and the 2006 *Evangelical Lutheran Worship* to depart from the traditional nomenclature regarding Advent.

11. See Massey Hamilton Shepherd, Jr., *The Oxford American Prayer Book Commentary* (New York: Oxford UP, 1950), p. 91.

12. Translated by Arthur Tozer Russell (1806-1874), *Common Service Book* no. 6; *Service Book and Hymnal* no. 11; translation of *The Lutheran Hymnal,* 1941, given in the *Lutheran Book of Worship* no. 23, the *Lutheran Service Book* no. 334, *Evangelical Lutheran Worship* no. 241: "O Lord, how shall I meet you."

13. Translated by Augustus Nelson (1863-1949), *Service Book and Hymnal* no. 9; "Prepare the royal highway" in the *Lutheran Book of Worship* no. 26, *Evangelical Lutheran Worship* no. 264; alt. in the *Lutheran Service Book* no. 343.; adapt. *Hymnal 1982* no. 65.

14. Translated by August Crull (1845-1923), the *Lutheran Book of Worship* no. 24, the *Lutheran Service Book* no. 350.

15. Translated by John Chandler (1806-1876), *Common Service Book* no. 4, *Service Book and Hymnal* no. 3; alt. in *The Lutheran Hymnal* no. 68 ("The Advent of our King"), the *Lutheran Book of Worship* no. 22, the *Lutheran Service Book* no. 331.

16. Percy Dearmer, *The Parson's Handbook* 12th ed. (London: Oxford UP, 1932), p. 113.

17. On liturgical color see J. Barrington Bates, "Am I Blue? Some Historical Evidence for Liturgical Colors," Studia Liturgica 13:1 (2003), pp. 75–88; Gilbert Cope, "Liturgical Colours," Studia Liturgica 7:4 (1970), pp. 40–49; "Colours, Liturgical," in *The New Westminster Dictionary of Liturgy and Worship* ed. Paul Bradshaw (Louisville: Westminster John Knox, 2002); Percy Dearmer, *The Parson's Handbook* 12th ed. (New York: Oxford UP, 1932), chapter 3, section 1; W. H. St. J. Hope and E. G. C. F. Atchley, *English Liturgical Colours* (New York: Macmillan, 1918); J. W. Legg, *Notes on the History of the Liturgical Colours* (1882); Henry E. Jacobs and John A. W. Haas, *The Lutheran Cyclopedia* (New York: Scribners, 1899), pp. 364–365; Paul Z. Strodach, *"Liturgical Colors," Memoirs of the Lutheran Liturgical Association* vol. VII (Pittsburgh, 1906), pp. 1–18; Ehud Spanier ed., *The Royal Purple and the Biblical Blue: Agaman and Tekhelet: the Study of Chief Rabbi Dr. Isaac Herzog on the Dye Industries in Ancient Israel and Recent Scientific Contributions* (Jerusalem: Keter, 1989).

18. Adrian Nocent, *The Liturgical Year* vol. 1 Advent, Christmas, Epiphany, trans. Matthew J. O'Connell (Collegeville: Liturgical Press, 1977), p. 96.

19. Patrick Regan, "Two Advents Compared: Ordinary and Extraordinary," Worship 84:6 (November 2010), p. 531.

20. *Liturgy of the Hours,* vol. I, p. 137; *Daily Prayer of the Church,* p. 25.

21. *Liturgy of the Hours,* vol. I, p. 137; *Daily Prayer of the Church,* p. 28.

22. *Liturgy of the Hours,* vol. I, p. 137.

23. *Liturgy of the Hours,* vol. I, p. 137; *Daily Prayer of the Church,* p. 33.

24. *Liturgy of the Hours,* vol. I, p. 144; *Daily Prayer of the Church,* pp. 103, 106.

25. Translation by John Chandler (1806-1876), *Daily Prayer of the Church* p. 128.

26. *Liturgy of the Hours,* vol. I, p. 145.

27. *Lutheran Book of Worship*, "The Entrance Hymn or Psalm is sung" (pp. 57, 78, 99; the Ministers Edition explains, "A classic Introit or an entire psalm may be sung in place of the hymn," p. 27. The *Lutheran Service Book* directs, after the Confession, "Introit, Psalm, or Entrance Hymn," pp. 152, 168, 186, 204, 214. The Leaders Desk Edition of *Evangelical Lutheran Worship*, p. 18, includes "a classic introit" among the various things that might be done during "Gathering."

28. See Jason J. McFarland, *Announcing the Feast: The Entrance Song in the Mass of the Roman Rite*. Collegeville: Liturgical Press, 2012.

29. Abraham Joshua Heschel, *Man's Quest for God* (New York: Scribner's, 1954), p. 35.

30. The example is a collect by Thomas Münzer, probably derived from a Latin collect and included in English translation in the Lutheran *Common Service Book* (1918) and the 1958 *Service Book and Hymnal* among three "Other Collects for Advent."

31. William Bright, *Ancient Collects* (Oxford and London: James Parker, 1875), p. 206. The quotation from Lord Macaulay is from his Essay on Milton.

32. Shepherd, p. 90; Marion J. Hatchett, *Commentary on the American Prayer Book* (New York: Seabury, 1981), pp. 165–166.

33. Luther D. Reed, *The Lutheran Liturgy* rev. ed. (Philadelphia: Muhlenberg Press, 1960), p. 466.

34. Translation by Catherine Winkworth given in the *Service Book and Hymnal* (1958) at no. 7; translation by Carl P. Daw, Jr. in the *Hymnal 1982* at nos. 61–62 as "Sleepers, wake! A voice astounds us."

35. Translation by Sarah Borthwick Findlater given in the *Service Book and Hymnal* at no. 14, altered to "Rejoice, rejoice, believers" in the *Lutheran Book of Worship* (1978) at no. 25 and in *Evangelical Lutheran Worship* (2006) at no. 244; further altered in the *Hymnal 1982* at no. 68. Laurenti, a Lutheran, was Cantor and Director of Music at the Roman Catholic cathedral in Bremen. The hymn was written for the Twenty-seventh Sunday after Trinity and is based on the Gospel appointed for that day, Matthew 25:1–13.

36. For a particularly egregious example see *Evangelical Lutheran Worship* no. 435.

37. For a translation and adaptation of the solemn blessings in the Leofric Missal, see Richard Tatlock, *An English Benedictional*. London: Faith Press, 1964. The Episcopal Church has provided a series of seasonal blessings in *The Book of Occasional Services 2003* (New York: Church Publishing, 2004), pp. 22–29.

38. *Liturgy of the Hours*, vol. I, p. 148; *Daily Prayer of the Church*, p. 25.

39. *Liturgy of the Hours*, vol. I, p. 148; *Daily Prayer of the Church*, p. 43.

40. William Bright, *Ancient Collects*, p. 16.

41. See William Bright, *Ancient Collects*, p. 17.

42. *Liturgy of the Hours*, vol. I, pp. 203–204; *Daily Prayer of the Church*, pp. 103–104.

43. *Liturgy of the Hours*, vol. I, p. 207.

44. The Sacramentary. Segment Two: Proper of Seasons. April 1994, p. 10.

45. The *Lutheran Book of Worship*, no. 37, alters it to "'Christ is near' we hear the cry"; *Evangelical Lutheran Worship*, no. 246, and the *Lutheran Service Book*, no. 345, alter it to "'Christ is near,' we hear it say."

46. A vigorous secular example of such a morning song is Robert Herrick's "Corinna's Gone A-Maying," which begins, "Get up! Get up for shame! The blooming morn/Upon her wings presents the god unshorn."

47. See Paul Tillich, *"Born in the Grave"* in *The Shaking of the Foundations*. New York: Scribner's, 1948.

48. *Liturgy of the Hours*, vol. I, p. 241; *Daily Prayer of the Church*, p. 76.

49. Translation based on William Bright, *Ancient Collects*, p. 18.

50. *Liturgy of the Hours*, vol. I, p. 256; *Daily Prayer of the Church*, p. 25.

51. Reed, p. 468.

52. Nocent, p. 162.

53. See Adam, p. 138.

54. See Paul Hartzell ed. *The Prayer Book Office*, p. 202.

55. *Liturgy of the Hours*, vol. I, p. 647; see *Daily Prayer of the Church*, p. 86.

56. *Liturgy of the Hours*, vol. I, p. 322; *Daily Prayer of the Church*, p. 113.

57. Translation from *Daily Prayer of the Church*, pp. 113–114.

58. Translation from *Daily Prayer of the Church*, p. 123; the reference to the chains of sin recalls the concluding prayer in A Penitential Office for Ash Wednesday in the 1928 Book of Common Prayer, p. 63, "though we be tied and bound with the chain of our sins."

59. *Liturgy of the Hours*, vol. I, p. 339; *Daily Prayer of the Church*, p. 132.

60. *Liturgy of the Hours*, vol. I, p. 1036; *Daily Prayer of the Church*, p. 93; *Common Service Book*, p. 128.

61. Translation from *Daily Prayer of the Church*, p. 133.

62. Martin Luther, Small Catechism, Explanation of the Third Article of the Apostles' Creed in The Book of Concord ed. Robert Kolb and Timothy J. Wengert (Minneapolis: Fortress, 2000), p. 355.

63. *Liturgy of the Hours*, vol. I, p. 347; *Daily Prayer of the Church*, p. 143.

64. Translation from *Daily Prayer of the Church*, p. 143.

65. Bernard, abbot, Homily 4, 8–9; *Liturgy of the Hours* vol. I, pp. 345; also given in *For All the Saints* ed. Frederick J. Schumacher with Dorothy A. Zelenko, vol. III (Delhi, N.Y.: American Lutheran Publicity Bureau, 1995), p. 111.

66. *Liturgy of the Hours*, vol. I, p. 346; *Daily Prayer of the Church*, p. 142.

67. *Liturgy of the Hours*, vol. I, p. 356; *Daily Prayer of the Church*, p. 155.

68. The translation is based on William Bright, *Ancient Collects*, p. 18; *Daily Prayer of the Church*, p. 155.

69. *Liturgy of the Hours*, vol. I, p. 364; *Daily Prayer of the Church*, p. 166.

70. Translation from *Daily Prayer of the Church*, p. 166.

71. *Liturgy of the Hours*, vol. I, p. 373; *Daily Prayer of the Church*, p. 175.

72. Translation from *Daily Prayer of the Church*, p. 175.

73. *Liturgy of the Hours*, vol. I, p. 1053; *Daily Prayer of the Church*, p. 103.

74. *Liturgy of the Hours*, vol. I, p. 338; *Daily Prayer of the Church*, pp. 131–132.

75. *Daily Prayer of the Church*, pp. 131–132; see *Liturgy of the Hours*, vol. I, pp. 336–337.

76. *Liturgy of the Hours*, vol. I, p. 309; *Daily Prayer of the Church*, p. 28.

77. *Liturgy of the Hours*, vol. I, p. 312; *Daily Prayer of the Church*, p. 107.

78. *Liturgy of the Hours*, vol. I, p. 315; *Daily Prayer of the Church*, p. 39.

79. *Liturgy of the Hours*, vol. I, p. 1124 (December 17-23); *Daily Prayer of the Church*, p. 115 (December 18); the antiphon also was the antiphon in previous Roman and Lutheran books for the Introit on the Eighteenth Sunday after Pentecost (Roman) or after Trinity (Lutheran).

80. Book of Common Prayer, p. 18.

81. Book of Common Prayer, pp. 205–206, 256–257, 929.

82. Harriet Reynolds Krauth Spaeth, *The Life of Adolph Spaeth, D.D., L.L.D.* (Philadelphia: General Council Publication House, 1916), p. 366.

83. *An Annotated Anthology of Hymns* ed. J. R. Watson (New York: Oxford UP, 2002), p. 314.

Chapter 3

1. Harald Buchinger, "On the Origin and Development of the Liturgical Year: Tendencies, Results, and Desiderata of Heortological Research," Studia Liturgica 40 (2010) p. 37.

2. Thomas J. Talley, *The Origins of the Liturgical Year*, 2nd ed. (Collegeville: Liturgical Press, 1986), p. 85; Paul F. Bradshaw and Maxwell E. Johnson, *The Origins of Feasts, Fasts, and Seasons in Early Christianity* (Collegeville: Pueblo, Liturgical Press 2011), pp. 140–141.

3. Adrian Nocent, *The Liturgical Year* vol. I Advent, Christmas, Epiphany. Trans. Matthew J. O'Connell (Collegeville: Liturgical Press, 1977), p. 191.

4. As given in altered form in *The Hymnal 1982* no. 87.

5. Paul Zeller Strodach, *The Church Year* (Philadelphia: United Lutheran Publication House, 1924), pp. 41–42.

6. Buchinger, *Studia Liturgica* 23.

7. Bradshaw and Johnson, p. 129.

8. Quoted in Adam, p. 125.

9. William Chatterton Dix, "As with gladness men of old" stanza 5. *Hymnal 1982* no. 119.

10. Leo the Great, Sermon 29.1, quoted by Nocent, p. 190.

11. Leo the Great, sermon 25.1.

12. Leo the Great, sermon 26, given in *For All the Saints*, vol. I, p. 162.

13. Fernand Cabrol, *The Year's Liturgy* vol. I (London: Burns, Oates, & Washbourne, 1938), p. 63. "The chronology is that of the system which was admitted in the time when this notice was written."

14. Bernard, *In vigilia Nativitatis Domini sermons* 3.1-2. Quoted in Nocent, p. 198.

15. *Daily Prayer of the Church*, pp. 198, 208; see *Liturgy of the Hours*, vol. I, pp. 394, 397.

16. *Liturgy of the Hours*, vol. I, p. 394.

17. Nocent, p. 197.

18. *The Church Book for the Use of Evangelical Lutheran Congregations* (Philadelphia: Lutheran Book Store, 1868), p. 41 under "Other Collects for the Season of Advent."

19. Book of Common Prayer (1979), p. 160: "O God, who makest us glad with the yearly remembrance of the birth of thy Son Jesus Christ...."

20. *Liturgy of the Hours*, vol. I, p. 394; *Daily Prayer of the Church*, p. 199.

21. *Liturgy of the Hours*, vol. I, p. 396; *Daily Prayer of the Church*, p. 202.

22. *Liturgy of the Hours*, vol. I, p. 397. See also p. 401.

23. *The Orthodox Study Bible* (Nashville: Thomas Nelson, 2008), p. 705.

24. O. B. Hardison, Jr. *Christian Rite and Christian Drama in the Middle Ages* (Baltimore: Johns Hopkins UP, 1965), p. 204.

25. See, for example, Marion J. Hatchett, *Commentary on the American Prayer Book* (New York: Seabury, 1981), p. 168.

26. See William E. Studwell, *Christmas Carols. A Reference Guide.* New York: Garland, 1984.

27. J. R. Watson ed., *An Annotated Anthology of Hymns* (New York: Oxford UP, 2002), p. 372.

28. *Liturgy of the Hours*, vol. I, p. 407; *Daily Prayer of the Church*, p. 283.

29. *Liturgy of the Hours*, vol. I, p. 399.

30. Antiphon at Morning Prayer on Christmas Day, *Liturgy of the Hours*, vol. I, p. 407; see *Daily Prayer of the Church*, p. 283.

31. *The English Hymnal* no. 18; *Hymns Ancient and Modern Revised* no. 57; abbreviated in *Service Book and Hymnal* no. 20, *Lutheran Book of Worship* no. 64, *Hymnal 1982* no. 77, *Lutheran Service Book* no. 385.

32. "Christians, awake, salute the happy morn," *Service Book and Hymnal* no. 19; *The English Hymnal* no. 21; in the *Hymnal 1982* no. 106 the line is "the earliest heralds of the Savior's name." The hymn has been much altered in various hymnals.

33. *On the Incarnation* 54. Literally, "He was humanized so that we might be deified."

34. Massey Hamilton Shepherd, Jr. *The Oxford American Prayer Book Commentary* (New York: Oxford UP, 1950), pp. 96–97.

35. Strodach, p. 44.

36. Psalm antiphon, second vespers on Christmas Day. *Liturgy of the Hours*, vol. I, p. 415.

37. Psalm antiphon, second vespers on Christmas Day, *Liturgy of the Hours*, vol. I, p. 416; *Daily Prayer of the Church*, p. 209.

38. Psalm antiphon, second vespers on Christmas 2, *Liturgy of the Hours*, vol. I, p. 499; *Daily Prayer of the Church*, p. 313, Morning Prayer.

39. Magnificat antiphon, second vespers on Christmas Day, *Liturgy of the Hours*, vol. I, p. 418; *Daily Prayer of the Church*, p. 218.

40. Nocent, p. 219.

41. Magnificat antiphon, December 26, *Liturgy of the Hours*, vol. I, p. 436; *Daily Prayer of the Church*, p. 226.

42. Antiphon on the Benedictus. *Liturgy of the Hours*, vol. I, p. 506; *Daily Prayer of the Church*, p. 311.

43. Antiphon on the Magnificat January 1. *Liturgy of the Hours*, vol. I, p. 487; *Daily Prayer of the Church*, p. 218.

44. Magnificat antiphon, Christmas 2, *Liturgy of the Hours*, vol. I, p. 494.

45. Responsory, Christmas Day, *Liturgy of the Hours*, vol. I, pp. 405–406; *Daily Prayer of the Church*, p. 295.

46. *Liturgy of the Hours*, vol. I, p. 404; *Daily Prayer of the Church*, p. 295.

47. *The Hours of the Divine Office in English and Latin* (Collegeville: Liturgical Press, 1963) vol. I, p. 1166.

48. Adam, p. 141.

49. Augustine, *City of God* 22.8.

50. The second stanza of the hymn "The Son of God goes forth to war" (*The Hymnal 1940*, no. 549, *Lutheran Book of Worship* no. 183).

51. The reading for December 26 in the Roman Catholic *Liturgy of the Hours*; also given in *For All the Saints* vol. III, pp. 140–141.

52. *Liturgy of the Hours*, vol. I, pp. 1257–1258; *Daily Prayer of the Church*, pp. 309–310.

53. Second Reading for December 26, by Fulgentius of Ruspe, *Liturgy of the Hours*, vol. I, p. 1257; *For All the Saints*, vol. III, p. 141.

54. *Liturgy of the Hours*, vol. I, p. 1259; *Daily Prayer of the Church*, p. 311.

55. *Liturgy of the Hours*, vol. I, p. 438.

56. *Jewish Study Bible* ed. Adele Berlin and Marc Zvi Brettler (New York: Oxford UP, 2004), p. 143 note on 18:5.

57. *Liturgy of the Hours* vol. I, p. 1272.

58. Reed, p. 476. The predecessor books (*Church Book, Common Service Book*) did not include the Holy Innocents on the calendar.

59. *Lutheran Worship* (St. Louis: Concordia, 1981), p. 117.

60. *Liturgy of the Hours*, vol. I, p. 1272; *Daily Prayer of the Church*, p. 329.

61. *The Lutheran Hymnal* (1941), no. 273, stanza 2; see *Hymns Ancient and Modern Revised*, no. 538.

62. *Liturgy of the Hours*, vol. I, p. 440; *Daily Prayer of the Church*, p. 241.

63. *Liturgy of the Hours*, vol. I, p. 1273; *Daily Prayer of the Church*, pp. 333–334.

64. The rule was preserved in Lutheran use in the 1960s by Arthur Carl Piepkorn, editor of the Lutheran Liturgy Edition of the Church Year Calendar published by the Ashby Company of Erie, Pennsylvania.

65. The name "The First Sunday of Christmas," introduced in *Evangelical Lutheran Worship* (2006), does not work when Christmas falls on a Sunday. In that case, Christmas Day becomes The First Sunday of Christmas. It is an unfortunate example of the imposition of a pattern ("of Advent," "of Christmas") even when that pattern manifestly does not work.

66. The nineteenth-century Lutheran liturgists were aware of F. E. Brightman's remark that "the Collect and Epistle (Rom. 4:8–14), adopted in the 1549 Book has 'altered the proportion of things, and in fact had turned the day into a commemoration of circumcision, rather than of the Circumcision of Our Lord, not to edification.'" The quotation is given in Massey Shepherd, *Oxford American Payer Book Commentary*, p. 105–106, and in Hatchett *Commentary on the American Prayer Book*, p. 169.

67. *Hymnal 1982*, no. 248, 249; *Common Service Book*, no. 36.

68. Noted by Strodach, pp. 57–58.

69. The description is J. R. Watson's in his *An Annotated Anthology of Hymns* (New York: Oxford UP, 2002), p. 187. The hymn text is printed by permission of Oxford University Press.

70. Responsory, Christmas Day, *Liturgy of the Hours*, vol. I, pp. 405–406; *Daily Prayer of the Church*, p. 295.

71. Adam, p. 149.

72. See Tristram P. Coffin, *The Book of Christmas Folklore*. New York: Seabury, 1973. See also Philip H. Pfatteicher, *New Book of Festivals and Commemorations* (Minneapolis: Fortress, 2008), p. 624.

73. "The Greens," *New York Times*, December 14, 1969. From the *New York Times* December 14 ©1969 the *New York Times*. All rights reserved. Used by permission and protected by the Copyright Laws of the United States. The printing, copying, redistribution, or retranmission of this Content without express written permission is prohibited. See also Bernd Brenner, *Inventing the Christmas Tree* trans. Benjamin A. Smith. New Haven: Yale UP, 2012

74. Wilhelm Löhe (1808-1872), a Lutheran pastor in the Bavarian village of Neuendettelsau, was acquainted with the tradition associated with this day and on his impressive liturgical calendar listed December 24 as the commemoration of Adam and Eve.

75. O. B. Hardison, Jr., pp. 179, 297.

76. Hardison, p. 223.

77. See *The Oxford Companion to the Year* ed. Bonnie Blackburn and Leofranc Holford-Strevens (New York: Oxford UP, 1999), especially, for Christmas, pp. 509–544.

78. See Philip H. Pfatteicher, "Robert Herrick's Child Priest," Literature and Theology 11:4 (December 1997), 403–407. See also *The Oxford Companion to the Year* ed. Bonnie Blackburn and Leofranc Holford-Strevens (New York: Oxford UP, 1999), pp. 487–488.

CHAPTER 4

1. Paul Zeller Strodach (d. 1947) had embraced this idea earlier in the century. See *The Church Year,* p. 62.

2. Paul F. Bradshaw and Maxwell E. Johnson, *The Origins of Feasts, Fasts, and Seasons in Early Christianity* (Collegeville: Liturgical Press, 2011), p. 137.

3. The first indisputable depiction of the Magus with dark skin only appeared in 1437, in Germany in the Wurznach altarpiece by Hans Multscher. Miranda Kaufmann, "A Subtle Bulwark of Canvas," *TLS* March 23, 2012 No. 5686, p. 8.

4. *Hymnal 1982,* no. 127; see the *Lutheran Book of Worship* no. 81, *The English Hymnal* no. 40.

5. *Hymnal 1982,* no. 128.

6. Sermon 31.1.

7. Gregory the Great, Sermons on the Gospels 10.2.

8. See Nicholas E. Denysenko, *The Blessing of Waters and Epiphany. The Eastern Liturgical Tradition.* Burlington, VT: Ashgate, 2012.

9. Antiphon to the canticle at Lauds on The Epiphany, *Liturgy of the Hours,* vol. I, p. 563.

10. Philip H. Pfatteicher ed., *Daily Prayer of the Church,* p. 283.

11. Maximus of Turin, Sermon 100 *de sancta Epiphania* 1, 3. *Liturgy of the Hours,* vol. I, pp. 612–613.

12. From stanza 2 of "A great and mighty wonder," *Service Book and Hymnal* no. 18, translated by John Mason Neale; *The English Hymnal* no. 19; *Hymns Ancient and Modern Revised,* no. 68; alt. in *Hymnal 1940* no. 18.

13. *Liturgy of the Hours,* vol. I, p. 642; *Daily Prayer of the Church,* p. 212.

14. *The Lutheran Hymnal* (1941), no. 131.

15. "The sinless one to Jordan came," *Hymnal 1982,* no. 120.

16. The hymn with a later doxology is in the *Hymnal 1982,* no. 131; *Lutheran Book of Worship,* no. 85. Translation of stanza 1 (no. 434) from the Hymn Book of the Anglican Church of Canada and the United Church of Canada © 1971. Used with permission.

17. *Liturgy of the Hours,* vol. I, p. 564; *Daily Prayer of the Church,* p. 299.

18. *Liturgy of the Hours,* vol. I, p. 573; *Daily Prayer of the Church,* p. 218.

19. *Liturgy of the Hours,* vol. I, p. 642; *Daily Prayer of the Church,* p. 211.

20. Psalm antiphon at first vespers of the Epiphany, *Liturgy of the Hours,* vol. I, p. 547; *Daily Prayer of the Church,* p. 198.

21. The older translation was "begotten of his Father before all worlds"; the *Quicunque vult,* the Athanasian Creed, declares of Jesus Christ, "He is God, begotten before all worlds from the being of the Father, and he is man, born in the world from the being of his mother." See the *Lutheran Book of Worship,* pp. 54–55; *Daily Prayer of the Church,* pp. 1585–1588.

22. Psalm antiphon at first vespers on the Epiphany, *Liturgy of the Hours,* vol. I, p. 549; *Daily Prayer of the Church,* p. 202.

23. Psalm antiphon at Lauds, *Liturgy of the Hours,* vol. I, p. 570.

24. Psalm antiphon Midmorning on the Epiphany, *Liturgy of the Hours,* vol. I, p. 568.

25. *Liturgy of the Hours,* vol. I, pp. 561–562; *Daily Prayer of the Church,* p. 297.

26. *Liturgy of the Hours,* vol. I, p. 637; *Daily Prayer of the Church,* p. 281.

27. Sermon 160, *Patrologia Latina* 52, 620–662; given in J. Robert Wright, *Readings for the Daily Office from the Early Church* (New York: Church Hymnal Corporation, 1991), pp. 48–49.

28. Strodach, p. 65.

29. Given on the Lutheran edition of the Church Year calendar published by the Ashby Company, Erie, Pennsylvania, ed. Philip H. Pfatteicher. The illustrative dates are those of 2012.

30. Adrian Nocent, *The Liturgical Year* vol. 1, trans. Matthew J. O'Connell (Collegeville: Liturgical Press, 1977), p. 217.

31. See the *Oxford Companion to the Year,* ed. Bonnie Blackburn and Leofranc Holford-Strevens (New York: Oxford UP, 1999), pp. 601–602.

32. Before Christianity came to northern Europe, February 1 was celebrated by the Celts as one of the four "cross-quarter" days that occurred between the equinoxes and the solstices. (The other days were May 1, August, 1, and November 1.) A prominent feature of the celebrations was the lighting of sacred fires in fields and in houses to encourage the strengthening of the sun.

33. Translation in the *Book of Occasional Services* for use in the Candlemas Procession.

34. *Liturgy of the Hours,* vol. III, p. 1351.

35. Slightly altered by Catherine Winkworth; *Common Service Book,* no. 51 stanzas 1 and 4.

36. (Lutheran) *Church Book* no. 149; *Common Service Book* (1918) no. 50; *Service Book and Hymnal* (1958), no. 142; *Lutheran Book of Worship* no. 184.

37. *Hymns Ancient and Modern Revised* no. 544; *The English Hymnal* no. 209; *Hymnal 1982* no. 259.

38. See the *Liturgy of the Hours,* vol. III, p. 1343.

39. *Hymnal 1982* no. 93, stanza 4; *The United Methodist Hymnal* (1989) no. 220, stanza 4; *Hymns Ancient and Modern Revised* no. 64, stanza 4, see also stanza 5:

> Though an infant now we view him,
> He shall fill his Father's throne,
> Gather all the nations to him;
> Every knee shall then bow down:
> Come and worship....

CHAPTER 5

1. *Lutheran Book of Worship Ministers Edition* (1978), p. 129. The address has been softened and not improved in the Leaders Desk Edition of *Evangelical Lutheran Worship* (2006), p. 617.

2. The first of the Ninety-five Theses. *Luther's Works,* vol. 31, p. 25.

3. Adrian Nocent, *The Liturgical Year,* vol. 2, Lent, trans. Matthew J. O'Connell (Collegeville: Liturgical Press, 1977) p. 19.

4. See Nocent, pp. 31, 19–20, 23, 25, 27, 42–43.

5. Gelasian and Gregorian sacramentaries; translation from William Bright's *Ancient Collects,* as revised in *Lesser Feasts and Fasts 2006* (p. 30).

6. *Liturgy of the Hours,* vol. II, p. 51; *Daily Prayer of the Church,* p. 1040.

7. John Chrysostom, *Homilies on the Statues,* Homily III, 11–12.

8. For further comment on the Address see Philip H. Pfatteicher, *Commentary on the Lutheran Book of Worship: Lutheran Liturgy in Its Ecumenical Context* (Minneapolis: Augsburg Fortress, 1990), pp. 224–226.

9. Nocent, pp. 28, 33, 36.

10. *Liturgy of the Hours,* vol. II, p. 212; *Daily Prayer of the Church,* p. 1005.

11. Harald Buchinger, "On the Origin and Development of the Liturgical Year: Tendencies, Results, and Desiderata of Heortological Research," Studia Liturgica 40:1–2 (2010), 24–28.

12. See Paul F. Bradshaw and Maxwell E. Johnson, *The Origins of Feasts, Fasts, and Seasons in Early Christianity* (Collegeville: Liturgical Press, 2011), pp. 89–119.

13. Nocent, pp. 35, 39.

14. *Common Service Book,* pp. 216–228; *Service Book and Hymnal* text edition (1967), pp. 463–477 and in the separate Lectionary *Epistles and Gospels Together with Lessons from the Old Testament from the Service Book and Hymnal* (1959), pp. 127–135.

15. Council of Laodicaea (ca. 363), Canon 52.

16. Paul F. Bradshaw and Maxwell E. Johnson, *The Origin of Feasts, Fasts, and Seasons in Early Christianity* (Collegeville: Liturgical Press, 2011) p. 90.

17. Bradshaw and Johnson, pp. 107–108.

18. Egeria 27:1.

19. One week of six days beginning with Clean Monday (the Monday before the Western Ash Wednesday) followed by four weeks of seven days each and concluding with six days through Friday of the final week, for a total of forty days.

20. William Bright, *Ancient Collects* (Oxford and London: James Parker, 1875), p. 208; quoted in Luther D. Reed, *The Lutheran Liturgy* rev. ed. (Philadelphia: Muhlenberg, 1960), p. 524.

21. Book of Common Prayer (1928), p. 31; *Common Service Book,* p. 46; *The Lutheran Hymnal* (1941), p. 45; *Service Book and Hymnal,* p. 148.

22. Reed, p. 447, quoting William Bright, who assumed that Pope Gelasius was the author of the sacramentary that bears his name.

23. The Church of the Advent, Boston.

24. Paul Zeller Strodach, *The Church Year* (Philadelphia: United Lutheran Publication House, 1924), p. 89.

25. So in the *Common Service Book*, p. 293: "Green. From and with Vespers of the Saturday before Septuagesima to Vespers of the day before Ash Wednesday"; *Service Book and Hymnal*, p. 277: "...to, but not including, Vespers of the day before Ash Wednesday." Other Lutheran books did not specify color use.

26. "Lent," *New Westminster Dictionary of Liturgy and Worship* ed. Paul Bradshaw. Louisville: Westminster John Knox, 2002.

27. For Carnival in Rome in the eighteenth century, see Johann Wolfgang von Goethe, *Italian Journey (1786-1788)*, trans. W. H. Auden and Elizabeth Mayer (New York: Pantheon, 1962), 445–469.

28. See Bonnie Blackburn and Leofranc Holford-Strevens, *The Oxford Companion to the Year* (New York: Oxford UP, 1999), pp. 602–608.

29. See C. L. Barber, *Shakespeare's Festive Comedy* (Princeton: University Press, 1959), chap. 1, "Introduction: The Saturnalian Pattern," especially the section, "Through Release to Clarification."

30. See Philip H. Pfatteicher, *Commentary on the Lutheran Book of Worship: Lutheran Liturgy in Its Ecumenical Context* (Minneapolis: Augsburg Fortress, 1990), pp. 222–223.

31. Philip H. Pfatteicher, *"Lent," New Proclamation Year B 2002-2003* (Minneapolis: Augsburg Fortress, 2002), pp. 142–143.

32. See Percy Dearmer, *The Parson's Handbook* 12th ed. (London: Oxford UP, 1932), pp. 450–451.

33. Nocent, p. 64.

34. Translated in *The Anglican Missal* (1995), p. A58.

35. Father Richard Herbel, *St. Augustine's House Newsletter*, Lent A.D. 2011.

36. 1928 Book of Common Prayer, pp. 60–63.

37. Luther D. Reed, *The Lutheran Liturgy* rev. ed. (Philadelphia: Muhlenberg Press, 1960) p. 492.

38. The translation is by William Bright in *Ancient Collects* (1875), p. 31.

39. Marion J. Hatchett, *Commentary on the American Prayer Book* (New York: Seabury, 1981), p. 400.

40. Massey H. Shepherd, Jr., *The Oxford American Prayer Book Commentary* (New York: Oxford UP, 1950), p. 218.

41. "Only-begotten, Word of God eternal," *The Hymnal 1982*, no. 361, stanza 4.

42. *Hymnal 1982* nos. 310, 311; *Service Book and Hymnal* no. 277.

43. *Hymnal of the Moravian Church* (1969) no. 432; (Lutheran) *Church Book* no. 447; *Common Service Book* no. 260; *Service Book and Hymnal* no. 532; *Lutheran Book of Worship* no. 341; *Evangelical Lutheran Worship* no. 624; *Lutheran Service Book* no. 718.

44. © 1939, 1966 by E. C. Schirmer Music Company, a division of ECS Publishing, www.ecspub.com Used by permission. *Lutheran Book of Worship* no. 557; alt. in *Evangelical Lutheran Worship* no. 881; and *The Presbyterian Hymnal* (1990) no. 554.

45. See Jerome Murphy-O'Connor, *The Holy Land* 5th ed. (New York: Oxford UP, 2008), pp. 37–38.

46. John Mason Neale described the hymn as "the most pathetic of medieval poems" ("pathetic" in the sense of arousing sympathetic sadness and compassion) as "Jerusalem the golden" is "the most lovely" and *Dies irae* "the most sublime."

47. The Lutheran *Church Book* (1868) followed by the *Common Service Book* (1918) and *The Lutheran Hymnal* (1941), which preserved the Latin names for the Sundays in Lent, curiously changed the tense of the verb from future to perfect, rendering it *invocavit,* "he called" instead of *invocabit.* The error was corrected in the 1958 *Service Book and Hymnal.* The error antedates the Reformation and is found in some north European Missals, probably because of a copyist's confusion of "b" with "v," which often look quite similar in script. Edward T. Horn III. *The Christian Year* (Philadelphia: Muhlenberg, 1957), p. 107.

48. Hatchett, p. 174.

49. Hatchett, p. 174.

50. Translation by William Bright, *Ancient Collects,* pp. 31–32; *Daily Prayer of the Church,* p. 930.

51. Joseph Sittler, "As Lent Begins," *The Lutheran,* February 27, 1963, p. 5.

52. *The Hymnal 1982,* no. 143. Translated by Maurice F. Bell (1862-1947). From The English Hymnal. Reproduced by Permission of CopyCat Music Licensing, LLC, obo Oxford University Press. All rights reserved.

53. Similar confidence in divine aid appears in the English Book of Common Prayer in the suffrages in Morning Prayer : "Give peace in our time, O Lord. Because there is none other that fighteth for us, but only thou, O God."

54. *The Hymnal 1982,* no. 146. Translated by James Quinn, SJ, from *Praise the Lord* (Geoffrey Chapman, 1972). Used by permission from Bloomsbury.

55. *The Hymnal 1982,* no. 142.

56. *Liturgy of the Hours,* vol. II, p. 61; *Daily Prayer of the Church,* p. 1030.

57. *Liturgy of the Hours,* vol. II, p. 93; *Daily Prayer of the Church,* p. 932.

58. Adolf Adam, *The Liturgical Year* (New York: Pueblo, 1981), p. 100.

59. International Commission on English in the Liturgy draft; *Daily Prayer of the Church,* p. 913.

60. Hatchett, p. 174.

61. Reed, p. 493.

62. See Bright, *Ancient Collects,* p. 31 no. 2.

63. The veiling may have been suggested by the conclusion of the Gospel appointed for this Sunday in the medieval lectionary that was in use until the final third of the twentieth century, John 8:46-59, "Jesus hid himself and went out of the temple."

64. See Percy Dearmer, *The Parson's Handbook* 12th ed. Rev. (London: Oxford UP, 1932), pp. 113–114.

65. The description derives from C. D. Smith, *The Royal Banners. A Tract for Passiontide* (London: The Church Union, Church Literature Association, n.d.), p. 9.

66. Strodach, p. 128.

67. *Liturgy and Worship. A Companion to the Prayer Books of the Anglican Communion* ed. W. K. Lowther Clarke and Charles Harris (London: SPCK, 1964 [1932]), p. 207. "Passion Week" appears in Roman Catholic and Anglican missals and was also current in Lutheran use.

68. Book of Common Prayer, p. 832; *Church Book*, p. 107 no. 59; *Common Service Book*, p. 139 no. 19; *Service Book and Hymnal*, p. 233 no. 113; *Lutheran Book of Worship*, p. 49 no. 220; *Evangelical Lutheran Worship*, p. 86; *Lutheran Service Book*, p. 310 no. 188.

69. *The Book of Concord* ed. Robert Kolb and Timothy J. Wengert (Minneapolis: Fortress, 2000), p. 355.

70. Reed, p. 528, quotes the Latin: *ut qui sine te esse non possumus secundum te vivere valeamus.*

71. Strodach, p. 204.

72. Reed, p. 535.

73. Reed, p. 536.

74. Strodach, p. 254.

CHAPTER 6

1. Among them the Episcopal Bishop of New York, Horace W. B. Donegan, prompting Bishop James Pike (in a noonday Lenten sermon at St. Thomas' Church on Fifth Avenue ca. 1965) to quip that Claudia Hernaman's hymn would have to be revised to "Lord, who threw out these forty days?"

2. See Roger Greenacre, *The Sacrament of Easter* (London: Faith Press, 1965), p. 54.

3. Melito of Sardis, "A Homily on the Pasch," given in *For All the Saints* ed. Frederick J. Schumacher vol. II (Delhi, NY: American Lutheran Publicity Bureau, 1995), p. 216.

4. See J. Gordon Davies, *Holy Week: A Short History* (Richmond, Virginia: John Knox, 1963), pp. 23–38. Also Jerome Murphy-O'Connor, *The Holy Land. An Oxford Archaeological Guide* 5th ed. New York: Oxford UP, 2008.

5. Adolf Adam, *The Liturgical Year* trans. Matthew J. O'Connell (New York: Pueblo, 1981), p. 107.

6. *The Hymnal 1982*, no. 104; *Lutheran Book of Worship* no. 74.

7. The Latin name *Palmarum* for the Sixth Sunday in Lent continues in Lutheran use, especially in Europe.

8. Jean Gaillard, *Holy Week and Easter* 3rd ed. trans. William Busch (Collegeville: Liturgical Press, 1964), p. 31.

9. *Liturgy of the Hours*, vol. II, p. 414; *Daily Prayer of the Church*, p. 1096.

10. *Liturgy of the Hours*, vol. II, p. 422; *Daily Prayer of the Church*, p. 1153.

11. *Liturgy of the Hours*, vol. II, p. 422.

12. Charles Coffin (1676–1749), *Instantis adventum Dei*, trans. John Chandler, "The advent of our God," *Service Book and Hymnal* no. 3; *Lutheran Book of Worship*, no. 22.

13. Adrian Nocent, *The Liturgical Year* vol. 2 Lent, trans. Matthew J. O'Connell (Collegeville: Liturgical Press, 1977), p. 195.

14. Translation from Gaillard, p. 39.

15. Gaillard, p. 35.

16. Greenacre, p. 55.

17. Greenacre, pp. 56–57.

18. See Chris Fenner, "Theodulf: Theologian at Charlemagne's Court, Poet, and Bishop of Orléans," The Hymn. A Journal of Congregational Song 63:1 (Winter 2012), 13–20.

19. *Service Book and Hymnal* no. 73; *English Hymnal* no. 620; *Hymns Ancient and Modern Revised* 99; *Hymnal 1982* no. 156 (stanza 3 altered); *Presbyterian Hymnal* (1990) nos. 90, 91 (stanzas 1, 2, 3, 5).

20. J. R. Watson ed. *An Annotated Anthology of Hymns* (New York: Oxford UP, 2002), p. 246. Watson (pp. 245–246) gives the original text of the hymn; it is slightly altered in the *Hymnal 1982* no. 156.

21. Luther D. Reed, *The Lutheran Liturgy* rev. ed. (Philadelphia: Muhlenberg, 1960), p. 498.

22. Massey H. Shepherd, Jr., *The Oxford American Prayer Book Commentary* (New York: Oxford UP, 1950), p. 134.

23. Philip H. Pfatteicher, *Commentary on the Lutheran Book of Worship* (Minneapolis: Fortress, 1990), p. 255 and note 129.

24. The current German *Evangelish Gesangbuch* (no. 85) attributes the hymn to Arnulf von Löwen and dates it "before 1250" (when Arnulf died). *Evangelical Lutheran Worship* (2006) gives the same attribution: Arnulf of Louvain.

25. Charles Porterfied Krauth (1823-1883) made an English translation of the section of the original Latin poem addressed to the hands, "Wide open are thy hands," *Service Book and Hymnal*, no. 66, altered in the *Lutheran Book of Worship*, no. 489.

26. *Service Book and Hymnal*, no. 88. The translation by Robert Seymour Bridges is given in the *Hymnal 1982*, nos. 168, 169.

27. *Kirchenbuch für Evangelisch-Lutherishe Gemeinden* (Philadelphia: United Lutheran Publication House, 1877), no. 554.

28. Ian Bradley ed., *The Book of Hymns* (New York: Testament Books, 1989), p. 318.

29. In its calendar, the 1979 Book of Common Prayer (p. 31) notes the "Lenten Season" and then separately "Holy Week." It was also clear in the previous American Prayer Book (1928, p. 134) that Holy Week was a separate liturgical season.

30. The terminology in referring to the days of Holy Week is universal (Roman Catholic, Anglican, Lutheran): "in Holy Week" following the pattern established

by the Sundays "in Lent." The distinction some make between "in" and "of" is not applied to Holy Week.

31. Paul Zeller Strodach, *The Church Year* (Philadelphia: United Lutheran Publication House, 1924), p. 136.

32. See *The Daily Prayer of the Church*, p. 1146, where the translation is credited to Canon Poole's student, Dean Dirk Van Dissel.

33. Massey H. Shepherd, Jr. *The Oxford American Prayer Book Commentary* (New York: Oxford UP, 1950), pp. 137–138.

34. *Liturgy of the Hours*, vol. II, pp. 433–434; *Daily Prayer of the Church*, p. 1169.

35. Strodach, p. 138.

36. Strodach, p. 140.

37. Tenebrae had a special power when it was sung in the Sistine Chapel, as numerous travelers testify. "As evening sinks, and the tapers are extinguished, one after another, at different stages of the service, the fading light falls dimmer and dimmer, on the reverend figures. The prophets and saints of Michael Angelo look down from the ceiling on the pious worshippers beneath; while the living figures of his Last Judgment, in every variety of infernal suffering and celestial enjoyment, gradually vanish in the gathering shade, as if the scene of horror had closed for ever on the one, and the other had quitted the darkness of earth for a higher world. Is it wonderful, that, in such circumstances, such music as that famed *Miserere,* sung by such a choir, should shake the soul even of a Calvinist?" Quoted in Kelly Grovier, "Secret Harmony. Mozart, Michelangelo, and the *Miserere Mei,*" *TLS* June 8, 2012 No. 5697, p. 14.

38. See Patrick Regan, "The Chrism Mass: Festival of the Priesthood. But Which One?" *Worship* 86:2 (March 2012), 124–139.

39. See Greenacre, pp. 15, 58.

40. *Purgatorio* VIII, lines 28-30. The translation is by John Ciardi.

41. Marion J. Hatchett, *Commentary on the American Prayer Book* (New York: Seabury, 1980) p. 177.

42. Tertullian, *De Oratione* 18.

43. Gaillard, p. 74.

44. In the Liturgy of St. John Chrysostom, just before receiving the precious Gifts, the communicants say, "Of thy mystical Supper, O Son of God, accept me today as a communicant, for I will not speak of thy Mystery to thine enemies, neither like Judas give thee a kiss; but like the thief I will confess thee: Remember me, O Lord, in thy kingdom."

45. Allan B. Warren III, Notes on the Liturgies of Holy Week at the Church of the Advent, Boston.

46. *Liturgy of the Hours*, vol. II, p. 466; *The Daily Prayer of the Church*, p. 1128.

47. *Liturgy of the Hours*, vol. II, p. 480, 490; *The Daily Prayer of the Church*, p. 1132.

48. *Liturgy of the Hours*, vol. II, p. 502; *The Daily Prayer of the Church*, p. 1137.

49. Michael Ramsey, *The Narratives of the Passion*. Contemporary Studies in Theology no. 1. (London: Mowbray, 1962), p. 24.

50. "Organ or other instrumental music is used to support the singing only," *Lutheran Book of Worship Ministers Edition*, p. 23; see *Evangelical Lutheran Worship Leaders Desk Edition*, p. 38.

51. William Bright, *Ancient Collects* (Oxford and London: James Parker, 1875), pp. 42–43.

52. The precise relationship between the Fourth Gospel and John "the beloved disciple" is a complicated matter. See, e.g., Raymond E. Brown, *The Gospel according to John I-XII* (Garden City, NY: Doubleday, 1966), pp. LXXXVII-CII.

53. John Chrysostom, Homily given in *From the Fathers to the Churches* ed. Brother Kenneth (London: Collins Liturgical Publishers, 1983), pp. 807–808. And in *For All the Saints*, vol. III, pp. 1067–1068.

54. *Common Service Book* (1918), pp. 156–158 *Service Book and Hymnal* (1958), pp. 236–237. The prayer had appeared without the rubric in the *Church Book* (1868) as General Prayer V.

55. In the *Service Book and Hymnal* (1958), p. 236, there was a bid and prayer "for the chief pastor of the Church, that the Lord God who called him to his office, may keep him in health and safety, for the good of the holy Church and the leadership of the people of God." Some, not unreasonably, interpreted "chief pastor" to refer to the pope.

56. See Pfatteicher, *Commentary on the Lutheran Book of Worship*, p. 249.

57. Egeria, 37.1–3; Paul F. Bradshaw and Maxwell E. Johnson, *The Origins of Feasts, Fasts, and Seasons in Early Christianity* (Collegeville: Liturgical Press, 2011), p. 63.

58. Book of Common Prayer, p. 281; *Daily Prayer of the Church*, p. 1208.

59. Book of Common Prayer, p. 282; *Daily Prayer of the Church*, p. 1215.

60. See the discussion in Philip H. Pfatteicher, *Commentary on the Lutheran Book of Worship*, pp. 251–254.

61. *Middle English Lyrics* ed. Maxwell S. Luria and Richard L. Hoffman (New York: Norton, 1974), no. 218, pp. 209–210. See also the lyrics "My folk, what habbe I do thee" by Friar William Herebert, no. 221, p. 212, and "My folk, now answere me" from the Commonplace Book of John Grimestone, no. 222, p. 213.

62. *Hymnal 1982* no. 158; *Service Book and Hymnal* no. 85; *Lutheran Book of Worship* no. 123. The translation is by Robert Seymour Bridges.

63. *Hymnal 1982* nos. 165, 166; *Lutheran Book of Worship* no. 118.

64. *Hymnal 1940* no. 63; *Service Book and Hymnal* no. 75.

65. See John Julian, *Dictionary of Hymnology*, p. 1220; J. R. Watson ed., *An Annotated Anthology of Hymns*, p. 29.

66. Tertullian, *Against Marcion* 3.

67. *Hymnal 1982* no. 162. Used by permission of Church Publishing. Stanza 2 trans. John Mason Neale, alt. in *Lutheran Book of Worship* nos. 124, 125.

68. Helen Waddell, *More Latin Lyrics from Virgil to Milton* (New York: Norton, 1977), p. 120.

69. Strodach, *The Church Year*, p. 145.

70. Edward T. Horn III, *The Christian Year* (Philadelphia: Muhlenberg, 1957), pp. 125–126; Luther D. Reed, *Worship: A Study of Corporate Devotion* (Philadelphia: Muhlenberg, 1959), p. 45.

71. (1) "Father forgive them" Luke 23:34; (2) "Today you will be with me in paradise" Luke 23:43; (3) "Behold your son; behold your mother" John 19:26, 27; (4) "My God, why have you forsaken me?" Matt. 27:46, Mark 15:34; (5) "I thirst" John 19:28; (6) "It is finished" John 19:30; (7) "Into your hands I commend my spirit" Luke 23:46.

72. *Service Book and Hymnal*, no. 87. See also *Daily Prayer of the Church*, pp. 1226–1227.

73. *Liturgy of the Hours*, vol. II. P. 498; *Daily Prayer of the Church*, p. 1223.

74. Gaillard, p. 102. See the imaginative portrayal of the event in the ancient homily for Holy Saturday in the *Liturgy of the Hours*, vol. II, pp. 496–498; *From the Fathers to the Churches* ed. Brother Kenneth (London: Collins, 1983), pp. 297–298; *For All the Saints*, vol. III, p. 1037.

75. *Liturgy of the Hours*, vol. II, p. 502; *Daily Prayer of the Church*, p. 1223.

76. Paraphrased by Howard Chandler Robbins in the *Hymnal 1982* no. 163; the *Hymnal 1940* no. 81.

77. Patrick Regan, "Paschal Vigil: Perfection of Salvation and Goal of Creation," Studia Liturgica 40:1–2 (2010), p. 144.

78. See "The Moon and the Mystery" in Philip H. Pfatteicher, *The School of the Church: Worship and Christian Formation* (Valley Forge, Pa.: Trinity Press International, 1995), pp. 76–83. See also, for a literary meditation, James Attlee, *Nocturne. A Journey in Search of Moonlight*. London: Hamish Hamilton, 2011.

79. See Gaillard, pp. 110–111.

80. Regan, *Studia Liturgica* p. 144.

81. Percy Dearmer, R. Vaughan Williams, Martin Shaw, *The Oxford Book of Carols* (New York: Oxford UP, 1964 [1928]), no. 180.

82. Regan, p. 145. For a full explication of the development and text of the Exsultet see Philip H. Pfatteicher, *Liturgical Spirituality* (Valley Forge, Pa.: Trinity Press International, 1997), pp. 86–92; Pfatteicher, *Commentary on the Lutheran Book of Worship*, pp. 264–273.

83. Regan, p. 149.

84. John Mason Neale, *Hymns of the Eastern Church* (1862), pp. 39–41.

85. For more on John Damascene see Philip H. Pfatteicher, *New Book of Festivals and Commemorations* (Minneapolis: Fortress, 2008), pp. 593–595.

86. J. R. Watson ed. *An Annotated Anthology of Hymns* (New York: Oxford UP, 2003), p. 14.

87. NRSV, NIV, NJB, "Greetings!"; NKJ, "Rejoice!"; CEV, "Peace be with you." REB, NAB, CEB replace quotation with description, "greeted them."

88. *Hymnal 1982* no. 210. The *Lutheran Book of Worship* no. 141 adds a doxology to Neale's original three stanzas.

89. Richard Crashaw, *"Easter Day," The Complete Poetry of Richard Crashaw* ed. George Walton Williams (New York: Norton, 1974), p. 26. The spelling here has been modernized.

CHAPTER 7

1. Translated by Ray Palmer, *Service Book and Hymnal* no. 62, stanza 4; see the *Lutheran Book of Worship* no. 101.

2. *The Hours of the Divine Office in English and Latin*, vol. II (Collegeville: Liturgical Press, 1964), p. 1215; Philip H. Pfatteicher ed., *The Daily Prayer of the Church* (Minneapolis: Lutheran University Press, 2005), p. 1355; see *Liturgy of the Hours*, vol. II, p. 675.

3. Patrologia Graecae 36, 617 quoted in Anscar J Chupungco, *"The Liturgical Year: The Gospel Encountering Culture,"* Studia Liturgica, 40:1–2 (2010), p. 55.

4. The Lutheran *Service Book and Hymnal* (1958) no. 93.

5. *Hymnal 1982* no. 199, the final stanza here altered to conform to Neale's translation.

6. Edward T. Horn III, *The Christian Year* (Philadelphia: Muhlenberg, 1957), p. 11.

7. Theodor H. Gaster, *Festivals of the Jewish Year* (New York: Morrow, 1953), p. 38.

8. Robert Alter, *The Book of Psalms. A Translation with Commentary* (New York: Norton, 2007), p. 482.

9. Included also in the *Hymnal 1982* nos. 417, 418.

10. Luther D. Reed, *The Lutheran Liturgy* rev. ed. (Philadelphia: Muhlenberg, 1960), p. 508.

11. Paul Zeller Strodach, *The Church Year* (Philadelphia: United Lutheran Publication House, 1924), pp. 151–152.

12. Massey H. Shepherd, Jr. *The Oxford American Prayer Book Commentary* (New York: Oxford UP, 1950), p. 163.

13. Augustine, *On the Gospel of St. John.* Tractate 120.2. On "gates" see Ps. 107:16; Isa. 26:2; 45:1–2; 62:10; Jer. 17:25; 22:4; Rev. 21:25.

14. See Ruth Ellis Messenger, *The Medieval Latin Hymn* (Washington, D.C.: Capital Press, 1953), pp. 35–52.

15. *Lutheran Book of Worship Ministers Edition*, p. 153: "The sequence hymn, no. 137, may follow."

16. *Hymnal 1982* no. 183; *Lutheran Book of Worship* no. 137; *Evangelical Lutheran Worship* no. 371; see also *Lutheran Service Book* no. 460. The full text, including an ugly couplet, "Mary's word believing/Above the tales of Jewry deceiving," is in *Hymns Ancient and Modern Revised* no. 138 and *The English Hymnal* no. 130.

17. See O. B. Hardison, Jr., *Christian Rite and Christian Drama in the Middle Ages* (Baltimore: Johns Hopkins UP, 1965), especially Essay 5; see also John Julian, *A Dictionary of Hymnology* 2nd ed. Rev. (1907), "Victimae Paschali."

18. Given in Julian, *Dictionary of Hymnology*, p. 1223; also in Ernest Edwin Ryden, *The Story of Christian Hymnody* (Rock Island, Illinois: Augustana, 1959), p. 47.

19. *Lutheran Book of Worship* no. 136; *Evangelical Lutheran Worship* no. 372; *Lutheran Service Book* no. 459.

20. Johann Wolfgang von Goethe, *Faust* Part 1, ll. 737–807. See *Goethe Faust Der Tragödie erster und zweiter Teil, Urfaust* ed. Erich Trunz (Munich: C. H. Beck, 2010), pp. 30–32.

21. *Service Book and Hymnal* no. 98; *Lutheran Book of Worship* no. 134; *Hymnal 1982* nos. 185, 186; *Evangelical Lutheran Worship* no. 370; *Lutheran Service Book* no. 458.

22. *The Works of Martin Luther* Philadelphia Edition (Philadelphia: Muhlenberg Press, 1932), vol. VI, p. 302. The "improvement" refers to the melody, not the text. See *Luther's Works* (Philadelphia: Fortress Press, 1965) vol. 53 Liturgy and Hymns, p. 255.

23. *Common Service Book* no. 112; *Service Book and Hymnal* no. 99; *Lutheran Book of Worship* no. 128; *Evangelical Lutheran Worship* no. 369; *Lutheran Service Book* no. 463; *Hymns Ancient and Modern Revised* no. 131.

24. Given in Richard Tatlock, *An English Benedictional* (Westminster: Faith Press, 1964), p. 48.

25. *Hymnal 1982* no. 624; the *Lutheran Book of Worship* no. 347; *Lutheran Service Book* no. 672.

26. *Lesser Feasts and Fasts 2006* (New York: Church Publishing, 2006), p. 71 no. 12. In the 1570 Roman Missal it was appointed for Easter Tuesday.

27. *Lesser Feasts and Fasts*, p. 67 no. 4.

28. *Daily Prayer of the Church*, p. 1329.

29. *Alleluia dulce Carmen* as in *Hymns Ancient and Modern Revised* no. 82, the *Service Book and Hymnal* no. 58; see *Hymnal 1982* no. 122, 123; *Lutheran Service Book* no. 417; *Evangelical Lutheran Worship* no. 318, *The English Hymnal* no. 63.

30. Massey H. Shepherd in his *Oxford American Prayer Book Commentary*, p. 166, identifies as a source of the wording of the collect an "Emmaus Litany" in *The St. Veronica Manual* (1896), compiled by a novelist, Genevieve Irons.

31. See Robert Payne, *The Holy Fire. The Story of the Early Centuries of the Christian Church in the Near East* (New York: Harper & Brothers, 1957), pp. 23–42.

32. *Daily Prayer of the Church*, p. 1329.

33. Shepherd, p. 165.

34. *Daily Prayer of the Church*, p. 1330.

35. Julian of Norwich, *Revelations of Divine Love*, chapter 58.

36. *Daily Prayer of the Church*, p. 1330.

37. European Lutheran use and the *Church Book* and the *Common Service Book* give *Misericordias* following the Vulgate Ps. 88 [89]:1. See also Horn, pp. 142–143.

38. Translation by Philip H. Pfatteicher based on a draft by the International Commission on English in the Liturgy.

39. Strodach, pp. 161–162.

40. Translation based on a draft by the International Consultation on English in the Liturgy.

41. Translation by Dirk van Dissel given in *Daily Prayer of the Church*, p.1336.

42. C. Frederick Barbee and Paul F. M. Zahl, *The Collects of Thomas Cranmer* (Grand Rapids: Eerdmans, 1999), p. 59. "This Collect is one of the high points of Anglican theology, a masterpiece of pure, perfect, prayed theology."

43. Translation by Philip H. Pfatteicher.

44. Reed, pp. 525–526.

45. The concluding two lines, the refrain, have been subject to various sorts of Vandalism by editors who found unacceptable Pierpoint's Tractarian theology with its reference to the divinity of Christ and to our offering of sacrifice. The text given here is from the Lutheran *Common Service Book* (no. 292) and the *Service Book and Hymnal* (no. 444), as Pierpoint wrote it. The lines were altered in the *Lutheran Book of Worship*, the *Hymnal 1940*, the *Hymnal 1982*, and elsewhere.

46. *Hymnal 1982* no. 409; *Service Book and Hymnal* no. 442. Compare the contemporaneous hymn by Isaac Watts, "I sing the almighty power of God/That made the mountains rise" from his 1715 collection for children in which it bore the descriptive title "Praise for Creation and Providence" given in the *Hymnal 1982* no. 398, *The Presbyterian Hymnal* (1990) no. 288, *The United Methodist Hymnal* (1989) no. 152.

47. From the apocryphal/deuterocanonlical *Song of the Three Young Men* in the NRSV as *The Prayer of Azariah and the Song of the Three Jews* vv. 35-65; see the *Lutheran Book of Worship* no. 18; the Book of Common Prayer pp. 47–49, 88–90; paraphrased in the *Lutheran Service Book* no. 930; adapted by St. Francis of Assisi in his Canticle of the Creatures, translated by William H. Draper (1855-1933) as "All creatures of our God and King" (*Hymnal 1982* no. 400).

48. *Hymnal 1982* no. 216; translation from *The English Hymnal* 1906.

49. Strodach, p. 170.

50. *Daily Prayer of the Church*, p. 1340.

51. Augustine, *Sermo de Ascensione Domini*, Mai 98, 1-2; given in *Liturgy of the Hours*, vol. II, p. 921.

52. John Chrysostom, *Sermon on the Ascension 2*.

53. *Hymnal 1982* no. 215, stanza 3. This stanza seems to be an exception to J. R. Watson's general objection that in this and in all Bishop Wordsworth's hymns "there is no theology, only contemplation" and that he has failed

"to articulate any ideas." (*The English Hymn. A Critical and Historical Study* [New York: Oxford, 1999], p. 407).

54. *Liturgy of the Hours* vol. 2, p. 817; *The Daily Prayer of the Church*, pp. 1417–1418.

55. *Liturgy of the Hours* vol. II, p. 933; *The Daily Prayer of the Church*, p. 1309.

56. See Adolf Adam, *The Liturgical Year* (New York: Pueblo, 1981), p. 89.

57. Johannes Tauler Sermon 23 trans. in Maria Shrady, *Johannes Tauler* (New York: Paulist Press, 1985).

58. Suggested by Strodach, p. 176; but see Reed, p. 516.

59. *Apostolic Constitutions* 5.20.

60. Adam, p. 89.

61. *Hymnal 1982* no. 516; *Lutheran Book of Worship* no. 508.

62. *Lutheran Book of Worship* no. 163; *Lutheran Service Book* no. 497; *Evangelical Lutheran Worship* no. 395.

63. F. A. March, *Latin Hymns with English Notes* (New York: American Book Company, 1874), p. 268. The reference is to Richard Chenevix Trench, *Sacred Latin Poetry* 3rd ed. London, 1874.

64. Caswall's text of 1849 is given in the (1917/1918) Lutheran *Common Service Book* no. 144, "Holy Spirit, Lord of light."

65. *Hymns Ancient and Modern Revised* no. 156; *Hymnal 1940* no. 109. For modern translations see *Hymnal 1982* nos. 226, 227, 228; also a version by Ray Palmer in the *Service Book and Hymnal* no. 121 and in *The Lutheran Hymnal* (1941) no. 227.

66. See Marion J. Hatchett, *Commentary on the American Prayer Book* (New York: Seabury, 1980), pp. 401–402.

67. *Liturgy of the Hours*, vol. II, p. 1015; *Daily Prayer of the Church*, p. 1258.

68. *Liturgy of the Hours*, vol. II, p. 1038; *Daily Prayer of the Church*, p. 1271.

69. *The Book of Concord. The Confessions of the Evangelical Lutheran Church* ed. Robert Kolb and Timothy J. Wengert (Minneapolis: Fortress, 2000), p. 357.

CHAPTER 8

1. The titles for these Sundays, derived from German sources, are from John W. Doberstein, *Minister's Prayer Book* (Philadelphia: Muhlenberg Press, 1959), pp. 72–76.

2. Noticed by Luther D. Reed, *The Lutheran Liturgy* rev. ed. (Philadelphia: Muhlenberg Press, 1960), p. 481.

3. *Daily Prayer of the Church* ed. Philip H. Pfatteicher (Minneapolis: Lutheran University Press, 2005), pp. 203, 271; see William Bright, *Ancient Collects* (Oxford and London: James Parker, 1875), p. 28.

4. *Lutheran Book of Worship* no. 83; *Lutheran Service Book* no. 401.

5. Maximus of Turin, *Sermo 100, de sancta Epiphania* 1, 3. See *Liturgy of the Hours*, vol. I, pp. 612–613.

6. *Liturgy of the Hours*, vol. I, p. 642; *Daily Prayer of the Church*, p. 211.

7. Reed, p. 486. The *Service Book and Hymnal,* including in its calendar the date of August 6 for the Transfiguration, attempted to lessen the emphasis on the Transfiguration in connection with the Epiphany season, appointing the Transfiguration propers only for the Sixth Sunday after the Epiphany but permitting their use on the Last Sunday after the Epiphany each year. The successor books reverted to the earlier Lutheran use.

8. The observance of August 6 as The Transfiguration is less common in Lutheran practice, although it is the date in Scandinavia, and this was reflected in the 1958 *Service Book and Hymnal* and (at least in a rubric) in the 1978 *Lutheran Book of Worship Ministers Edition,* p. 14.

9. Reed, p. 486. On the observance of August 6, see Philip H. Pfatteicher, *New Book of Festivals and Commemorations* (Minneapolis: Fortress, 2008), pp. 377–379.

10. Paul Zeller Strodach, *The Church Year* (Philadelphia: United Lutheran Publication House, 1924), p. 88.

11. *Hymnal 1982* nos. 136, 137; *Lutheran Book of Worship* no. 80.

12. Irenaeus, *Against Heresies* Book IV, 20.5–7.

13. Fernand Cabrol, *Liturgical Prayer. Its History and Spirit* (New York: Kenedy, 1922), p. 45; quoted in Reed, p. 296.

14. *Hymnal 1982* no. 122, 123. The unaltered version of stanza 3 is found in the *Service Book and Hymnal* no. 58:

> Alleluia cannot always
> Be our song while here below;
> Alleluia our transgressions
> Make us for a while forego;
> For the solemn time is coming
> When our tears for sin must flow.

15. For example, *The Daily Office* ed. Herbert Lindemann (St. Louis: Concordia, 1965), p. 697.

16. Strodach, p. 74.

17. Marion J. Hatchett, *Commentary on the American Prayer Book* (New York: Seabury, 1981), p. 171.

18. *Hymnal 1982* no. 443. Translated by J. Howard Rhys (b. 1917), adapted and altered by F. Bland Tucker (1895-1984). Used by permission of Church Publishing.

19. *Daily Prayer of the Church,* p. 611.

20. Martin Luther, *The Large Catechism,* The First Commandment; in *The Book of Concord* ed. Robert Kolb and Timothy Wengert (Minneapolis: Fortress, 2000), p. 386.

21. The *Lutheran Book of Worship* (1978), p. 10 and *Evangelical Lutheran Worship* (2006), p. 15. See Philip H. Pfatteicher, *Commentary on the Lutheran Book of Worship,* p. 314 and *New Book of Festivals and Commemorations* (Minneapolis: Fortress, 2008), pp. 38–39.

22. The 1662 Book of Common Prayer translation modernized in *The Daily Prayer of the Church*, p. 611.

23. Massey H. Shepherd, Jr., *The Oxford American Prayer Book Commentary* (New York: Oxford UP, 1950), p. 115.

24. *Daily Prayer of the Church*, p. 612.

25. *Daily Prayer of the Church*, p. 612.

26. Marion J. Hatchett, *Commentary on the American Prayer Book* (New York: Seabury, 1981), pp. 172–173.

27. Strodach, p. 180, correcting the date Strodach cites.

28. Reed, p. 519.

29. See Patrick Prétot, "Sacramental Theology and the Celebration of the Mystery of Christ in the Liturgical Year: An Approach," Studia Liturgica 40:1–2 (2010), p. 135.

30. *Service Book and Hymnal* no. 138; *Hymns Ancient and Modern* no. 159, without stanza 5. The original poem in Faber's *Jesus and Mary* (1849) has eleven stanzas beginning "Have mercy on us, God most high." The six stanzas in the *SBH* are stanzas 2-5, 10, and 11 of the original.

31. *Lutheran Book of Worship* no. 165; *Hymnal 1982* no. 362. In the original, line 10 reads, "Though the eye of sinful man thy glory may not see."

32. J. R. Watson ed. *An Annotated Anthology of Hymns* (New York: Oxford UP, 2002), pp. 244–245.

33. See the prayer for Trinity Sunday, "O God, who hast made thyself known to us as Trinity in Unity and Unity in Trinity, in order that we may be informed of thy love and thy majesty: Mercifully grant that we may not be terrified by what thou hast revealed of thy majesty, nor tempted to trespass upon thy mercy by what we know of thy love for us; but that by the power of thy Spirit we may be for ever drawn to thee in true adoration and worship; who livest and reignest, one God, world without end." John E. W. Wallis and Leslie M. Styler, *Euchologium Anglicanum* (London: SPCK, 1963), p. 50; also given in *Daily Prayer of the Church*, p. 1589.

34. *Lutheran Book of Worship*, p. 54; *Daily Prayer of the Church*, pp. 1585, 1587.

35. See Philip H. Pfatteicher, *Commentary on the Lutheran Book of Worship* (Minneapolis: Augsburg Fortress, 1990), pp. 444–445.

36. John Henry Newman, *An Essay in Aid of a Grammar of Assent* into. By Nicholas Lash (Notre Dame: Notre Dame UP, 1979), pp. 117–118.

37. *Lutheran Book of Worship*, pp. 54–55; *Lutheran Service Book*, pp. 319–320; *Daily Prayer of the Church*, pp. 452, 458, 705, 1585–1589.

38. This despite the effusion of Urban IV in the Bull *Transiturus* instituting the feast, "The faithful will come eagerly to the churches, and then the clergy and people will rejoice together. They will raise songs of praise; and the hearts and voices of all, their mouths and lips, shall sound forth the joy of salvation. Faith shall sing. Hope shall dance. Charity exult. Devotions praise. Purity sing, and virture be celebrated."

39. *Hymnal 1982* no. 320, "Zion, praise thy Savior singing," a doctrinal exposition of the real presence closely following the *Summa Theologicae*.

40. *Collects and Prayers for Use in Church* (Philadelphia: the Board of Publication of the United Lutheran Church in America, 1935), p. 50 no. 88; altered in *Service Book and Hymnal* (1958), p. 220 no. 12 to "the founding of this congregation."

41. Anscar J. Chupungco, "The Liturgical Year: The Gospel Encountering Culture," Studia Liturgica 40:1–2 (2010), p. 50. The figure of Christ the Pantocrator (ruler over all) adorns the inner dome of every church in the Byzantine tradition.

42. The description derives from Malcolm Muggeridge, *The End of Christendom* (Grand Rapids: Eerdmans, 1980), "we acknowledge a king men did not crown and cannot dethrone."

43. *Service Book and Hymnal* no. 508. Also *The Presbyterian Hymnal* (1990) no. 378; *United Methodist Hymnal* (1989) no. 421.

44. *Liturgy of the Hours*, vol. I, p. 197; *Daily Prayer of the Church*, p. 28. See Zech. 9:9.

45. *Liturgy of the Hours*, vol. I, p. 139; *Daily Prayer of the Church*, p. 86.

46. *Liturgy of the Hours*, vol. I, p.139, 926; *Daily Prayer of the Church*, pp. 104, 116.

47. *Liturgy of the Hours*, vol. I, p. 217; *Daily Prayer of the Church*, p. 52.

48. *Liturgy of the Hours*, vol. I, p.154; *Daily Prayer of the Church*, p. 123.

49. *Liturgy of the Hours*, vol. I, p. 186; *Daily Prayer of the Church*, p. 166.

50. *Liturgy of the Hours*, vol. I, p. 139; *Daily Prayer of the Church*, p. 35.

51. *Liturgy of the Hours*, vol. I, p. 148; *Daily Prayer of the Church*, p. 35.

52. *Liturgy of the Hours*, vol. I, p. 207; *Daily Prayer of the Church*, p. 37.

53. *Liturgy of the Hours*, vol. I, p. 315; *Daily Prayer of the Church*, p. 39.

54. *Liturgy of the Hours*, vol. I, p. 1069; *Daily Prayer of the Church*, p. 167.

55. John Betjeman ed., *Altar and Pew* (London: Hulton, 1959), pp. 42f.

56. Book of Common Prayer (1928), p. li; *Common Service Book*, p. 295; *Service Book and Hymnal*, p. 278; *Lutheran Book of Worship Ministers Edition*, pp. 13–14.

57. Reed, p. 520.

58. Strodach, p. 198.

59. Strodach, p. 186, 196, 239; Reed, p. 525.

60. Strodach, p. 198, 199; Reed, p. 526.

61. Strodach, p. 216, 239; Reed, p. 532, 533.

62. Strodach, p. 239; Reed, p. 540.

63. See Reed, p. 548: this Gospel was first found in T. H. Hesshusen of Helmstadt in 1580 and eventually became the accepted Gospel for the Last Sunday after Trinity in Lutheran church orders.

64. Translation by Catherine Winkworth as in *Daily Prayer of the Church*, pp. 889–891; see the *Common Service Book* no. 521, *The Lutheran Hymnal* (1941) no. 619, the *Lutheran Book of Worship* no. 348, the *Lutheran Service Book* no. 674.

65. The Book of Common Prayer on the Fourth Sunday after Trinity used the same Epistle and Gospel but the Collect is appointed for the Fifth Sunday after Trinity.

66. Strodach, pp. 189–191. See also p. 221.

67. *Evangelical Lutheran Worship* carries this so far as to replace the Book of Common Prayer and Revised Common Lectionary designation of a Sunday as "Proper XXX" with "Lectionary XXX," a practice peculiar to that book.

68. The Roman Catholic commission had considered and quickly rejected a continuous reading of the Old Testament as impractical because of its length.

69. William Bright, *Ancient Collects* (Oxford and London: James Parker, 1895), p. 208; see also Strodach, pp. 193–194. Samuel A. Bridges Stopp, *"The Collects," Memoirs of the Lutheran Liturgical Association,* vol. V (Pittsburgh, 1906), p. 48, and also C. Frederick Barbee and Paul F. M. Zahl, *The Collects of Thomas Cranmer* (Grand Rapids: Eerdmans, 1999), p. 78, quote Dean E. M. Goulburn, *The Collects of the Day* (1883): "When the Goths, the Huns, and the Vandals were hovering over the moribund Roman Empire, like a flight of vultures preparing to pounce upon a dying camel in the desert as soon as the breath is out of his body, there was certainly some point, and there was likely to be some sincerity, in such a prayer."

70. Reed, p. 527. See also Barbee and Zahl, p. 84.

71. Hatchett, p. 188.

72. Shepherd, pp. 190–191.

73. Translation by Dirk van Dissel; given in *The Daily Prayer of the Church,* p. 616.

74. Hatchett, p. 189.

75. Reed, p. 481.

76. Translation by Dirk van Dissel; given in *The Daily Prayer of the Church,* pp. 617–618.

77. Barbee and Zahl, p. 76.

78. International Commission on English in the Liturgy draft, revised by Philip H. Pfatteicher.

79. Translation by Dirk van Dissel; given in *The Daily Prayer of the Church,* pp. 618–619.

80. Shepherd, p. 200.

81. Strodach, p. 204.

82. Barbee and Zahl, p. 80.

83. Canto III, line 85. See Eph. 2:15.

84. Reed, p. 527.

85. Strodach, p.199.

86. International Commission on English in the Liturgy draft, revised by Philip H. Pfatteicher.

87. Hatchett, p. 192.

88. Hatchett, pp. 192–193.

89. Reed, p. 531; Strodach, p. 216.

90. Reed, p. 534; Hatchett, p. 194.

91. Translation by Philip H. Pfatteicher based on a draft translation by the International Commission on English in the Liturgy.

CHAPTER 9

1. *Daily Prayer* ed. Eric Milner-White and George Wallace Briggs (London: Oxford UP, 1941); *The Daily Prayer of the Church*, p. 1541.

2. *Parish Prayers* ed. Frank Colquhoun (London: Hodder and Stoughton, 1967); *The Daily Prayer of the Church*, p. 1540.

3. Martin Luther, "An Argument in Defense of All the Articles of Dr. Martin Luther Wrongly Condemned in the Roman Bull" (1521), trans. Charles M. Jacobs in *Works of Martin Luther*, vol. 3 (Philadelphia: Muhlenberg Press, 1930), p. 31. The translation was revised and weakened in *Luther's Works*, vol. 32 (Philadelphia: Fortress Press, 1958), p. 24.

4. Dietrich Bonhöffer, *The Cost of Discipleship* (1937, rev. ed. 1959), begins with the two sentences, "Cheap grace is the deadly enemy of our Church. We are fighting to-day for costly grace."

5. Evelyn Underhill, *Worship* (New York: Harper & Bros., 1936), p. 81.

6. Wording in the 1979 Book of Common Prayer; the Roman and Lutheran forms are comparable.

7. Underhill, *Worship*, pp. 250.

8. Robert Louis Wilken, "Sanctorum Communio: For Evangelicals and Catholics Together," Pro Ecclesia 11:2 (Spring 2002), p. 166. The whole essay, pp. 159–166, builds on the suggestion of J. N. D. Kelly, *Early Christian Creeds* 3rd ed. (London: Longmans, 1972). See also Timothy Ware, *The Orthodox Church* new ed. (New York: Penguin, 1997), pp. 255–257.

9. See, e.g., Charles Freeman, *Holy Bones, Holy Dust. How Relics Shaped the History of Medieval Europe.* (New Haven: Yale UP, 2011).

10. St. Anthony's Chapel on Troy Hill in Pittsburgh, Pennsylvania, was built to house the largest collection of relics (some 5000) outside of the Vatican, gathered by its nineteenth-century pastor, Father Suitbert Mollinger, on his numerous trips to Europe.

11. Dom Gregory Dix, *The Shape of the Liturgy* (Westminster: Dacre Press, 1945), pp. 744–745.

12. *Liturgy of the Hours*, vol. IV, p. 1536. The *Common Service Book*, p. 249, and the *Service Book and Hymnal*, p. 263, use the antiphon in the Burial of the Dead as an antiphon to the Nunc Dimittis.

13. The translation in the 1979 Book of Common Prayer.

14. Given in J. R. Watson ed., *An Annotated Anthology of Hymns* (New York: Oxford UP, 2002), pp. 200–201. The more familiar abbreviated version is given in the *Hymnal 1982* no. 526, "Let saints on earth in concert sing." Watson also points the reader to Isaac Watts's "There is a land of pure delight," *Service Book and Hymnal* no. 583; *Hymnal 1940* no. 586; *Hymns Ancient and Modern Revised* no. 285; *The English Hymnal* no. 498.

15. The Church's calendar of saints celebrates just three earthly birthdays: Jesus on December 25; his mother on September 8; and his forerunner on June 24.

16. Martin Luther, "The Holy and Blessed Sacrament of Baptism 1519," *Luther's Works*, vol. 35 (Philadelphia: Muhlenberg, 1960), pp. 30–31.

17. Luther, "The Holy and Blessed Sacrament of Baptism," pp. 39, 41.

18. Martin Luther, "On the Councils of the Church" (1539), *Luther's Works*, vol. 41 (Philadelphia: Fortress, 1966), pp. 148–166. Luther thought so highly of these *notae ecclesiae* that he suggested, "I would even call these seven parts the seven sacraments...." (pp. 165–166).

19. Noted by W. K. Lowther Clarke in *Liturgy and Worship. A Companion to the Prayer Books of the Anglican Communion*, ed. W. K. Lowther Clarke and Charles Harris (London: SPCK, 1964 [1932]), p. 212.

20. Trans. Michael W. Holmes, *The Apostolic Fathers* 3rd ed. (Grand Rapids: Baker Academic, 2007), p. 227.

21. See Louis Bouyer, *Liturgical Piety* (Notre Dame: Notre Dame UP, 1955), p. 218. See also Philip H. Pfatteicher, *New Book of Festivals and Commemorations* (Minneapolis: Fortress, 2008), pp. 513–516.

22. *Hymnal 1982* no. 237: John Mason Neale's translation slightly altered in stanza 3.

23. See Maxwell E. Johnson, "Sub Tuum Praesidium: The Theotokos in Christian Life and Worship before Ephesus," Pro Ecclesia 17:1 (Winter 2008), 52–75; also Bradshaw and Johnson, *The Origins of Feasts, Fasts, and Seasons in Early Christianity*, chapter 20, pp. 196–214.

24. Löhe's calendar may be seen in Philip H. Pfatteicher, *New Book of Festivals and Commemorations*, pp. 644–652.

25. John Macquarrie, *Principles of Christian Theology* 2nd ed. (New York: Scribner, 1977), p. 237. See also Philip H. Pfatteicher, *New Book of Festivals and Commemorations*, pp. 477–479.

26. John Henry Newman, *Apologia Pro Vita Sua*, Part III "History of My Religious Opinions to the Year 1833."

27. Thomas Traherne, *Centuries* (New York: Harper & Bros., 1960), Century I, sections 81, 85, pp. 41, 43–44. The "resentments" of every soul are to be understood in the older sense of strong feelings, sentiments.

28. *Hymnal 1982*, no. 623.

29. Sermon 2, given in the *Liturgy of the Hours*, vol. IV, pp. 1526–1527, the Second Reading for All Saints' Day.

30. *Service Book and Hymnal* no. 594, which has the original of stanza 2 "They were mourning here below/And wet their couch with tears." The *Hymnal 1982* no. 253 weakens the intensity of the opening by making it plural: "Give us the wings of faith." See J. R. Watson, ed. *An Annotated Anthology of Hymns*, pp. 137–138.

CHAPTER 10

1. Thomas Karshan, "Nabokov in Bed," *Times Literary Supplement*, February 4, 2011, p. 4.

2. Gilbert K. Chesterton, *Orthodoxy* (New York: John Lane, 1908), pp. 148–149, 150.

3. See the "Tables and Rules for Finding the Date of Easter Day," Book of Common Prayer, pp. 880–883.

4. For a thoughtful consideration of such apparent dislocations, see Anscar J. Chupungco, "The Liturgical Year: The Gospel Encountering Culture," Studia Liturgica 40:1–2 (2010), 46–64.

5. "Burnt Norton," II in T. S. Eliot, *Collected Poems 1909-1962* (New York: Harcourt, Brace & World, 1963), p. 177.

6. "Burnt Norton," V in Eliot, *Collected Poems*, p. 180.

7. T. S. Eliot, "Little Gidding," V. *Collected Poems*, pp. 207, 208.

8. From the opening poem, "Morning," of his *The Christian Year* (1827); *Hymnal 1982* no. 10; *Service Book and Hymnal* no. 201.

9. Paul Zeller Strodach, *The Church Year* (Philadelphia: United Lutheran Publication House, 1924), p. 25.

10. Canto xxxiii, lines 142–145. *The Comedy of Dante Alighieri. Cantica III Paradise* trans. Dorothy L. Sayers and Barbara Reynolds (Baltimore: Penguin, 1962), p. 347.

11. See John Freccero, *Dante: The Poetics of Conversion* ed. Rachel Jacoff (Cambridge: Harvard UP, 1986), especially the essay "Pilgrim in a Gyre."

12. M. H. Abrams, *Natural Supernaturalism: Tradition and Revolution in Romantic Literature* (New York: Norton, 1971), pp. 183–184. On the ascending spiral in Coleridge see *PMLA* 101:5 (1986), pp. 848–856.

13. Pius XII, *Mediator Dei* 51.

14. Hermann Dietzfelbinger (1908-1984), Bishop of the Lutheran territorial church in Bavaria, *Deutsches Pfarrerblatt*, February 15, 1955, quoted in *Minister's Prayer Book* ed. John W. Doberstein (Philadelphia: Muhlenberg, 1959), p. 230, rev. in *For All the Saints* ed. Frederick J. Schumacher with Dorothy Zelenko, vol. II (Delhi, NY: American Lutheran Publicity Bureau, 1995), pp. 230–231.

15. See Philip H. Pfatteicher, "Caravaggio's Conception of Time in His Two Versions of the Supper at Emmaus," Source: Notes in the History of Art 7:1 (Fall 1987), pp. 9–13.

16. Venerable Bede, Homily 21, given in *From the Fathers to the Churches* ed. Brother Kenneth (London: Collins, 1983), p. 745.

17. From a sermon preached by Allan B. Warren III at the Church of the Advent in Boston, March 6, 2011, the Last Sunday after the Epiphany.

18. From a sermon on the transfiguration of our Lord by Anastatius of Sinai, bishop, *Liturgy of the Hours*, vol. IV, p. 1286.

19. *Hymnal 1982* no. 657; *Service Book and Hymnal* no. 397; *Lutheran Book of Worship* no. 315.

20. Note the hymn drawn from the Liturgy of St. James by Charles William Humphreys (1840-1921), "From glory to glory advancing," *Hymnal 1982* no. 326.

21. Sermon 129/L quoted in Walter Knowles, "Holy Week in Hippo: The Weeks Surrounding Easter in a North African Parish," Studia Liturgica 40:1–2 (2010), p. 163.

22. Roman Missal trans. *Service Book and Hymnal.* Note the version in the Book of Common Prayer, which, in an effort to soften the assertion of *theosis*, in fact appeals more to pride: "and in their sight ascended into heaven, to prepare a place for us; that where he is, there we might also be, and reign with him in glory."

23. *New Revised Standard Version*: "participants of the divine nature"; *Revised English Bible*: "may come to share in the very being of God"; *New Jerusalem Bible*: "share the divine nature."

24. See *The Orthodox Study Bible* (Nashville: Thomas Nelson, 2008), p. 1692. See also Timothy Ware, *The Orthodox Church* rev. ed. (New York: Penguin, 1997), pp. 231–238.

25. See, for example, J. Todd Billings, "The Catholic Calvin," Pro Ecclesia 20:2 (Spring 2011), pp. 120–134.

26. George Florovsky, *Bible, Church, Tradition: An Eastern Orthodox View* (Belmont, Mass.: Nordland, 1972), p. 38.

27. "I come to the garden alone" (*United Methodist Hymnal* [1989] no. 314) is perhaps the most egregious example of such a picture, but there are other hymns such as "Blessed assurance, Jesus is mine" (*United Methodist Hymnal* no. 369; *The Presbyterian Hymnal* [1990] no. 341; *Evangelical Lutheran Worship* [2006] no. 638) that are similarly individualistic and self-centered.

28. Malcolm Muggeridge, *Jesus Rediscovered* (New York: Bantam Doubleday Dell, 1969), p. 65.

A Short Glossary

Antiphon. (1) A verse from the Bible or a brief liturgical composition sung or said before and after a psalm or a canticle to highlight a particular theme or meaning. (2) A verse sung or said by itself, as in the Entrance Antiphon or the Communion Antiphon of the Latin Rite.

Benedictus. *Benedictus Dominus Deus,* the song of Zechariah at the birth of his son John the Baptist (Luke 1:68-79), sung daily in Lauds at daybreak, looking toward the time when "the dawn from on high will break upon us."

Bergamo sacramentary. A ninth-century sacramentary of the Ambrosian rite of Milan.

Compline (pronounced COM-plin). The final hour of the daily office, prayed before going to sleep. In the Roman Catholic Liturgy of the Hours, Compline is called Night Prayer.

Computus. The collection of rules by which the date of Easter is calculated. In earlier times, before calendars were easily available, a knowledge of the computus was an essential part of the training of the clergy.

Concurrence. The situation when two festivals fall on successive days so that **second vespers** of the first overlaps **first vespers** of the second festival. The propers of the more important festival take **precedence** and prevail. The collect of the more important festival is said first; the collect of the second is said next. See **occurrence.**

Entrance Antiphon. In the Roman sacramentary an **Antiphon,** usually from the historic **Introit** of the day, sung as the ministers of the Eucharist enter and approach the altar at the beginning of the Eucharist. Sometimes the name is applied to the entire Introit.

Feria (Latin, weekday). A weekday not a Sunday or a festival; a day that is neither a feast nor a fast.

First Vespers. Evening Prayer marking the beginning of a festival or day according to the pattern of Genesis 1 ("There was evening and there was morning, the first day."); second vespers is prayed on the following evening to conclude the day.

Gelasian sacramentary. A Vatican sacramentary of the mid-eighth century, the oldest known Roman sacramentary in which the feasts are ordered according to the liturgical year. Its attribution to Pope Gelasius (492-496) is mistaken, although the name remains in use.

Graduale Romanum. The Roman Church's official book for the choir, as the **Sacramentary** is for the priest, the Book of the Gospels for the deacon, and the Lectionary for the reader. It is the primary source for the processional texts of the Mass with their music (Entrance, Offertory, Communion) and for the chants after the First Reading (the Gradual) and before the Gospel (the Alleluia or Tract). The sources can be traced to the ninth century.

Gregorian sacramentary. A family of sacramentaries ascribed to Pope Gregory I (590-604) and containing elements composed by him.

Introit. A liturgical song consisting of an antiphon and a psalm verse with the Gloria Patri sung to accompany the entrance of the ministers of the Eucharist, marking the beginning of the liturgy and announcing a principal theme of the day.

Invitatory. An invitation to praise, used as an antiphon to the Venite (Psalm 95) in Morning Prayer. It is a variable **proper** that changes with the day or season. Sometimes "invitatory" is used of the antiphon and the Venite together, since they function as a single invitation to praise, "Come, let us sing to the Lord."

Kalendar. A variant of "calendar" used in certain Anglican quarters to preserve the Middle English spelling and to distinguish the ecclesiastical from the secular calendar.

Lauds. Morning Praise, the principal morning hour of the Daily Office, prayed as the sun rises.

Leonine sacramentary. The earliest collection of prayers according to the Roman rite, ascribed to Pope Leo the Great (d. 461). The manuscript of the early seventh century draws on material from the fifth and sixth centuries. Also known as the Verona sacramentary, from the city where it is preserved.

Magnificat. The song of Mary (Luke 1:46-55) on the occasion of her visit to Elizabeth during their mutual pregnancies, sung daily at vespers, celebrating God's revolutionary activity.

Matins (Mattins). The first of the traditional hours of prayer in the daily office, originally prayed at midnight. In Anglican and Lutheran circles, the medieval Matins was combined with Lauds and elements of Prime to create the office called Morning Prayer or Matins.

Missal. A book containing the services of the church for the use of those who minister at the altar. In the tenth century the missal included all the texts of the Mass, including choir anthems and lessons, as the celebrant took on himself all the roles previously assigned to a number of ministers and choristers. As the term is used in this book, the Roman Missal is the official liturgical book of the entire Latin Rite Roman Catholic Church in use from 1570 to 1970.

Mozarabic. The use of that part of Spain that was under Moorish (Arab) rule after

711 until 1085; sometimes called the Visigothic rite, since the Visigoths occupied Spain after 470, and recognized the liturgy as the official rite in 633.The Mozarabic (Moz-AR-a-bic) rite dates from perhaps 400; its use is now limited to the Cathedral in Toledo.

Nocturn(s). Prayer during the night; one of the three divisions of Matins in the medieval breviary.

Nunc Dimittis. The song of Simeon (Luke 2:29-32) at the presentation of the infant Jesus in the temple, sung daily at Compline, praising God for the revelation of his great work and gift of peace.

Occurrence. The situation when two festivals fall on the same day. In such a case, the greater festival takes **precedence** and prevails; the lesser festival is postponed until the next open date.

Office hymn. A hymn appointed for use in the daily office; the practice is first mentioned in the *Rule* of St. Benedict (ca. 540). The office hymns at vespers have traditionally dealt with creation on successive days of the week following the pattern of Genesis 1.

Precedence. The priority of one festival over another when the two fall on the same date. Example: when a Sunday in Lent falls on March 25, the Feast of the Annunciation, the Lenten Sunday takes precedence and the Annunciation is moved to the next open date, usually the next day, Monday.

Propers. The variable liturgical texts of a service, which change according to the day or season of the liturgical year in contrast to the ordinary, or fixed parts of the liturgy. In the fullest form, the propers of the Eucharist consist of the Introit or entrance antiphon, the Collect, Lesson, Psalm, Epistle, Gradual or Tract, Gospel, Offertory antiphon, Offertory prayer, Proper Preface, Communion antiphon, post-Communion, Seasonal Blessing.

Responsory. A liturgical response to the readings in daily prayer, particularly Morning Prayer, in which scripture verses or liturgical compositions based on scripture are arranged so as to comment on the lesson just read. The form of the responsory consists of a refrain sung after a brief series of verses. The traditional responsories at Matins are among the oldest and finest liturgical compositions in the Church's possession.

Roman sacramentary. As the term is used in this book, the Sacramentary of Paul VI of 1970, revised 1985, third edition 2002.

Sacramentary. The liturgical book containing the text of the Eucharist and the Propers but not the Lessons nor those parts of the Mass that are sung by the choir.

Sarum. The use of Salisbury Cathedral in England, a medieval modification of the Roman rite from the latter eleventh century. By 1457 it had become the use of nearly the whole of England, Wales, and Ireland.

Second Vespers. Evening Prayer marking the conclusion of a festival that began with first vespers on the eve of the day.

Suffrages (from the Latin *suffragia*, petitions). A series of brief prayerful petitions.

Verona sacramentary. Another name for the **Leonine sacramentary.**

Vespers. Evening Prayer or Evensong, the hour of daily prayer prayed as the sun
  sets; with Morning Prayer it is one of the two principal hours of daily prayer.

Bibliography

Adam, Adolf. *The Liturgical Year. Its History and Its Meaning after the Reform of the Liturgy.* Trans. Matthew J. O'Connell. New York: Pueblo, 1981.

Alexander, J. Neil. *Waiting for the Coming: The Liturgical Meaning of Advent, Christmas, Epiphany.* Washington, D.C.: Pastoral Press, 1993.

Berger, Rupert and Hans Hollerweger eds. *Celebrating the Easter Vigil.* Trans. Matthew J. O'Connell. New York: Pueblo, 1983.

Bouyer, Louis. *Liturgical Piety.* Notre Dame, Ind.: University of Notre Dame Press, 1955.

Bradshaw, Paul F. and Maxwell E. Johnson. *The Origins of Feasts, Fasts, and Seasons in Early Christianity.* Collegeville, Minn.: Liturgical Press, 2011.

Buchinger, Harald. "On the Origin and Development of the Liturgical Year: Tendencies, Results, and Desiderata of Heortological Research," Studia Liturgica 40: 1–2 (2010), 14–45. A most helpful summary of the current state of the questions with abundant bibliographies. The entire number of *SL* deals with the Liturgical Year.

Bynum, Caroline Walker. *Christian Materiality. An Essay on Religion in Late Medieval Europe.* Brooklyn, N.Y.: Zone Books, 2011.

_____. *Holy Feast and Holy Fast.* Berkeley: University of California Press, 1988.

Connell, Martin F. *Eternity Today.* Vol. 1 On God and Time, Advent, Christmas, Epiphany, Candlemas. Vol. 2 Sunday, Lent, The Three Days, The Easter Season, Ordinary Time. London and New York: Continuum, 2006.

_____. *An Introduction to the Church's Liturgical Year.* Chicago: Loyola Press, 1997.

The Daily Prayer of the Church ed. Philip H. Pfatteicher. Minneapolis: Lutheran University Press, 2005.

Davies, J. Gordon. *Holy Week: A Short History.* Ecumenical Studies in Worship No. 11. Richmond, Va.: John Knox, 1963.

Donovan, Kevin. "The Sanctoral," chapter IV.2 of *The Study of Liturgy* rev. ed. Ed Cheslyn Jones et al. New York: Oxford UP, 1992.

Eliade, Mircea. *Cosmos and History. The Myth of the Eternal Return.* New York: Harper & Row, 1959.

Farmer, David. *The Oxford Dictionary of Saints* 5th ed. rev. New York: Oxford UP, 2011.

Gaster, Theodor H. *Festivals of the Jewish Year. A Modern Interpretation and Guide.* New York: Morrow, 1953.

Greenacre, Roger. *The Sacrament of Easter: An Introduction to the Liturgy of Holy Week.* Studies in Christian Worship No. 4. London: Faith Press, 1965.

Gunstone, John T. A. *Christmas and Epiphany.* London: Faith Press, 1967.

_____. *The Feast of Pentecost.* London: Faith Press, 1967.

Hardison, O. B., Jr. *Christian Rite and Christian Drama in the Middle Ages.* Baltimore: Johns Hopkins UP, 1965.

Heinz, Donald. *Christmas: Festival of Incarnation.* Minneapolis: Fortress, 2010.

Horn, Edward T. III. *The Christian Year.* Philadelphia: Muhlenberg Press, 1957.

Irwin, Kevin. *Advent and Christmas. A Guide to the Eucharist and Hours.* New York: Pueblo, 1986.

_____. *Easter. A Guide to the Eucharist and Hours.* New York: Pueblo, 1991.

_____. *Lent. A Guide to the Eucharist and Hours.* New York: Pueblo, 1990.

Johnson, Maxwell E. ed. *Between Memory and Hope: Readings on the Liturgical Year.* Collegeville: Liturgical Press, 2000.

Liturgy of the Hours 4 vols., New York: Catholic Book Publishing Co., 1975.

Martimort, A. G. et al. *The Church at Prayer IV.* Collegeville: Liturgical Press, 1986.

McArthur, A. Alan. *The Evolution of the Church Year.* London: SCM, 1953.

McManus, Frederick R. *The Rites of Holy Week.* Patterson, N.J.: St. Anthony Guild Press, 1956.

Melhorn, Nathan R. "The Ecclesiastical Calendar," Memoirs of the Lutheran Liturgical Association vol. III (Pittsburgh, 1906), pp. 17–27.

Nichols, Bridget ed. *The Collect in the Churches of the Reformation.* London: SCM, 2010.

Nocent, Adrian. *The Liturgical Year.* 4 vols. Trans. Matthew J. O'Connell. Collegeville: Liturgical Press, 1977.

The Oxford Companion to the Year. An Exploration of Calendar Customs and Time-Reckoning ed. Bonnie Blackburn and Leofranc Holford-Strevens. Oxford University Press, 1999.

Parsch. Pius. *The Church's Year of Grace.* Trans. William G. Heidt. 5 vols. Collegeville: Liturgical Press, 1962.

Pfatteicher, Philip H. *Commentary on the Lutheran Book of Worship: Lutheran Liturgy in Its Ecumenical Context.* Minneapolis: Augsburg Fortress, 1990. Chapters 5 and 6.

_____. *Holy Week.* Proclamation 6, Series B: Interpreting the Lessons of the Church Year. Minneapolis: Fortress, 1995.

_____. "Lent," New Proclamation Year B, 2002-2003. Minneapolis: Fortress, 2002.

_____. *Liturgical Spirituality.* Valley Forge, Pa.: Trinity Press International, 1997, pp. 32–141.

_____. *New Book of Festivals and Commemorations: A Proposed Common Calendar of Saints.* Minneapolis: Fortress, 2008.

_____. *The School of the Church: Worship and Christian Formation.* Valley Forge, Pa.: Trinity Press International, 1995. Chapters 5 and 6.

Porter, H. Boone. *The Day of Light.* Washington: Pastoral Press, 1987 [1960].

_____. *Keeping the Church Year.* New York: Seabury, 1977.

Regan, Patrick. "The Fifty Days and the Fiftieth Day," Worship 55 (May 1981), 194–218.

_____. *Advent to Pentecost. Comparing the Seasons in the Ordinary and Extraordinary Forms of the Roman Rite.* Collegeville, Minn.: Liturgical Press, 2012.

Rorsdorf, Willy. *Sunday: The History of the Day of Rest and Worship in the Earliest Centuries of the Christian Church.* Trans. A. A. K. Graham. Philadelphia: Westminster, 1968.

Strodach, Paul Zeller. *The Church Year. Studies in the Introits, Collects, Epistles, and Gospels.* Philadelphia: United Lutheran Publication House, 1924.

Studwell, William E. *Christmas Carols: A Reference Guide.* New York: Garland, 1984.

Talley, Thomas J. *The Origins of the Liturgical Year.* Emended 2nd edition. Collegeville: Liturgical Press, 1991.

Weiser, Francis X. *Handbook of Christian Feasts and Customs: The Year of the Lord in Liturgy and Folklore.* New York: Harcourt, Brace, and World, 1952.

Index

Note: individual hymns are listed under the entry "Hymns."